A PRACTITIONER'S GUIDE TO

Commercial Arbitration

A PRACTITIONER'S GUIDE TO

Commercial Arbitration

EDITED BY

Marvin J Huberman

IRWIN LAW

Published in 2017 by

Irwin Law Inc.
14 Duncan Street
Suite 206
Toronto, ON
M5H 3G8
www.irwinlaw.com

ISBN: 978-1-55221-462-6
e-book ISBN: 978-1-55221-463-3

Library and Archives Canada Cataloguing in Publication

A practitioner's guide to commercial arbitration / edited by Marvin J. Huberman.

Includes bibliographical references and index.
Issued in print and electronic formats.
ISBN 978-1-55221-462-6 (softcover).—ISBN 978-1-55221-463-3 (PDF)

1. Arbitration and award—Canada. I. Huberman, Marvin J. (Marvin Joel), 1958–, author II. Title: Commercial arbitration.

KE8618.P73 2017 347.71'09 C2017-905464-3
KF9085.P73 2017 C2017-905465-1

Printed and bound by CPI Group (UK) Ltd, Croydon, CR0 4YY

1 2 3 4 5 21 20 19 18 17

Summary Table of Contents

Detailed Table of Contents

Preface

"When will mankind be convinced and agree to settle their difficulties by arbitration?"

— BENJAMIN FRANKLIN

Arbitration can be a highly effective alternative commercial dispute resolution process outside of court. Indeed, arbitration is and has historically been a widely used method for resolving commercial conflicts arising out of domestic and international corporate and commercial transactions. It has tremendous potential to resolve disputes with confidentiality, economy, efficiency, finality, durability, neutral expertise, impartiality, fairness, and more party-sensitive and satisfactory outcomes than traditional litigation.

But for arbitration to fully realize its perceived benefits, expectations, and promise as a means of effectively resolving commercial disputes, many circumstances must combine:

- informed and consenting parties that understand the advantages and disadvantages and the techniques and concepts of arbitration
- respect for and a healthy attitude toward ADR (the initialism for alternative or appropriate dispute resolution) and its goals, values, principles, and challenges
- well drafted — that is, clear and robust — arbitration clauses and agreements that (1) address what is and what is not arbitrable and (2) contain fair and reasonable provisions,

dealing with the award and enforcing and challenging the award, and the signatures of authorized representatives of the parties who understand what is being agreed to

- the selection of high-quality arbitrators who understand their multifaceted roles, ethical obligations, powers, and limitations and who can effectively perform those roles, obligations, and powers
- a fair process that is truly responsive to the needs, interests, and objectives of the disputing parties, beginning with the pre-arbitration phase and continuing through the arbitration hearing and the postarbitration stages of the proceeding
- selection of the right forum and venue for the arbitration

Above all, however, effective commercial arbitration is all about shaping and controlling the entire arbitral process — namely, arbitral management. As ADR guru and Harvard Law Professor Frank Sander said, "One must fit the forum to the fuss"; that is, one must analyze the particular dispute and then find the appropriate forum to assist in facilitating its resolution.[1] The correct process for the specific dispute and the particular disputants must be selected. An appropriate neutral arbitrator trained in ADR should be retained to tailor the process and explore creative approaches to dispute resolution to maximize the chances for optimal innovation and mutually beneficial solutions having regard to the three Ps: the People, the Problem, and the Process. Once combined, these circumstances will maximize the chances of achieving the goals of ADR: a faster, cheaper, and better dispute resolution process than traditional adversarial litigation in court.

To be sure, a comprehensive arbitration plan must be devised (ideally) collaboratively by the arbitrator, counsel, and the disputants working cooperatively for the fair, efficient, and effective conduct of the particular arbitral proceedings, having regard to the resources available. Unnecessary and unproductive steps and lengthy hearings should be avoided. Instead, the time and resour-

1 Frank EA Sander, "Fitting the Forum to the Fuss: A User-Friendly Guide to Selecting an ADR Procedure" (1994) 10 *Negotiation* 49.

ces of the parties, their counsel, and the arbitrator must be used professionally, wisely, and efficiently from the initial stages to the disposition of the arbitration proceeding. This requires flexibility, creativity, and innovation that is responsive to the individual needs, interests, and objectives of the stakeholders. One size does not fit all arbitration cases.

It is therefore imperative that each and every arbitration proceeding be carefully designed and effectively case managed. This requires not simply a hope but a strategy. Initial pre-arbitration conferences should be conducted as soon as practicable and followed by a first procedural (case management) order, subsequent pre-arbitration conferences, scheduling orders, and a final procedural (case management) order. Effective arbitral management requires that the arbitrator be actively involved in formulating, monitoring, modifying, controlling, and executing the arbitration plan, as appropriate in the circumstances of the particular case, to assure compliance with the plan. Cooperation, collaboration, and professionalism from counsel for the parties, and their clients, are also needed, especially given the increasing complexity, variety of issues, time demands, and costs of commercial arbitration. The arbitral process must be managed so that the needs and interests of the particular parties and the dispute are met. Moreover, it must be recognized that the overall goal of the arbitration plan is an expeditious, inexpensive, and just determination of the case, tailored to the needs and interests of the particular parties in light of the existing resources, including those not only of the parties but also of the arbitrator.

So what should we do? How do we get from here to there? Where do we begin? In this book, we heed the advice in Lewis Carroll's *Alice's Adventures in Wonderland*: "'Begin at the beginning,' the King said, very gravely, 'and go on till you come to the end: then stop.'"

I hope this book will (1) dispel the notion that one size fits all in dispute resolution, especially in commercial arbitration, (2) evoke greater interest in commercial arbitration and help move us toward full realization of its promise as a means of effective dispute resolution, and (3) serve as a practical guide for all those who have an interest in or are passionate about commercial arbitration. Let us know what you think.

Marvin J Huberman, LLB, LLM.
BARRISTER, MEDIATOR, CHARTERED ARBITRATOR
CERTIFIED SPECIALIST IN CIVIL LITIGATION

This book is dedicated to my mentor and friend
The Honourable Coulter A Osborne, QC,
a renowned Canadian arbitrator and former
Associate Chief Justice of Ontario.

In him wisdom and prudential judgment,
learning and competence, sophistication and
high ethical standards are combined.

part one

The Beginning

Great is the art of beginning, but greater is the art of ending.

— HENRY WADSWORTH LONGFELLOW

chapter one

An Introduction to Commercial Arbitration

ANTHONY DAIMSIS & MARINA PAVLOVIĆ

A. PRELIMINARY REMARKS

As the world becomes ever more interconnected, states, state institutions, and international organizations increasingly rely on arbitration to resolve their disputes.[1] A question that is often asked is, why choose arbitration over the courts? The answer is entirely subjective. What is good and advantageous for one party is not always relevant to another. In an international context, where parties' domestic court systems may differ significantly, international arbitration is seen as a better alternative to the courts because it allows each party to avoid appearing and litigating before the other side's home court. By choosing arbitration, the parties maintain the decision maker's neutrality. If this is important to the parties, then it is easy to answer that arbitration is better than the courts, at least for parties that prioritize the neutrality of a dispute's forum.[2]

1 See Karl-Heinz Böckstiegel, "The Role of Arbitration within Today's Challenges to the World Community and to International Law" (2006) 22:2 *Arbitration International* 165, online: https://doi.org/10.1093/arbitration/22.2.165.

2 See Jan Paulsson, "International Arbitration Is Not Arbitration" (2008) 2 *Stockholm International Arbitration Review* 1.

Another reason to prefer arbitration to the courts, both domestically and internationally, is that it allows parties a great deal of freedom to craft and tailor the process. Private arbitration parallels this freedom by allowing parties to select the very rules and laws that govern the resolution of their disputes. Perhaps even more striking is that parties also play a hand in choosing *who* will resolve their disputes. This stands in stark contrast to most national court systems, where parties rarely select their judges or decide the framework of laws applicable to their disputes.

This chapter will introduce the reader to arbitration's basic mechanics. Subsequent chapters pick up various discrete topics and handle them in greater depth. Readers who are new to arbitration will benefit from this chapter as it lays down the basic legal framework and introduces some critical theories unique to arbitration. But even the readers who are more familiar with arbitration may benefit from a refresher on where arbitration sits within the Canadian legal landscape and internationally.

This chapter is divided into four main sections, below. The first sets arbitration within the broader dispute resolution system. The second introduces arbitration's legal framework in Canada both from a domestic and from an international perspective. Distinctions are drawn, where necessary, between legislation governing domestic arbitration and legislation governing international arbitration. Additionally, international arbitration requires an understanding of two significant legal instruments on international commercial arbitration: the United Nations *Convention on the Recognition and Enforcement of Foreign Arbitral Awards* (the *New York Convention*)[3] and the *UNCITRAL Model Law on International Commercial Arbitration*.[4] These two legal instruments and their accompanying *travaux préparatoires* are vital sources in international commercial

3 10 June 1958, 330 UNTS 3, online: www.uncitral.org/pdf/english/texts/arbitration/NY-conv/New-York-Convention-E.pdf.

4 21 June 1985, UN Doc A/40/17, annex 1 [1985 *UNCITRAL Model Law*], with amendments adopted 7 July 2006, UN Doc A/61/17, annex 1, online: www.uncitral.org/pdf/english/texts/arbitration/ml-arb/07-86998_Ebook.pdf [*UNCITRAL Model Law*].

arbitration.[5] More importantly, these two legal instruments are critical to understanding the Canadian legal framework for international commercial arbitration as the *New York Convention* and the *UNCITRAL Model Law*, through adoption and implementation, structure Canada's international commercial arbitration legislation. Internationally, these instruments are also the foundation for many modern legislative enactments on international commercial arbitration.[6] Consequently, any discussion of arbitration is incomplete without reference to these legal instruments.

The third main section, below, considers some foundational theories unique to arbitration, such as why an arbitration agreement is often treated as a separate agreement and why arbitrators retain competence to determine their own jurisdiction. This last point often shocks newcomers, but we expect that once understood, the reader will appreciate its purpose and its necessity to the arbitration system.

The fourth section briefly explains the processes that come into play during arbitration. For example, this section explains

---

5 Although *travaux préparatoires* do not constitute a primary interpretive source, in *Thomson v Thomson*, [1994] 3 SCR 551 at para 40, La Forest J for the majority of the Supreme Court of Canada wrote that it "would be odd if in construing an international treaty to which the legislature has attempted to give effect, the treaty were not interpreted in the manner in which the state parties to the treaty must have intended. Not surprisingly, then, the parties made frequent references to this supplementary means of interpreting the Convention, and I shall also do so." In almost every instance where Canadian legislators have implemented the *New York Convention* and the *UNCITRAL Model Law*, specific reference to relevant *travaux préparatoires* has been made. And while many of these references are only to the *UNCITRAL Model Law*'s 18th session of the commission, as argued by Binder, "a thorough understanding of the issues surrounding the Model Law can only be obtained by an analysis of *all* major documents published during the drafting . . . ." [emphasis in original] in Peter Binder, *International Commercial Arbitration and Conciliation in UNCITRAL Model Law Jurisdictions*, 2d ed (London, Sweet & Maxwell, 2005).

6 According to the United Nations Commission on International Trade Law, the *UNCITRAL Model Law* has been adopted or used to fashion international commercial arbitration legislation in over 60 jurisdictions. At the time of writing, there are 157 parties to the *New York Convention*.

how parties may use arbitration rules to support their legal framework or how parties may appoint and remove arbitrators. Since these matters are taken up in subsequent chapters, this section merely serves to whet the reader's appetite.

B. ARBITRATION EXPLAINED

Arbitration is a procedure whereby parties appoint one or more persons called arbitrators to finally render a binding decision. A sole arbitrator or panel of arbitrators makes up what is known as an arbitral tribunal. An arbitral tribunal's decision is called an award.

Using the familiar court system as a comparator, one can view arbitrators as fulfilling the role of judges and arbitral tribunals as akin to courts. Just as judges ascertain facts, scrutinize evidence, and interpret the law to reach a decision (or judgment), arbitrators ascertain facts, scrutinize evidence, and interpret the law to reach an award. By agreeing to arbitrate, parties undertake to abide by the arbitrator's award. Where a party does not voluntarily comply with the award, legislation ensures that the party will not shirk its responsibility. Since one of the purposes of using arbitration is to move away from the court system, the grounds to appeal arbitral awards are limited. Although reviewing awards is dealt with in greater detail in subsequent chapters, for introductory purposes it is useful to know that under Canadian legislation a great deal of deference is shown to arbitral awards.

1) Fundamental Features

While there are many reasons to opt for arbitration, one of the most common reasons is for the parties to tailor arbitral tribunals to fit their needs. Specifically, if parties believe that their arbitrators should possess certain skills, they may include such stipulations in their agreements or seek arbitrators who possess those skills. This is not the case with the court system. Although certain Canadian courts have specialized commercial courts, their dockets are often backlogged, and parties are not guaranteed to have their case heard by a judge who specializes in the area of law on which the case centres. Another advantage of arbitration, particularly in cross-border, multilingual settings, is that the parties can choose arbitrators fluent in the case's languages. This allows the arbitrators to appreciate the sometimes subtle linguistic differences that can colour certain business transactions.

Arbitrators are also generally not bound by precedent or complex systems of law (e.g., conflicts of law rules). What this means is that although arbitrators nevertheless look to how national laws handle a particular problem and may take note of these approaches, their hands are not tied to rules of law that may or may not be appropriate given the trade practice and usages associated with a particular trade and applicable to the dispute. While it is true that many modern laws do seek to defer to trade practices, for parties there is a measurable difference between an arbitrator who has practised in a particular trade and is familiar with particular trade practice or usages and a generalist judge, who may be unfamiliar with the same practice or usages.

In principle, arbitrations are private and confidential. Privacy and confidentiality is often a significant concern to businesses. For example, a major distributor with a dispute concerning a business-sensitive element of its distribution network may hesitate to put this information before a court and consequently before its competitors. At the same time, the distributor may still need to resolve what could be a costly dispute. Arbitration allows such a company to resolve the dispute quickly and by a panel of specialists with the added value that its sensitive business information will not be revealed to the public or its competitors.

Arbitration — at least international arbitration — is principally a one-level system with a limited right of appeal. This is especially true in countries that have adopted the *UNCITRAL Model Law* or drafted legislation approximating it. Once an arbitral tribunal has rendered its award, setting it aside is not an easy task. For example, if a party shows that the arbitral tribunal was corrupted or that one party was not treated equally and therefore could not present its case, then the award could be set aside, effectively nullifying it. However, absent such egregious grounds, courts often show deference to an award and enforce it as if it were a judgment of the court. It is perhaps the ease with which awards are enforceable that makes arbitration such an attractive option.

2) Distinguishing Arbitration from Litigation

Court litigation is expensive, time-consuming, and procedurally heavy. In addition, judges are generalists and rarely specialize in any one area of the law. Arbitration, as an alternative to litigation, values efficiency and uses decision makers who possess specialized knowledge. This simple point is often overlooked. Arbitration is not intended to imitate or follow cumbersome court procedures. And yet more and more often it appears that the underlying reasons for including arbitration clauses in clients' contracts are lost on many counsel, who advance protracted discovery requests, interrogatories, and other similar procedural requests, which obfuscate arbitration proceedings and turn them into a paler shade of litigation.

Perhaps the best way to distinguish between arbitration and litigation is to consider the benefits and drawbacks of both. An important benefit of arbitration is that the dispute is most often resolved at a single-level and in a single place, rather than in multiple courts. For example, in arbitration, one hearing may take a few days, but once it is over, most of the process is done. This is unlike the court system, where a dispute may go through a multi-level appeal process. While it is not suggested that judges lack specialized knowledge, it is hard to dispute that an arbitrator who has practised in a particular area for decades is in a better position to understand and to finally make a decision more in line with the parties' expectations. One of the more important elements of arbitration is how significantly parties participate in shaping the process, rather than its being shaped by rules of civil procedure and evidence, and other court rules.

Privacy, finality, and enforceability of awards rank high on the list of reasons why arbitration is favoured over litigation.

3) Comparison with Other ADR Mechanisms

Arbitration is generally classified under the generic umbrella of alternative dispute resolution (ADR). An important goal of any ADR process is to resolve disputes while preserving relationships and to create a productive working environment between the parties. Arbitration does not always fulfill this goal; more often than not, it can be just as acrimonious as any litigation in court.

a) Mediation

Mediation is a process whereby a mediator, a neutral third party, facilitates a resolution of a dispute. A mediator is not a decision maker. The mediator's role is to help the parties reach a settlement. Except for court-mandated mediation, mediation is a non-binding process. The parties retain full control of the process and can leave the mediation at any time. Consequently, mediators, unlike arbitrators, do not impose decisions on the parties. To reach a settlement, the parties must voluntarily accept a settlement.

Generally, mediation is confidential, and parties cannot use any proposals or offers discussed during the mediation in any future litigation. Additionally, a mediator's skill set is very different from an arbitrator's. Mediators use various skills, particularly active listening, questioning, negotiating, and creating options, to help the parties work out *their own* solution to their dispute. A compromise is often involved but not in the sense of splitting the difference. The goal is to find a win-win solution, in which both sides achieve something they want.

Mediation is an interests-based process. In reaching a solution, the parties take into account many subjective interests. One of mediation's strengths is that the parties can consider interests such as their future relationship in deciding whether to accept a decision. This is in stark contrast to arbitration, where the parties hand over control to the arbitrators. Arbitration is a rights-based process. It uses an objective standard—the applicable law. Arbitration is different from mediation because the parties are not seeking to convince the other side. Instead, they are seeking to convince the arbitrators.

Mediation is well-suited to continuing business relationships. It is also good for parties that wish to maintain complete control over the process. But because mediation requires cooperation, it is not well-suited to disputes where the parties have opposing views or interpretations of the law. Arbitration is closer to win-lose adversarial proceedings, and once parties are engaged in arbitration, preserving relationships is not always important or possible. Especially in large arbitrations, everything comes out in the wash.

b) Conciliation

Conciliation is a process "whereby parties request a third person or persons ('the conciliator') to assist them in their attempt to reach an amicable settlement of their dispute arising out of or relating to a contractual or other legal relationship."[7] The conciliator acts as a facilitator and cannot impose a solution on the parties. Conciliation and mediation are quite similar, and in fact the terms are often used interchangeably. If a difference between conciliation and mediation exists, perhaps it is that a conciliator may offer an opinion whereas a mediator guides parties to create their own solution.

C. CANADA'S ARBITRATION LEGAL FRAMEWORK

1) Emergence of Arbitration in Canada

The origins of Canada's arbitration framework are deeply rooted in its colonial history. Even though Canada officially ceased to be a British colony with the passage of the *Statute of Westminster, 1931*, Canada's common law provinces continued to follow the

7 *UNCITRAL Model Law on International Commercial Conciliation*, 24 June 2002, UN Doc A/57/17, art 1, online: www.uncitral.org/pdf/english/texts/arbitration/ml-conc/03-90953_Ebook.pdf.

English common law. Indeed, until 1949 the Judicial Committee of the Privy Council of Great Britain was the court of final appeal throughout Canada. And until provincial legislatures drafted their own arbitration legislation, the English *Arbitration Act, 1889* was the operative international arbitration legislation in the nine common law provinces. In Quebec, early arbitration development followed that in France.[8] As a result of the *Quebec Act, 1774*,[9] which restored French civil law to the province of Quebec, and because arbitration is a matter that falls under the legislative competence of the provinces, Quebec's arbitration law has followed its own path. The *Civil Code of Quebec* and the Quebec *Code of Civil Procedure* resemble the corresponding French codes, in particular France's *Code Napoléon*. Nevertheless, in the context of Canada's arbitration framework, the distinctions between civil law and common law are less pronounced because provincial arbitration legislation follows principles enshrined in the *New York Convention* and the *UNCITRAL Model Law*. Indeed, neither the *New York Convention* nor the *UNCITRAL Model Law* would have entered into force had all the provinces not agreed to the accession and adoption of the two legal instruments.

Before Canada acceded to the *New York Convention* and adopted the *UNCITRAL Model Law*, Canadian domestic law had been unfriendly to international commercial arbitration. The early arbitration legislation of Canada's common law provinces tracked English arbitration legislation and was marked by heavy judicial supervision of the arbitral process. Although Quebec drew from French law, its early arbitration laws remained virtually unchanged, except for a minor amendment to the Quebec *Code of Civil Procedure* in 1966.[10] Despite Quebec's historical reliance on French law, English law remains the principal influence on Canadian arbitration

8 See Louis Marquis, "L'influence du modèle juridique français sur le droit québécois de l'arbitrage conventionnel" (1993) 45:3 *Revue internationale de droit comparé* 577, online: www.persee.fr/doc/ridc_0035-3337_1993_num_45_3_4728.

9 14 Geo III, c 83.

10 Which recognized *clauses compromissoires* as well as *compromis*.

law, though Canadian courts also rely on other Commonwealth, notably Australian, and US authority. While Quebec courts still rely on and even apply French commentaries, the ultimate appellate court remains the Supreme Court of Canada.

What took Canada so long to join the rest of the world, which had already updated its arbitration laws? Canada's apathy was due to a belief that the Canadian justice system was not in need of any adjustments to handle international commercial arbitration, especially in light of the Canadian legal tradition's favouring litigation over arbitration. Furthermore, Canada was known for fair and unbiased courts, so it was difficult to see a need for an "alternative" adjudicative process.

A conference held in Quebec City in 1985 marked an important turning point for international commercial arbitration in Canada. During this meeting, which brought together important authorities on international commercial arbitration from around the world, the Canadian government announced that Canada would accede to the *New York Convention* and adopt the *UNCITRAL Model Law*. It must be noted that an important push came from the then attorney general of British Columbia, Brian RD Smith, and the then justice minister of Canada, John Crosbie.[11] This decision has also had an important effect on Canada's domestic arbitration, and it was certainly a watershed moment for the overall growth of arbitration in Canada.

As Canada's arbitration statutes are based on the *New York Convention* and the *UNCITRAL Model Law*, we begin by examining how the separation of powers doctrine under Canada's *Constitution Act, 1867*[12] has been interpreted to allow the federal Parliament[13] and each provincial and territorial legislature to separately enact arbitration legislation based on these two legal instruments. Next,

11 See David R Haigh, QC, Alicia K Kunetzki, & Christine M Antony, "International Commercial Arbitration and the Canadian Experience" (1995) 34 *Alberta Law Review* 137.

12 (UK), 30 & 31 Vict, c 3, reprinted in RSC 1985, Appendix II, No 5.

13 In this chapter, "Parliament" refers to the federal legislature, and "legislature" is reserved for the provincial parliaments.

we review the *New York Convention* and the *UNCITRAL Model Law*, which duplicates certain provisions of the *New York Convention* and clarifies others. The *UNCITRAL Model Law* is more elaborate than the *New York Convention* as it was intended to serve as a comprehensive guide for legislators to use to fashion their national and international arbitration legislation. Again, as many of the *UNCITRAL Model Law*'s provisions are examined in more detail in subsequent chapters, our review of them in this chapter is limited to broad points of interest.

2) Constitutional Framework

Part VI of the *Constitution Act, 1867* provides for the distribution of legislative powers between Parliament and the provincial legislatures.[14] Section 92 of the *Constitution Act, 1867* specifies the classes of matters over which the provincial legislatures have exclusive competence while section 91 specifies the classes of matters over which Parliament enjoys exclusive legislative authority.[15] Section 2 of the *Constitution Act, 1871* empowers Parliament to create additional provinces and territories as well as to delimit their powers.[16] Thus, by federal statutes, Parliament conferred onto Canada's three territories powers similar to those that the provinces enjoy over the classes of matters enumerated in section 92.[17]

However, arbitration is not an enumerated class in either section 91 or section 92. Consequently, the question arises whether arbitration falls within Parliament's residual power by virtue of section 91 or whether it falls within one of the classes of matters enumerated in section 92. Since arbitration agreements are contracts and since section 92(13) provides that "property and civil rights in the province" are within exclusive provincial competence,

14 Above note 12.

15 Parliament retains a residual power to legislate in matters not specified in section 92 of the Act.

16 (UK), 34 & 35 Vict, c 28, reprinted in RSC 1985, Appendix II, No 11.

17 *Yukon Act*, SC 2002, c 7, s 18; *Northwest Territories Act*, SC 2014, c 2, s 2 s 18; *Nunavut Act*, SC 1993, c 28, s 23(1)(e)–23((1)(l).

the private contractual right to enter into, and be bound by, arbitration agreements is caught by section 92(13) and falls within provincial legislative competence. Furthermore, as section 92(14) confers exclusive competence on provincial legislatures to administer justice within the province, this section has been held to mean that matters regarding the court enforcement of arbitral awards are within provincial competence, as it is the provinces that hold the power to constitute courts, which, in turn, enjoy jurisdiction over both provincial and federal matters.[18]

Although provincial and territorial legislatures enjoy core competence in the area of arbitration, this competence is not exclusive. Parliament is competent where at least one of the parties to an international commercial arbitration is Her Majesty in right of Canada, a departmental corporation, or a Crown corporation or where the arbitration relates to maritime or admiralty matters.[19] Therefore, where a matter does not fall within one of these discrete categories, provincial or territorial legislation applies to the dispute. Most importantly, federal legislation applies where Canada is pursued under its investment obligations, like those under NAFTA's Chapter 11.

3) International Arbitration

a) The *New York Convention*

The *New York Convention* is an international treaty regulating the enforcement of foreign arbitration *agreements* and *awards*. Its inception marked a turning point in international commercial arbitration by creating a simple method for parties to enforce their arbitration agreements and awards in any state party to the treaty. Under the *New York Convention*, courts of a signatory state may refuse enforcement only on limited grounds. Unlike earlier conventions on the subject of arbitration, the *New York Convention*

18 See *Desputeaux v Éditions Chouette (1987) inc*, 2003 SCC 17 at para 43.

19 See *Commercial Arbitration Act*, RSC 1985, c 17 (2nd Supp), s 5.

shifts the burden onto the losing party to establish the grounds on which a court should refuse to enforce the arbitration award.[20]

i) A Foreign Award

The meaning of a foreign award under the *New York Convention* must be explained since this concept defines the scope of awards subject to the convention. As far as arbitral awards go, the *New York Convention* applies only to foreign arbitral awards: "awards made in the territory of a State other than the State where the recognition and enforcement of such awards are sought."[21] An award is assigned nationality under the *New York Convention* based on the country in which the arbitration takes place. The parties' nationality is irrelevant. This contrasts with other legal instruments on international commercial arbitration that use the term "international" and require either that the parties come from different countries or that the transaction occurs in a different country (hence international) to trigger the instrument's application.[22]

The first paragraph of article 1 of the *New York Convention* expands the definition by stating that "arbitral awards not considered as domestic awards in the State where their recognition and enforcement are sought" are considered foreign for the purposes of recognition and enforcement. This wording is intended to cover particular instances where certain countries apply a flexible view of "nondomestic" arbitration. For example, if two parties from the same country buy and sell goods inside their own country but if the goods come from a third country, certain countries accept that an award arising from this transaction is "nondomestic."

20 See Anthony R Daimsis, "Canada's Indoor Arbitration Management: Making Good on Promises to the Outside World" in Chios Carmody, ed, *Is Our House in Order? Canada's Implementation of International Law* (Montreal & Kingston, ON: McGill-Queen's University Press, 2010) 174.

21 Above note 3, art 1(1).

22 See, for example, *UNCITRAL Model Law*, above note 4; *European Convention on International Commercial Arbitration*, 21 April 1961, 484 UNTS 349; *Inter-American Convention on International Commercial Arbitration*, 30 January 1975, OASTS No 42.

In these countries, under the expanded definition found in article 1, the *New York Convention* would apply.

Finally, the *New York Convention* deliberately omits a definition of domestic awards. This makes sense because the convention does not apply to domestic awards. Domestic arbitration awards are subject to domestic statutes. Consequently, the *New York Convention* does not override signatory states' domestic provisions relating to domestic arbitration. Under the convention, the arbitral awards that do not fit within its definition of foreign awards are domestic awards, which are subject to distinct domestic rules.

ii) Recognition and Enforcement

There is a full discussion on recognizing and enforcing arbitration awards in a later chapter. However, it is appropriate here to signal what these terms mean as they are included in the full title of the *New York Convention* (*Convention on the Recognition and Enforcement of Foreign Arbitral Awards*).

Recognition of an arbitration award is the process whereby a party seeks a national court's formal approval of the rights flowing from the award. The enforcement of awards subsumes their recognition. Recognition is the formal act of a court not merely approving or recognizing the rights that flow from an award but using its imperium to convert the award into a formal court order. As a result, a recognized arbitration award benefits from all the rights enjoyed by a decision from the recognizing court.

The difference between recognition and enforcement is subtle but important. A motion seeking recognition of an award can be used to block attempts to raise court proceedings on issues that have already been decided in arbitration proceedings. For example, if an arbitral tribunal has found in its award that Party A did not breach a contract with Party B and if Party B nevertheless then sues before a national court on the same alleged breach, Party A can ask the court to recognize the findings of the arbitration award and effectively end court proceedings based on the principle of *res judicata*. Recognition is also useful where court litigation raises issues not covered by the arbitration agreement that led to an award but also raises issues dealt with in the award. In this case, Party A will ask the court to recognize those issues already dealt with in the award for the purposes of issue estoppel.

Where a party seeks enforcement of an award, it is usually because the arbitration award includes some form of compensation. Using the same example as above, if Party A in addition to having been exonerated from any breach has also been awarded costs, or perhaps has been successful in a counterclaim, Party A may ask a court to enforce the award. Enforcement transforms the award into an order of the court allowing Party A to seize the property of Party B to satisfy the award.

b) The *UNCITRAL Model Law*

The *New York Convention* is quite clear in that it applies to the recognition of foreign awards and arbitration agreements. In this way, the convention distinguishes between what it considers domestic and nondomestic arbitration. In doing so, however, it also reinforces the separation between international and domestic arbitration. This was a conscious choice driven by states not yet being willing to surrender full control over arbitrations conducted within their territory.

The success of the *New York Convention* convinced the General Assembly of the United Nations that a model law on international commercial arbitration that was capable of adoption by states as a blueprint for internal legislation on the subject would further contribute to the establishment of a unified legal framework for arbitration.[23]

The *UNCITRAL Model Law* began as a proposal to reform the *New York Convention* with respect to some very specific but unresolved issues in international commercial arbitration.[24] This led

---

23 See *Report of the Working Group on International Negotiable Instruments on the Work of Its Thirteenth Session* (New York, 7–18 January 1985), UNCITRAL Docs, 18th Sess, UN Doc A/CN.9/261.

24 It was the Asian-African Legal Consultative Committee (AALCC) that initially suggested drafting a protocol to the *New York Convention* to deal with what the AALCC perceived to be a lacuna in international commercial

to a report from the United Nations Commission on International Trade Law (UNCITRAL) that concluded that the best way to harmonize and improve on the state of arbitration laws of different countries was to draft a model law made up of uniform provisions.[25] The use of a model law capable of adoption by like-minded states in lieu of the traditional treaty-style agreements marked an important shift from the perspective of international harmonization. As the traditional means for like-minded states wishing to solidify agreements on a subject was to sign on to a treaty, adopting a model law to use as internal legislation signified an evolution in international integration of uniform views on law.

When UNCITRAL undertook a global survey of national arbitration laws, it became apparent that national laws on arbitration were considerably different. In its report, UNCITRAL noted areas of considerable divergence: the power of the parties to determine the applicable law, the arbitral tribunal's jurisdiction to decide on its own jurisdiction, restrictive judicial control over the composition of the tribunal, and nationality requirements for arbitrators.[26] Such idiosyncratic elements of national law were seen as barriers to a harmonized arbitration procedure adaptable to international commercial parties. A model law would eliminate such idiosyncrasies and include only those elements of arbitration practice that were recognized and accepted as international standards.

The *UNCITRAL Model Law* reflects a worldwide consensus on the principles and important issues of international arbitration practice. It covers each stage of the arbitral process from the arbitration agreement to the recognition and enforcement of the arbitral award. It attempts to do this in a relatively simple form

arbitration. The suggestion was rejected because it was thought that the *New York Convention*'s success should not be risked by a protocol aimed at amending it. Instead, a model law was suggested as an alternative means of satisfying the AALCC's concerns. For a cogent overview of the preliminary work on the *UNCITRAL Model Law*, see Binder, above note 5 at 9ff.

25 "Further Work in respect of International Commercial Arbitration," UNCITRAL Docs, 12th Sess, UN Doc A/CN.9/169 (1979).

26 *Ibid* at para 8.

and succeeds in doing so. Because of its simple but thorough form, many states including most Canadian jurisdictions simply use the *UNCITRAL Model Law* as their international commercial arbitration legislation with few or no amendments.

It is important to note, however, that although the *UNCITRAL Model Law* covers each stage of the arbitration, it does not deal with each stage exhaustively. The model law provides a framework for parties to use to tailor arbitration proceedings to their specific needs. It does this by leaving great discretion in the hands of the parties, and where the parties have not decided, it provides that the arbitral tribunal may fill the gaps.[27] Because of its construction, the model law places party autonomy at the forefront. As much as possible, the *UNCITRAL Model Law* confirms the idea that the parties should be in control of how their arbitration proceeds. This freedom, however, is not an unfettered one. The model law includes safety clauses and guidelines, which ensure that the parties may not abuse, deliberately or otherwise, their autonomy.[28] These provisions borrow from concepts of natural justice and place an emphasis on fairness. For example, *UNCITRAL Model Law* article 18 requires that above all the parties are to be treated equally and are to be provided with a full opportunity to present their case. If one party is permitted to submit written submissions, then the other party must also be permitted to do so.[29] This equality requirement is considered the *UNCITRAL Model Law*'s backbone, and article 18 is touted as one of the model law's two salient provisions.[30]

27 Above note 4, art 19.

28 See *ibid*, art 18, requiring that parties are to be treated equally.

29 The *UNCITRAL Model Law* does not, however, take a position on whether arguments must be presented orally or in writing, or on other technical points such as the length of memoranda. This makes sense given that there is no international consensus on such points. A useful document often used by arbitrators is the *UNCITRAL Notes on Organizing Arbitral Proceedings* (Vienna: UNCITRAL, 2012), online: www.uncitral.org/pdf/english/texts/arbitration/arb-notes/arb-notes-e.pdf. These notes are used to tailor the proceedings to meet the needs of the parties and the particular arbitration.

30 The other is *UNCITRAL Model Law*, above note 4, art 19.

i) The UNCITRAL Model Law's *2006 Amendments*

In 2006, UNCITRAL amended the model law to further align it with developments in international practice. In March 2017, Ontario enacted the *International Commercial Arbitration Act, 2017*, which incorporated these amendments.[31] Three prominent changes to the 1985 *UNCITRAL Model Law*, and to the previous Ontario international commercial arbitration act in particular, are worth mentioning.

The first relates to the formal requirements for creating a valid arbitration agreement. Arbitration agreements under both the *New York Convention* and the 1985 *UNCITRAL Model Law* must be in writing.[32] At first glance, this requirement appears straightforward. But, as the following examination will show, this seemingly innocuous requirement is not without ambiguity. It may also appear outmoded and overrigid given all the jurisdictions that do not object to oral contracts in general.[33] Even Canadian contract law permits parties to use oral contracts covering a wide range of subjects. In line with this, the domestic arbitration acts of British Columbia and Alberta both permit oral arbitration agreements.[34] However, both provinces' international commercial arbitration acts as well as comparable acts of other Canadian jurisdictions require writ-

31 SO 2017, c 2, Schedule 5.

32 *New York Convention*, above note 3, art 2; 1985 *UNCITRAL Model Law*, above note 4, art 7. The "in writing" requirement is explained in Section E(4), below in this chapter.

33 There are persuasive arguments from noted authorities that it is illogical for parties to be able to enforce rights stemming from oral agreements to buy and sell valuable goods yet escape the related obligation to arbitrate simply because agreement on this latter point has been reached orally: see Neil Kaplan, QC, "Is the Need for Writing as Expressed in the New York Convention and the Model Law Out of Step with Commercial Practice?" (1996) 12:1 *Arbitration International* 27, online: https://doi.org/10.1093/arbitration/12.1.27.

34 The *Arbitration Act*, RSBC 1996, c 55, s 1, defines an "arbitration agreement" as "a written or oral term of an agreement between 2 or more persons to submit present or future disputes between them to arbitration, whether or not an arbitrator is named, but does not include an agreement to which the *International Commercial Arbitration Act* applies." The *Arbitration Act*, RSA 2000, c A-43, s 5(1), states that an "arbitration agreement need not be in writing."

ten arbitration agreements.[35] Interestingly, in most other areas of arbitration theory, international norms tend to be more lenient than their domestic counterparts.[36] The international trend appears headed toward a loosening of the "in writing" requirement under national laws on international arbitration, and the 2006 amendments are a step in that direction. Ontario's new act incorporating the 2006 amendments allows parties to form an arbitration agreement if "its content is recorded in any form, whether or not the arbitration agreement or contract has been concluded orally, by conduct, or by other means."[37] This significant departure now allows parties to use recording technology to evidence the agreement and shifts the means for proving an agreement away from, what many deem, anachronistic forms of evidence. This is a marked departure, in particular, from the standard found in the *New York Convention*.

---

35 Federal legislation: *Commercial Arbitration Act*, above note 19, Schedule 1, art 7(2). Territorial legislation: *International Commercial Arbitration Act*, RSY 2002, c 123, Schedule, art 7(2); *International Commercial Arbitration Act*, RSNWT 1988, c I-6, Schedule B, art 7(2); *International Commercial Arbitration Act*, RSNWT (Nu) 1988, c I-6, Schedule B, art 7(2). Provincial legislation reproducing *UNCITRAL Model Law*, above note 4, art 7: *International Commercial Arbitration Act*, RSA 2000, c I-5, Schedule 2, art 7(2); *The International Commercial Arbitration Act*, SS 1988–89, c I-10.2, Schedule, art 7(2); *The International Commercial Arbitration Act*, CCSM c C151, Schedule B, art 7(2); *International Commercial Arbitration Act*, RSO 1990, c I.9, Schedule, art 7(2) [1990 ON *ICAA*], now replaced with new act, above note 31; *International Commercial Arbitration Act*, RSNB 2011, c 176, Schedule B, art 7(2); *International Commercial Arbitration Act*, RSNS 1989, c 234, Schedule B, art 7(1); *International Commercial Arbitration Act*, RSPEI 1988, c I-5, Part II, art 7(2); *International Commercial Arbitration Act*, RSNL 1990, c I-15, Schedule B, art 7(2). Provincial legislation based on *UNCITRAL Model Law*, above note 4, art 7, with slight variations: *International Commercial Arbitration Act*, RSBC 1996, c 233, s 7; *Civil Code of Quebec*, CQLR c CCQ-1991, art 2640 [CcQ].

36 The best-known example is the restrictive grounds for setting aside and refusing recognition and enforcement of international arbitration awards. Under domestic arbitration legislation, the right of appeal and judicial review resembles the national court option. The recognition, enforcement, and setting aside of international arbitration awards is dealt with exhaustively in Chapters 9 & 10.

37 Above note 31, Schedule 2, art 7(3).

The second important amendment relates to interim measures. Parties often seek interim measures in international arbitration to ensure that the very purpose of the arbitration is not frustrated while awaiting the arbitral tribunal's decision on the merits, to regulate party conduct during the arbitral proceedings, or to conserve evidence. The 1985 *UNCITRAL Model Law* placed two important restrictions on arbitral-ordered interim measures. The first was that these measures could relate only to the subject matter of the dispute. The second was that they could be directed only against parties to the dispute. Quite significantly, the 1985 *UNCITRAL Model Law* was silent on whether and how to enforce interim measures. The 2006 amendments have changed this. Under these amendments, interim measures are enforced in the same way that final arbitral awards are enforced. This is a significant change because it now gives teeth to what were considered by some toothless arbitral orders. To be fair, even before the 2006 amendments, Ontario's legislation had taken the bold step of allowing enforcement of these measures.[38] Ontario was the lone Canadian jurisdiction to do this. But the 2006 *UNCITRAL Model Law* amendments went even further than the earlier Ontario amendment by allowing what the 2006 *UNCITRAL Model Law* calls "preliminary orders." These orders allow one party to seek on an *ex parte* basis an order from the tribunal directing the targeted party to not take any measure that would frustrate an award. Given the extreme nature of such orders, they are not enforceable, and parties may agree to opt out of this regime.

The third amendment worth mentioning is the addition of article 2A. This new provision more or less put into writing what most seasoned practitioners had already known: The *UNCITRAL Model Law* should be interpreted bearing in mind its international

38 Ontario's previous Act (1990 ON *ICAA*, above note 35, s 9) explained that interim measures should for enforcement purposes be treated like final awards. Other jurisdictions that similarly enforced interim measures before the 2006 amendments included England (s 42(1) of its 1996 arbitration act), Germany (ZPO § 1041(2)), New Zealand (art 17 of its international arbitration act), and Switzerland (PIL art 183(2)).

nature and the need to promote uniformity in its application. But this addition is nevertheless important for at least two reasons. First, it sets down a rule of interpretation distinct from domestic legislation. When interpreting the *UNCITRAL Model Law,* users should consult its *travaux préparatoires* to understand what the drafters intended by the wording of any article. Additionally, decision makers should look to how other *UNCITRAL Model Law* jurisdictions interpret and apply the model law. Both these methods meet the uniformity mandate that article 2A speaks to and that is in stark contrast to the typical method, certainly under Canadian law, of interpreting domestic legislation.

ii) *Domestic Arbitration Framework*

Adoption of the *UNCITRAL Model Law* created a great deal of uniformity in the area of international commercial arbitration. The Uniform Law Conference of Canada prepared the *Uniform Arbitration Act,* which was modelled after the *UNCITRAL Model Law,* with a goal of harmonizing and modernizing domestic arbitration framework. However, the model law had to be adapted to domestic arbitration, and its terminology was "somewhat domesticated and expanded for the assistance of Canadian users."[39] While the objective of the *Uniform Arbitration Act* was to unify domestic arbitration legislation and bring it in line with international standards, complete uniformity has not yet been achieved. Seven provinces have adopted the *Uniform Arbitration Act*: Alberta, Saskatchewan, Manitoba, Ontario, New Brunswick, Nova Scotia, and Prince Edward Island.[40] British Columbia has substantially similar legislation, but Newfoundland and Labrador, Yukon, Northwest Territories, and Nunavut still have pre-1985 arbitration acts based on the English

39 Uniform Law Conference of Canada, *Uniform Arbitration Act* (1990) at 2-3, online: www.ulcc.ca/en/home/117-josetta-1-en-gb/uniform-actsa/arbitration-act/1391-uniform-arbitration-act-1990.

40 The *Uniform Arbitration Act* was adopted by the Uniform Law Conference of Canada in 1990 and amended in 1995 and again in 2002. Alberta adopted the 2002 version, and the Quebec legislation, based on the *UNCITRAL Model Law,* is seen as similar. The remaining provinces adopted either the 1990 version or the 1995 version.

Arbitration Act, 1889. Quebec has adopted the *UNCITRAL Model Law* for both international and domestic arbitrations. In provinces that had adopted the *Uniform Arbitration Act*, the *Act* applies to all arbitrations that are not excluded by the Act itself. The *International Commercial Arbitration Act* (*UNCITRAL Model Law)* applies to the arbitrations that are excluded under the domestic Act. The Uniform Law Conference of Canada has recently issued a discussion paper to serve as a basis for future reform of the *Uniform Arbitration Act*.[41]

Table 1.1, below, lays out Canada's arbitration legislation for both domestic and international arbitration.

41 Uniform Law Conference of Canada, "Domestic Arbitration in Canada: Proposals for a New Uniform Arbitration Act — Discussion Paper" (June 2015), online: www.ulcc.ca/images/stories/2015_pdf_en/2015ulcc0007.pdf.

Table 1.1: Canada's Arbitration Legislation

Jurisdiction	Domestic arbitration	International arbitration: *New York Convention*[*] Integral[‡]	International arbitration: *New York Convention*[*] Incorporated[§]	International arbitration: *New York Convention*[*] Commercial reservation	International arbitration: *UNCITRAL Model Law*[†] Integral[‡]	International arbitration: *UNCITRAL Model Law*[†] Incorporated[§]
Federal	*CAA*, RSC 1985, c 17 (2d Supp)	*UNFAACA*, RSC 1985, c 16 (2d Supp)		Yes		*CAA*, RSC 1985, c 17 (2d Supp)
Yukon	*AA*, RSY 2002, c 8	*FAAA*, RSY 2002, c 93		Yes	*ICAA*, RSY 2002, c 123	
Northwest Territories	*AA*, RSNWT 1988, c A-5	*ICAA*, RSNWT 1988, c I-6		Yes	*ICAA*, RSNWT 1988, c I-6	
Nunavut	*AA*, RSNWT (Nu) 1988, c A-5	*ICAA*, RSNWT (Nu) 1988, c I-6		Yes	*ICAA*, RSNWT (Nu) 1988, c I-6	
British Columbia	*AA*, RSBC 1996, c 55	*FAAA*, RSBC 1996, c 154		Yes		*ICAA*, RSBC 1996, c 233
Alberta	*AA*, RSA 2000, c A-43	*ICAA*, RSA 2000, c I-5		Yes	*ICAA*, RSA 2000, c I-5	
Saskatchewan	*AA, 1992*, SS 1992, c A-24.1	*EFAAA, 1996*, SS 1996, c E-9.12		Yes	*ICAA*, SS 1988–89, c I-10.2	
Manitoba	*AA*, CCSM c A120	*ICAA*, CCSM c C151		Yes	*ICAA*, CCSM c C151	

* Above note 3.
† Above note 4.
‡ Included in Act as a separate annex or schedule, in certain cases following interpretive and explanatory notes.
§ Incorporated into Act with modifications.

AA: (The) Arbitration Act
CAA: Commercial Arbitration Act
EFAAA: The Enforcement of Foreign Arbitral Awards Act
FAAA: Foreign Arbitral Awards Act
ICAA: (The) International Commercial Arbitration Act
UNFAACA: United Nations Foreign Arbitral Awards Convention Act

Jurisdiction	Domestic arbitration	International arbitration: *New York Convention*[*] Integral[‡]	International arbitration: *New York Convention*[*] Incorporated[§]	International arbitration: *New York Convention*[*] Commercial reservation	International arbitration: *UNCITRAL Model Law*[†] Integral[‡]	International arbitration: *UNCITRAL Model Law*[†] Incorporated[§]
Ontario	*AA, 1991*, SO 1991, c 17	*ICAA, 2017*, SO 2017, c 2, Sch 5		Yes	*ICAA, 2017*, SO 2017, c 2, Sch 5	
Quebec[**]	CcQ, CQLR c CCQ-1991; CcP, CQLR c C-25.01		CcQ, CQLR c CCQ-1991; CcP, CQLR c C-25.01	No		CcQ, CQLR c CCQ-1991; CcP, CQLR c C-25.01
New Brunswick	*AA*, SNB 2014, c 100	*ICAA*, RSNB 2011, c 176		Yes	*ICAA*, SNB 1986, c I-12.2	
Nova Scotia	*AA*, RSNS 1989, c 19	*ICAA*, RSNS 1989 c 234		Yes	*ICAA*, RSNS 1989, c 234	
Prince Edward Island	*AA*, RSPEI 1988, c A-16	*ICAA*, RSPEI 1988, c I-5		Yes	*ICAA*, RSPEI 1988, c I-5	
Newfoundland and Labrador	*AA*, RSNL 1990, c A-14	*ICAA*, RSNL 1990, c I-15		Yes	*ICAA*, RSNL 1990, c I-15	

** Quebec's legislation applies to both domestic and international arbitration. The principles of the *New York Convention* and the *UNCITRAL Model Law* are incorporated into Quebec's civil and procedural codes.

AA: (The) Arbitration Act
CAA: Commercial Arbitration Act
EFAAA: The Enforcement of Foreign Arbitral Awards Act
FAAA: Foreign Arbitral Awards Act
ICAA: (The) International Commercial Arbitration Act
UNFAACA: United Nations Foreign Arbitral Awards Convention Act

D. FOUNDATIONAL PRINCIPLES OF THE ARBITRATION AGREEMENT

1) The Doctrine of Separability

An arbitration agreement is itself an independent and separate agreement. It is a contract. When this separate agreement is contained inside another contract (like a sale of goods contract), the parties have, in effect, agreed to not one but two contracts. The first contract is the main container contract (e.g., the sale of goods contract), and the second contract is the arbitration agreement contract. This surprises many since this separate arbitration contract may simply be a clause inside the larger contract. The effect of this separateness can be quite dramatic, but, as explained below, it is necessary.

The autonomous nature of the agreement to arbitrate is essential to the proper functioning of the arbitral process. If an arbitration agreement were never independent from the contract to which it relates (the container contract), its fate would remain always tied to that of the container contract. Tying their fates together would create a difficulty that arbitration would have to overcome. If a container contract suffers from a defect that goes to the root of its existence, then all the clauses within it should, logically, suffer from this same fate, including the clause that represents the arbitration agreement. This cause-and-effect logic leads to a conundrum that if left unresolved could undermine the arbitration process. If a container agreement suffers a defect that renders it void *ab initio*, how can we rely on an arbitration agreement contained in a contract that the law deems never to have existed? The doctrine of separability was developed to solve this conundrum: An arbitration agreement is a separate and independent agreement. In Canada, both domestic and international arbitration legislation recognizes the separability doctrine.[42]

42 See, for example, *Arbitration Act, 1991*, SO 1991, c 17, s 17(2) [ON *AA, 1991*]; CcQ, above note 35, art 2642; *UNCITRAL Model Law*, above note 4, art 16(1).

The separability doctrine seems quite shocking at first, but when placed in context, it is an indispensable aspect of arbitration law. Without it, parties could always raise arguments, even if unfounded, against the container contract, and the effects of those arguments could undermine the arbitration process. This is one reason why the separability doctrine is necessary.

2) *Kompetenz-Kompetenz*

Just like the doctrine of separability, *kompetenz-kompetenz* (or competence-competence) is necessary to the arbitral process. In its simplest form, *kompetenz-kompetenz* stands for the following: arbitrators are competent (the first *kompetenz*) to determine their own jurisdiction (the second *kompetenz*). What this means is that where parties attempt to thwart the arbitral process by raising defences that call into question an arbitral tribunal's jurisdiction, that very tribunal is competent to decide the matter of its own jurisdiction. In this way, the doctrine creates a disincentive to parties' launching jurisdictional challenges.

Both domestic and international arbitration legislation recognizes this doctrine. For example, Ontario's domestic *Arbitration Act, 1991* explains that an "arbitral tribunal may rule on its own jurisdiction to conduct the arbitration and may in that connection rule on objections with respect to the existence or validity of the arbitration agreement."[43]

3) Arbitrability

"Arbitrability" is a term of arbitration art and refers to the concept that some matters may be resolved through arbitration while others may not. The decision to restrict matters capable of settlement through arbitration vests with each jurisdiction. Some use legislation, others use caselaw, and still others rely on public policy to determine the scope of arbitrability. But whichever

43 ON *AA, 1991*, above note 42, s 17(1).

method is used to restrict what matters may proceed to arbitration, it is critical to determine whether the dispute contemplated by an arbitration agreement is actually one that the relevant jurisdiction sanctions.

Obvious examples of matters that may not resort to arbitration to resolve disputes are those matters affecting the public, like those regulated by criminal law. More difficult questions arise where public interest and private interests converge. For example, while the common law provinces allow arbitration in the realm of family law, Quebec does not.[44]

4) The "In Writing" Requirement

a) The *New York Convention*'s "In Writing" Requirement

Despite amending its international arbitration legislation to bring it in line with the 2006 amendments to the *UNCITRAL Model Law*, the Ontario Act also includes the *New York Convention* that includes the "in writing" requirement as do all of Canada's other jurisdictions. Therefore, a discussion of the convention's "in writing" requirement is necessary.

Article II(1) of the *New York Convention* requires contracting states to recognize a written arbitration agreement:

> Each Contracting State shall recognize an agreement in writing under which the parties undertake to submit to arbitration all or any differences which have arisen or which may arise between them in respect of a defined legal relationship, whether contractual or not, concerning a subject matter capable of settlement by arbitration.[45]

This provision begins by explaining that only written arbitration agreements are capable of recognition under the *New York Convention*. Of course, contracting states are free to draft separate national laws governing international arbitration with standards

44 CcQ, above note 35, art 2639.

45 Above note 3.

that are more lenient than the convention's "in writing" requirement. However, any awards recognized pursuant to such more lenient national laws are not *New York Convention* awards and consequently cannot benefit from the recognition directive of the convention.[46] The central issue, then, is determining the precincts of the *New York Convention*'s "in writing" requirement.

Article II(2) of the *New York Convention* defines an agreement in writing as follows: "The term 'agreement in writing' shall include an arbitral clause in a contract or an arbitration agreement, signed by the parties or contained in an exchange of letters or telegrams."[47] This provision explains that where an arbitral clause or agreement is signed by the parties or if unsigned contained in an exchange of letters or telegrams, the *New York Convention*'s "in writing" requirement is met.

The *travaux préparatoires* on the *New York Convention* reveal two policy reasons for requiring a written agreement. The first is to ensure that the parties know that they are agreeing to arbitrate, that is, that the parties have turned their minds to the decision to allow an arbitrator to resolve a dispute in place of a judge.[48] Of course, a party may nevertheless argue that it did not turn its mind to this consequence, but from an evidentiary perspective, a written agreement, especially a signed one, is difficult to argue away.[49]

---

46 Contracting states that do not require the written form for international arbitration agreements include Belgium, France, Italy, the Netherlands, Sweden, and Switzerland. Interestingly, these states are not *UNCITRAL Model Law* jurisdictions *sensu stricto* and are not identified as such on UNCITRAL's website.

47 Above note 3.

48 AJ Vandenberg, *The New York Arbitration Convention of 1958. Towards a Uniform Judicial Interpretation* (Deventer, NL: Kluwer Law and Taxation Publishers, 1981) at 173.

49 The Working Group found in its discussions three reasons justifying a written agreement: (1) to evidence the conclusion of the agreement, (2) to identify the parties to the agreement, and (3) to serve as a warning that the parties have given up their inherent right to go before a national court: see Binder, above note 5 at 2-400.

The second policy reason is to create a uniform standard across jurisdictions.[50]

At the time that the *New York Convention* was drafted, there was a divergence in national laws regarding the form of arbitration agreements.[51] Because the 1923 Geneva *Protocol on Arbitration Clauses* and the 1927 Geneva *Convention on the Execution of Foreign Arbitral Awards*, which regulated international arbitration at the time, did not set form standards for arbitration agreements, parties to those conventions relied on domestic standards to determine whether to enforce awards arising from arbitration agreements.

This made the enforcement of arbitration awards unpredictable, since different countries and their courts had different understandings of what was a valid and enforceable arbitration agreement. It was expected that article II of the *New York Convention* would remedy these divergences by setting a uniform standard for arbitration agreements that contracting states would apply. And this, in turn, would lead to more predictability in the enforcement of arbitration awards. For the most part, it has. For the 157 parties to the *New York Convention*, article II is a rule of substantive law that is directly applicable, and where an arbitration agreement falls under the convention, the formal requirements of article II take precedence over any national law.[52] Consequently, decision makers (judges and arbitrators) who interpret these agreements are expected to apply the standards of article II when the issue of formal validity arises.

---

50 Whether art II remains a uniform standard has recently been questioned. However, what cannot be questioned is that at the time, the *New York Convention*'s drafters intended art II to be a uniform standard: see Albert Jan van den Berg, *The* New York Arbitration Convention *of 1958: Towards a Uniform Judicial Interpretation* (Deventer: Kluwer Law and Taxation, 1981).

51 Although the *New York Convention*, above note 3, dates to 1958, its drafting began years earlier.

52 This would also hold true under art 27 of the *Vienna Convention on the Law of Treaties*, 23 May 1969, 1155 UNTS 331 [*Vienna Convention*].

b) The 1985 *UNCITRAL Model Law*'s Broader "In Writing" Definition

Although broader than article II of the *New York Convention*, article 7(2) of the 1985 *UNCITRAL Model Law* was deliberately drafted to not stray too far from the *New York Convention* to ensure that awards from model law jurisdictions would be enforceable in convention states.[53] The writing requirement reads as follows:

New York Convention, article II(2)	*UNCITRAL Model Law*, article 7(2)
The term "agreement in writing" shall include an arbitral clause in a contract or an arbitration agreement, signed by the parties or contained in an exchange of letters or telegrams.	The arbitration agreement shall be in writing. An agreement is in writing if it is contained in a document signed by the parties or in an exchange of letters, telex, telegrams or other means of telecommunication which provide a record of the agreement, or in an exchange of statements of claim and defence in which the existence of an agreement is alleged by one party and not denied by another. The reference in a contract to a document containing an arbitration clause constitutes an arbitration agreement provided that the contract is in writing and the reference is such as to make that clause part of the contract.

Travaux préparatoires confirm that while article 7 was intended to address some of the *New York Convention*'s strict requirements, it was also intended to not conflict with the convention's article II. Therefore, as a starting point, originating oral agreements cannot be recognized under the 1985 *UNCITRAL Model Law* except where it provides for a waiver.[54]

The 1985 *UNCITRAL Model Law* widens the scope of the "in writing" definition in three ways. First, the model law's language is more expansive and allows for the formation of arbitration

53 Please note that the discussed provisions changed after the 2006 amendments. See Section D(3)(b)(i).

54 Binder, above note 5 at 284 n 14.

agreements by any means of telecommunication that provide a record of the agreement. This includes exchanges by electronic mail, a means of communication that has not always been well-received under the *New York Convention.* Second, article 7(2) allows tacit acceptance of, or implied consent to, arbitration through the exchange of statements of claim and defence in which the existence of an agreement is alleged by one party and not denied by the other. This could allow parties to proceed to arbitration based on a questionable original arbitration agreement. Third, article 7(2) accounts for the common trade practice of incorporating into a contract a term, in this case an arbitration clause, by reference to another document. The article requires, however, that the contract be in writing and that the reference be such as to make that clause part of the contract.

Finally, due to the time limit for raising objections in *UNCITRAL Model Law* article 16(2), an otherwise defective agreement might be overlooked and in this sense deemed acceptable under the model law. This is not unlike the estoppel argument used when the *New York Convention* applies. Each of these points is addressed in more detail below.

i) Exchange of Letters, Telex, Telegrams, or Other Means of Telecommunication Which Provide a Record of the Agreement

Much as with the *New York Convention,* parties can use an exchange of written documents to evidence the agreement to arbitrate and meet the "in writing" requirement under the *UNCITRAL Model Law.* The focus remains on the exchange element, which requires that one party send and that the other party return the communication evidencing the arbitration agreement.

However, with the addition of the phrase "other means of telecommunication which provide a record of the agreement," the *UNCITRAL Model Law* lays to rest the question whether the list of forms of communication (letters and telegrams under the *New York Convention*) is exhaustive.[55] Indeed, the model law expands

55 1985 *UNCITRAL Model Law,* above note 4, art 7(2).

on the convention by taking into account modern advances in technology while also leaving room for future advances.[56] Underlying article 7 is the requirement that whatever method is used to prove the exchange of telecommunication, a record of the agreement is ascertainable. In light of the advances in telecommunications, this provision should be read together with the *UNCITRAL Model Law on Electronic Commerce,* which Canada and a number of other states have either adopted wholly or incorporated into legislation.[57] Electronic commerce legislation of this kind adopts a functional equivalent approach that determines how the purpose and function of traditional contracts can be satisfied using electronic commerce.

ii) Exchange of Statements of Claim and Defence in Which the Existence of an Agreement Is Alleged by One Party and Not Denied by the Other

The "in writing" requirement in the *UNCITRAL Model Law* is satisfied when an arbitration agreement is alleged by one party in a statement of claim and not denied by the other party in a statement of defence. As the wording of article 7 demonstrates, a formal original arbitration agreement is not required.[58] While this may appear counterintuitive considering the emphasis placed on formal validity of arbitration agreements, when viewed from the perspective of a submission agreement (a post-dispute arbitration agreement, which is as valid as an arbitration clause), the solu-

56 See *International Commercial Arbitration: Analytical Commentary on Draft Text of a Model Law on International Commercial Arbitration — Report of the Secretary-General,* UNCITRAL Docs, 18th Sess, UN Doc A/CN.9/264 (1985) art 7 at para 7 [*Analytical Commentary on* UNCITRAL Model Law].

57 12 June 1996, UN Doc A/51/17, Annex 1. The *Uniform Electronic Commerce Act* (online: www.ulcc.ca/en/uniform-acts-new-order/older-uniform-acts/703-electronic-commerce/1793-uniform-electronic-commerce-act-consol-2011), which was adopted in 1999 by the Uniform Law Conference of Canada and uses the *UNCITRAL Model Law on Electronic Commerce* as a source, is the basis for all Canadian legislation on the subject except Quebec's *Act to Establish a Legal Framework for Information Technology,* CQLR c C-1.1, which is based on the *UNCITRAL Model Law on Electronic Commerce.*

58 1985 *UNCITRAL Model Law,* above note 4, art 7(2).

tion provided by the *UNCITRAL Model Law* is consistent. It deems an agreed written agreement where one party alleges an arbitration agreement in a statement of claim and where the other party, on reading that agreement, does not deny its existence. Given that statements of claim and defence are signed, the signature requirement is also met. In practice, this might allow parties to rectify an otherwise flawed agreement to arbitrate by simply not referencing the flaws in statements of claim and defence or even by treating the submissions as the formal arbitration agreement. The statements of claim and defence would thereby become the consensual written agreement to arbitrate, much like a submission agreement.

iii) Reference Is Such as to Make That Clause Part of the Contract

Under the *New York Convention*, only specific references to the arbitration agreement contained in the referenced document will satisfy the "in writing" requirement. This means that under the *New York Convention*, to validly incorporate an arbitration clause by reference, the reference must not merely refer to a separate contract containing an arbitration clause but must specify the arbitration clause. But even this principle is not consistently respected across *New York Convention* signatory jurisdictions. The *UNCITRAL Model Law* allows a general reference to a document containing an arbitration agreement instead of requiring an explicit reference to the arbitration agreement contained in the referenced document.[59] It is sufficient that the parties may access the document containing the clause at the time that the contract is formed.[60]

59 See *Analytical Commentary on* UNCITRAL Model Law, above note 56, art 7 at para 8; *Report of the Working Group on International Contract Practices on the Work of Its Seventh Session* (New York, 6–17 February 1984), UNCITRAL Docs, 17th Sess, UN Doc A/CN.9/246 at para 19.

60 See *Corporacion Transnacional de Inversiones, SA de CV and STET International, SpA* (1999), 45 OR (3d) 183 (SCJ), aff'd (2000), 49 OR (3d) 414 (CA).

iv) Estoppel or Waiver

Due to the time limit for raising objections in *UNCITRAL Model Law* article 16(2), an otherwise defective agreement might be overlooked and in this sense deemed acceptable under the model law. But while this is true on a simple reading of the text, parties should proceed with caution, especially where the enforcing state relies on the stricter *New York Convention* requirements. Under the convention, the only means to overcome a defective agreement is to raise the defence of estoppel when a party seeks to prevent recognition and enforcement of the award. As good faith is an inherent principle of the *New York Convention*,[61] it is arguable that a party that has taken part in arbitration hearings without objection and has presented a thorough argument may be precluded from raising a defect in the arbitration agreement that could have been raised at an earlier stage.

E. IMPORTANT PROCEDURAL ASPECTS OF ARBITRATION

1) Arbitration Rules

Arbitration rules complete the procedural framework for arbitration. Arbitration rules can be in the form of pre-set rules published by arbitration institutions, stand-alone rules for use in ad hoc proceedings, rules published under the auspices of international organizations such as the United Nations, or rules drafted by the parties. Whichever the choice, the selection of arbitration rules is an offshoot of party autonomy as the parties select, or draft, their own rules.

It is important to realize that arbitration rules are not law — they are distinct from any legal system. Confusion on this point is understandable since prominent international arbitration insti-

61 Because the *New York Convention* is a treaty, it is subject to a good faith interpretation despite the nonretroactive rule in the *Vienna Convention*, above note 52: see *Case Concerning Kasikili/Sedudu Island (Botswana/Namibia)*, [1999] ICJ Rep 1045.

tutes designate themselves as "courts" despite not actually being courts, as most people understand the term.[62]

Arbitration rules fill the gaps that legislation leaves open. They cover simple procedural matters like time limits for the exchange of statements of claim and defence, and more complex matters related to when and how a party initiates arbitral proceedings. Arbitration rules also delineate an arbitral tribunal's powers and obligations. For example, rule 42 of the International Chamber of Commerce *Rules of Arbitration* places a "soft" mandate on the arbitral tribunal to ensure that it drafts its award with a view to ensuring the award is effective and therefore enforceable.[63]

2) Arbitrators

It surprises many to learn that anyone of sound mind may act as an arbitrator. Unlike judges, arbitrators require no formal training or law degrees and need not have ever been a member of any law society. This is why it is possible to see an engineer or other expert act as an arbitrator, particularly in highly technical or specialized areas. For example, in commodities arbitration, it is far more common to have an industry specialist act as an arbitrator than a lawyer.

The only restriction on arbitrators is that they remain neutral. Neutrality is often discussed in terms of independence and impartiality. As this topic is addressed in a later chapter, it is sufficient for introductory purposes to note that arbitrators must remain

---

62 As the London Court of International Arbitration (LCIA) explains on its website, the "Arbitration Court of the LCIA is a body of eminent arbitrators which is the final arbiter for the proper application of the LCIA Rules. Its key functions include appointing Tribunals, determining challenges to arbitrators and controlling costs. There is no connection between the LCIA and any State Court" ("Frequently Asked Questions: About the Institution," online: www.lcia.org/Frequently_Asked_Questions.aspx).

63 International Chamber of Commerce, *Rules of Arbitration* (current as of 1 March 2017), online: https://iccwbo.org/dispute-resolution-services/arbitration/rules-of-arbitration.

impartial and independent of the parties that they arbitrate. Otherwise their awards may be annulled.

3) Interim and Provisional Measures and Remedies

Arbitrators, like judges, may have injunctive-like powers. The extent of such powers is set by arbitration rules and applicable arbitration legislation. Often, arbitration commentary notes that interim and provisional measures go by many names without further addressing the considerable differences underlying legislative linguistic choices. Different jurisdictions treat these measures differently. Some jurisdictions consider them matters of substance while others consider them matters of procedure. Dismissing provisional measures as merely flora of another name without study seems imprudent. An important albeit subtle difference exists between the common law's provisional remedies and the civil law's protective measures.

Provisional remedies, in the form of remedial measures, serve to remedy, redress, or compensate a wrong that has occurred or risks continuing to occur. Provisional remedies address these needs by protecting parties' rights until the final award. They also help to protect any final award. Labelled "provisional," they rely on a principal demand for relief determined at a later date. Provisional remedies encompass two broad categories. The first category affects property, most often via attachment or garnishment orders and sequestering or seizing orders. Known generically as holding orders, these orders allow parties to request that property be held as security to satisfy a final award. The second category regulates party conduct. Interlocutory injunctions and similar directives usually make up this latter category. These remedies seek to maintain the status quo pending a dispute's final resolution by ordering a party to take certain actions or refrain from taking certain actions that risk prejudicing its opponent's legal rights.

What most distinguishes provisional remedies from protective measures is how the former can be temporally nonlinear as they can redress both past and future harm. An order to pay undisputed sums in arrears is an example of a provisional remedy that seeks to redress a past injury. Although an order to pay up sums in arrears could also be seen as a protective measure, an important difference is that requesting "protection" will usually require the requesting party to establish that harm is likely to materialize if the measure is not ordered, whereas a remedy seeking merely to restore the status quo requires proving only that the act causing the harm occurred or continues to occur. Protective or conservatory measures seek to protect against future harm by preserving shriftless rights. Establishing that one's opponent is intent on dissipating its assets to avoid compensating an expected damage award makes a suitable case for protective measures, and in such a case, an arbitral tribunal may order the opponent to place sums in escrow to avoid a fruitless final award.

Aside from Quebec, however, most provinces outline what measures arbitral tribunals may order in arbitrations and classify them as interim measures. These measures usually have two important restrictions. The first is that these measures may relate only to the subject matter of the dispute. The second is that arbitrators may direct them only against parties to the dispute. Three basic grounds exist to order interim measures in arbitration practice: (1) to ensure that the very purpose of the arbitration is not frustrated while awaiting the pronouncement and enforcement of the arbitral tribunal's decision on the merits, (2) to regulate the conduct of and the relations between the parties during the arbitral proceedings, and (3) to conserve evidence and regulate its administration.

This short introduction should now set the stage for the reader to delve deeper into discrete areas of arbitration practice, procedure, and theory.

chapter two

Drafting ADR and Arbitration Clauses for Commercial Contracts

WENDY EARLE

A. INTRODUCTION

Litigation has changed in the last thirty years. We have moved from a time when many, if not most, disputes were tried to a time when 98 percent of disputes are settled without a trial.[1] The Ontario *Rules of Civil Procedure*[2] were designed to provide a fair process to parties going to trial on any type of issue, regardless of its complexity, size, or nature. While there have been significant changes to the Ontario *Rules* over the years and while there are new court directions and initiatives designed to promote dispute resolution outside of a trial, too many cases, if not most, grind through the various litigation steps prescribed by the Ontario *Rules* — pleading, documentary production, oral discoveries, motions about the documentary production and oral discoveries, pretrial hearings, etc. — until the parties, worn down by the accumulated legal fees, worn out by the drain on their time and emotional resources, and terrified by the ever-present risk of losing and having to pay costs, settle. The process is unsatisfying, costly, emotionally draining,

1 See Julie Macfarlane, *The New Lawyer: How Settlement Is Transforming the Practice of Law* (Vancouver: UBC Press, 2008) at 7–9.

2 RRO 1990, Reg 194 [Ontario *Rules*].

and not particularly just. Real people, as opposed to wealthy corporations and very wealthy people, cannot afford it anymore and are effectively denied access to justice.

The focus of this chapter is on whether arbitration can do better and whether arbitration clauses (both pre- and postdispute) can be designed to (1) avoid time-consuming disputes about the arbitration clause and process and (2) foster "fair, quick and cost-effective"[3] dispute resolution by empowering the arbitrator to customize the process to enable the parties to obtain the information that they require to resolve their dispute (whether by hearing or settlement) in an efficient manner.

My starting point will be to examine three common errors made in drafting arbitration clauses that complicate and delay dispute resolution, frequently causing the parties to argue endlessly and at great expense about matters that have virtually nothing to do with the actual dispute itself. Next I will explore the role that procedure plays in promoting fair, quick, and cost-effective dispute resolution and how procedure can promote or obstruct this goal. I will explore how the traditional approach to procedure in pre- and postarbitration clauses poses challenges to counsel, parties, and arbitrators and how modifying the traditional approach so as to impose more responsibility on the arbitrator for designing and managing the arbitration process increases the chances of achieving fair, quick, and cost-effective dispute resolution.

B. THE THREE COMMON ERRORS IN ARBITRATION CLAUSES WHICH PROMOTE LITIGATION

Pre- and postarbitration clauses are complex provisions that require the consideration of many different issues. It is beyond the

3 The phrase "fair, quick and cost-effective" is taken from the decision of Brown J in *Farrell v Kavanagh*, 2014 ONSC 905, Schedule A at para 1 (Commercial List). This case, together with Brown J's decision in *George Weston Ltd v Domtar Inc*, 2012 ONSC 5001 [*George Weston*], should be read as offering a wealth of ideas on how parties can work creatively with the judiciary in litigation to customize procedure to meet the needs of a particular case at all stages.

scope of this chapter to cover all the different points that the draftsperson should think about when preparing these clauses. I have included at the end of this chapter a checklist, as Appendix 1, taken from my book *Drafting ADR and Arbitration Clauses for Commercial Contracts*,[4] that may assist practitioners in this regard. In this section, I want to highlight three common errors made particularly in predispute arbitration clauses that have led to an uncommon amount of litigation while offering little to the parties in the way of promoting the resolution of their dispute.

1) Common Error Number One: Unclear Arbitration Clauses

The ultimate time and money waster is litigation about the meaning and intention of an arbitration clause. Section 1 of the Ontario *Arbitration Act, 1991* defines an "arbitration agreement" to mean "an agreement by which two or more persons agree to submit to arbitration a dispute that has arisen or may arise between them."[5] The "agreement" must be clear, unequivocal, and mandatory, not permissive — the parties must agree that all disputes arising under the agreement *shall* be referred to final and binding arbitration, not *may*. The agreement must be one that cannot be revoked by either party; it cannot be conditional on the future agreement of one or both parties or subject to one of the parties having the right to rescind it unilaterally.[6]

The arbitration agreement should also clearly set out exactly what disputes are being referred to an arbitrator. In this respect, arbitration clauses are often described as being either universal, that is, ones that refer all disputes arising under the particular agreement in question to binding arbitration, or particular, that is, ones that refer only certain specified types of disputes to binding

4 (Toronto: Carswell, 2001) (loose-leaf).

5 SO 1991, c 17.

6 For an example of an arbitration clause that was set aside for lack of clarity, see *Benner and Associates Ltd v Northern Lights Distribution Inc*, [1995] OJ No 626 (Gen Div).

arbitration. Usually, the universal type is the clearest and most straightforward, if only because it avoids arguments as to whether any particular dispute is included or not included in the arbitrator's jurisdiction.

It is prudent when drafting a universal arbitration clause to add the words "including all disputes respecting the validity of this agreement" after the words "all disputes arising under this agreement." In *Premium Nafta Products Ltd v Fili Shipping Co*,[7] the parties' litigation over whether an allegation that the underlying contract was invalid because it had been procured by bribery should be determined by the arbitrator or by the courts went all the way to the House of Lords. The predispute arbitration clause referred "[a]ny dispute arising under this charter" to arbitration. The House of Lords, per Lord Hoffmann, concluded that the allegation should be determined by the arbitrator and made the following helpful and sensible comments:

> In approaching the question of construction, it is therefore necessary to inquire into the purpose of the arbitration clause. As to this, I think there can be no doubt. The parties have entered into a relationship, an agreement or what is alleged to be an agreement or what appears on its face to be an agreement, which may give rise to disputes. They want those disputes decided by a tribunal which they have chosen, commonly on the grounds of such matters as its neutrality, expertise and privacy, the availability of legal services at the seat of the arbitration and the unobtrusive efficiency of the supervisory law. Particularly in the case of international contracts, they want a quick and efficient adjudication and do not want to take the risks of delay and, in too many cases, partiality, in proceedings before a national jurisdiction.
>
> If one accepts that this is the purpose of an arbitration clause, its construction must be influenced by whether the parties, as rational businessmen, were likely to have intended that only some of the questions arising out of their relationship were to be submitted to arbitration and others were to be de-

7 [2007] UKHL 40 [*Premium Nafta*].

> cided by the courts. Could they have intended that the question of whether the contract was repudiated should be decided by arbitration but the question of whether it was induced by misrepresentation should be decided by a court? If, as appears to be generally accepted, there is no rational basis on which businessmen would be likely to wish to have questions of the validity or enforceability of the contract decided by one tribunal and questions about its performance decided by another, one would need to find very clear language before deciding that they must have had such an intention . . . .
>
> In my opinion the construction of an arbitration clause should start from the assumption that the parties, as rational businessmen, are likely to have intended any dispute arising out of the relationship into which they have entered or purported to enter to be decided by the same tribunal. The clause should be construed in accordance with this presumption unless the language makes it clear that certain questions were intended to be excluded from the arbitrator's jurisdiction.[8]

Unfortunately, the Canadian courts have not yet had an opportunity to consider *Premium Nafta*, and not all the caselaw in Canada is as sensitive to the practical intentions of businessmen.[9] It is therefore prudent to include an express reference to "disputes respecting the validity of this agreement" in the language defining the scope of the arbitrator's jurisdiction. Helpful as the House of Lords decision in *Premium Nafta* is, one must have some sympathy for the parties that incurred all that time and legal expense going to the House of Lords on an issue that brought them no closer at all to resolving their substantive dispute.

8 *Ibid* at paras 6–7 and 13.

9 Some cases in Ontario have been deferential to parties choosing to have their dispute determined by arbitration, most particularly the decisions of the Ontario Court of Appeal in *Ontario Medical Assn v Willis Canada Inc*, 2013 ONCA 745, and *Haas v Gunasekaram*, 2016 ONCA 744, which reflect much of the thinking in *Premium Nafta*. Some cases reflect that thinking much less so: see, for example, *2156775 Ontario Inc (cob D'Angelo Brands) v Just Energy Ontario LP*, 2014 ONSC 3276.

As in all things, there are exceptions that prove the rule. Universal arbitration clauses can offer clarity in many situations, but they can prove to be a disaster in others. For example, consider an ordinary lease of commercial real property. The commercial lease is governed by the *Commercial Tenancies Act*,[10] which provides for a range of summary procedures and efficient self-help remedies to address common breaches of the lease, including nonpayment of rent, eviction, and relief from forfeiture. A universal arbitration clause referring all such disputes to arbitration would add only cost and complexity. For this reason, arbitration clauses in commercial leases are usually limited to setting rent on a lease renewal.[11] A similar argument can be made, and has been made,[12] in the context of shareholders' agreements where shareholders have the benefit of summary processes under the *Business Corporations Act*.[13]

2) Common Error Number Two: Unreasonable and Unworkable Time Limits

It is tempting for parties to predispute arbitration clauses to agree to timelines for various stages or steps of the arbitration and, sometimes, for the entire arbitration process. Sometimes these timelines mimic the Ontario *Rules* as in "The applicant shall have 30 days from the date that the arbitrator is appointed to deliver a statement of its position; the respondent shall deliver its statement of its position within 30 days of receipt of the applicant's statement of position." These are relatively harmless except when

10 RSO 1990, c L.7.

11 Sadly, rent on lease renewal arbitration clauses have given rise to an inordinate amount of litigation that has done little to resolve the complexities involved: see Wendy Earle, "Arbitrating the Value of Property: Approaches and Challenges" in T Archibald & M Cochrane, eds, *Annual Review of Civil Litigation 2004* (Toronto: Carswell, 2004) 189.

12 See Robert Wisner, "Arbitration Clauses and Shareholder Disputes: Are 'Fussy Distinctions' Undermining Efficient Dispute Resolution?" *McMillan Litigation Bulletin* (August 2015), online: www.mcmillan.ca/Files/183610_Arbitration%20Clauses%20and%20Shareholder%20Disputes.pdf.

13 RSO 1990, c B.16.

every single step conceivable in the process is given a timeline, which can easily result in a process that is either unnecessarily drawn out or unrealistically short, depending on the nature, size, and complexity of the actual dispute.

More problematic are the clauses that contain statements like "The arbitration of the dispute will be completed within 60 days of the appointment of the arbitrator" or "The arbitration hearing shall take place no later than 45 days following the appointment of the arbitrator." These place the arbitrator in a difficult position: on the one hand, the arbitrator is bound to respect and give effect to the intentions and agreements of the parties; on the other hand, the arbitrator has a clear statutory obligation to ensure that both parties have the benefit of due process, that they have an opportunity to present their case fully and to respond to the case presented by the other side. Unreasonable time limits cause the arbitrator to be pulled in two directions at once because it is often impossible to give effect to an unreasonable time limit and to ensure that both parties have the benefit of due process. Invariably one or the other party will feel that due process has been denied or that the intentions of the arbitration agreement have not been respected and will apply to the court for relief — perhaps even to have the arbitrator's award set aside. Once again, the parties find themselves in a court, spending time and fees on matters that are far removed from the merits of their substantive dispute.

3) Common Error Number Three: Stepped ADR Clauses

Stepped ADR clauses are clauses that provide for the parties to go through a series of stepped ADR processes before either one can start the arbitration process. Sometimes these clauses are referred to as multitiered ADR clauses. Typically, the parties are required to arrange a meeting of senior executives from each party to try to resolve the dispute, perhaps followed by a meeting of even more senior executives. There may be a mediation step as well. Each step usually has a timeline that prohibits the parties from moving to the next step until the timeline has expired. Often the clauses require the parties to act "in good faith" in going through the steps. These clauses are surprisingly common and very popular, particularly in the United States. There seems to be a romantic and folksy idea that if only the litigating parties could just talk to one another before the lawyers get in there and make everything worse, the dispute will just evaporate.

Like most arbitration practitioners, I dislike these clauses. Here is why:

1) Unless both parties agree to dispense with the steps, both parties must comply with them. They must in good faith try to resolve their dispute on a consensual basis in various ways. Unfortunately, they have to do so at the point when they know the least about their own case and the other side's. They have no documents, no summaries of evidence, no cross-examinations, no expert evidence, and often no pleadings except, maybe, a brief statement of position. They are often negotiating blindly, with no meaningful basis on which to make a principled decision.
2) The steps are time-consuming and inevitably require the parties to incur significant costs, particularly legal costs, as lawyers have to learn the case, prepare the participants for the meetings and mediation, prepare briefs for the other side, the senior executives, or the mediator, and attend. Rarely do the steps take the parties closer to acquiring the information that would enable them to make a principled settlement decision. In fact, the various steps postpone the arbitration process and the "day of reckoning" element of the arbitration hearing itself, which often does pressure the parties to think through their options.
3) The early stages of a dispute are often filled with strong emotions — anger, distrust, and disappointment. Over time, particularly after the parties have garnered more information about the strengths and weaknesses of their position, these emotions often dissipate, allowing for more rational thinking.

In summary, stepped clauses impose good faith negotiations of various formats on parties that are not ready to negotiate and likely not minded to negotiate. The result is often an expensive pantomime where everyone goes through the motions of having good faith discussions and mediation but actually uses the delay for their own agenda, which may or may not be helpful. In a worst-case scenario, one side may take steps that are profoundly detrimental to the other side's interests. Assuming that the innocent party can meet the test for an interlocutory injunction, it can go to the court for relief, but then the parties have the burden and significant cost of running *two* processes at once: the injunction application, which is intensely adverse, and the good faith negotiations, where everyone is pretending to be constructive and positive.

The caselaw on stepped clauses gives us fine examples of parties that, apparently as a matter of principle, refused to go through with the pantomime of negotiation and mediation steps. Unfortunately, the courts have not been particularly supportive. In *British Cable & Wireless Plc v IBM United Kingdom Ltd*,[14] British Cable, after two levels of unsuccessful negotiations, refused to go through with a mediation required before resort to arbitration could be made in a stepped dispute resolution clause. IBM applied to stay the arbitration until British Cable participated in the required mediation. The English High Court, per Colman J, accepted IBM's position and stayed the arbitration until the parties went through the mediation process. Once again, one is left wondering at the enormous expense and time consumed by the parties on (1) the court application and then on (2) the mediation that British Cable did not wish to participate in, both of which did absolutely nothing to advance the resolution of the substantive dispute between the parties.

While there have been a number of cases that have held that an agreement to negotiate is merely an agreement to agree and therefore unenforceable,[15] a recent decision in England of Teare J

14 [2002] 2 All ER (Comm) 1041.

15 *Walford v Miles*, [1992] 2 AC 128 (HL); *Sul-America CIA Nacional De Seguros SA v Enesa Engenharia SA*, [2012] 1 Lloyd's Rep 671 (CA); *Wah v Grant Thornton*, [2013] 1 Lloyd's Rep 11 (Ch).

concluded that an agreement to have "friendly discussions" over a *continuous four-week period*, that is, within a defined time frame, as a prerequisite to arbitration was enforceable.[16] One wonders at the time and legal costs incurred by the parties in *Emirates Trading Agency v Prime Minerals* examining the record of the meetings over the continuous four-week period, before the arbitrator and then the court, in an exploration of whether the "discussions" were or were not sufficiently "friendly" or were or were not sufficiently "continuous" over the four-week period.

C. DESIGNING THE PROCESS FOR ARBITRATION — TRADITIONAL AND NEW APPROACHES

I turn now to consider the process of arbitration, that is, the steps that the parties must take to present their own case fully and fairly to the arbitrator and to respond fully and fairly to the case presented by the other side. The process is fundamentally about the parties' exchanging information. The information required for the presentation of a case before an arbitrator is the same as the information required to engage in principled settlement discussions. It is important to ask at the outset what information the parties need to engage in principled settlement discussions or to go to an arbitration hearing. In my view, the information needed falls into three categories:

1) *The legal strengths and weaknesses of each party's case*: Lawyers can provide this, but to be meaningful a legal opinion requires an understanding of which facts are likely to be proven and which facts not proven. This leads to the second category:
2) *The facts*: Facts come in two categories: (a) facts that are obvious or can be readily ascertained or agreed on and (b) facts that are disputed and cannot be readily agreed on. The more facts in (b), the more difficult, time-consuming, and expensive it will be to determine the matters in dispute and the more uncertain the outcome. The purpose of the process is,

16 *Emirates Trading Agency v Prime Mineral Exports*, [2014] EWHC 2104.

or should be, to give the parties the information that they require to reduce the number of facts in (b) as much and as soon as possible, whether by access to relevant documents and data or examination of witnesses. After this process, the parties can assess the facts in (a) to determine the likelihood of a successful outcome and the facts in (b) to gauge the uncertainties in proceeding to final adjudication. Where a case has many facts in (a), the parties should be able to narrow the issues, simplify the process, and predict the outcome of adjudication on the merits with some degree of success, all of which would suggest that settlement negotiations have real promise. Where a case has many facts in (b), the significant uncertainties, costs, and time involved would also suggest that negotiations may be successful but for a different reason: the exercise of having the dispute fairly adjudicated would be too expensive and uncertain to be worthwhile.[17]

3) *Expert evidence*: This is not relevant in all cases, but in some cases it is central. Where it is required, significant time and expense can be saved if the parties can agree on (a) the instructions given to the experts including the assumptions that they should make in giving their opinion and (b) where relevant, the methodologies that they should apply. These are issues where, in the absence of agreement of counsel, a preliminary

---

17 I question whether human fact-finding, by a judge or arbitrator, is ever worth the effort. In his wonderful book *A Thousand Times More Fair: What Shakespeare's Plays Teach Us about Justice* (New York: HarperCollins, 2011), Kenji Yoshino makes the point that there is no such thing as an infallible human fact-finder, which is why the transition from supernatural fact-finding (i.e., trial by coals, battle, compurgation, and the like) took place so slowly. The justification offered in support of findings of fact by a judge or arbitrator is usually superficial at best, and the findings of fact are all but impossible to appeal. Yoshino, *ibid* at 92, asks whether human fact-finding is just another way of "letting an inscrutable but definitive authority help us negotiate a world that is, and will remain, largely opaque to human apprehension." If so, we have actually not moved that far from supernatural fact-finding at all. In my mind, this invites the question of why we bother with the exercise at all, particularly if we can avoid it?

ruling by the arbitrator can save significant amounts of time and money.

The perennial difficulty with the second and third categories above is that often there is no obvious way to limit the amount of information in these categories that might just possibly prove helpful to one side or the other. There is always another body of documents or data, another witness, another subject area for questioning, or another expert for counsel to argue over. A line has to be drawn somewhere to prevent, or end, hugely expensive and time-consuming quarrels about what information in these categories should be provided in any given lawsuit. The Ontario *Rules* attempt to address this issue by requiring that orders and directions given by the court be "proportionate to the importance and complexity of the issues, and to the amount involved, in the proceeding."[18] The practical problem is that frequently such orders and directions are made only at the end of a costly, drawn-out battle over productions or refusals or cross-examinations.[19] In a well-managed case, it should be possible to draw the line earlier, and with less time and effort spent arguing about it.

When the parties have these three categories of information, they are usually in a position to make a reasoned assessment of the strengths and weaknesses of their case and engage in a principled settlement discussion — or, alternatively, arbitrate their case. This is the moment when the dispute is ripe for negotiation with, or without, mediation and when the chances of a fair and principled settlement are at their highest. The threat of an imminent arbitration hearing or trial motivates settlement discussions like nothing else, which explains why government directions that impose early mandatory mediation and stepped ADR clauses often fail so dismally.[20] By the same token, the more steps and time re-

18 Above note 2, r 1.04(1.1).

19 See, for example, *George Weston*, above note 3.

20 See The Honourable Chief Justice Warren K Winkler, *Evaluation of Civil Case Management in the Toronto Region: A Report on the Implementation of the Toronto Practice Direction and Rule 78* (Toronto: Court of Appeal for Ontario, 2008) at 9–10, online: www.ontariocourts.ca/coa/en/ps/reports/rule78.pdf.

maining before a final hearing of some sort, the less motivated and pressured the parties are to settle. The goal and purpose of any arbitration process, therefore, should be to enable the parties to acquire these three categories of information as soon as possible, with as few unnecessary steps and delays as possible. In my view, achieving this goal requires an arbitration process fashioned specifically for the actual dispute—and informed by knowledge of the specific categories of information required to resolve it. Achieving this goal also requires that the arbitrator work closely with the parties to fashion the process and thereafter manage it to ensure that it is implemented as the parties intended. Once it is implemented, the arbitrator, in consultation with the parties, is in the best position to determine the point at which settlement negotiations are most likely to succeed, and to support and encourage the parties to pursue such discussions as required.[21]

Typical pre- and postarbitration clauses do not address the arbitration process in this way but rather provide for it in one of four ways:

1) They incorporate by reference the rules of a well-known arbitration institution, which may or may not also be named to administer the arbitration. The rules of most reputable arbitration institutions are detailed and cover most things, if not everything, covered by the rules of civil procedure of a common law jurisdiction. They can differ from one another in significant ways. Once parties agree to them, it is essential that counsel follow them.[22]
2) They provide that the parties will proceed by analogy to the rules of civil procedure of a named common law jurisdiction.
3) They provide that the parties agree to arbitrate in accordance with rules agreed on by the parties that are set out in the agreement or in an attached schedule. These rules tend to be a miniversion of the rules of civil procedure of a common law jurisdiction, complete with timelines.

21 For example, by appointing a mediator.

22 See *Bell Canada v The Plan Group* (2009), 96 OR (3d) 81 (CA).

4) They incorporate by reference the statutory framework under which the arbitration is to take place. In Ontario, this is usually the *Arbitration Act, 1991*[23] or the *International Commercial Arbitration Act, 2017*,[24] which incorporates the *UNCITRAL Model Law on International Commercial Arbitration*. Both statutes include basic procedural rules, and the expectation of the parties is that they will agree upon supplementary rules as required, failing which the arbitrator will rule on any procedural issues.

It should be noted that all four of these approaches, which are found most commonly in predispute arbitration clauses, are used largely by solicitors who may be unfamiliar with the practicalities of procedure in either the litigation or the arbitration context and who, in addition, are necessarily ignorant of the actual dispute to which the procedural regime they have selected will apply. This is ironic and troublesome given that it is the arbitrator who is responsible for ensuring that the parties receive due process and whose decisions will be picked over in any judicial review of her actions by the courts of the seat of the arbitration that supervise the arbitration.[25]

There are strengths and challenges with each of these four approaches. The first three represent detailed one-size-fits-all regimes, which are designed to apply equally to small matters, involving small amounts of documents or issues purely of law, and to large complex cases, involving millions of documents and perhaps allegations of fraud and bad faith with significant issues of credibility. In some cases, rules with such particularity are definitely required; in others, they most definitely are not. Advocates of these approaches argue that they provide a measure of certainty and familiarity as to what will happen, which provides comfort to counsel and clients alike. They also argue that

23 Above note 5.

24 SO 2017, c 2, Schedule 5.

25 *Mungo v Severino* (15 October 1995), Doc RE 178/95 (Ont Ct Gen Div), Campbell J, additional reasons (5 November 1995), Doc RE 178/95 (Ont Ct Gen Div): "For the disappointed arbitral litigant, jurisdiction and natural justice are good pickings."

it is open to the parties to amend the rules to suit the dispute at any time. While this sounds reasonable, more often than not one party will perceive it to be in its own interest to not change the rules. Sometimes, it will see a strategic advantage in a long and complex process. Often, it will see agreeing to change as giving in. Alternatively, counsel will fear the risk of giving up a procedural step to which their client is entitled by agreement, which could result in their being accused of missing something or losing an opportunity to learn something favourable to their case.

The fourth approach, which I call the statutory rules option, can work well for experienced counsel who take the time and effort to figure out and to work with the arbitrator to identify the procedural steps that the particular dispute requires so that it can be decided in a fair, quick, and cost-effective way. This approach has the benefit that counsel focus on the procedure required at a point when they are familiar with the actual dispute to be arbitrated. It has the advantage that the parties and their counsel are not burdened with a lengthy set of rules that they then have to agree to set aside in whole or in part.

Too often, counsel and clients take the easy route and agree to take one of the first three approaches — for all the not very good reasons set out above. It is a pity when counsel trade away one of arbitration's great advantages — its flexibility of approach — to secure the certainty of inflexibility. These traditional procedural approaches have not served the reputation of arbitration well and have even led to the view that it is just a more expensive form of traditional litigation.[26] We need to do better. We need to take a new approach that preserves and, indeed, exploits the flexibility available to arbitrators.

A new approach must do three things: (1) ensure that the procedure for the arbitration is determined when the arbitrator, the parties, and their counsel know the dispute and what it is about

26 See Quinn Emanuel Urquhart & Sullivan LLP, "The Case against Arbitration: Do the Doubters Have a Point?" *Lexology USA* (6 December 2011), online: www.lexology.com/library/detail.aspx?g=76145cb6-bb5b-4937-b6d9-8d57c855d467; Michelle Lore, "Making the Case — Arbitration Isn't Quicker, Cheaper" *Minnesota Lawyer* (19 February 2010).

and can customize the procedure to enable the parties to acquire the types and amount of information necessary to resolve the particular dispute as soon as reasonably possible; (2) entrust the design of and decisions respecting the arbitration process to the arbitrator, who bears the responsibility of ensuring that the process is fair and impartial and, hopefully, has the experience and expertise to fulfill his obligations in this regard; and (3) give the arbitrator powers to support and facilitate settlement discussions at a point when the dispute is ripe for negotiation or mediation. I would suggest that a provision in the pre- or postarbitration clause modifying the statutory rules option along the following lines has a better chance of promoting a fair, quick, and cost-effective resolution of a dispute than any of the approaches traditionally taken:[27]

1) The arbitration shall be conducted in accordance with the Ontario *Arbitration Act, 1991*, SO 1991, c 17.
2) Within 10 days following the appointment of the arbitrator, the arbitrator shall arrange a meeting with counsel for all parties (the "Initial Meeting"). The purpose and goal of the Initial Meeting is for the arbitrator to hear submissions from counsel on the procedural steps and schedule leading to the arbitration that will best ensure that the merits of this particular case will be determined quickly, cost-effectively, and fairly in a way that is proportionate to the importance and complexity of the issues and the amount involved in the dispute.
3) In preparation for the meeting, the arbitrator may require:
    a) That the parties exchange statements of position setting out the nature of the dispute and the facts and law material to their positions; and
    b) That counsel for the parties meet and attempt to reach agreement on:

27 I would like to express my sincere gratitude to Ken Glasner, QC, Arbitrator, for allowing me to peruse his standard letter to counsel directing them to attend an initial meeting with him with the goal of customizing the arbitration process to fit the requirements of the dispute. This letter provided me with many of the ideas and suggestions in this section and in this proposed clause in particular.

i) The issues/information/matters that are preventing the parties from reaching a settlement and the information required by the parties in order to either negotiate a settlement or proceed to arbitration;
ii) Facts that can be agreed upon;
iii) Facts that the parties cannot agree upon;
iv) The legal issues that are fundamental to the dispute;
v) The bodies of documents and data that each party absolutely requires to review in order to fairly assert or respond to the issues that are fundamental to the dispute, and a process for providing same as soon as reasonably possible in a cost-effective way;
vi) The identity of the key persons whose evidence is necessary in order to determine the dispute and the most effective and efficient way to obtain and test this evidence; if discoveries are required, a process for addressing relevance, refusals, and undertakings;
vii) The need for expert evidence; definition of the issues and the process and instructions to be given to the expert(s), how best to obtain and test such evidence;
viii) Whether the parties can reach an agreed statement of facts on some or all of the issues;
ix) Whether the parties can agree on a common book of admissible documents the authenticity of which is not in dispute and an agreement identifying documents disputed on the grounds of authenticity;
x) Whether there are issues that can be determined in a summary manner — i.e., by a motion for a summary award, and the process for same;
xi) Whether an arbitration hearing is required and, having regard to the various options to a conventional trial-type hearing identified in paragraph 36 of *Weston v Domtar*, how the evidence might be most cost-efficiently presented;
xii) Timelines for the steps required and counsel's best estimate for the duration of the arbitration; and

xiii) Whether a mediation or some other negotiation support would assist the parties, the identity of the mediator or negotiation support, timing, how to select the mediator if the parties cannot agree, and any other issues respecting negotiation of a fair and principled settlement of the matters in dispute.

4) Prior to the Initial Meeting, the arbitrator may require the parties to make written submissions on all of the items set out in (3), setting out all matters agreed to and those matters not agreed to with the position of the parties.

5) Within 10 days of the Initial Meeting, the arbitrator shall issue an award setting out the procedure for the arbitration of the dispute that is most likely to lead to a quick, cost-effective, and fair resolution of the matters in dispute and is proportionate to the importance and complexity of the issues and to the amount involved in the proceeding.

A provision of this type gives the arbitrator and counsel an opportunity to fashion a process for the arbitration that is proportionate to the dispute and as fair, quick, and cost-effective as it can be while ensuring that the parties have the benefit of due process. The provision will be most effective where the parties and their counsel are truly motivated to get to the heart of the issues in dispute as quickly as possible and where the arbitrator is sufficiently experienced to guide and supervise the parties in the design and implementation of the customized process. Where one of the parties is not so motivated or perhaps even motivated to drag things out, at least that reality will become quickly apparent to the arbitrator at an early stage. Parties that are interested in adding some teeth to the arbitration clause may consider a provision allowing the arbitrator to take into account the positions taken by a party in the initial meeting in the exercise of the arbitrator's discretion to award costs at the end of the day.[28]

---

28 A comprehensive standard predispute arbitration clause is included at the end of this chapter, as Appendix 2, to provide ideas and inspiration. Like any precedent, it should not be adopted blindly but always reviewed crit-

Unfortunately, a provision of the type reproduced above will be of minimal assistance where counsel for both parties (and perhaps even the arbitrator as well) have no motivation to streamline the process. Sadly, because of the way both counsel and arbitrators are usually compensated, an unspoken but significant financial incentive discourages fair, quick, and cost-effective arbitration procedure, just as it discourages fair, quick, and cost-effective litigation procedure. The longer and more drawn out the process, the more everyone gets paid. Until clients press persistently for changes to the way their counsel (and arbitrators) are paid, achieving fair, quick, and cost-effective dispute resolution by any method will face significant obstacles, regardless of how the arbitration clause is drafted.

The last forty years have seen adjudicated dispute resolution, whether by litigation or arbitration, become like the game of polo — a sport for kings, an unattainable luxury for everyone else. This poses an alarming threat to a democratic society and represents a failure for the legal profession, which is supposed to defend that society and its rights. The courts are trying creative ways to address the problems. Arbitration, which has the advantage of a tradition of flexibility, must do likewise if it is to retain its credibility. The key is for counsel and arbitrators to seize and use arbitration's flexibility in approach to create proportionate, fair, quick, and cost-effective procedures while avoiding the temptation to copy the traditional, safe, and familiar procedures of litigation. My hope is that this chapter contributes some ideas to the dialogue that must take place on the subject.

---

ically in the context of the particular contract, circumstances, and parties considering including it in their contract.

APPENDIX 1

Checklist: Significant Matters That Must Be Addressed in the Arbitration Agreement and Other Significant Issues

1) Significant Matters That Must Be Addressed in the Arbitration Agreement
    a) The Parties' Agreement to Submit Disputes to Arbitration
        - Nonarbitrators
        - Emergency Arbitrators
        - Project Arbitrators
    b) The Scope of the Arbitrator's Jurisdiction
    c) Starting the Arbitration Process: When and How
    d) Selecting the Arbitrator
        - Multiple Parties
        - Avoiding Court-Appointed Arbitrators

        i) Arbitration Institutions
        ii) Roster of Arbitrators
        iii) Arbitrators with Special Expertise
    e) The Number of Arbitrators
    f) Procedural Issues
    g) Ensuring All Parties Are Bound by the Arbitration Agreement
    h) Successors, Assigns, and Other Related Parties
    i) Time Frames Governing Various Steps in the Arbitration Process
    j) The Principles and Standards Governing the Arbitrator's Decision
        i) Law Including Equity
        ii) Objective Standards/Terms of Reference
        iii) Valuation of Business and Shares
            a. Valuation of Business
                A. The Income Concept
                B. The Market Concept
                C. The Cost Concept
            b. Valuation of Shares
        iv) Valuation of Real Property
            a. Ground Leases

f) Power of the Arbitrator to Award Interest on Any Monetary Amount Awarded
g) Procedure for Enforcing the Award
h) Language of Arbitration
i) Survival of the Arbitration Agreement beyond Termination or Expiry of the Contract
j) Consolidation of More Than One Arbitration
k) Arbitration and Class Proceedings
l) Continued Performance of an Agreement
m) Continuance of the Arbitration Where One Party Abandons or Does Not Participate in the Process
n) Subsequent Arbitration Agreements
o) Arbitrations and the Ontario *Limitations Act, 2002*
p) Dismissal for Want of Prosecution

APPENDIX 2

A Standard Arbitration Clause for a New Era

1) Any dispute, controversy, or claim arising out of or in connection with or relating to this Agreement, or the performance, breach, termination, or validity thereof, shall be finally settled by arbitration.
2) The arbitration shall be conducted by a single arbitrator having no financial or personal interest in the business affairs of either of the parties or any close personal or social connection with either of them. The arbitrator shall be appointed jointly by agreement of the parties, failing which an arbitrator shall be appointed by order of a judge of the Superior Court of Justice of Ontario, on application by either party. Absent agreement or award in the arbitration to the contrary, the arbitrator's fees and expenses shall be paid by the parties jointly.
3) The arbitration shall be conducted in accordance with the Ontario *Arbitration Act, 1991*, SO 1991, c 17.
4) Within 10 days following the appointment of the arbitrator, the arbitrator shall arrange a meeting with counsel for all parties (the "Initial Meeting"). The purpose and goal of the Initial Meeting is for the arbitrator to hear submissions from counsel on the procedural steps and schedule leading to the arbitration that will best ensure that the merits of this particular case will be determined quickly, cost-effectively, and fairly in a way that is proportionate to the importance and complexity of the issues and the amount involved in the dispute.
5) In preparation for the meeting, the arbitrator may require:
    a) That the parties exchange statements of position setting out the nature of the dispute and the facts and law material to their positions; and
    b) That counsel for the parties meet and attempt to reach agreement on:
        i) The issues/information/matters that are preventing the parties from reaching a settlement and the infor-

mation required by the parties in order to either negotiate a settlement or proceed to arbitration;

ii) Facts that can be agreed upon;

iii) Facts that the parties cannot agree upon;

iv) The legal issues that are fundamental to the dispute;

v) The bodies of documents and data that each party absolutely requires to review in order to fairly assert or respond to the issues that are fundamental to the dispute, and a process for providing same as soon as reasonably possible in a cost-effective way;

vi) The identity of the key persons whose evidence is necessary in order to determine the dispute and the most effective and efficient way to obtain and test this evidence; if discoveries are required, a process for addressing relevance, refusals, and undertakings;

vii) The need for expert evidence; definition of the issues and the process and instructions to be given to the expert(s), how best to obtain and test such evidence;

viii) Whether the parties can reach an agreed statement of facts on some or all of the issues;

ix) Whether the parties can agree on a common book of admissible documents the authenticity of which is not in dispute and an agreement identifying documents disputed on the grounds of authenticity;

x) Whether there are issues that can be determined in a summary manner — i.e., by a motion for a summary award, and the process for same;

xi) Whether an arbitration hearing is required and, having regard to the various options to a conventional trial-type hearing identified in paragraph 36 of *Weston v Domtar*, how the evidence might be most cost-efficiently presented;

xii) Timelines for the steps required and counsel's best estimate for the duration of the arbitration; and

xiii) Whether a mediation or some other negotiation support would assist the parties, the identity of the mediator or negotiation support, timing, how to select the mediator if the parties cannot agree, and any other issues respecting negotiation of a fair and principled settlement of the matters in dispute.

6) Prior to the Initial Meeting, the arbitrator may require the parties to make written submissions on all of the items set out in (5), setting out all matters agreed to and those matters not agreed to with the position of the parties.
7) Within 10 days of the Initial Meeting, the arbitrator shall issue an award setting out the procedure for the arbitration of the dispute that is most likely to lead to a quick, cost-effective, and fair resolution of the matters in dispute and is proportionate to the importance and complexity of the issues and to the amount involved in the proceeding.
8) The arbitrator shall have the authority to award any remedy or relief that a court could order or grant in accordance with this Agreement, including without limitation specific performance of any obligation created under this Agreement, the issuance of an interim, interlocutory, or permanent injunction, and the imposition of sanctions for abuse or frustration of the arbitration process, including dismissal of the claimant's claim or the respondent's defence for want of prosecution or lack of diligence in moving to the arbitration hearing.
9) The arbitral award shall be in writing, stating the reasons for the award, and shall be final and binding on the parties with no rights of appeal. The award may include an award of costs, including some or all of the legal fees and disbursements and fees and expenses of the arbitrator. In exercising his discretion in this regard, the arbitrator may consider:
   a) Success of either party in the final outcome;
   b) Positions taken at the Initial Meeting that, in the arbitrator's opinion, were unreasonable or uncooperative or that tended to complicate, lengthen, or make the process more costly, without a compelling justification based upon one party's best interests;
   c) Breach of confidentiality under (11) below;

d) Poor behaviour by either the parties or their counsel that tended to undermine the arbitration process or exacerbate tensions between the parties or their counsel; or
e) Any other issue the arbitrator, in his sole discretion, considers relevant or important in determining whether a party should pay costs and in what amount.

10) Judgment upon the award may be entered by any court having jurisdiction thereof or having jurisdiction over the relevant party or its assets.
11) The arbitration shall be kept confidential, and the existence of the proceeding and any element of it (including but not limited to any pleadings, briefs, or other documents and experts' reports submitted and exchanged, and testimony or other oral submissions and any awards) shall not be disclosed beyond the arbitrator, the parties, their counsel, and any person necessary to the conduct of the proceeding, except as may be lawfully required in a judicial proceeding relating to the arbitration or otherwise.

chapter three

Shifting the Paradigm: Moving from Litigation to Arbitration

KENNETH J GLASNER, QC

It is not the strongest species that survive, nor the most intelligent, but the ones who are most responsive to change.

— CHARLES DARWIN

A. INTRODUCTION AND SCOPE OF THIS CHAPTER

The practice of law and the development and acceptance of mediation and arbitration have changed dramatically since I was first appointed as an arbitrator in 1967 — in my third year of law. The playing field has changed. The acceptance of problem solving by clients and their counsel has grown notwithstanding pockets of resistance.

The present challenge is how to impart to lawyers the need to redirect their reasoning, and their competitive spirit, in advising their clients on resolving issues. Experience has taught me that lawyers, like other professionals, have some resistance to change — not only change in process (e.g., the rules of court) but also change in terms of a paradigm shift — the change from one way of thinking to another.

This concern is not limited to litigators who spend their time using the "have hammer — all nails" approach by seeking resolution only in the public courts. It also relates to the need for solicitors to understand, for example, that tacking on an arbitration clause from some precedent in a contract without understanding the divorce process has serious and unacceptable consequences for their clients.

After much consideration, I thought it best to deal with the subject matter not by preparing some academic paper but by setting out in some eclectic fashion primary information for the reader, providing, wherever possible, considerations for the practitioner entering this problem solving area — with an emphasis on domestic arbitration.

I have in this exercise relied upon papers I have written in the past together with papers and information gleaned from colleagues. Most of the caselaw and legislation referred to is from British Columbia. There is corresponding caselaw and legislation in other provinces.

Hopefully, you will take "a view from the balcony" with the result that you further understand the benefits for your clients of various forms of arbitration.

B. LEGAL CULTURE: THE SETTING

Legal culture has changed in the last thirty years. The skill set of lawyers of the 1970s is inadequate for problem solving in this decade. Professor Julie Macfarlane, in her book *The New Lawyer*, notes as follows:

> The new lawyer takes on all the traditional professional responsibilities of counsel as well as some additional ones. These include the responsibility to educate the client on a range of alternate process options, to establish a constructive relationship with the other side that does not undermine her loyalty to her client, to commit to the good faith use of appropriate conflict resolution processes and to model good faith bargaining, attitudes, to anticipate pressures to settle, and to advocate strongly for a consensus solution that meets, above all, the needs of her client. It is in relation to these additional responsibilities that the new lawyer faces the greatest challenges in developing an appropriate professional response to new (or reconfigured) ethical dilemmas.[1]

1 Julie Macfarlane, *The New Lawyer: How Settlement Is Transforming the Practice of Law* (Vancouver: UBC Press, 2008) at 221.

Rodney MacDonald, in a discussion paper, cites the Australian Law Reform Commission: "'significant and effective long term reform [of the system of civil litigation] may rely as much on changing the culture of legal practice as it does on procedural or structural change to the litigation system. In particular, lawyers, their clients and the courts may need to change the ways in which they perceive their relationships and responsibilities.'"[2]

Compare the following words from a paper by Peter Behie, QC, with those in the quotation below from Professor Macfarlane's book:

> It is hardly controversial to suggest that you and your client should know where a file is headed. As the inimitable Yogi Berra said, "If you don't know where you're going, you'll end up somewhere else." The development of a road map will fulfill this role. More importantly, the early development of a game plan or roadmap is essential if you are to solve your clients' problems in the most efficient way and in a manner that puts the client in the driver's seat (two goals that I also take to be not controversial) . . . .
>
> I spent the first many years of my practice transforming my clients' problems and concerns into legal issues and the [*sic*] advancing those legal issues through the litigation process. I undertook this kind of approach in a rather unexamined sort of way. I simply saw myself as and referred to myself as a commercial litigator. I formed litigation strategies sometimes only vaguely related to clients' problems and, I am embarrassed to admit, without a keen awareness of the costs (both soft and hard) of delivering these legal outcomes.
>
> I began to realize that this approach was impoverished. It often did not deliver results that clients expected or wanted, or did so at a price that was unacceptably high. Clients routinely reported feeling disaffected and dissatisfied. Worse still, I sometimes felt that my training and understanding of the process became an impediment to solutions and outcomes. Often disputes

2 Rodney MacDonald, "Legal Culture" (Civil Justice Reform Working Group Discussion Paper, 23 February 2005) at 2.

were not being resolved, not because the parties were not willing to resolve them, but rather because counsel, caught in the system, resisted resolution. More information was required; a higher level of understanding of the intricacies of the facts was needed; discoveries had to be completed. These I began to see were my needs not necessarily my clients' needs . . . .

Now, I say that what I do is solve clients' business problems often with, but not exclusively through, the litigation process. I also resist the temptation to merely transform clients' problems into legal problems and only address the latter and ignore the former. Clearly, one must apply legal analysis to the problems and use case law as a predictor of outcomes. The analysis should not, however, presuppose that litigation is inevitable or if the process is issued, that a trial is certain. The litigation trial should not wag the dog. When I use the litigation process I do so with an eye on the clients' commercial problem all [*sic*] times.

It is against that backdrop that I turn to the initial assessment. It goes without saying that if one's job is to solve commercial problems then the initial assessment has to focus on identifying what those problems are and developing a strategy that addresses the resolution of these commercial problems.

The goal, then, of the initial assessment is to form a strategy based on a clear understanding of the client's goals. It is my view that this strategy should be reduced to writing sent to and reviewed with the client. It should include the following:

(a) a description of the client's goals as you understand them together with the facts as you apprehend them;
(b) clear options for the client which should include options short of or separate from litigation;
(c) an honest estimate of the costs of each option;
(d) some rough time lines for each option;
(e) an analysis of the legal issues (both on liability and damages) and outcomes; and
(f) the probability of success to at least the litigation options (based on your judgment of the risks).

> There a [*sic*] number benefits to doing this. This road map will force discipline into your thinking from the outset, make you accountable to the client as the matter moves forward and gives the client the clearest possible picture of what lies ahead. It is a road map that will help you and your client avoid, as Yogi said, ending up somewhere else. In providing this road map, you will be allowing the client to exercise control over the decision making. In my view, it is no longer adequate to say that the litigation road has too many unexpected turns to undertake such any [*sic*] analysis or provide a road map. You can — and indeed must — explain the uncertainty of litigation and the difficulty of precision . . . .
>
> The first meeting is critical. You will want to expand on the information that has been provided to you. But more importantly, you will want to ask what the client wants to achieve. You must divine the client's goals; what they want, need and what can be done. You should obviously pay attention to the context in which the problem arises. Consider the relationships at play. Often I deal with shareholders' disputes in which the falling out is between old and dear friends or even family members. You must be attuned to these sorts of dynamics and they should weigh heavily on the judgment you bring to bear on [*sic*]course of action.[3]

Professor Macfarlane quotes a lawyer as saying "'I mean, we're trained as pit bulls, I'm not kidding you, I mean we're trained pit bulls and pit bulls just don't naturally sit down and have a chat with a fellow pit bull, the instinct is to fight and you just get it from the first phone call. I'm bigger and tougher and strong and better than you are.'"[4]

---

3 Peter Behie, QC, "Some Thoughts on the Initial Assessment and the Road Map of Dispute Resolution" (Paper delivered at the Dispute Resolution Conference of The Continuing Legal Education Society of British Columbia, Vancouver, BC, 26 May 2006).

4 Quoted in Macfarlane, above note 1 at 13.

And what of the client? How have clients viewed the culture of civil litigation? It was the British humourist Jerome K Jerome who wrote the following:

> If a man stopped me in the street, and demanded of me my watch, I should refuse to give it to him. If he threatened to take it by force, I feel I should, although not a fighting man, do my best to protect it. If, on the other hand, he should assert his intention of trying to obtain it by means of an action in any court of law, I should take it out of my pocket and hand it to him, and think I had got off cheaply.[5]

The Honourable George W Adams, QC, in his book *Mediating Justice*, comments on the present judicial culture:

> Lawyers increasingly distrust one another. The profession is no longer a seamless cadre of legal professionals. Recessions and the economics of lawyering have also increased the number of inexperienced lawyers willing to handle lawsuits. The courts have been slow to adopt modern management techniques to administer the growing caseloads primarily because our traditional conception of justice encourages judges to be passive, disinterested and impartial. Dealing primarily with "private" disputes, judges have tended to leave the pace of pursuit to the parties.[6]

We live in a cost-conscious global society where people want to solve their problems now — not in five years — and as inexpensively as possible. The late Honourable Willard Zebedee Estey, QC, wrote, "Disputes, unlike wine, do not improve by aging."[7]

When I refer to costs, it is not only to financial costs but also to emotional and productive costs. Many business people want to

5 Jerome K Jerome, *Three Men in a Boat and Three Men on a Bummel*, ed by Geoffrey Harvey (Oxford: Oxford University Press, 1998) at 217. Jerome was an English writer and humourist of the late nineteenth century.

6 The Honourable George W Adams, QC, *Mediating Justice: Legal Dispute Negotiations* (Toronto: CCH Canadian, 2003) at 3.

7 The Honourable Willard Z Estey, QC, "Foreword" in D Paul Emond, ed, *Commercial Dispute Resolution: Alternatives to Litigation* (Aurora, ON: Canada Law Book, 1989) at v.

solve their conflicts and get on with business. Many times, they would like to repair their long-term relationship with the other litigant.

Both business executives and their lawyers share a behavioural pattern. Former US Chief Justice Warren E Burger noted the following:

> A common thread pervades all courtroom contest: Lawyers are natural competitors, and once litigation begins they strive mightily to win using every tactic available. Business executives are also competitors, and when they are in litigation, they often transfer their normal productive and constructive drives into the adversary contest. Commercial litigation takes business executives and their staffs away from the creative paths of development and production and often inflicts more wear and tear on them than the most difficult business problems. The plaintive cry of many frustrated litigants echoes what Learned Hand implied: "There must be a better way."[8]

These words appear to be consistent with the view of the Australian Law Reform Commission, noted above, suggesting the need for the involvement of lawyers, their clients, and the courts in this paradigm change.

The relationship between private decision makers — namely, arbitrators — and public decision makers — namely, judges — is the subject of a paper by John Bolton in which he quotes Lord Woolf, who was delivering a paper entitled "Why Can't an Arbitrator Be Just Like a Judge?" Lord Woolf turns the tables and asks, in essence, "Why can't a judge be just like an arbitrator?"[9] He is, of course, referring to the flexibility that arbitrators have in dealing with issues in dispute.

---

8 Quoted in Ernest G Tannis, *Alternative Dispute Resolution That Works* (North York, ON: Captus Press, 1989) at 129.

9 Quoted in John Bolton, "Why Can't an Arbitrator Be Just Like a Judge?" (February 1996) *Arbitration* 34.

In July 1996, Lord Woolf's *Access to Justice* report was published suggesting well over 100 changes to the civil litigation process.[10] One of the suggestions was the expansion of the Calderbank offer, a concept that now forms, in part, the amendment to Rule 9-1 of the British Columbia *Supreme Court Civil Rules*.[11] Since 1980, section 11 of the British Columbia *Arbitration Act* has granted an arbitrator discretion in awarding costs.[12] A Calderbank offer is a useful tool in the hands of a party that has made a fair settlement offer on a without prejudice basis, save as to costs (and where costs in British Columbia can be full indemnity).

C. PAST AND PRESENT METHODS OF RESOLVING DISPUTES

Some years ago, the *Lawyers Weekly* set out the pros and cons of various dispute resolution methods. I reproduce this information as Table 3.1, below, with certain modifications.[13]

Table 3.1: Past and Present Methods of Resolving Disputes — Pros and Cons

	Pros	*Cons*
Duel	• usually done at dawn (so it will not interfere with the workday)	• out of fashion • might get killed
Coin toss	• cheap • simple • a penny will do	• arbitrary
War	• good for business • great stories for grandchildren	• might get killed • world might end • determines not who is right but who is left

10 Lord Harry Kenneth Woolf, *Access to Justice: Final Report to the Lord Chancellor on the Civil Justice System in England and Wales* (London: Her Majesty's Stationery Office, 1996).

11 BC Reg 168/2009.

12 RSBC 1996, c 55.

13 See *Lawyers Weekly* (pre-2000) [specific citation unavailable].

	Pros	Cons
Bare fists	• good exercise • cheap	• might need cosmetic surgery afterwards • dry-cleaning bill for blood on shirt
Litigation	• respectable • great fees (if you can collect them)	• expensive • drags on forever
ADR	• cheaper than litigation • quicker than litigation • pick your own decision maker or mediator • private • now very popular • most clients prefer it once they understand it • client driven	• used to be seen as flaky • misunderstood by those who are not on the "inside"

D. ARBITRATION'S RELATIONSHIP TO LITIGATION

The relationship between arbitration and litigation formed part of the subject matter addressed by Newbury JA in *MacKinnon v National Money Mart Co* where she cited Deschamps J in *Dell Computer Corp v Union des consommateurs*:

> The neutrality of arbitration as an institution is one of the fundamental characteristics of this alternative dispute resolution mechanism. Unlike the foreign element, which suggests a possible connection with a foreign state, arbitration is an institution without a forum and without a geographic basis . . . . *Arbitration is part of no state's judicial system . . . the arbitrator has no allegiance or connection to any single country . . . . In short, arbitration is a creature that owes its existence to the will of the parties alone . . . .*
>
> To say that the choice of arbitration as a dispute resolution mechanism gives rise to a foreign element would be tantamount to saying that arbitration itself establishes a connection to a given territory, and this would be in outright contradiction to the very essence of the institution of arbitration: its neutrality. This institution is territorially neutral; it contains no foreign element.

Furthermore, *the parties to an arbitration agreement are free, subject to any mandatory provisions by which they are bound, to choose any place, form and procedures they consider appropriate*. They can choose cyberspace and establish their own rules. It was open to the parties in the instant case to refer to the *Code of Civil Procedure*, to base their procedure on a Quebec or U.S. arbitration guide or to choose rules drawn up by a recognized organization, such as the International Chamber of Commerce, the Canadian Commercial Arbitration Centre or the NAF. The choice of procedure does not alter the institution of arbitration in any of these cases. *The rules become those of the parties, regardless of where they were taken from*.[14]

E. MEDIATION VERSUS ARBITRATION

Mediation, a form of controlled negotiation, does the following:

1) looks to the future
2) focuses on relationships
3) seeks to restructure relationships
4) results in custom-made solutions
5) provides a role for the clients

In contrast, arbitration does the following:

1) looks to the past
2) focuses on facts
3) seeks to establish fault or liability
4) has winners and losers
5) is dominated by lawyers

Some of the advantages of arbitration as opposed to litigation are as follows:

1) Arbitration is generally less expensive than litigation, although it is not cheap unless carefully planned in advance.
2) The matter can if the parties cooperate be heard promptly.

14 2009 BCCA 103 at para 26, citing *Dell Computer Corp v Union des consommateurs*, 2007 SCC 34 at paras 51–52 [emphasis and ellipses added by Newbury JA].

3) The evidence is heard in private.
4) The process and the award are generally confidential.
5) Parties can determine who the decision maker will be (a great advantage over the court system). One can have the best case possible and still run the risk of losing by drawing an inexperienced decision maker.
6) The process — namely, the rules of arbitration — can be determined by the consent of the parties as opposed to the process's being governed by a specified set of rules or the parties' being required to adopt such rules.

The lawyer's role in arbitration is similar to the lawyer's role in litigation: The lawyer is an identifier, selector, and marshaller of evidence. In fact, one text describes the litigator's role as that of a historian and litigation as largely a process of recreating historical facts.[15] One needs only to look at the division of time spent on a case. The majority of time is spent gathering and presenting the evidence as opposed to gathering and arguing the law.

During the process of dispute resolution, the client and his counsel deal with an evaluation of risk taking, by which I mean an assessment of risk — namely, the cost if things go wrong and the probability of that occurring. If the cost is high, the probability must be minimized. If the cost is low, the probability may be allowed to increase according to the client's personal assessment of acceptable risk.

Risks are controlled in the following ways:

1) elimination of risk
2) elimination of activities that produce undue risk
3) insuring for otherwise uncontrolled risk
4) informed consent of the client
5) establishment of standards, controls, and regulations

These approaches come into play in any dispute either as a proactive or as a reactive procedure.

---

15 David A Binder & Paul Bergman, *Fact Investigation: From Hypothesis to Proof* (St Paul, MN: West Publishing, 1984) at 4–7.

F. THE PROACTIVE ARBITRATOR: APPLYING MANAGEMENT PRINCIPLES TO ARBITRATION

By espousing the *proactive* arbitrator, I mean active rather than passive conduct by the arbitrator. The management skills required by an arbitrator are many. She is not, in fact, a public judge while still having judge-like powers, with the ability to bind the parties in a manner similar to that of a judge. An arbitrator is a decision maker. When an arbitrator acts as decision maker in the arbitration process, one party may be happy, and one party may not be. It is important for the arbitrator to ensure that she writes a decision that clearly explains to the unsuccessful party the reasons for the decision. If not, the arbitrator will be performing economic suicide.

There have been criticisms by lawyers and their clients of arbitrators who have failed to take a leading role in controlling the proceedings from the commencement of the arbitration to its completion. Such control is, I suggest, without arrogance, required in most arbitrations. Generally, counsel prefer an arbitrator who manages the whole hearing process so that decisions are made promptly, clearly, and concisely. People like to win, but when they do not win, they need to know that the process has been fair. Arbitrators need confidence in their expertise and experience, coupled with a working knowledge of business and management. One must remember that the arbitrator relies on the parties to perform his directions and orders so that the process works smoothly.

This process requires preplanning on the part of the arbitrator with substantial input from the parties, their counsel, or both, including deciding whether they are going to conform to a specific set of rules, adapt their own rules, or do both. Other forms of appropriate dispute resolution may be used. For example, it is not uncommon in certain situations to use Med-Arb (mediation-arbitration) or, in some cases, Arb-Med (arbitration-mediation).

The structure and process should evolve, and everyone should know what has to be done, who will be doing it, and within what time frame. Throughout this process, the arbitrator must have a clear idea of the necessary personal duties and responsibilities while retaining command of the proceedings. This form of discipline and control must be evident, together with, hopefully, a trace of humility and gentle humour.

The process may commence with correspondence sent out by the arbitrator setting out a prehearing agenda and inviting counsel for input on the agenda. This letter is generally followed by a prehearing meeting preferably at an office to decide a number of issues. The alternative is to hold a conference call. By taking this approach, one ensures that no one is caught off guard or is subjected to trial by ambush.

It is important for an arbitrator to anticipate, think ahead of possible developments, and in a timely fashion to make the parties aware of events to come. The proceedings should be controlled with flexibility. The arbitrator must be prepared to make clear decisions and offer directions at critical stages. What is more, the parties must be aware of the arbitrator's objective at all times, which is to ensure that natural justice (procedural justice) and common sense, based on good commercial practice, prevail.

I suspect that no arbitrator comes close to being a Solomon, but certain leadership qualities are essential. Derek Sharp lists those qualities:

1. Knowing and understanding what is wanted by the parties and communicating it to all involved.
2. Creating a personal atmosphere, having the right appearance, body language, voice quality and formulating the appropriate package with flair.
3. Demonstrating integrity, fairness, truthfulness and the confidence to act alone.
4. Having the confidence to dominate encounters, meetings and hearings, being able to set the scene, begin to set the pace, keep control, manage change and stop proceedings when appropriate.
5. Remaining calm in crises, absorbing stress, standing off to see the whole problem, creating order from chaos, giving

simple, clear directions and knowing how to get relief from the tension after each crisis is resolved.

6. Making the parties aware of where their authority, responsibility and accountability lie and ensuring that each party performs their role and focuses on the desired results.
7. Maintaining discipline by establishing ground rules of behavior, being punctual and reliable and by offering a good example.
8. Gauging the place and timing of action, knowing the right moment to intervene, being consistent in directions and stimulating action by the parties at the right time.
9. Ensuring balanced, harmonious progress, tying up loose ends, giving clear directions on time and maintaining continuity and enthusiasm.
10. Maintaining good morale — we are all human and the best results are based on trust, recognition, rewards, satisfaction and fulfilment, allowing people maximum freedom of action.[16]

Bonita Thompson, QC, writes that most "of the problems that can plague the arbitration process can be avoided by":

1. choosing counsel who are knowledgeable in the process;
2. choosing highly experienced arbitrators;
3. using rules of procedure that provide for an efficient and timely disposition of the arbitration;
4. citing the arbitration in a jurisdiction with laws that are supportive of the arbitral process.[17]

G. PARTICULAR CHALLENGES FOR COMMERCIAL ARBITRATORS

One of the greatest challenges faced by an arbitrator occurs when one party attempts to delay the process, thereby lengthening the

16 Derek Sharp, "Applying Management Principles to Arbitration" (February 1996) *Arbitration* 6 at 6.

17 Bonita Thompson, QC, "Commercial Dispute Resolution: A Practical Overview" in Emond, ed, above note 7, 89 at 118.

proceedings, adding to their costs and expenses, and antagonizing the other parties and their counsel.

An attempt to delay the process can come in the following forms:

1) jurisdictional challenge
   - the substantive law applied to the dispute
   - the governing law regarding the arbitration procedure
   - the validity of the arbitration clause
   - the rules of the administering organization
2) discovery challenge
3) perceived procedural irregularity
   - arbitrator's impartiality
   - unfair treatment by the arbitrator

While arbitrators have no ability to control delays before their appointment, after their appointment they can exercise good and active management skills from the preliminary hearing stage to the rendering of the final award, which will make the process move to a prompt conclusion, thereby giving effect to the positive aspects of private arbitration.

H. THE ATTITUDE OF BRITISH COLUMBIA'S COURTS TO ARBITRATION

The British Columbia Court of Appeal in *Hayes Forest Services Limited v Weyerhaeuser Company Limited*, a decision written by Chiasson JA, a judge well versed in the law of arbitration, stated as follows:

> Commercial arbitration is a private dispute resolution process designed to enable parties to deal with disputes efficiently, effectively and economically. In this case, applicable legislation is the *Commercial Arbitration Act*, R.S.B.C. 1996, c. 55 (the "*Act*"). Although the *Act* provides in s. 14 that arbitral awards are "final and binding on all parties", s. 31 gives parties a right to appeal to the court "any question of law arising out of the award", either by agreement or with leave of the court. Section 32 contains a limited privative clause.

> The parties expressed clearly their intention to resolve disputes efficiently and effectively by agreeing to arbitrate before a single arbitrator to be selected from an agreed list of named persons . . . .
>
> In my view, a core value of the arbitration process — the efficient and effective resolution of private disputes — has been lost in this case, in part, because rather than simply ensuring the rights of the parties were determined on sound legal principles, the court usurped the function of the arbitrator and exceeded the authority granted to it by s. 31 of the *Act* . . . .
>
> The Commission [referring to the Law Reform Commission of British Columbia and its 1982 report on arbitration] noted that the case-stated procedure was much criticized as increasing the cost and inefficiency of arbitration and had this to say at 72:
>
> > Although arbitrations are intended to provide a less expensive and less cumbersome method of resolving disputes than litigation in the courts, the setting aside of an award can sometimes make arbitration a more costly and a less satisfactory procedure than litigation. It can also make a mockery of the two principal objectives of arbitration, namely early finality and a determination outside the courts.[18]

In August 2014, the Supreme Court of Canada rendered a seminal decision for the business and arbitral communities in *Sattva Capital Corp v Creston Moly Corp*.[19] Justice Rothstein, writing for the Court, established a number of principles including those regarding the deference to be given to commercial arbitrators and the limits of appeal, coupled with a practical, common sense approach to interpreting contracts:

> Nevertheless, judicial review of administrative tribunal decisions and appeals of arbitration awards are analogous in some respects. Both involve a court reviewing the decision of a non-judicial

18 2008 BCCA 31 at paras 1–2, 4, and 31.

19 2014 SCC 53 [*Sattva*].

> decision-maker. Additionally, as expertise is a factor in judicial review, it is a factor in commercial arbitrations: where parties choose their own decision-maker, it may be presumed that such decision-makers are chosen either based on their expertise in the area which is the subject of dispute or are otherwise qualified in a manner that is acceptable to the parties. For these reasons, aspects of the *Dunsmuir* framework are helpful in determining the appropriate standard of review to apply in the case of commercial arbitration awards.[20]

The dispute that led to *Sattva* was submitted to arbitration in February 2008. The case was heard in late September and early October. The arbitration award was released in December 2008 by Leon Getz, QC, a seasoned commercial arbitrator and retired professor of corporate law at the University of British Columbia. The award rejected the position taken by Creston Moly. The story of the leave to appeal proceedings that followed the rendering of the arbitration award is a sad commentary on the leave to appeal process. The entire arbitration was conducted and concluded within approximately ten months of the dispute's arising. The final resolution, which came with the rendering of the Supreme Court decision, took another five and a half years.

Consider only one of those benefits: the timeliness of the arbitration proceedings when contrasted with the glacial pace of the court process. In the end, what the arbitrator accomplished in less than a year in the prelude to the *Sattva* case provided the parties with more value than what the court system laboured mightily to deliver in almost six. It will now be appropriate for provincial legislatures in Canada to consider amendments to the arbitration statutes that govern arbitration appeals. The subject of legislative change is a topic for the Uniform Law Conference of Canada (ULCC) in its current review of domestic arbitration legislation.[21]

---

20 *Ibid* at para 105.

21 See Kenneth J Glasner, QC, & William G Horton, "Judicial Review of Commercial Arbitration Awards North of the 49th Parallel" (2014) 32:10 *Alternatives to the High Cost of Litigation* 151, online: http://dx.doi.org/10.1002/alt.21553.

Within a year of the Supreme Court's *Sattva* decision, the British Columbia Court of Appeal dealt with a commercial dispute in *Boxer Capital Corp v JEL Investments Ltd*. The court, citing *Sattva*, made the following comments:

> Commercial Arbitration is intended to provide a speedy and, in the vast majority of cases, final determination of the issue or issues between the parties. The issues between the sophisticated commercial parties in the present case are not terribly complex. They involve the construction of a joint venture agreement. Yet I count two separate arbitrations and nine judicial proceedings to date in this saga. Surely that procedural history is inconsistent with the objectives of commercial arbitration.
>
> . . .
>
> This was recently confirmed by the Supreme Court of Canada in *Sattva Capital Corp. v. Creston Moly Corp.*, 2014 SCC 53, a decision released shortly after the appellant filed its factum in this appeal. In *Sattva*, Mr. Justice Rothstein for the Court observed that an appeal from an arbitral award "takes place under a tightly defined regime specifically tailored to the objectives of commercial arbitrations and is different from judicial review of a decision of a statutory tribunal" (at para. 104). In general, parties *choose* to submit their dispute to arbitration; they also choose the number and identity of their arbitrator or arbitrators. This means that the judicial review framework developed in *Dunsmuir v. New Brunswick*, 2008 SCC 9, "is not entirely applicable" to appeals from arbitral awards (*ibid.*). For example, while the *Dunsmuir* framework merely affords deference to an administrative tribunal's factual findings, the *Arbitration Act* "*forbids* review of an arbitrator's factual findings" (*ibid.*, emphasis added).
>
> . . .
>
> *Sattva* held that questions of contractual interpretation should almost always be regarded as questions of mixed fact and law (at para. 50). (Historically they were seen as questions of law.) This means that, after *Sattva*, leave will rarely be granted to appeal an arbitral award on a question of contractual in-

> terpretation. (If *Sattva* had been decided earlier, leave arguably would not have been granted to appeal the parties' initial arbitral award and this lengthy saga would have been avoided.).
>
> . . .
>
> Finally, when leave is granted to appeal an arbitral award, it is important for the reviewing court to strictly honour the boundaries of the question or questions of law on which leave was granted. The appeal is not one at large. The reviewing court must constantly remind itself of the narrow question or questions before it, lest it improperly expand its search for error into areas that go beyond those questions, let alone areas that go beyond the scope of the dispute referred by the parties to the arbitrator. I proceed on this basis.[22]

The *Boxer* case is yet another sad commentary on the leave to appeal process. The first arbitration award was made in March 2009, and the dispute, after many appearances at various levels of the courts and a second arbitration award, was finally resolved by the Court of Appeal in June 2015.

In November 2016, the Supreme Court heard an appeal from the British Columbia Court of Appeal in *Urban Communications Inc v BCNET Networking Society*. In upholding the Court of Appeal's decision, the Supreme Court dismissed the appeal by Urban Communications from the bench.[23] In its reasons, the Court of Appeal had stated, "*Sattva* changed the approach to be taken on commercial leave to appeal applications and, if granted, on consideration of the merits of the appeal from an arbitrator's award."[24]

In 2016, the Ontario Court of Appeal dealt with a case where both the arbitrator's reasons and the court's reasons were reasonable. Justice of Appeal MacPherson in *Ottawa (City) v Coliseum Inc* referred to an earlier (January 2016) Ontario Court of Appeal decision in *Popack v Lipszyc* linking private consensual arbitration with the need for judicial deference:

---

22 2015 BCCA 24 at paras 3, 7, 9, and 11 [*Boxer*].

23 2016 SCC 45.

24 2015 BCCA 297 at para 53.

In a similar vein, in *Popack v. Lipszyc*, 2016 ONCA 135, 262 A.C.W.S. (3d) 841, Doherty J.A. linked the fact of a private consensual arbitration with the need for judicial deference to the result of that arbitration in this fashion, at para. 26:

> In addition to the generally applicable principles that urge deference in the review of all discretionary decisions, the nature of the specific order under appeal can also enhance the deference rationale. The application judge exercised her discretion in the context of a review of an award rendered in a private arbitration before a panel chosen by the parties to determine the dispute between them. *The parties' selection of their forum implies both a preference for the outcome arrived at in that forum and a limited role for judicial oversight of the award made in the arbitral forum.* The application judge's decision to not set aside the award is consistent with the well-established preference in favour of maintaining arbitral awards rendered in consensual private arbitrations. [Emphasis added, citations omitted.][25]

After referring to *Sattva*, MacPherson JA stated, "In my view, the arbitrator's reasoning was entirely faithful to this approach. His reasoning and result simply cannot attract the label 'unreasonable'."[26] Accordingly, the application judge had erred by setting aside the arbitrator's interpretation of the Minutes of Settlement at issue and substituting her own. The fact that the application judge's interpretation was also reasonable did not affect the result, as the arbitrator was owed deference on his reasonable interpretation.[27]

It appears that, at least in Ontario, when both the arbitrator's and the court's reasons are reasonable, the arbitrator's reasons will prevail.

25 2016 ONCA 363 at para 33.

26 *Ibid* at para 44.

27 *Ibid.*

I. ARBITRATION CLAUSES: DOS AND DON'TS FOR LAWYERS

While arbitration offers significant advantages over litigation, poorly drafted arbitration clauses (referred to as pathological clauses) not only lead to costly and time-consuming delays but also fail to meet the intentions and expectations of the parties — in particular, those that have entered into contracts to achieve some rational commercial purpose. Counsel should attach the same importance to a dispute resolution clause as they do to any other fundamental term of the agreement.

Agreements to arbitrate are formed either (1) during the negotiation of a contract or (2) after a dispute has arisen. The preferred sequence is to negotiate an arbitration process before entering into the main contract, not after acrimony has developed. The arbitration clause stands separate and apart from the main agreement. I refer you to *Premium Nafta Products Ltd v Fili Shipping Co*:

> On the other hand, if (as in this case) the allegation is that the agent exceeded his authority by entering into a main agreement in terms which were not authorized or for improper reasons, that is not necessarily an attack on the arbitration agreement. It would have to be shown that whatever the terms of the main agreement or the reasons for which the agent concluded it, he would have had no authority to enter into an arbitration agreement. Even if the allegation is that there was no concluded agreement (for example, that terms of the main agreement remained to be agreed) that is not necessarily an attack on the arbitration agreement. If the arbitration clause has been agreed, the parties will be presumed to have intended the question of whether there was a concluded main agreement to be decided by arbitration.
>
> . . .
>
> That is not this case, however. The appellants' argument was not that there was no contract at all, but that they were entitled to rescind the contract including the arbitration agreement because the contract was induced by bribery. Allegations

> of that kind, if sound, may affect the validity of the main agreement. But they do not undermine the validity of the arbitration agreement as a distinct agreement. The doctrine of separability requires direct impeachment of the arbitration agreement before it can be set aside. This is an exacting test. The argument must be based on facts which are specific to the arbitration agreement. Allegations that are parasitical to a challenge to the validity to the main agreement will not do. That being the situation in this case, the agreement to go to arbitration must be given effect.[28]

Considerations in domestic arbitration may be different from those in international arbitration. The starting point should be to carefully review the statutes that will be applicable in the client's case. Provisions dealing with costs, confidentiality, restrictions on the court, and a plethora of other matters must be considered in *each* case. There are few cases where one can apply a standard arbitration clause that will meet the needs and commercial expectations of the client. In addition, consideration must be given to a set of rules (such as institutional rules) dealing with the process that will govern, to whether rules will be decided on an ad hoc basis, or to a blending of the two.

The following is a checklist of dos and don'ts for considering arbitration clauses:[29]

1) *Do* the following:
    - have a clear, unequivocal agreement to arbitrate
    - consider the dispute resolution clause early in negotiations
    - consider whether to include a formal pre-arbitration procedure, for example, mediation

28 [2007] UKHL 40 at paras 18 and 35.

29 A number of these points were set out in an article by Karen Birch of Allen & Overy in the United Kingdom. While this article was available on Allen & Overy's website before 2010, it has since been removed. A copy is on file with the author. For another excellent arbitration clause checklist, see Barry Leon & Jana Stettner, "Arbitration Clause Checklist" (2008) 19:3 *Advocates' E-Brief* 3, online: www.advocates.ca/assets/files/pdf/e-brief/E-brief_Spring_08a.pdf.

- make an informed choice between institutional and ad hoc arbitration, and read any relevant rules (In British Columbia, I direct your attention to section 22 of the *Arbitration Act.*[30])
- specify the seat, or formal place, of arbitration
- specify an odd number of arbitrators, the manner of appointment, and if it is an ad hoc arbitration the appointing authority, if any
- specify the language of arbitratio
- consider the scope of the agreement to arbitrate
- specify the governing law
- consider whether a waiver of judicial review or appeal of the tribunal's decisions is desirable and enforceable (Subject to the applicable arbitration legislation, see, for example, sections 23, 31, and 35 of the *Arbitration Act,*[31] the parties should clearly state their intention with respect to appeals. Notwithstanding *Sattva,*[32] their joint intention should include that the decision of the arbitrator shall be final and binding and shall not be subject to appeal on a question of fact, law, or mixed fact and law.)
- consider providing for joinder or consolidation of disputes if the situation involves multiple parties or contracts (This is important in construction disputes.)
- obtain an understanding of the client's business, including whether products or services are sold within the province, the country, or another state
- consider the nature of relief that an arbitrator may impose, having regard to the law in the particular jurisdiction
- consider the effect of an arbitration clause on other agreements where the parties have other agreements in place[33]

---

30 Above note 12.

31 *Ibid.*

32 Above note 19.

33 See *Dancap Productions Inc v Key Brand Entertainment, Inc*, 2009 ONCA 135.

- consider that the client may wish to rely on the legal principles of *res judicata* and issue estoppel when the other party wishes to re-arbitrate the same issues[34]
- consider that in a recent English decision, the court considered the doctrine of abuse of process where after an arbitral award had been issued, a third party commenced court proceedings basically revisiting in a court of law what one of the parties to the arbitration thought had been settled at arbitration[35] (The lesson to solicitors is to ensure that all parties to a contract and those that rely directly on the contract buy in and are committed to the arbitral process *ab initio*.)

2) *Don't* do the following:
   - assume that dispute resolution provisions do not really matter
   - assume that arbitration is the best option for all disputes
   - assume that all jurisdictions are supportive of arbitration
   - blindly adopt an arbitration clause from another agreement
   - draft an arbitration clause without examining the rest of the agreement and related agreements
   - choose more than one governing law or seat (It is important to remember that the substantive rights may be different from the procedural law, or the *lex arbitri*. Generally, the seat of the arbitration will be the *lex arbitri*. This is one of the reasons why Canada is well-suited for international arbitration.)
   - choose arbitration rules that are inconsistent with the arbitration clause without specifying that such rules are being amended by agreement
   - assume that "split clauses," which give one party the option to arbitrate or litigate while the other party can only litigate, are valid in all jurisdictions

34 See *Ennax Energy Corp v TransAlta Generation Partnership*, 2015 ABCA 383.
35 See *Michael Wilson & Partners Ltd v Sinclair*, [2017] EWCA Civ 3.

- include restrictive criteria for the qualifications of arbitrators that may make it difficult or impossible to appoint suitable arbitrators
- specify as an appointing authority a person, position, or institution unless you are sure that she or it exists and will be willing to make the appointment
- assume that arbitration will be confidential (If the parties want confidentiality, provide for it expressly.)

J. CONFIDENTIALITY OF ARBITRATION AWARDS

One of the benefits of private arbitration is the assumption that not only will the process attendant upon the arbitration be confidential but also the award. Where an award is being reviewed by a court, a request may be made to the presiding judge that the award be sealed. Clearly, in his reasons, the judge would be careful with how he expresses his views on the contents of the award.

Consideration should be given to the following in drafting a confidentiality clause:

1) whether the issue of confidentiality is recognized by the law of the venue of the arbitration
2) whether the governing arbitral body has a confidentiality provision included in its rules

The importance of confidentiality was raised in *Emmott v Michael Wilson & Partners Ltd*.[36] There are circumstances where an award may not be kept confidential, including the following:

1) The subject matter of the dispute is required to be reported as material to the financial condition of a public company.
2) Disclosure is required by shareholders, partners, creditors, or others having a legitimate business interest.
3) One or more parties are subject to a fiduciary duty to disclose.
4) Parties have a duty of disclosure to their insurers.

36 [2008] EWCA Civ 184.

5) Parties are obliged to disclose evidence from the arbitration in a subsequent proceeding.

Consideration of these circumstances will help in designing the most appropriate confidentiality clause, as it relates not only to the process but also to the award.

K. *KOMPETENZ-KOMPETENZ*: JURISDICTION

Kompetenz-kompetenz (or competence-competence) refers to the tribunal's power or competence, in the first instance, to rule on its jurisdiction. Delays and court challenges would undermine the arbitral process if this were not so.

Jurisdictional challenges are sometimes made by a party seeking to have the court declare that the arbitrator lacks jurisdiction to hear a particular matter. This form of application is generally brought together with an application for a stay of proceedings. Both the *Arbitration Act*[37] and the *International Commercial Arbitration Act*[38] address the arbitrator's jurisdiction.

Section 22(1) of the *Arbitration Act* states, "Unless the parties to an arbitration otherwise agree, the rules of the British Columbia International Commercial Arbitration Centre for the conduct of domestic commercial arbitrations apply to that arbitration."[39] Rule 20(1) of the International Commercial Arbitration Centre's domestic commercial arbitration rules states, "The arbitration tribunal may rule on its own jurisdiction, including ruling on any objections with respect to the existence or validity of the arbitration agreement."[40]

Section 16 of the *ICAA* states as follows:

37 Above note 12.

38 RSBC 1996, c 233 [*ICAA*].

39 Above note 12, s 22(1).

40 The British Columbia International Commercial Arbitration Centre, *Domestic Commercial Arbitration: Rules of Procedure* (Vancouver: BCICAC, 1998) r 20(1), online: http://bcicac.com/wordpress/wp-content/uploads/2016/12/DCARulesofProcedureAmendedJune1998.pdf.

16(1) The arbitral tribunal may rule on its own jurisdiction, including ruling on any objections with respect to the existence or validity of the arbitration agreement, and for that purpose,

(a) an arbitration clause which forms part of a contract must be treated as an agreement independent of the other terms of the contract, and

(b) a decision by the arbitral tribunal that the contract is null and void must not entail ipso jure the invalidity of the arbitration clause.[41]

L. ENFORCEMENT OF ARBITRATION AWARDS

Under section 29 of the *Arbitration Act*, with leave of the court, an award may be enforced in the same manner as a judgment or order of the court. Judgment is entered in the terms of the award.[42]

Under section 35, and subject to section 36, of the *ICAA*, "an arbitral award, irrespective of the state in which it was made must be recognized as binding and, on application to the Supreme Court, must be enforced."[43] This is consistent with Canada's being a signatory to the United Nations *Convention on the Recognition and Enforcement of Foreign Arbitral Awards* (the *New York Convention*).[44] Over 150 countries have ratified the convention, the purpose of which is to give certainty to the issue of award enforceability, rather than having it depend on each country's national laws.

M. COSTS

In 1980, British Columbia amended section 11 of the *Arbitration Act* to give arbitrators discretion to award full indemnity for legal costs incurred by a party to the arbitration.[45]

---

41 Above note 38, s 16.

42 Above note 12, s 29.

43 Above note 38, ss 35 & 36.

44 10 June 1958, 330 UNTS 3, online: www.uncitral.org/pdf/english/texts/arbitration/NY-conv/New-York-Convention-E.pdf.

45 Above note 12, s 11.

N. UNCONSCIONABILITY

Arbitration clauses have become commonplace in national and international consumer contracts, or contracts of adhesion. Coupled with the proliferation of these "standard form contracts" (take a look at your credit card contract) are arbitration clauses very favourable to one of the parties (e.g., the credit card issuer). The American courts have considered a number of these arbitration clauses to be unconscionable.

Paul Marrow sets out criteria for identifying procedural and substantive unconscionability.[46] In terms of procedural unconscionability, the following factors are to be considered:

1) Is the contract standard form?
2) Is the suspect clause boilerplate?
3) Was the clause hidden or made nonconspicuous?
4) Is the language used incomprehensible to a layperson?
5) Was there gross inequality in bargaining power?
6) Was there exploitation of a weakness such as lack of sophistication or education?

In terms of substantive unconscionability, the following factors are to be considered:

1) Is there significant price disparity?
2) Are there private penalties?
3) Is there a denial of a basic right or remedy?
4) Are there liquidated damages?
5) Are there disclaimers?
6) Are there covenants not to compete?
7) Are there limitations on remedies?
8) Is there an absence of mutuality concerning access to the judicial system?
9) Is there predispute mandatory arbitration?

46 Paul Bennett Marrow, "Policing Contracts for Unconscionability: Guidelines for International Arbitrators Subject to the Scrutiny of US Courts" (2007) 73:4 *Arbitration* 382 at 385–86, online: https://papers.ssrn.com/sol3/papers.cfm?abstract_id=1080357.

Marrow goes on to write as follows:

> Substantive unconscionability is about terms that operate in an unfair or unreasonable fashion. Within the context of mandatory arbitration, a group of factual situations have emerged raising questions about fairness and reasonableness:
>
> 1. Clauses that permit one party to select the arbitrator or specify qualifications.
> 2. Clauses that specify inconvenient locations for the arbitration proceedings.
> 3. Clauses that unnecessarily require one party or the other to incur burdensome expenses in the pursuit of a claim in arbitration.
> 4. Clauses that give the drafter the right to unilaterally alter the terms for arbitration.
> 5. Clauses that alter existing rights and remedies, examples being clauses that shorten a statute of limitations period or restrict the authority of arbitrators to impose punitive damages otherwise permissible by law.
> 6. Clauses that restrict class actions.
> 7. Clauses that lack mutuality, i.e. relegate one party to arbitration and give the other flexibility to pick and choose between arbitration and access to the judicial system.[47]

O. GOVERNING LAWS AND JURISDICTIONAL CLAUSES

The drafter of an arbitration agreement must distinguish between the governing law and jurisdiction. When the parties come from different jurisdictions, an attempt to deal with both concepts with the same wording may lead to confusion. The parties may agree on the jurisdiction of one party or the other, or they may agree on a third jurisdiction. Each choice brings into play different legal systems.

The following is an example of what may be considered an acceptable clause in British Columbia:

47 *Ibid* at 387–88.

> All disputes arising out of or relating to this contract, or the breach, termination, or validity thereof, shall be settled by arbitration. The arbitration shall be conducted in accordance with the *International Commercial Arbitration Act* of British Columbia. The seat of the arbitration shall be Vancouver, British Columbia, and the arbitration shall be conducted in the English language.

P. INTERNATIONAL ARBITRATION

My comments about international arbitration will be limited to (1) a 2015 White & Case survey report on international arbitration[48] and (2) making a pitch for Canada as the ideal place for international arbitration.

While international arbitration has been criticized for excessive delays and costs, the stakeholders consider it to be a better alternative than international litigation. A comprehensive study of international arbitration can be found in the White & Case report. The following are some of the key conclusions of the report:

- 90% of respondents indicate that international arbitration is their preferred dispute resolution mechanism, either as a stand-alone method (56%) or together with other forms of ADR (34%).
- "Enforceability of awards" is seen as arbitration's most valuable characteristic, followed by "avoiding specific legal systems," "flexibility" and "selection of arbitrators".
- "Cost" is seen as arbitration's worst feature, followed by "lack of effective sanctions during the arbitral process", "lack of insight into arbitrators' efficiency" and "lack of speed".

---

48 White & Case LLP, International Arbitration Practice Group & Queen Mary University of London, Centre for Commercial Law Studies, School of International Arbitration, *2015 International Arbitration Survey: Improvements and Innovations in International Arbitration* (London: White & Case, 2015), online: www.whitecase.com/sites/whitecase/files/files/download/publications/qmul-international-arbitration-survey-2015_0.pdf.

- The majority of respondents do not favour an appeal mechanism on the merits in either commercial or investment treaty arbitration.
- A growing concern in international arbitration is a perceived reluctance by tribunals to act decisively in certain situations for fear of the award being challenged on the basis of a party not having had the chance to present its case fully ("due process paranoia") . . . .
- The five most preferred arbitral institutions are the ICC, LCIA, HKIAC, SIAC and SCC.[49]

Q. CANADA AS THE IDEAL PLACE FOR INTERNATIONAL ARBITRATION

Justice Barry Leon, (formerly) of Torys LLP, sets out a compelling argument in his paper "Canada on the World Stage in International Arbitration":

> The reason why Canada is a good place for international arbitration can be summarised in three words: supportive, accessible and acceptable. First, Canada's laws and its courts are supportive of arbitration. Canada has modern arbitration statutes. In fact, it led the way in implementing Model Law international arbitration statutes and acceding to the New York Convention. Canadian courts are as independent and competent as any in the world. Recent decisions dealing with *Kompetenz-Kompetenz*, subject-matter arbitrability, the scope of arbitration clauses, and recognition and enforcement of awards have consistently reaffirmed the support that Canadian courts will give to arbitration and indicated a strong judicial policy favouring arbitration.
>
> Secondly, Canada is acceptable to most of the world as a place for arbitration because it has a multicultural society, a reputation for fairness and neutrality, and both common and civil law systems. From the perspective of many Americans, although Canada is foreign, it is a known commodity. Even though there are marked

49 *Ibid* at 2 [footnote omitted].

> differences between Canada and the United States, Americans appreciate and are comfortable with Canada's common law system; legal culture; litigation system (for example, an adversarial system with limited documentary and oral discovery) and style; use of the English language; and approaches to doing business. These similarities are appreciated by people in other common law jurisdictions too, with the added attraction that Canadians are similar to, but are not, Americans. People in Continental Europe, Latin America, Asia and other parts of the civil law world may also appreciate that Canadians are similar to, but are not, Americans. Canada has less of what they see as undesirable aspects of the US legal system. Canada is more international in outlook, has a civil law tradition and is an English/French bilingual country.
>
> Thirdly, Canada is accessible — its major cities are well connected by air to almost all business centres in the world. It has good hearing facilities, with easy access to all modern technologies. For people in many leading business centres, Canada's time zones are more convenient than those in many other potential places for arbitration. Also, it is not insignificant that for arbitration participants from some parts of the world, Canada is easier to enter than the United States. And Canada's major cities are attractive places in which to spend time and are reasonably priced.[50]

In its construction, the *ICAA*[51] reflects the *UNCITRAL Model Law on International Commercial Arbitration*,[52] which is consistent with the legislation of the many states that have signed onto the model law. Enforcement of foreign awards in British Columbia is governed by the *Foreign Arbitral Awards Act*,[53] which incorporates the *New York Convention*.[54]

---

50 Justice Barry Leon, "Canada on the World Stage in International Arbitration" (2006) 72 *Arbitration* 143 at 143–46.

51 Above note 38.

52 21 June 1985, UN Doc A/40/17, annex 1, with amendments adopted 7 July 2006, UN Doc A/61/17, annex 1, online: www.uncitral.org/pdf/english/texts/arbitration/ml-arb/07-86998_Ebook.pdf [*UNCITRAL Model Law*].

53 RSBC 1996, c 154.

54 Above note 44.

The combination of the *UNCITRAL Model Law* and the *New York Convention* coupled with courts that are supportive of arbitration makes for a positive culture for international arbitration in Vancouver, Calgary, Toronto, and elsewhere north of the forty-ninth parallel.

R. UNIFORM LAW CONFERENCE OF CANADA

After extensive discussions and input from the arbitration community, and with the assistance of working groups, the ULCC recently dealt with both discussion papers on a new uniform international commercial arbitration act and proposals for a new uniform domestic arbitration act in Canada. Currently, the Ontario legislature is dealing with a new international arbitration act based upon the ULCC recommendations.

In December 2016, the ULCC adopted a revised *Uniform Arbitration Act*,[55] the purpose of which is to harmonize arbitral legislation in the provinces and territories. Gerald Ghikas, QC, of Vancouver led the two working groups' significant efforts that resulted in the suggested changes.

Recently, the minister of justice for British Columbia formed an arbitration advisory group to provide input on reforming and updating the *Arbitration Act* and the *ICAA*.[56] J Kenneth McEwan, QC, and Ludmila B Herbst note that

> Canada was, in fact, the first country to adopt the Model Law, and British Columbia was the first jurisdiction to adopt the Model Law anywhere in the world. British Columbia was particularly interested in attracting arbitration business as is reflected in the preamble to its *International Commercial Arbitration Act*, which was essentially a reworked version of the Model Law.[57]

---

55 Uniform Law Conference of Canada, "Domestic Arbitration in Canada: Proposals for a New Uniform Arbitration Act — Discussion Paper" (June 2015).

56 Above notes 12 and 38.

57 J Kenneth McEwan, QC, & Ludmila B Herbst, *Commercial Arbitration in Canada: A Guide to Domestic and International Arbitrations* (Aurora, ON: Canada Law Book, 2004) (loose-leaf) at 1-10.

S. CONCLUSION

I can do no better than to quote former master of the rolls Sir Anthony Clarke's paper "The Woolf Reforms: A Singular Event or an Ongoing Process?":

> Changing the rules is one thing; changing how the rules are interpreted and applied is another thing entirely. The most perfect system implemented imperfectly is an imperfect system . . . .
>
> In my opinion, Woolf's greatest insight was the realization that discrete structural and procedural reforms were not both necessary and sufficient conditions for successful reform. Woolf proposed explicitly that not only should there be structural and procedural reform but that our litigation culture had to change as well. If the discrete structural and procedural reforms were to achieve the end of enabling litigation to be conducted expeditiously and economically, litigation had to be carried out in a radically different way.[58]

Someone once said, "As a businessman, if I don't listen to the market, I am not in business. If I were an attorney, I'd make sure I was involved in Alternative Dispute Resolution, because it may well be the service that the market will demand and I will have to offer in the future."[59]

The purpose of this chapter has been to provide the reader with an overview of domestic arbitration in Canada with the hope that the subject matter covered in an eclectic fashion will encourage both the solicitor and the litigator to adopt a more flexible problem solving approach where the parties have opted for some form of binding process other than litigation. To do otherwise would commit counsel to continue roaming in Jurassic Park.

58 Anthony Clarke, "The Woolf Reforms: A Singular Event or an Ongoing Process?" in Déirdre Dwyer, ed, *The Civil Procedure Rules Ten Years On* (Oxford: Oxford University Press, 2009) 32 at 43–44.

59 Quoted in Tannis, above note 8 at 131.

T. EPILOGUE

There are many sources of information available to both in-house and outside counsel on understanding the practical aspects of arbitration. The following are some of my favourites:

1) *Drafting ADR and Arbitration Clauses for Commercial Contracts* by Wendy Earle[60]
2) any material published by the International Institute for Conflict Prevention and Resolution, commonly called CPR and located in New York[61]
3) any publication by Richard Susskind
4) the following four books written by Professor Ugo Draetta:
   - *Behind the Scenes in International Arbitration*[62]
   - *Counsel as Client's First Enemy in Arbitration?*[63]
   - *Monads or Triads: Conflict and Cooperation among Arbitrators*[64]
   - *On the Side of In-House Counsel*[65]
5) any article written by Wendy Earle, Thomas G Heintzman, QC, William (Bill) Horton, Justice Barry Leon, and Michael MacIlwrath
6) *Arbitration Law of Canada: Practice and Procedure* by J Brian Casey[66]
7) *Commercial Arbitration in Canada: A Guide to Domestic and International Arbitrations* by J Kenneth McEwan, QC, and Ludmila B Herbst[67]
8) *Getting Past No: Negotiating in Difficult Situations* by William Ury[68]

---

60 (Toronto: Carswell, 2001) (loose-leaf).
61 Online: www.cpradr.org/.
62 (Huntington, NY: Juris, 2011).
63 (Huntington, NY: Juris, 2014).
64 (Huntington, NY: Juris, 2016).
65 (Huntington, NY: Juris, 2012). Each of these hardcover books is approximately 130 pages and very reasonably priced.
66 3d ed (Huntington, NY: Juris, 2017).
67 Above note 57.
68 (New York: Bantam Books, 1993). This is the source of my modified phrase "a view from the balcony": see Section A, above in this chapter.

chapter four

Arbitrator Selection

KEN McEWAN

A. INTRODUCTION

It has been said that the most important decision in an arbitration is the selection of the arbitral tribunal. Unlike litigation, where the adjudicator is assigned, in arbitration the arbitral tribunal is not a permanent entity and must be selected by the parties. Having made the decision that arbitration is the best resolution mechanism for their dispute, the parties are also best placed to determine the adjudicator.[1]

This requires counsel to have a thorough understanding of their client's case at a very early stage. Selecting the tribunal requires understanding not only the basic facts but also the case that counsel are planning to present, including the themes that will be advanced. Without a thorough understanding of the case, counsel cannot expect to properly assess the particular qualities to seek in an arbitrator.

1 See Emilia Onyema, "Selection of Arbitrators in International Commercial Arbitration" (2005) 8:2 *International Arbitration Law Review* 45 at 45.

It has also been said that arbitration will only be as good as the arbitrators conducting it.[2] The arbitral tribunal is tasked with not just making the decision at the end of the day but running the hearing of the dispute. Selecting the "best possible" arbitrator in this context means choosing an arbitrator with the "requisite qualifications and experience to understand the facts and issues in the case and the case management skills to see that it proceeds efficiently and does not get sidetracked."[3]

A discussion of the selection of arbitrators can proceed in two parts: the process of selecting arbitrators and which arbitrators to select through that process.[4]

B. THE SELECTION PROCESS

The first step in any arbitration should be to examine the applicable arbitration clause specified in the contract. In many cases, the clause itself will dictate how proceedings are to be commenced or what rules will govern the process. It is important to note that even when a procedure has been specified, the parties can agree to change the procedure, provided that it is by consent. Once the parties have agreed to be bound by a specific set of rules, they have agreed to have the applicable organization administer the arbitration to the extent that the rules provide, including assist in the selection of arbitrators and their rate schedule.[5] Counsel should consider whether a given arbitration needs an administering or-

2 See Doak Bishop & Lucy Reed, "Practical Guidelines for Interviewing, Selecting and Challenging Party-Appointed Arbitrators in International Commercial Arbitration" (1998) 14:4 *Arbitration International* 395 at 395, online: https://doi.org/10.1093/arbitration/14.4.395.

3 Raymond G Bender Jr, "Critical First Steps in Complex Commercial Arbitration: Appointing Qualified Arbitrators and Staging the Preliminary Conference" (2009) 64:1 *Dispute Resolution Journal* 28 at 30.

4 See James H Carter, "The Selection of Arbitrators" (Paper delivered at the Worldwide Forum on the Arbitration of Intellectual Property, 3–4 March 1994).

5 See J Brian Casey, "Choosing an Arbitration Organization and an Arbitrator" (2007) 26:1 *Advocates' Journal* 22 at 22.

ganization to assist in matters such as overseeing the proceeding, providing arbitrator suggestions, finding spaces for hearings, administering billing, and collecting the fees.[6] There are a variety of organizations available to assist with arbitrations, both domestically and internationally.

1) Domestic Arbitration

Most arbitrations in Canada are performed ad hoc, without an arbitral organization overseeing the process. Instead, parties agree on preliminary matters including the choice of arbitrators and the applicable rules before the tribunal is constituted.[7] There are four main arbitral institutions in Canada, available to administer arbitrations should the parties wish one to do so: the ADR Chambers, ADR Institute of Canada, British Columbia International Commercial Arbitration Centre, and Canadian Commercial Arbitration Centre.

2) International Arbitration

Outside of Canada, the major international arbitration organizations include the International Centre for Dispute Resolution (ICDR) (which is the international wing of the American Arbitration Association), International Centre for Settlement of Investment Disputes (ICSID), International Chamber of Commerce (ICC), London Court of International Arbitration (LCIA), United Nations Commission on International Trade Law (UNCITRAL), and World Intellectual Property Organization (WIPO). These organizations continue to update their rules to adapt to changing practices in arbitration, with the oldest standing rules being from 2006.[8]

---

6 See *ibid* at 24.

7 See *ibid* at 22.

8 The ICC introduced its most recent rules in 2012 and amended them in 2017, to come into effect on 1 March 2017. The current ICDR, LCIA, and WIPO rules all came into effect in 2014. The UNCITRAL arbitration rules were most recently revised in 2013. The ICSID *Convention on the Settlement of*

3) Number of Arbitrators

Arbitral tribunals are generally made up of one or three arbitrators, each number having its own specific benefits and drawbacks. Most arbitral organizations specify certain circumstances in which to use a specific number of arbitrators.[9]

One arbitrator is usually quicker to appoint than three, and having only one arbitrator will usually result in a cheaper arbitration. While sole arbitrators may be appointed upon joint proposal, statistics compiled by the ICC suggest that in that forum, at least, institutional intervention is the norm.[10] Cost savings can be

Investment Disputes between States and Nationals of Other States rules are the oldest, having come into effect in 2006, after a two-year period of public consultations.

9 The Inter-American Commercial Arbitration Commission *Rules of Procedure* (as amended and in effect 1 April 2002), online: www.adr.org/sites/default/files/Inter-American%20Commercial%20Arbitration%20Commission%20Rules-%20English.pdf [IACAC *Rules*], specify that there shall be three arbitrators unless otherwise agreed by the parties. The ICC *Rules of Arbitration* (current as of 1 March 2017), online: https://iccwbo.org/dispute-resolution-services/arbitration/rules-of-arbitration [ICC *Rules*], specify at art 12 that there shall be either one or three arbitrators with the default being one arbitrator unless it appears to the court that the dispute warrants three arbitrators. The LCIA *Arbitration Rules* (effective 1 October 2014), online: www.lcia.org/Dispute_Resolution_Services/lcia-arbitration-rules-2014.aspx [LCIA *Rules*], state at art 5.8 that a sole arbitrator shall be appointed unless the parties have agreed in writing to have a larger tribunal or unless the LCIA court specifies that three (or more) arbitrators are required. The UNCITRAL *Arbitration Rules* (with new art 1, para 4, as adopted in 2013), online: www.uncitral.org/pdf/english/texts/arbitration/arb-rules-2013/UNCITRAL-Arbitration-Rules-2013-e.pdf [UNCITRAL *Rules*], specify in art 7 that if "the parties have not previously agreed on the number of arbitrators, and if within 30 days after the receipt by the respondent of the notice of arbitration the parties have not agreed that there shall be only one arbitrator, three arbitrators shall be appointed." The WIPO *Arbitration Rules* (effective from 1 June 2014), online: www.wipo.int/amc/en/arbitration/rules [WIPO *Rules*], state in art 14 that when no number has been specified by the parties, a sole arbitrator will be utilized unless in the opinion and discretion of the WIPO Arbitration and Mediation Center the dispute requires three arbitrators.

10 According to ICC statistics for 2007, 83.7 percent of sole arbitrators were appointed by the ICC court upon proposal by national committees or dir-

achieved with a sole arbitrator if scheduling and deliberation delays can be minimized.[11] But the cost of the arbitrators themselves is only a minimal portion of the total costs of arbitration. ICC statistics state that about 82 percent of the costs of arbitration are party representation costs, with the arbitrator fees composing only a portion of the remaining 18 percent.[12] Thus, depending on the nature of the case, the marginal cost difference between one and three arbitrators may easily be exaggerated.

In international matters in particular, there are significant benefits to having three members on the arbitral tribunal, including the ability to name one of the three arbitrators directly. Being able to choose one arbitrator and having a hand in choosing the third increases the predictability of the arbitral panel, and increases party confidence in the integrity of the process.[13] It is also thought to increase the quality of the award although there has been some debate about this in the academic literature.[14] The addition of co-arbitrators is believed to reduce the likelihood of an eccentric result,[15] but this has been contrasted with the amount of power that the presiding arbitrator can have in a three-member panel in certain circumstances.[16] Some commentators have expressed concern about the potential for party-appointed arbitrators to show bias, a potential that is thought to be eliminated by the use of a sole arbitrator. However, a skilled presiding arbitrator

---

ectly whereas only 41.3 percent of chairmen were so appointed by the ICC court: ICC, "2007 Statistical Report" (2008) 19:1 *ICC International Court of Arbitration Bulletin* 1 at 9. See also Pierre A Karrer, "One or Three Arbitrators?" (2010) 1 *Yearbook on International Arbitration* 91 at 97.

11 See Wendy Miles, "International Arbitrator Appointment" (2002) 57:3 *Dispute Resolution Journal* 36 at 41.

12 See Karrer, above note 10 at 101.

13 See Carter, above note 4.

14 See Jennifer Kirby, "With Arbitrators, Less Can Be More: Why the Conventional Wisdom on the Benefits of Having Three Arbitrators May Be Overrated" (2009) 26:3 *Journal of International Arbitration* 337.

15 See Miles, above note 11 at 41.

16 See, for example, the IACAC *Rules*, above note 9, art 28: "The arbitral tribunal shall adopt its decision by a majority vote. When there is no majority, the decision shall be made by the president of the tribunal."

together with protections that allow for challenging biased arbitrators should allay any such concern.[17] In this regard, it is essential to understand at the outset of any international arbitration the cultural norms of the jurisdictions involved and the expectations of the parties as to the role of party-appointed arbitrators.

In the end, the parties should decide what fits their dispute the best, having regard to the complexity of the case, the amount in dispute, the expediency required, and considerations of cost.[18] Another factor that should be considered is whether three arbitrators are required to instill confidence in the arbitration, and therefore increase party participation.[19]

4) Selecting Arbitrators

Each arbitral institution has its own specific procedure to follow regarding how to select the arbitral panel. In the case of three-arbitrator panels, each party will appoint an arbitrator of its choosing, and the presiding arbitrator (referred to as the chairman or, more recently, the president of the arbitration) will be chosen either by consent of the parties, or party-appointed arbitrators, or by the independent appointing authority.[20]

a) Party-Appointed Arbitrators

The ability to choose your own arbitrator in a three-member tribunal is an entitlement intended to instill further confidence in the arbitral proceedings. While party-appointed arbitrators are still bound to be independent and impartial, counsel will often attempt to select an arbitrator who will look favourably upon their client's case. It is for this reason that party-appointed arbitrators have also been referred to as "nonneutral" arbitrators. Previously,

17 See Karrer, above note 10 at 96.

18 See Miles, above note 11 at 41.

19 See Kirby, above note 14 at 342.

20 See AA de Fina, "The Party Appointed Arbitrator in International Arbitrations — Role and Selection" (1999) 15:4 *Arbitration International* 381 at 381, online: https://doi.org/10.1093/arbitration/15.4.381.

party-appointed arbitrators in some countries were truly nonneutral. However, in international arbitration, this is not looked upon favourably.[21] AA de Fina discusses the seemingly contradictory status of party-appointed arbitrators as follows:

> On its face, the concept of party appointed or so-called non-neutral arbitrators and their potential role in an arbitral tribunal may appear inconsistent with a fundamental tenet requiring matters in dispute to be dealt with by independent and impartial judges. However, party autonomy, the consensual nature of arbitration, and the particular ability of the parties jointly to direct and formulate procedure, allow the parties' expectation to be accommodated in manners unavailable through judicial proceedings.[22]

The benefit to the appointing party is obvious in that it is able to ensure that there is at least one member on the tribunal who is if not sympathetic to its case at least able to understand or have more direct knowledge of the case that the party is trying to present. This can be accomplished by selecting an arbitrator with specific expertise in a given area or a certain tendency to arbitrate in a specific manner.[23] In this way, a party is able to assist in ensuring that the tribunal has at least one member who will move the process forward in what that party considers a fair and considered manner.[24] While the arbitrator is unable to advocate on behalf of the party that appointed her, she can serve a useful role in guiding the proceeding. However, there is a delicate balance to maintain between ensuring that a party's case is being properly heard and crossing the line into impropriety and advocacy on a

21 See Peter Morton, "Selection and Appointment of Party-Nominated Arbitrators" (Paper delivered at the K&LNG International Arbitration Symposium, 23 March 2006).

22 Above note 20 at 382.

23 See Richard Chernick, "Selecting Party Arbitrators" (2014) 34:4 *Association of Business Trial Lawyers Report* 1 at 4.

24 See Andreas F Lowenfeld, "The Party-Appointed Arbitrator in International Controversies: Some Reflection" (1995) 30:1 *Texas International Law Journal* 59 at 65.

party's behalf, which could ultimately necessitate the removal of the arbitrator.[25]

Jennifer Kirby describes achieving this balance and the role of the co-arbitrator in terms of "being mindful of the interests of the party that nominated him. At the shallow end of the pool, this means, for example, listening sympathetically to that party's case and taking a particular interest to ensure it is fully understood and considered by the members of the tribunal."[26] This could, for example, be as simple as the party-appointed arbitrator's choosing to ensure that he carefully inspects the documents before him, which would encourage the other arbitrators to do the same.[27]

The appointment of the party-appointed arbitrator can be especially important in international arbitration, where language and cultural differences can play into the arbitral proceeding. As de Fina points out, a "party to a transnational dispute presenting its case before a tribunal which is of itself composed of persons of differing cultural, legal and language backgrounds can have legitimate cause for concern that its contentions and arguments might not be fully understood or appreciated."[28] The idiosyncrasies of language can present difficulties in the understanding of the law applicable to an arbitration, especially in contract interpretation. Andreas Lowenfeld describes the case of *faux amis*, or false friends — words that appear the same but have different meanings in different languages.[29] This issue can be further compounded where arbitrators come from different legal backgrounds and where, for example, a civil lawyer is presented with a common law case.

b) Sole or Presiding Arbitrators

Ideally, a sole or presiding arbitrator will be appointed by consent. The parties are best situated to understand their dispute and as-

25 See de Fina, above note 20 at 382.

26 Above note 14 at 345.

27 See Lowenfeld, above note 24 at 65.

28 Above note 20 at 382.

29 Above note 24 at 65.

sess the arbitrator best qualified to adjudicate it. Agreement at the outset on a procedure for jointly nominating an arbitrator will increase the likelihood of coming to a consensus. Parties often adopt the list procedure utilized by many arbitral organizations: Counsel for the parties compile a joint list of arbitrators that is then examined, and arbitrators are either struck or ranked to see whether an agreement can be reached. Parties can either engage in this procedure on an ad hoc basis in an attempt to reach a consensus or agree to be bound by the results.[30]

When co-arbitrators are tasked with the appointment of the presiding arbitrator,[31] each is permitted to solicit the opinion of the party that appointed her but is not bound by that party's suggestions.[32] Such discussions must be managed carefully to avoid inappropriate communications about the merits of the case disguised as input on a potential presiding arbitrator.[33] Party-nominated arbitrators should attempt to agree on a third nominee if possible, but, depending on the two co-arbitrators appointed, it may be impossible to find a consensus, whether due to differing ideologies or merely a lack of common acquaintances who they would feel comfortable appointing.[34] Nevertheless, it is in the best interests of the process for the co-arbitrators to come to a consensus as they are served by finding a presiding arbitrator who they know they can get along with throughout the arbitral proceeding and who they can expect to do a professional job. Interpersonal dynamics are important on a panel, and can have a substantial impact on the case itself.[35]

---

30 See Carter, above note 4.

31 See, for example, the WIPO *Rules*, above note 9, art 17(c), which states that the two party-appointed arbitrators have twenty days after the appointment of the second arbitrator to nominate a third arbitrator who will preside over the arbitration.

32 See Carter, above note 4.

33 See Bishop & Reed, above note 2 at 426.

34 See Carter, above note 4.

35 See Charles J Moxley Jr, "Selecting the Ideal Arbitrator" (2005) 60:3 *Dispute Resolution Journal* 24 at 26.

Where the parties are unable to agree on a sole arbitrator or where co-arbitrators are unable to agree on a presiding arbitrator, various rules have been established for the correct procedure to follow. Under the WIPO *Rules*, the WIPO Arbitration and Mediation Center (the Center) sends an identical list of candidates to each party, and the parties are to mark up the list with their deletions and then number the remaining candidates in order of preference.[36] Where this process does not result in a mutually agreeable nomination, the Center retains the discretion to nominate an arbitrator of its own choosing. The UNCITRAL *Rules* mandate a similar list procedure, where the appointing authority once again retains the discretion to appoint should a consensus not be reached.[37] The ICC *Rules*, however, in the absence of agreement, permit the court to "appoint each member of the arbitral tribunal and . . . designate one of them to act as president. In such case, the Court shall be at liberty to choose any person it regards as suitable to act as arbitrator."[38] In practice, this means that the court will invite a national committee of the ICC (from a country other than the countries of the parties) to make proposals on the arbitrator or arbitrators to be appointed.

C. DECIDING ON AN ARBITRATOR

1) Desired Qualifications

An ideal arbitrator has been described as someone who is "wise, experienced, fair, knowledgeable in the applicable law and the subject of the dispute, available to serve without serious time constraints and reasonable in their fees and other charges."[39] Some academics have suggested that only lawyers or legally trained persons are appropriate to fill the panel chair due to

36 WIPO *Rules*, above note 9, art 19.

37 UNCITRAL *Rules*, above note 9, art 8 & 9.

38 ICC *Rules*, above note 9, art 12(8).

39 Carter, above note 4.

the requirements of that position.[40] Legally trained persons are well equipped to provide tribunal reasons and deal with difficult questions of jurisdiction, law, and statutory interpretation. However, as each arbitration is unique, the qualifications or qualities that make up the ideal arbitrator for a given dispute are ultimately variable. Although some qualifications are consistent across arbitrations and therefore sometimes set out in the institutional guidelines themselves, it is largely up to counsel and the parties themselves to dictate what their ideal candidate will look like. Each individual dispute, with its unique interests, will require its own carefully crafted balance of qualifications to identify the best arbitrators for the panel.[41]

a) Arbitrators in General

Every arbitrator is required to be impartial and neutral as these are the characteristics that allow arbitrators to move forward with integrity and to issue unbiased decisions.[42] It has been suggested that the next most important characteristic is the ability and curiosity to learn about both the law and the technical aspects of the case, as this makes the presentation of the arbitration much easier.[43]

i) *Impartiality and Independence*

While it is preferable to appoint an arbitrator who understands the party's legal and cultural background and will sympathize with the party's position, the characteristics of impartiality and independence are directly embodied in the rules of most arbitral institutions. The Inter-American Commercial Arbitration Commission (IACAC) *Rules* state at article 5(6) that the IACAC shall have "regard to such considerations as are likely to secure the ap-

40 See, for example, Miles, above note 11 at 39.

41 Fernando Dias Simões, "Powered by Expertise: Selecting Arbitrators in Energy Disputes" (2015) 8:6 *Journal of World Energy Law & Business* 501 at 505, online: https://doi.org/10.1093/jwelb/jwv032.

42 See Bender Jr, above note 3 at 31.

43 See Karrer, above note 10 at 100.

pointment of independent and impartial arbitrators."[44] The ICC *Rules* specify at article 11(1) that "every arbitrator must be and remain impartial and independent of the parties involved in the arbitration."[45] Article 5.5 of the LCIA *Rules* establishes a duty on each arbitral candidate to continue to disclose any circumstances that "are likely to give rise in the mind of any party to any justifiable doubts as to his or her impartiality or independence."[46] The ICSID *Rules of Procedure for Arbitration Proceedings* require that each arbitrator sign a declaration stating his impartiality and independence.[47] Arbitrators who do not sign this form are deemed to have resigned. Previously, party-appointed arbitrators did not have to be impartial in United States–based disputes. This ap-

44 Above note 9, art 5(6).

45 Above note 9, art 11(1).

46 Above note 9, art 5.5.

47 ICSID, *Rules of Procedure for Arbitration Proceedings* (April 2006), applicable to proceedings under the ICSID *Convention on the Settlement of Investment Disputes between States and Nationals of Other States*, r 6(2), online: http://icsidfiles.worldbank.org/icsid/icsid/StaticFiles/basicdoc/partF.htm [ICSID *Rules*]. The text of this declaration is contained in rule 6(2):

> To the best of my knowledge there is no reason why I should not serve on the Arbitral Tribunal constituted by the International Centre for Settlement of Investment Disputes with respect to a dispute between ____________________ and ____________________.
>
> I shall keep confidential all information coming to my knowledge as a result of my participation in this proceeding, as well as the contents of any award made by the Tribunal.
>
> I shall judge fairly as between the parties, according to the applicable law, and shall not accept any instruction or compensation with regard to the proceeding from any source except as provided in the Convention on the Settlement of Investment Disputes between States and Nationals of Other States and in the Regulations and Rules made pursuant thereto.
>
> Attached is a statement of (a) my past and present professional, business and other relationships (if any) with the parties and (b) any other circumstance that might cause my reliability for independent judgment to be questioned by a party. I acknowledge that by signing this declaration, I assume a continuing obligation promptly to notify the Secretary-General of the Centre of any such relationship or circumstance that subsequently arises during this proceeding.

pears to have changed in recent years because in international disputes any partiality of party-appointed arbitrators is considered unacceptable.[48] As a purely practical matter, it is to a party's advantage to have an impartial arbitrator who will decide the case on the facts and law before her as she will not lose credibility in front of her fellow arbitrators when carrying out deliberations.[49]

ii) Neutrality

Neutrality in this context refers to the nationality of an arbitrator. As Doak Bishop and Lucy Reed state, "Reality dictates that the nationality of the parties will always be a factor in the appointment of international arbitrators. When the parties appoint their own arbitrators, they will often favor an arbitrator of their own nationality or at least of common cultural and jurisprudential background."[50] Choosing an arbitrator with the same nationality as one of the parties could appear to tip the scales in that party's favour initially, and this is part of the reason why many arbitral institutions, to prevent any appearance of bias in the proceedings, do not permit a presiding arbitrator with the same nationality as one of the parties without the express consent of the other party.[51]

---

48 See Carter, above note 4.

49 See Morton, above note 21.

50 Bishop & Reed, above note 2 at 401.

51 See, for example, the ICC *Rules*, above note 9, art 13(5):

> The sole arbitrator or the president of the arbitral tribunal shall be of a nationality other than those of the parties. However, in suitable circumstances and provided that none of the parties objects within the time limit fixed by the Court, the sole arbitrator or the president of the arbitral tribunal may be chosen from a country of which any of the parties is a national.

The ICSID *Rules*, above note 47, contain a similar albeit stricter provision at rule 1(3):

> The majority of the arbitrators shall be nationals of States other than the State party to the dispute and of the State whose national is a party to the dispute, unless the sole arbitrator or each individual member of the Tribunal is appointed by agreement of the parties. Where the Tribunal is to consist of three members, a national of either of these States may not be appointed as an arbitrator by a party without the agreement

This issue goes to the very essence of why party-appointed arbitrators are important to the parties. A party-appointed arbitrator who understands the ins and outs of daily life in the legal system of the appointing party is better suited to make a well-informed judgment about the merits of the case and can provide this insight to the neutral presiding arbitrator.

There may be some situations where it is impractical or inappropriate to disqualify an arbitrator on the basis of shared nationality with one of the parties. Where, for example, there is an agreement to arbitrate in a specific location, be bound by the law of a country, or dealings have been principally in a particular nation, it may make sense to appoint an arbitral tribunal composed of arbitrators of a specific nationality as they are likely more appropriate for that specific dispute.[52] Arbitrators from the country where the arbitration is to occur are likely better suited to arbitrate under the law of that country.[53]

The LCIA *Rules* set out in article 6 some of the practical considerations in assessing nationality: persons who have citizenship in more than one country are treated as nationals of each country; citizens of the European Union are regarded as nationals of its different member countries and not as having the same nationality; and the "nationality of a party shall be understood to include those of its controlling shareholders or interests."[54]

Despite the rules to the contrary, if a party selects a co-arbitrator with the same nationality as the opposing party and if the opposing party selects a co-arbitrator with the same nationality,

of the other party to the dispute. Where the Tribunal is to consist of five or more members, nationals of either of these States may not be appointed as arbitrators by a party if appointment by the other party of the same number of arbitrators of either of these nationalities would result in a majority of arbitrators of these nationalities.

52 See Carter, above note 4.

53 See Christopher R Drahozal, "Arbitrator Selection and Regulatory Competition in International Arbitration Law" in Christopher R Drahozal & Richard W Naimark, eds, *Towards a Science of International Arbitration: Collected Empirical Research* (The Hague: Kluwer Law International, 2005) 167.

54 Above note 9, art 6.

the ICC will consider there to be no objection to the appointment of a chairman with the nationality of the opposing party.[55]

iii) Expertise

The ability to have adjudicators with knowledge tailored to the parties' specific dispute is a distinct advantage of arbitration. Arbitrators can be chosen specifically for their expertise, which results in increased procedural efficiency and predictability.[56] It is advisable, however, not to focus too strongly on ensuring that the arbitrators have the relevant technical expertise, as when technical expertise is considered in concert with other qualifications, such as having arbitration experience, this can narrow the number of candidates available for the arbitration.[57]

It is also important to remember that arbitrators may have the assistance of expert testimony during the arbitration to assist them in their decisions, so specific expertise in the relevant field may not be necessary.[58] A lack of "process" expertise can cause much greater strife in the arbitration than a lack of technical expertise.[59]

iv) Other Characteristics

Doak Bishop, Craig Miles, and Roberto Aguirre Luzi describe at least six characteristics that should be considered when selecting an arbitrator: "integrity, intelligence, attention to detail, personality and stature, expertise, and general predisposition."[60] Other qualifications that have been suggested as necessary are business acumen,[61] judicial temperament,[62] case management skill,[63] avail-

55 See Morton, above note 21.

56 See Carter, above note 4.

57 See *ibid.*

58 See Morton, above note 21.

59 See Moxley Jr, above note 35 at 27.

60 Doak Bishop, Craig Miles, & Roberto Aguirre Luzi, "Interviewing and Selecting Arbitrators" (2007) 6:1 *Latin Lawyer* 46 at 47.

61 See Bender Jr, above note 3 at 32.

62 See *ibid.*

63 See *ibid* at 33.

ability,[64] language ability, and view of the manner in which a contract should be interpreted (for example, literal or according to context).[65]

Each side has the right to satisfy itself that the arbitrator it nominates has the requisite experience and knowledge in the field relating to the dispute.[66]

b) Sole or Presiding Arbitrators

While the characteristics required of party-appointed arbitrators are also required of sole or presiding arbitrators, these arbitrators should also possess additional characteristics. Due to the extra decision-making powers of sole or presiding arbitrators, it is particularly useful, if at all possible, for these arbitrators to be from the country where the arbitration is to take place.[67]

A sole or presiding arbitrator must also have the ability to manage the arbitral process, as delays and inefficiencies can build up with an inexperienced or passive arbitrator who lets counsel dictate the procedure. A presiding arbitrator must be able to control the (1) parties, (2) other members of the tribunal, and (3) requirements of the relevant arbitration rules and applicable law.[68]

2) Acquiring Information

After the desired arbitrator qualifications have been determined, information must be gathered to identify which candidates possess these qualifications. While one method of acquiring this information is through interviews with the candidates themselves (discussed in the following section), there are various other ways of assessing the suitability of arbitral candidates. The idea is to

64 See Carlos A Matheus López, "Practical Criteria for Selecting International Arbitrators" (2014) 31:6 *Journal of International Arbitration* 795 at 798.

65 See Morton, above note 21.

66 See LCIA, "Arbitration and Mediation — The Basics," online: www.lcia.org/Dispute_Resolution_Services/Arbitration_and_Mediation_The_Basics.aspx, cited in Miles, above note 11 at 38.

67 See Drahozal, above note 53.

68 See Thomas H Webster, "Selection of Arbitrators in a Nutshell" (2002) 19:3 *Journal of International Arbitration* 261.

gather as much information as possible about each prospective candidate. Such information may include the candidates' professional background and affiliations, experience as counsel in similar cases, professional and academic publications, nationality, and, perhaps most importantly, past experience as arbitrators in comparable cases.[69]

The first step in assessing a candidate should be to review the candidate's professional background and biographical information. This will provide indications of where to look for additional information about the potential arbitrator and should provide insight into his arbitration experience and whether he will be able to provide references or have publications available to read. It is recommended that counsel review whatever publications a potential arbitrator has written, as this may provide insight into that arbitrator's opinions on a variety of topics related to the arbitration.[70] It is also possible to gather information about an arbitrator through word of mouth. The purpose of conducting these information searches is to determine whether a candidate possesses the qualifications desired or whether she harbours any pre-existing bias that would be prejudicial to the arbitration.[71]

There is currently a movement to request the publication of more arbitral awards as this will help facilitate the selection of arbitrators. But this runs squarely into parties' concern for the confidentiality of past arbitral awards.[72] It may also be in arbitrators' best interests to have their arbitral awards published when possible as this would assist in advertising the quality of their services.[73] Arbitrators are increasingly required to be more entrepreneurial and sophisticated to attract clients, which has necessitated their expansion into publishing articles, speaking at

69 See Simões, above note 41 at 508.

70 See Moxley Jr, above note 35 at 26. Webster, "Selection of Arbitrators in a Nutshell," above note 68.

71 See Charles B Lewis, "The Art of Picking an Arbitrator" (2008) 22 *CBA* [Chicago Bar Association] *Record* 38 at 43.

72 See AA de Fina, "Selecting Arbitrators" (1990) 3:1 *Corporate and Business Law Journal* 58 at 64.

73 See Simões, above note 41 at 517.

conferences, or organizing academic or industry-targeted initiatives such as seminars and workshops.[74] In other forums, arbitrators are subject to the same advertising and market pressures as any other professionals providing a service, and available materials should be considered in that light.[75]

Finally, parties should remember that arbitrators get paid only when they have been chosen as adjudicators for a dispute.

3) Arbitrator Interviews

While previously contentious, the practice of interviewing potential arbitrators has gained greater acceptance with the publication of relevant guidelines. These guidelines aim to ensure that candidate interviews do not jeopardize the integrity of the arbitral process by jeopardizing the independence and impartiality of arbitrators. Guidelines are intended to instill confidence in the fairness of the process and avoid any appearance of partiality.[76]

Commentators have suggested that interviews occur at the office of the arbitral candidate, last no longer than thirty minutes, and do not occur over food or drinks, regardless of who is paying the bill. It is said to be common sense that the longer the interview, the more likely the conversation is to wade into improper areas.[77] The Chartered Institute of Arbitrators has suggested that candidates tape the interview process and disclose it to the other side, but it has also been suggested that this is extreme when taking careful notes should be enough to show that no improper conduct occurred.[78]

Discussions at an arbitral candidate interview can include a wide range of topics including the identities of the parties, coun-

74 See *ibid* at 507.

75 See *ibid*.

76 See Bishop, Miles, & Luzi, above note 60 at 47.

77 See Bishop & Reed, above note 2 at 424.

78 See Mark W Friedman, "Regulating Judgment: A Comment on the Chartered Institute of Arbitrators' Guidelines on the Interviewing of Prospective Arbitrators" (2008) 2:2 *Dispute Resolution International* 288 at 289.

sel, and witnesses; the estimated timing and length of the hearings; information about the general nature of the case sufficient to ascertain the candidate's suitability for determining the issues at stake; whether he has disclosures that he would be required to make; whether he can commit the appropriate amount of time to the dispute; his qualifications including his background and resume; his publications and where to locate them; whether he has previously appeared as an expert witness and, if so, what positions were taken; previous arbitral service and whether his decisions are available; whether he feels competent to handle the dispute; and whether there is background information that may raise suspicions of bias.[79]

It is important that the interview not exceed these boundaries of proper conversation as this could lead to the challenge of an otherwise suitable candidate or, even worse, the annulment of an arbitral award after the process is complete and after the award has been made.[80] One is advised to err on the side of caution when conducting an interview with a potential candidate for this reason.

Carlos A Matheus López gives seven practical suggestions for conducting an arbitral candidate interview:

(1) The interview must be conducted in the office of the candidate.
(2) The delegation responsible for the interview should be headed by an external attorney hired by the party concerned with the designation.
(3) The interview cannot be conducted during a lunch or similar gathering, no matter who covers the expenses.
(4) The interview should be restricted to a time limit, which will normally be of thirty minutes.
(5) The candidate must take note of the discussion, which may be revealed to the other arbitrators and parties.
(6) If they are appointed, the arbitrator must inform the other arbitrators of the content of the interview which they held with the party that appointed them.

79 See Bishop, Miles, & Luzi, above note 60 at 47.
80 See Friedman, above note 78 at 288.

(7) All these previous issues should be discussed before the interview with the representative of the designating party.[81]

D. AFTER ARBITRATOR SELECTION

1) Remuneration

Ad hoc arbitrations should specify the amount of remuneration of arbitrators in advance. It is increasingly common in ad hoc arbitrations with three-arbitrator panels for a common rate to be set for all and for the overall cost to be shared between the parties. Otherwise, as remuneration of arbitrators can be an uncomfortable subject, some arbitral institutions have established relevant rules. The WIPO *Rules* specify at article 71 that the "amount and currency of the fees of the arbitrators and the modalities and timing of their payment shall be fixed by the Center, after consultation with the arbitrators and the parties, in accordance with the Schedule of Fees applicable on the date on which the Request for Arbitration is received by the Center."[82] The UNCITRAL *Rules* address the payment of arbitrator fees at articles 41(1) and (2):

> (1) The fees and expenses of the arbitrators shall be reasonable in amount, taking into account the amount in dispute, the complexity of the subject matter, the time spent by the arbitrators and any other relevant circumstances of the case.
>
> (2) If there is an appointing authority and it applies or has stated that it will apply a schedule or particular method for determining the fees for arbitrators in international cases, the arbitral tribunal in fixing its fees shall take that schedule or method into account to the extent that it considers appropriate in the circumstances of the case.[83]

The LCIA *Rules* state at article 28.1 that the "costs of the arbitration other than the legal or other expenses incurred by the parties

81 López, above note 64 at 805.
82 WIPO *Rules*, above note 9, art 71.
83 UNCITRAL *Rules*, above note 9, art 41(1) & (2).

themselves (the 'Arbitration Costs') shall be determined by the LCIA Court in accordance with the Schedule of Costs. The parties shall be jointly and severally liable to the LCIA and the Arbitral Tribunal for such Arbitration Costs."[84] Lastly, the ICC *Rules* specify at articles 38(1) and (2) that the fees of the arbitrators will be decided in accordance with the currently published scales and that the Court will have the discretion to "fix the fees of the arbitrators at a figure higher or lower than that which would result from the application of the relevant scale should this be deemed necessary due to the exceptional circumstances of the case."[85]

2) Conflicts

The rules of most arbitral institutions require arbitrators to make disclosures concerning their independence and impartiality either early before appointment or early on in the proceedings, with a continuing obligation should any additional disclosures be required.[86] The leading set of rules on conflicts, the *International Bar Association Guidelines on Conflicts of Interest in International Arbitration*, was published in 2004 after two years of research and consultation, and was recently updated in 2014.[87] These guidelines set out a number of principles as well as specific situations that create different disclosure requirements for arbitrators. The guidelines specifically state that making a disclosure does not automatically imply the existence of a conflict of interest, nor should it automatically

84 LCIA *Rules*, above note 9, art 28.1.

85 ICC *Rules*, above note 9, art 38(1) & (2).

86 See, for example, ICC *Rules*, above note 9, art 11(2):

> a prospective arbitrator shall sign a statement of acceptance, availability, impartiality and independence. The prospective arbitrator shall disclose in writing to the Secretariat any facts or circumstances which might be of such a nature as to call into question the arbitrator's independence in the eyes of the parties, as well as any circumstances that could give rise to reasonable doubts as to the arbitrator's impartiality.

Article 11(3) specifies that this disclosure obligation is an ongoing obligation of the arbitrator.

87 See Morton, above note 21.

create a presumption in favour of the arbitrator's disqualification.[88] Specific situations that are likely to occur in arbitration practice have been divided into four nonexhaustive lists:

1) *Nonwaivable red list*: The factual situations that fall into the two red lists create an "objective conflict of interest from the point of view of a reasonable third person having knowledge of the relevant facts and circumstances."[89] The nonwaivable red list covers situations that derive from the principle that no person can be a judge in her own cause. Therefore, there is no ability to waive the conflict in these situations. Examples of situations that would fall into this list include where the arbitrator has a significant financial or personal interest in one of the parties and where the arbitrator has acted as an adviser or legal counsel to the party and derived significant financial income from the relationship.
2) *Waivable red list*: This list covers situations that are serious but not as severe as those in the nonwaivable red list. Situations falling into this list may be waived but only by express consent of both parties. Examples of situations that would fall into this list include where the arbitrator has provided legal advice or an expert opinion on the dispute to a party, where a close family member of the arbitrator holds a significant financial interest in the outcome of the dispute, and where the arbitrator is a lawyer in the same law firm as the counsel to one of the parties.
3) *Orange list*: This list covers situations that may give rise to doubts as to the arbitrator's impartiality or independence in the eyes of the parties themselves. The arbitrator has a duty to disclose these situations. Once such a disclosure is made, if no timely objection is made, the parties are deemed to have ac-

88 International Bar Association, *IBA Guidelines on Conflicts of Interest in International Arbitration* (London: IBA, 2014) Part II(4), online: www.ibanet.org/Publications/publications_IBA_guides_and_free_materials.aspx.

89 *Ibid*, Part II(2).

cepted the arbitrator.[90] Examples of situations that would fall into this list include where the arbitrator has provided services for one of the parties or had other involvement in the case in the past three years, where the arbitrator and another arbitrator are members of the same law firm, and where there is a close personal friendship between the arbitrator and a director of the supervisory board of a party.

4) *Green list*: This list covers situations where no appearance of and no actual conflict of interest exists from an objective point of view. There is no duty to disclose situations in this list.[91] Examples of situations that would fall into this list include where the arbitrator has previously expressed a legal opinion in print regarding a topic relating to the legal dispute, where the arbitrator has previously served as an arbitrator with another arbitrator on the panel, and where the arbitrator has an insignificant amount of shares in one of the parties where the shares are publicly traded.

Regardless of the applicability of these, or other, guidelines, in any arbitration it is not in the interests of either the parties or the tribunal for conflicts not to be identified, raised, and properly resolved at the outset. This is equally true for ad hoc arbitrations and those conducted under institutional auspices.

3) Challenging Arbitrators

As the parties' confidence in the process is of vital importance to a successful arbitration, arbitral institutions have designated procedures for the challenge of arbitrators to resolve issues of bias or conflict when they arise. Applicable legislation also provides relief, including for corrupt or fraudulent acts or on grounds of bias.[92]

The ability to challenge an arbitrator is not limitless, however, and most organizations limit the time for a challenge to within

90 *Ibid*, Part II(3).

91 *Ibid*, Part II(7).

92 See, for example, the *Arbitration Act, 1991*, SO 1991, c 17, s 46.

thirty days of a party's becoming aware of the conduct that it wishes to challenge. The ICC *Rules* at article 14 state that a "challenge of an arbitrator, whether for an alleged lack of impartiality or independence, or otherwise, shall be made by the submission to the Secretariat of a written statement specifying the facts and circumstances on which the challenge is based."[93] The challenge must be made "either within 30 days from receipt by that party of the nomination of the appointment or confirmation of the arbitrator, or within 30 days from the date when the party making the challenge was informed of the facts and circumstances on which the challenge is based if such date is subsequent to the receipt of such notification."[94] The ICSID *Rules* set out their disqualification procedure in article 57: "A party may propose to a Commission or Tribunal the disqualification of any of its members on account of any fact indicating a manifest lack of the qualities required by paragraph (1) of Article 14."[95] Under the LCIA *Rules*, article 10.1, the LCIA retains the ability to challenge arbitrators on its own behalf:

> The LCIA Court may revoke any arbitrator's appointment upon its own initiative, at the written request of all other members of the Arbitral Tribunal or upon a written challenge by any party if: (i) that arbitrator gives written notice to the LCIA Court of his or her intent to resign as arbitrator, to be copied to all parties and all other members of the Arbitral Tribunal (if any); (ii) that arbitrator falls seriously ill, refuses or becomes unable or unfit

---

93 ICC *Rules*, above note 9, art 14.

94 *Ibid.*

95 ISCID *Rules*, above note 47, art 57. Article 14(1) of the ICSID *Convention on the Settlement of Investment Disputes between States and Nationals of Other States*, 18 March 1965, 575 UNTS 159, online: https://icsid.worldbank.org/en/Documents/resources/2006%20CRR_English-final.pdf, reads as follows: "Persons designated to serve on the Panels shall be persons of high moral character and recognized competence in the fields of law, commerce, industry or finance, who may be relied upon to exercise independent judgment. Competence in the field of law shall be of particular importance in the case of persons on the Panel of Arbitrators."

> to act; or (iii) circumstances exist that give rise to justifiable doubts as to that arbitrator's impartiality or independence.[96]

However, article 10.3 limits the time for a challenge to only fourteen days: "A party challenging an arbitrator under Article 10.1 shall, within 14 days of the formation of the Arbitral Tribunal or (if later) within 14 days of becoming aware of any grounds described in Article 10.1 or 10.2, deliver a written statement of the reasons for its challenge to the LCIA Court, the Arbitral Tribunal and all other parties."[97]

4) Replacing Arbitrators

Once a vacancy has arisen on an arbitral tribunal, whether through a challenge or another circumstance, a procedure is necessary to replace the missing arbitrator. It is highly preferable for the tribunal once constituted to remain the same so as not to have to replicate any portion of the proceedings that has already occurred. A vacancy can occur for a number of reasons, including a challenge, death, or resignation.[98]

The ICSID has arguably one of the most comprehensive sets of rules for vacancies, with a provision even specifically noting that after a tribunal has been constituted and after proceedings have begun, the composition of the tribunal should remain unchanged unless a death, incapacitation, or resignation of an arbitrator results in a vacancy.[99] Rule 11 of the ICSID *Rules* states that "a vacancy resulting from the disqualification, death, incapacity or resignation of an arbitrator shall be promptly filled by the same method by which his appointment had been made."[100] However, before the tribunal is constituted, the replacement of arbitrators

96 LCIA *Rules*, above note 9, art 10.1.

97 *Ibid*, art 10.3.

98 See Chiara Giorgetti, "The Arbitral Tribunal: Selection and Replacement of Arbitrators" in Chiara Giorgetti, ed, *Litigating International Investment Disputes: A Practitioner's Guide* (Leiden, NL: Brill Nijhoff, 2014) 145.

99 See *ibid*.

100 ISCID *Rules*, above note 47, r 11.

is much easier, as set out in rule 7: "each party may replace any arbitrator appointed by it and the parties may by common consent agree to replace any arbitrator."[101]

While some arbitral rules, such as the UNCITRAL *Rules*, specify that the original process used to appoint an arbitrator will be used to find her replacement,[102] the ICC *Rules* give the ICC discretion to choose the appointing procedure that it wishes to follow.[103] The LCIA also retains the discretion to determine its own process for replacing a removed arbitrator.[104]

E. CONCLUSION

A successful arbitration is one that is resolved according to a fair process and one whose result reflects the informed and deliberate consideration of the dispute by a tribunal having the necessary expertise to appreciate its particular nuances. This can be reliably achieved only through the careful selection, in terms of both procedure and substance, of arbitrators with expertise suited to the task.

---

101 *Ibid*, r 7.

102 The UNCITRAL *Rules*, above note 9, art 15 states as follows:

> Subject to paragraph 2, in any event where an arbitrator has to be replaced during the course of the arbitral proceedings, a substitute arbitrator shall be appointed or chosen pursuant to the procedure provided for in articles 8 to 11 that was applicable to the appointment or choice of the arbitrator being replaced. This procedure shall apply even if during the process of appointing the arbitrator to be replaced, a party had failed to exercise its right to appoint or to participate in the appointment.

103 The ICC *Rules*, above note 9, art 15(4) provides, "When an arbitrator is to be replaced, the Court has discretion to decide whether or not to follow the original nominating process."

104 The LCIA *Rules*, above note 9, art 11.1 reads as follows:

> In the event that the LCIA Court determines that justifiable doubts exist as to any arbitral candidate's suitability, independence or impartiality, or if a nominee declines appointment as arbitrator, or if an arbitrator is to be replaced for any reason, the LCIA Court may determine whether or not to follow the original nominating process for such arbitral appointment.

chapter five

Arbitration Independence and Bias: Testing the Limits

GRAEME MEW

A. INTRODUCTION

This chapter focuses on challenges to arbitral awards based on allegations of bias or procedural breaches said to be of sufficient magnitude to render the resulting awards unfair.

Notwithstanding the overarching demand for fairness and equal treatment of the parties to an arbitration, there is as a practical matter a degree of tolerance for imperfections in the arbitral process, whether as a result of perceived bias or failure to adhere to agreed-upon procedures. This reality is considered in the following sections through an analysis of a number of cases, focusing on the three introduced below.

In *Jacob Securities Inc v Typhoon Capital BV*, an award was challenged because it was alleged that an arbitrator's independence had been compromised by his failure to disclose that his former law firm had acted for the underwriters of and for a prospective investor in a project that was the subject of a commercial arbitration.[1]

1 2016 ONSC 604 [*Typhoon Capital*]. The author of this decision is the author of this chapter. Nothing in this chapter is intended to analyze or explain this court decision.

Even if a particular arbitrator has no apparent conflict of interest or bias, if an arbitral institute with appointing authority is insufficiently independent of the parties, the fairness of the arbitral process itself could be compromised. A decision of the German Federal Court of Justice, the *Bundesgerichtshof*, in a long-running dispute between Claudia Pechstein, a German speed skater, and the International Skating Union over an antidoping rule violation addressed concerns arising from how arbitrators are appointed and by whom to cases heard by a sports arbitral institution, the Court of Arbitration for Sport.[2]

In *Popack v Lipszyc*, the tribunal — a rabbinical court — met *ex parte* with a rabbi who had been the arbitrator in a previous attempted arbitration between the parties.[3] One of the parties moved to have the award set aside. The application judge agreed that the *ex parte* meeting without notice to the parties had breached the procedure that the parties had agreed upon but concluded that she would not set aside the award despite the procedural error by the panel because the error had not affected the reliability of the result, fairness, or appearance of the fairness of the process. Her decision was affirmed by the Court of Appeal.

Also discussed are a number of English cases that illustrate where the line is drawn between errors made by arbitrators that do not render the process as a whole unfair and errors that do.

B. INDEPENDENCE AND BIAS GENERALLY

It is trite to say than an arbitrator should be independent of the parties and act impartially.[4] Arbitrators exercise a function that

2 *Pechstein/International Skating Union*, 7 June 2016. The decision in German can be accessed, online: http://juris.bundesgerichtshof.de/cgi-bin/rechtsprechung/document.py?Gericht=bgh&Art=pm&Datum=2016&Sort=3&anz=97&pos=0&nr=75021&linked=urt&Blank=1&file=dokument.pdf. An English translation is online: www.tas-cas.org/fileadmin/user_upload/Pechstein___ISU_translation_ENG_final.pdf.

3 2016 ONCA 135, aff'g 2015 ONSC 3460.

4 While both domestic and international arbitration laws in Canada require arbitrators to be independent of the parties and to act impartially re-

is by its nature judicial.[5] The first qualification of a judge is the ability to make independent and impartial decisions, free of extraneous influence.[6] And so it is with arbitrators too. Although written in the context of the English *Arbitration Act 1996*, the following statement in *ASM Shipping Ltd of India v TTMI Ltd* could apply equally to Canadian arbitration legislation: "The right to a fair hearing by an impartial tribunal is fundamental; the Act is founded upon that principle and the Act must be construed accordingly."[7]

But many different elements can affect an arbitrator's actual or perceived independence. Arbitrators are challenged on a variety of grounds including bias, conflict of interest, and having an inappropriate connection to or having had communications with a party or a witness. And then there are more subtle threats to independence, for example, an arbitrator's asking himself what will be the consequences for his future engagement in similar cases if he is perceived to have made the "wrong" decision in this one. The gravamen of all such challenges is the lack, or the loss, of the arbitrator's independence.

Whereas there are institutional and operational arrangements designed to safeguard the independence of judges, the same cannot be said for arbitrators. Arbitrators are in business. They compete

---

gardless of whom the arbitrator was appointed by, there are arbitration processes that contemplate different standards: see, for example, rule 6.1 of the *ARIAS • U.S. Rules for the Resolution of U.S. Insurance and Reinsurance Disputes* (2014), online: www.arias-us.org/wp-content/uploads/2016/09/ARIASU.S.-Rules.pdf, which requires that party-appointed arbitrators only be "disinterested" (meaning that no member of the panel shall be under the control of either party and that no member of the panel shall have a financial interest in the outcome of the arbitration): "The Panel shall consist of three Disinterested arbitrators, one to be appointed by the Petitioner, one to be appointed by the Respondent and the third to be appointed by the two Party-appointed arbitrators. The third arbitrator shall serve as the umpire, who shall be Neutral."

5 See *Szilard v Szasz*, [1955] 1 DLR 370 at 371, Rand J.

6 See Canadian Judicial Council, *Ethical Principles for Judges* (Ottawa: CJC, 2004) r 2 at Commentary 3.

7 [2005] EWHC 2238 (Comm) at para 39(3), Morison J [*ASM Shipping*].

for work with other arbitrators. Although judges and arbitrators share the same duty to make decisions without regard to whether those decisions are popular or not, the pressures and perceived personal consequences of an unpopular decision faced by judges and arbitrators may be different. Judges are more likely to face public criticism and may feel that their career advancement (to the extent that it is influenced by nonjudges) could be jeopardized. But judges are tenured. For the arbitrator, reputational damage can and often will have financial consequences. Can it be said with confidence that an arbitrator will never be influenced, even unwittingly, by the impact that her decision will have on future appointments?

That said, arbitrators cannot, and are not expected to, come to their task with their mind and predispositions wiped clean. All neutral decision makers bring their life experiences and social, cultural, and educational background to the table. Arbitrators will often have particular expertise or industry experience. Indeed, it is usually some or all of an arbitrator's distinctive qualities that lead to him being nominated for appointment in the first place.

To the extent that the appointment process gives a party the opportunity to participate in the selection of the arbitrator, that party will want to get appointed a candidate who the party thinks may view its case favourably. This is particularly so if there are three arbitrators and if each party gets to nominate one arbitrator (in such arrangements the third arbitrator, who will usually chair the panel, is commonly selected by the two party-appointed arbitrators or by an appointing authority). A leading author on arbitration law and practice, Professor Martin Hunter observes that the optimal party-nominated arbitrator is "someone with the maximum predisposition towards my client, but with the minimum appearance of bias."[8]

---

8 Martin Hunter, "Ethics of the International Arbitrator" (1987) 53 *Arbitration* 219 at 223.

The selection of arbitrators and the considerations and strategy that go into that process is a subject meriting its own chapter (see Chapter 4). The point, for the purposes of a discussion of arbitrator independence, is that complete arbitrator neutrality is neither achievable nor expected. This raises the question, how neutral is "neutral"? An unhelpful answer would be that it depends on the nature of the forum and the subject matter of the arbitration. But there are some principles that apply generally to most forms of arbitration.

C. THE REASONABLE APPREHENSION STANDARD

Actual bias on the part of a judge or arbitrator does not have to be established. It is the existence of a reasonable apprehension of bias, and not the existence of actual partiality, by which bias is judged.[9]

The leading Canadian articulation of the test for reasonable apprehension of bias is found in the Supreme Court of Canada's decision in *Committee for Justice and Liberty v Canada (National Energy Board)*:

> [T]he apprehension of bias must be a reasonable one, held by reasonable and right minded persons, applying themselves to the question and obtaining thereon the required information. In the words of the Court of Appeal, that test is "what would an informed person, viewing the matter realistically and practically — and having thought the matter through — conclude. Would he think that it is more likely than not that Mr. Crowe, whether consciously or unconsciously, would not decide fairly."[10]

This test is equally applicable to an arbitrator who acts in a judicial or quasi-judicial capacity. In *Szilard v Szasz*, the Supreme Court observed, in the context of an arbitration award that had been set aside, "It is the probability or the reasoned suspicion

9 See *Ghirardosi v British Columbia (Minister of Highways)*, [1966] SCR 367.

10 [1978] 1 SCR 369 at 394 [*Committee for Justice and Liberty*].

of biased appraisal and judgment, unintended though it may be, that defeats the adjudication at its threshold. Each party, acting reasonably, is entitled to a sustained confidence in the independence of mind of those who are to sit in judgment on him and his affairs."[11]

When will the circumstances give rise to a reasonable apprehension of bias on the part of an arbitrator? That was the central issue in the *Typhoon Capital* case.[12] The dispute giving rise to the arbitration was a claim by the applicant, Jacob Securities, that it was entitled to compensation from the respondent, Typhoon Capital, because it had introduced the latter to a third-party investor. That claim was disputed. The parties then entered into an arbitration agreement and appointed a retired lawyer as arbitrator, who ultimately dismissed the applicant's claim. At the time of his appointment, the arbitrator advised that he had no previous dealings with the parties and that, accordingly, there was no conflict that would prevent him from acting as arbitrator. He did not, however, conduct a conflict search with respect to clients of his former firm. In the aftermath of the award, it emerged that the arbitrator's former firm had acted for the third-party investor. The applicant claimed that this circumstance created a reasonable apprehension of bias and sought to have the arbitral award set aside, and a new arbitrator appointed.

The court concluded that it could not consider the applicant's challenge to the award on the basis of article 12(2) of the 1985 *UNCITRAL Model Law on International Commercial Arbitration*,[13] which allows for a challenge to an arbitrator's appointment where circumstances exist giving rise to justifiable doubts as to the arbitrator's impartiality or independence. The court held that article 12 — and its companion, article 13(2), enshrining the default pro-

11 Above note 5 at 373.

12 Above note 1.

13 21 June 1985, UN Doc A/40/17, annex 1, online: www.uncitral.org/pdf/english/texts/arbitration/ml-arb/06-54671_Ebook.pdf [*UNCITRAL Model Law*], being the Schedule to the *International Commercial Arbitration Act*, RSO 1990, c I.9.

cess for challenging an arbitrator — had no application to a challenge of an award made after the final award was released and when the arbitrator was *functus officio*. However, the court did find that it had jurisdiction to hear the application on the basis that a challenge to an award based on reasonable apprehension of bias amounted to a claim of unequal treatment, which would be contrary to article 18 and hence properly brought under articles 34 and 36 of the *UNCITRAL Model Law*, which concern the setting aside and nonrecognition of awards not in accordance with the model law.

The court first adverted to the objective test for reasonable apprehension of bias articulated by the Supreme Court in the *Committee for Justice and Liberty* case[14] and the strong presumption of judicial and arbitrator impartiality. The case boiled down to the question of whether the connection between the arbitrator's former firm and the third-party investor would raise a reasonable apprehension of bias in the mind of a reasonable and informed person. The court concluded that it would not, especially as the arbitrator had not worked on any matters involving the investor while he had been at his former firm and had no knowledge of his former firm's connection with the third-party investor. Ultimately, the court ruled that the connection between the arbitrator and the third-party investor was too remote to establish a reasonable apprehension of bias: "to raise any concern as to the Arbitrator's partiality would require far more than has been established by the applicant."[15]

Of perhaps more interest and greater novelty was the applicant's alternative argument that the arbitrator had a positive obligation to conduct a conflicts check with his former firm. The applicant claimed that because the arbitrator had failed to conduct an adequate investigation of possible conflicts of interest, it had been deprived of the opportunity to make a fully informed decision when it had agreed to the appointment of the arbitrator.

---

14 Above note 10.

15 *Typhoon Capital*, above note 1 at para 50.

According to that argument, on the test for reasonable apprehension of bias, an objective person would expect an arbitrator to be proactive in seeking out any possible conflicts with his former law firm, which would include requesting a conflict search with that firm.

The court agreed with the proposition that an arbitrator who was currently a partner of or who otherwise currently worked for a law firm had a positive duty to investigate any potential conflicts of interest with her law firm to satisfy her disclosure obligations. The same considerations, however, did not apply to situations involving the arbitrator's former, as opposed to current, law firm. The court was aware of no authority that imposed on a judge, recently appointed or otherwise, a duty to ask her former firm to conduct conflict searches for the names of all the parties to the cases that she dealt with. Judges could not possibly know or be expected to know every client that their former firms acted for, and nor could arbitrators:

> I do not see why the position of an arbitrator who is in independent practice and who is no longer associated with a law firm should be any different . . . . The notion that a judge or arbitrator must make a concerted effort to search for hitherto unknown conflicts from a firm that he or she no longer works with would be a burdensome exercise and [a] wholly disproportionate response to the duty to disclose.[16]

Finally, and perhaps most importantly, as a practical matter, the very wide scope of the disclosure obligation being proposed by the applicant was unrealistic in light of the duty of confidentiality owed by law firms to their clients: "As a practical matter, firms such as [the arbitrator's former firm] owe an obligation to their clients not to disclose confidential information to third parties, which would include former partners and lawyers."[17] The arbitrator was simply not in a position to conduct the kind of

16 *Ibid* at para 58.

17 *Ibid* at para 59.

conflicts search proposed by the applicant. In the end, the applicant failed to rebut the presumption of impartiality that attached to the arbitrator.

D. INSTITUTIONAL BIAS

The *Pechstein* case addressed bias from the perspective of alleged structural imbalances in the process of appointing arbitral panels.[18] It was a veritable legal saga that engaged the theme of arbitral independence.

Claudia Pechstein, the German speed skater, was found to have violated the new antidoping policy of the International Skating Union (ISU) and was given a two-year competition ban on 5 March 2009. Pechstein appealed the ban to the Court of Arbitration for Sport (CAS), in Lausanne, pursuant to the arbitration agreement in her skating licence. The CAS dismissed her appeal,[19] and she then brought her case to the Swiss Federal Tribunal, the normal appeal route after a CAS decision. Unsuccessful before the Swiss Federal Tribunal,[20] she then sued in the Bavarian regional court (*Landesgericht*). The *Landesgericht* ruled that the arbitration clause in her skating licence — mandating the jurisdiction of the CAS in disputes between athletes and their union — was invalid but would not grant Pechstein a remedy on the principle of *res judicata*. She then appealed to the Bavarian *Oberlandesgericht* (*OLG*), which released its decision on 15 January 2015.[21]

18 Above note 2.

19 CAS 2009/A/1912 & 1913, online: http://static.isu.org/media/108941/arbitral-award-cas.pdf; www.centrostudisport.it/PDF/TAS_CAS_ULTIMO/48.pdf.

20 *Claudia Pechstein v International Skating Union*, 4A_612/2009 (English translation and annotation, online: www.swissarbitrationdecisions.com/limited-judicial-review-of-awards-independence-of-cas-reaffirmed?search=%22Claudia+Pechstein%22).

21 *Pechstein/International Skating Union*, OLG München [2015] Az U 1110/14 Kart, online: https://openjur.de/u/756385.html (unofficial English translation of portions of the decision by Antoine Duval, online: http://papers.ssrn.com/sol3/papers.cfm?abstract_id=2561297).

The decision of the *OLG* was something of a bombshell. It held that the arbitration clause in Pechstein's licence was contrary to German antitrust law and therefore refused, on the basis of the 1958 United Nations *Convention on the Recognition and Enforcement of Foreign Arbitral Awards* (the *New York Convention*), to enforce the CAS decisions concerning the skater. German antitrust law was engaged, said the *OLG*, because sports governing bodies (such as the ISU) are monopolists and are in a position to dictate more onerous arbitration terms to athletes than would be obtained in a competitive market. But that did not end the analysis as the *OLG* appreciated the practical need to resolve sporting disputes in a uniform way by subjecting them to the jurisdiction of the CAS.

The problem was not simply the monopolistic position of entities such as the ISU. It was also the structural makeup of the CAS, whose closed list of potential arbitrators was said to be heavily influenced by international sports governing bodies, such as the ISU. That structural imbalance was even more manifest in the selection of the president of an arbitral panel because such a person was nominated by the president of the CAS Appeals Division, himself appointed by the International Council of Arbitration for Sport (ICAS), and at the relevant time, fourteen of the twenty members of the ICAS had ties to sports governing bodies, like the ISU. The connection between sports governing bodies and arbitrators acting under the auspices of the CAS was perceived to structurally compromise the fairness of the CAS arbitral process. Antoine Duval has paraphrased the *OLG*'s ruling thus: "in light of the monopolistic position of the ISU and the lack of independence of CAS panels, the imposition of an arbitration clause depriving the athlete of her constitutional right to a judge constitutes a breach of German antitrust law."[22]

The case was appealed by the ISU to the German Federal Court of Justice, the *Bundesgerichtshof* (*BGH*), which released its ruling

22 Antoine Duval, "The *Pechstein* Ruling of the *Oberlandesgericht München* — Time for a New Reform of CAS?" *Asser International Sports Law Blog* (19 January 2015), online: www.asser.nl/SportsLaw/Blog/post/the-pechstein-ruling-of-the-oberlandesgericht-munchen-time-for-a-new-reform-of-cas.

on 7 June 2016. The *BGH* reversed the *OLG*, ruling that although the ISU was a monopoly, recourse to the CAS ensured that athletes would get a fair hearing, especially as they had a subsequent right of appeal to the Swiss Federal Tribunal. "The plaintiff signed the arbitration agreement of her own free will," observed the *OLG*. The *BGH* observed that the plaintiff had signed the arbitration agreement of her own free will. The fact that she was required by others to do so, or else she would not have been able to compete, did not invalidate the agreement.[23] The *OLG* regarded the CAS as independent and impartial and commented that its uniform standards and speedy decisions provided advantages for athletes as well as sports governing bodies.

The *Pechstein* saga has engendered a good deal of commentary and criticism, and it has focused attention on the important issue of arbitral independence. By virtue of this saga, the CAS has become a kind of paradigm for how arbitral institutions should or should not be organized, depending on one's point of view.

Andrew Vaitiekunas, of RMIT University in Australia, has recently published a book in this area, *The Court of Arbitration for Sport: Law-Making and the Question of Independence*.[24] It addresses the CAS's role in the generation of a *lex sportiva*, that is, a transnational sports law. One of the concerns of Vaitiekunas's book is to measure the independence of the CAS against generally accepted standards of judicial independence. Because of the influence exerted by sports governing bodies on the appointment of ICAS members — and more indirectly on the appointment of arbitrators from the CAS's closed list — Vaitiekunas finds the institutional independence of the CAS to be wanting: "the potential

23 Above note 2 at paras 55–56.

24 Andrew Vaitiekunas, *The Court of Arbitration for Sport: Law-Making and the Question of Independence* (Berne: Stämpfli, 2014). See also Antoine Duval, "Book Review: Questioning the (In)dependence of the Court of Arbitration for Sport" *Asser International Sports Law Blog* (20 November 2015), online: www.asser.nl/SportsLaw/Blog/post/book-review-questioning-the-in-dependence-of-the-court-of-arbitration-for-sport; Antoine Duval, "Book Review: Questioning the (In)dependence of the Court of Arbitration for Sport" (2016) 15:3–4 *International Sports Law Journal* 253.

influence that the Olympic governing bodies may be perceived to exercise over ICAS and the CAS secretary general is inconsistent with judicial independence norms which require judicial matters to be exclusively within the responsibility of the judiciary."[25]

Some of the themes of Vaitiekunas's critique are taken up and developed by Antoine Duval, of the TMC Asser Institute in The Hague.[26] Duval is especially welcoming of the *OLG*'s ruling in *Pechstein* as a harbinger of future reform.[27] As may be expected, he is critical of the *BGH*'s decision in the same action and unconvinced by the *BGH*'s conclusion that Pechstein had freely signed the arbitration agreement with the ISU. As a matter of fact and reality, Duval asserts, CAS arbitration is always forced arbitration. The *BGH*'s conclusion that the arbitration agreement in *Pechstein* granted a right of appeal to the Swiss Federal Tribunal — thus obviating any need for recourse to the German courts — is also unpersuasive to Duval. He makes the point that that the Swiss Federal Tribunal is known to be sympathetic to the CAS and concludes, rather topically, "[w]inning an appeal against a CAS award in front of the SFT is a bit like Leicester City winning the Premier League, an oddity."[28]

The decision of the *BGH* in this saga evidently came as a relief to the CAS. In a subsequent media release, the CAS acknowledges a mood for further change:

> Although the [*BGH*] decision represents a ratification of the current CAS system, the CAS will continue to listen and analyze the requests and suggestions of its users, as well as of judges and legal experts in order to continue its development, to improve and evolve with changes in international sport and best practices in international arbitration law with appropriate reforms. For example, since 2009 and the resolution of the case Pechstein/ISU,

25 Vaitiekunas, above note 24 at 193.

26 Online: www.asser.nl/SportsLaw/Blog/post/the-bgh-s-pechstein-decision-a-surrealist-ruling.

27 Above note 21.

28 Above note 26.

> a procedure for legal aid has been implemented to assist athletes without sufficient financial means to access to CAS arbitration. A real diversity in the composition of ICAS has also been achieved with a majority of members not linked to sports organizations and an equal representation of men and women.[29]

Other commentators have suggested that CAS may wish to take further steps to preserve its independence by giving athletes further opportunity to influence the list of arbitrators and becoming more transparent about how the chair of a panel is nominated.[30]

E. ERRORS BY ARBITRATORS: DRAWING THE LINE

Even if a procedural error has been made by an arbitrator that creates the possibility of prejudice to both sides — for example, an *ex parte* meeting of an arbitral tribunal with a witness in a proceeding — courts will not disturb an arbitral award where there has been no real unfairness or no real practical injustice. So much is evident from the case of *Popack v Lipszyc*.[31]

This case concerned an arbitral award of a rabbinical court. Before releasing its decision, the arbitral tribunal met with Rabbi Schwei, a prior adjudicator in the dispute between the parties, without either of the parties being present. One of the parties had asked the tribunal to hear from Rabbi Schwei, and the other had indicated that it did not object, but notice of the actual meeting was not given to the parties. After the award, the applicant, Popack, sought to have it set aside for reasons of procedural irregularity.

29 CAS, "Media Release: Statement of the Court of Arbitration for Sport (CAS) on the Decision Made by the German Federal Tribunal (*Bundesgerichtshof*) in the Case between Claudia Pechstein and the International Skating Union (ISU)" (7 June 2016), online: www.tas-cas.org/fileadmin/user_upload/Media_Release_Pechstein_07.06.16_English_.pdf.

30 Mathias Wittinghofer & Sylvia Schenk, "A Never Ending Story: Claudia Pechstein's Challenge to the CAS," online: http://kluwerarbitrationblog.com/2016/06/14/a-never-ending-story-claudia-pechsteins-challenge-to-the-cas.

31 Above note 3.

In terms of jurisdiction, the court did not accept the respondent's argument that the parties had contracted out of article 34 of the *UNCITRAL Model Law*[32] in their arbitration agreement, and, accordingly, it considered the application on its merits. On those merits, and construing the relevant terms of the parties' arbitration agreement, the court found that the private meeting of the arbitral tribunal with Rabbi Schwei was a breach of the agreement and satisfied the prerequisites for potential relief under article 34(2)(a)(iv) of the *UNCITRAL Model Law*.

The relief sought by the applicant — to have the award set aside — was not automatically mandated by article 34 but lay in the application judge's discretion. In considering whether to engage that discretion, the application judge essentially conducted a balancing exercise, weighing the possible prejudice to the parties flowing from the impermissible *ex parte* communication by the tribunal against the actual prejudice that would result if the arbitral award were set aside. In that balancing exercise, it was significant that the terms of the arbitration agreement precluded a transcript and any reasons for the decision in making the arbitral award. Accordingly, although there was the *possibility* of prejudice to both sides, the application judge could not practically go any further — there was no practical information that would substantiate that possibility of prejudice. Balancing this mere possibility of prejudice against the actual and certain prejudice that would result if the award were set aside — because a material witness had died in the interim and would thus be unavailable at any subsequent hearing — the application judge concluded that this was not an appropriate case to set aside the arbitral award.

That decision was upheld by the Ontario Court of Appeal, which observed that the decision to not set aside the award was consistent with the well-established preference in favour of maintaining arbitral awards rendered in consensual private arbitrations. The Court of Appeal looked to international jurisprudence from the New Zealand Court of Appeal and the Federal Court of

---

32 Above note 13.

Australia to consider the kind of balancing exercise that would justify the exercise of judicial discretion under article 34(2) of the *UNCITRAL Model Law*, in terms of both the nature of the procedural breach and its impact on the proceedings.

In the Court of Appeal's view, "all of the factors identified by the application judge as relevant to the exercise of her discretion were properly considered in deciding whether the improper *ex parte* meeting with Rabbi Schwei produced 'real unfairness' or 'real practical injustice'."[33] A particularly salient consideration for the Court of Appeal in concluding that the application judge had made no error in declining to exercise her discretion under article 34(2) of the *UNCITRAL Model Law* was the ability of the parties to effectively and fairly redo the arbitration process should the award be set aside. As noted above, a material witness in the proceedings had died and would have been unavailable in the event of any further adjudication.

A subsequent Court of Appeal panel in *Ottawa (City) v Coliseum Inc* endorsed the approach taken in *Popack v Lipszyc*, emphasizing in particular — in the context of the standard of review to be applied to an arbitrator's decision — that "the parties' selection of their forum implies both a preference for the outcome arrived at in that forum and a limited role for judicial oversight of the award made in the arbitral forum."[34] All in all, a procedural error going to an arbitrator's neutrality, such as an *ex parte* communication by an arbitrator or an arbitration panel, will not necessarily be fatal to an arbitral award if no substantial unfairness or injustice results.

This issue has recurred in a number of English cases. The principle of arbitral impartiality underlies the English *Arbitration Act 1996*. Section 68 of the Act gives the High Court the authority to set aside arbitral awards on the ground of "serious irregularity" that has caused substantial injustice to the applicant.[35] *Norbrook*

33 Above note 3 at para 36.

34 2016 ONCA 363 at para 33, quoting *Popack v Lipszyc*, above note 3 at para 26, Doherty JA.

35 *Arbitration Act 1996* (UK), c 23, s 68.

Laboratories Ltd v Tank illustrates the kind of circumstances that will mandate the setting aside of an arbitral award where there has been biased conduct on the part of an arbitrator that amounts to serious irregularity under the Act.[36]

The dispute in this case concerned the purchase of an allegedly defective methanol recovery plant by the plaintiff, Norbrook. The arbitration that ensued was conducted under the *Arbitration Rules* of the Institution of Chemical Engineers (IChemE). The arbitrator was nominated by the president of the institution and was himself a chartered engineer. Over the course of the arbitration, two key sets of events occurred. The first set involved *ex parte* communications by the arbitrator with one of the parties; the second set involved *ex parte* communications by the arbitrator with witnesses to the dispute. Justice Colman's analysis of the different aspects of these communications that might amount to serious irregularity is worthy of careful consideration.

The arbitrator's *ex parte* communications with one of the parties were by telephone, which was a significant factor in Colman J's ultimate conclusion that this kind of contact amounted to a failure to properly conduct the proceedings. An especially problematical aspect of telephone conversations for the court was that, in the ordinary course, telephone conversations leave no record:

> The making of direct unilateral telephone contact by the Arbitrator with the parties is generally to be deprecated for it inevitably gives rise to the risk that evidence or submissions will be put before the Arbitrator in circumstances where no record is kept of what has been said and without the opposing party's awareness and therefore of an opportunity of challenging it. That is why Arbitrators invariably communicate with the parties in writing on even the most trivial matters of administration and do so by copying in the opposite party.[37]

36 [2006] EWHC 1055 (Comm) [*Norbrook*].

37 *Ibid* at para 132.

Evidently, as the subject matter of the telephone calls involved administrative affairs rather than substantive legal issues, the arbitrator supposed that it was acceptable for him to make unilateral telephone calls. "In this," observed Colman J, "he was wrong."[38]

After these telephone calls, the solicitors for one of the parties protested, and the arbitrator agreed to adopt a system of written communication with both parties. Notwithstanding this agreement, the arbitrator then took the "extremely unorthodox" step of communicating directly with one of the parties by telephone apparently because he could not get a clear response from that party's solicitors on a legal issue.[39] This subsequent communication signified three different kinds of mistake to Colman J. First, it revealed a failure to appreciate the rationale for avoiding unilateral telephone communications. Second, it was a departure from the normal procedure in English (and Canadian) arbitrations: Where one party is legally represented, it is conventional to communicate with that party solely through its solicitors. Third, the question on which the arbitrator sought to contact the party — concerning notice given under rule 16.2 of the IChemE *Arbitration Rules* — had already been answered in a previous letter from that party's solicitors.

These mistakes amounted to a failure on the part of the arbitrator to properly conduct the proceedings. And yet this failure did not cause substantial injustice to either party. The "extremely unorthodox" phone call with one of the parties was immediately brought into the open and led to no decision adverse to the parties that the arbitrator would not otherwise have reached. This was not the case, however, with the second set of *ex parte* communications in the arbitration.

The arbitrator made direct contact with three potential witnesses, all of whom were potentially able to speak to the operation of the plant run by the claimant in the arbitration. These communications were in the form of private telephone conver-

38 *Ibid.*

39 *Ibid* at para 134.

sations except for one written communication to one of the witnesses. The arbitrator was unsuccessful in obtaining statements from any of those witnesses, and these conversations were not disclosed by the arbitrator.

These contacts were highly problematical because an arbitrator in contact with a factual witness might be exposed to information that might influence his judgment — whether consciously or unconsciously — on a matter in dispute. Thus, observed Colman J, it was "absolutely axiomatic that the parties should at the very least have the opportunity of access to what the witness or potential witness has said to the Arbitrator so as to enable that party to refute any statement adverse to its case or to rely upon any statement supportive of its case."[40] Justice Colman had no difficulty in concluding that these communications created a procedural irregularity within the meaning of section 68 of the *Arbitration Act 1996* and revealed that the arbitrator had failed to conduct the proceedings fairly in accordance with section 33. The next step in the analysis was the question of whether that failure had caused substantial injustice to one or both of the parties.

In finding that the conduct of the arbitration had led to substantial injustice, Colman J referred to Morison J's observations in *ASM Shipping*[41] for the proposition that where a properly informed independent observer would conclude that there was a real possibility of bias on the part of an arbitrator, that would be a species of serious irregularity causing substantial injustice to an applicant under the Act. On the facts of *Norbrook*, those considerations were amplified because the arbitrator was a sole arbitrator, acting without any collegial restraint or oversight on the ultimate decision. Accordingly, Colman J concluded that where a fair and properly informed independent observer would perceive a real possibility of bias in any award already made, substantial injustice would normally be inferred. The arbitrator's direct contact with the three potential witnesses exposed him to information

40 *Ibid* at para 139.

41 Above note 7.

that, consciously or unconsciously, could have influenced him in the decision that he did make — a costs decision under rule 16.3 of the IChemE *Arbitration Rules* — and that might have later influenced him in his final award.

Justice Colman also added an interesting gloss on the arbitrator's stated determination to address the risk of bias by putting any improper witness comments "out of his mind." This determination, said Colman J, was no answer to the risk of bias: "The essential attribute of objective impartiality is not to be achieved by subjective self-discipline."[42] Ultimately, the arbitral award was set aside, and the arbitrator was removed, notwithstanding the considerable additional expense that course of action would entail at that stage of the proceedings.

It should be pointed out that the result in *Norbrook* is unusual. Section 68(3) of the *Arbitration Act 1996* makes clear that even in the event of serious irregularity, remission to the arbitral tribunal is the default option under the statute. Matters will not be remitted to the tribunal only in cases where it would be inappropriate to do so. *Norbrook* is therefore a paradigm case of those unusual circumstances where such remission would be inappropriate.

In *Secretary of State for the Home Department v Raytheon Systems Ltd*, Akenhead J referred to *Norbrook* for the proposition that there are shades of serious irregularity within the meaning of the *Arbitration Act 1996* and that "the more serious the irregularity the more likely it is that setting aside [the arbitral award] may be the appropriate remedy."[43]

F. CONCLUSION

No doubt there are further adjustments that can be made to allay the types of concerns that have been expressed in cases such as *Pechstein*. And no doubt there are plenty of other examples of arbitral tribunals susceptible to criticisms similar to those levelled

42 Above note 36 at para 155.

43 [2015] EWHC 311 at para 16.

against the CAS. As with governance issues generally, there is (and should be) an increased awareness of, and hence vigilance for, appearances of conflict and bias. But if arbitration is to remain an effective dispute resolution option, there needs to be a greater tolerance for structural, procedural, and evidentiary imperfections than would be the case in the court system. In particular, arbitral institutions established to serve the needs of a particular industry, sector, or activity will inevitably have ties to the parties for whose benefit they exist. If there is no forgiveness for imperfections that do not lead to an unjust result, much of the efficacy of arbitration will be lost.

As always, the challenge is finding the right balance.

chapter six

"Evidence First" Arbitration: A Conceptual Framework for Arbitration Efficiency

WILLIAM G HORTON

A. COURT LITIGATION AND ACCESS TO JUSTICE

About ten years ago, I decided to become a full-time arbitrator. One of the factors that moved me in this direction, after thirty years of practising commercial litigation for national and international business clients, was a deep and growing dissatisfaction with the ability of court-based litigation to deliver results that were cost-effective, timely, or even, in many instances, reflective of the legal merits of the case.

As to cost-effectiveness and timeliness, it occurred to me that there are few if any issues that arise in the business world for which cost and time are secondary or irrelevant. The litigation of business disputes seems to be a notable exception. Court cases are regularly conducted on the basis that only a result achieved through an arcane, lengthy, and laborious process can be viewed as a legitimate outcome. Considerations of cost and time are subordinated to this belief, which is inculcated by counsel and readily accepted by clients. It is, therefore, unsurprising that costs routinely approach or exceed the economic value of the dispute and that the resolution of the dispute is routinely delayed well beyond the point at which the utility of a resolution has significant benefit to the parties. In commercial disputes, access to justice is defined not as much by the ability of the parties to afford the dispute resolution process as by the ability of the process to deliver a result at a reasonable cost and in a reasonable time having regard to the business context. Furthermore, while cost may not be a factor in commercial disputes with very large financial implications, the timeliness of adjudication can be, and almost always is, critical. In these respects, court litigation fails businesses in both small and large disputes.

As to the results' reflecting the merits of the case, the fact that cost and time regularly exceed what is justifiable from a business perspective means that as the litigation grinds on, pressure will build to the point where one or both sides will seek a resolution primarily to bring an end to the pain of the litigation process. The parties may resort to negotiation or mediation. But in these processes, the cost and inefficiency of the litigation process itself will figure prominently as reasons for bringing the dispute to an end. Indeed, the problem of how to allocate litigation costs that have dwarfed the original dispute often proves to be the main challenge.

Mediation may produce finality, but in the absence of an effective adjudicative process, the result produced by mediation is more likely to reflect the power balance, or imbalance, between the parties and their respective abilities to absorb the costs and delays imposed by the litigation process. Thus, the cost and inefficiency of the litigation process will be primary factors in shaping the terms of a settlement.

Because commercial disputes are almost never concluded by court litigation within the business cycle in which they occur, settlement of a dispute will often be brought about not by the Herculean efforts and brilliance of advocates over a number of years but by changes in the circumstances of the parties that have no relationship to what has been occurring in the litigation, such as insolvency, sale of the business, or developments in market conditions or technology — not to mention normal human events such as death and reconciliation.

Despite the emphasis on perfection in procedure and on correctness in the application of the law, less than 5 percent of all cases filed with a court will actually be determined by applying the law to the facts. If the main goal of the *Rules of Civil Procedure* were to *prevent* cases litigated in the courts from being adjudicated, that goal would be achieved in over 95 percent of all cases.[1] Surely, I reasoned, a better process must exist. Arbitration holds out that promise. But often, the same lawyers using more or less the same procedures in arbitration as in court actions tend to achieve similar results, leading to the same complaints.

Since arbitration is based on consent, the question then arises whether there are choices that can be made by the parties and their counsel, as well as by arbitrators, that will deliver more cost-effective and timely results to those — possibly not everybody — for whom these considerations are important.

B. WHAT MAKES COURT LITIGATION COST SO MUCH AND TAKE SO LONG

It is worth spending a bit of time to consider certain key features of the normal court litigation process that contribute the most to the buildup of cost and delay. Once we have identified those features, we can and should try to avoid them in an efficient arbitration process.

1 It has been consistently reported in Canada over many years that less than 5 percent of all cases filed with a court reach trial: see, for example, The Honourable Neil C Wittmann, Chief Justice, Court of Queen's Bench of Alberta, "Judicial Dispute Resolution in the Court of Queen's Bench: Making Resolution Accessible" (2016) 25:1 *Canadian Arbitration and Mediation Journal* 14 at 19, online: http://adric.ca/wp-content/uploads/2016/06/ADRIC_JOURNAL_2016_Vol25_No1.pdf. My own experience as an arbitrator is that well over 50 percent of the cases in which I am appointed will result in an award, almost always within about twelve months and usually within about six months.

1) Loopiness

While we think of normal court litigation as taking place in stages, it is more revealing to think of it as taking place in loops. Broadly speaking, there are seven loops:

1) pleadings loop
2) document disclosure loop
3) discovery loop
4) expert evidence loop
5) interlocutory motion loop
6) trial loop
7) development of the law loop

Each loop anticipates later loops and may be reactivated by one of them. No loop is ever fully complete until a trial judgment is pronounced — and perhaps not even then.

Pleadings may be amended, and arguably should be amended, at any subsequent stage as new information and documents emerge. They may even be amended at the appeal stage to re-characterize the proven facts with a different legal theory.[2] While documents may be referenced or produced in any of the loops, new documents may emerge even during the trial and give rise to the need for amendments to the pleadings or even further discoveries. Expert reports, which are timed to come at a fixed interval before the trial of the action, presumably after all facts and documents have been disclosed and probed, may themselves give rise to new legal or factual theories or inquiries. Finally, the pleadings and every subsequent stage of the process may be informed by the possibility that the law will develop or be clarified as a result of the lawsuit itself to rectify what are perceived to be existing weaknesses in the legal basis of a claim or defence.

2 See, for example, *Clement v McGuinty* (2001), 18 CPC (5th) 267 (Ont CA). See also *Haikola v Arasenau* (1996), 27 OR (3d) 576 (CA). In a system where prejudice is defined as something that cannot be compensated in costs or cured by an adjournment, is it surprising that cases end up costing too much and taking too long?

Interlocutory motions and appeals create more loops in which a variety of judges who will not be involved in the final adjudication are tasked to participate. As these judges will not wish to foreclose a line of evidence or analysis that the trial judge may find useful, there is a tendency for their rulings to be permissive rather than preclusive. This contributes, along with the other factors mentioned, to the elaboration of the dispute rather than its refinement over the course of the litigation.

The adjournment of the trial on multiple occasions to accommodate other loops, and which is sometimes due to the lack of court resources, creates yet another loop. Counsel with only modest levels of tactical acumen can use all of these loops to considerable advantage. In the hands of seasoned practitioners, these loops can become nooses.

2) Stop and Go

As a result of what I have described as the "loopiness" of court procedure, there are frequent pauses in the process when the parties and their counsel recalibrate each element of the process in light of the most recent events. Often this will result in long delays during which work on the file by one or both sides will be postponed while further inquiries are made or actions taken. Every time the file is put down and taken up again, it is necessary for counsel to refamiliarize themselves with the matter at an additional cost to their clients. And each time that happens, it occurs in the context of some new information or development that may cause one or more of the loops in the process to be reactivated as counsel seek to maximize their chances of success (or minimize their chances of failure) with reference to the new information or development. If the original claims or defences falter, new claims or defences are added. The overall effect is reminiscent of the circus act where a performer seeks to keep multiple plates spinning at the top of multiple poles by running among them to attend to the plate most in need of a bit more spin.

The simplest cases can thus take two or more years to process. A complicated case may take as much as ten years to reach trial.

3) Anticipation

Until the presentation of evidence at trial, everything that occurs in a court litigation process merely anticipates what may or may not happen at trial. In chess, there is a saying that the threat is greater than the fulfillment. In litigation, it is all threat, and in the vast majority of cases, there is never any fulfillment in the sense of an adjudicated outcome.

Every fact that is in a pleading may not be proved or provable. Every document that is produced may not be relied upon by any party. Documents that have been produced may be referenced at trial by a witness in a way that was not anticipated by the discovery process. Lengthy examinations for discovery are conducted largely for the purpose of determining what the evidence of the other side will be at trial or trying to pin the opponent down to a particular version of events. Those examinations for discovery may not be referred to at all at trial. Alternatively, selective portions may be read in as evidence often giving rise to contextual objections. Sometimes witnesses who answered questions on their examinations for discovery using certain language may use different language at trial or give different answers, giving rise to issues as to whether or not they have contradicted what they said before or whether what they said before was not fully understood, perhaps as a result of a flawed question.

All of the foregoing is attributable to the fact that from an evidentiary standpoint, nothing actually happens until the trial. Everything that precedes the trial is therefore some combination of provable fact, optimistic or wishful thinking, idle threat, tactical overstatement, and outright prevarication.

4) Ambiguity and Anxiety

All of the aforementioned features of court litigation produce elevated levels of ambiguity and anxiety over a protracted time frame. Each party seeks to maximize its flexibility in terms of how it will present its claims or defences at trial while it seeks to minimize the other side's flexibility.

In the context of an adversarial process, these elements often and predictably lead to mistrust and significant escalations in the dispute that in turn appear to justify irrational levels of emotional and financial investment in the litigation process itself, which often disregard the objective value or time sensitivity of the dispute.

C. HOW ARBITRATION CAN BE DIFFERENT

One of the reasons why evidence in a court proceeding is not presented in a definitive manner until the trial is because that is when the trial judge makes her first appearance. In arbitration, the adjudicator is present from the outset. A neutral and objective presence, in the form of a person or persons chosen by the parties themselves or by an institution in which they have reposed confidence, is available to oversee the entire process from beginning to end. While the final decision on the merits can be pronounced only after the process is complete and after all the parties have had an opportunity to present their case, steps in the adjudicative process can begin immediately and continue in real time until the award is rendered.

Whereas in normal court proceedings a trial date is not set until most if not all preliminary phases of the litigation process have been completed (and given the vicissitudes of litigation, it would generally be foolhardy to do so before), in arbitration a final hearing date is usually one of the first matters that is settled. It is a testament to the efficiency of true arbitration processes (when they are employed) that the final hearing date rarely changes. The expectation is that the parties and the arbitrator will work toward completing the hearing on the set schedule, if for no other reason than that is what makes sense in terms of the nature and scope of the dispute.[3]

---

3 As with many other individual features of arbitration, the fixed trial date can be duplicated in court proceedings, but often the realities of the court system neutralize the benefit. I know of one case in which a party seeking to stay court proceedings in favour of arbitration was told by the motions judge that

In setting the final hearing date, the arbitrator commits to work with the parties to ensure that all parties will be treated fairly and given an opportunity to present their case within the agreed time frame. In my view, there should be no implication that the values of procedural fairness or the disclosure of relevant information within the power and control of any party will be compromised. Rather, the commitment is to work diligently, pragmatically, and cooperatively toward ensuring that these goals are met. I will say more about this shortly.

Often, counsel or arbitrators who come to arbitration from a litigation background conceive of arbitration as simply a speeded up version of litigation. Using this conception, they adopt the *Rules of Civil Procedure*, or some variation of them, and follow the same process as in court litigation but agree on shorter time frames for each stage. This almost never works. The reasons are obvious if one considers the aforementioned points about normal litigation procedure. The loops and resulting dynamics described above will almost certainly ensure that no agreed-upon time frame will ever be met. Disputes will arise regarding such matters as the particularity of the pleadings, the ability of the parties to review all their documents before deciding what to produce, the scheduling of examinations for discovery, and additional information or documents required to complete expert reports. In my experience, arbitrations that are conducted on this basis simply replicate most if not all of the problems of litigation and are extremely difficult to keep on track.

D. EXAMPLE FROM INTERNATIONAL ARBITRATION

An example of another approach may be drawn from international arbitration. While there is considerable variability among different rules and approaches, one feature stands out: the extent to which

he would give the parties a fixed date for the trial in a year and would personally supervise the litigation if they stayed in the court system. Unfortunately, when the trial date arrived, the judge had been moved to another court, and no other judge was available to make good on the commitment.

parties are required to present the actual evidence in support of their claims or defences at an early stage and as the process unfolds.

Both a claimant and a respondent are expected to deliver with their initial pleading all of the documents on which they rely. After pleadings are delivered, the parties are expected to exchange one or two rounds of "memorials" that will typically be accompanied by the witness statements and expert reports on which they rely (or that they put forward by way of reply in the second round). In their statements or reports, witnesses will reference or attach all the documents on which they rely.

The memorials are what we might call briefs or facta and detail both the facts and the legal theory and authorities on which each party relies. Thus, subject to documentary production, all of the evidence is put forward immediately following the close of pleadings together with each party's explanation of exactly how the testamentary and documentary evidence supports the claim that it is making. In the second round of memorials, each party is expected to put forward the evidence and legal arguments that contradict the position taken by the other party in the first round. Little is left to the imagination—and nothing to anticipation—by the time the two rounds of memorials have been completed.

Leave of the tribunal is required before further evidence is allowed. All that remains is for witnesses to be cross-examined at the final hearing. Because there is no need to repeat impeaching facts that are already to be found in the factual record, cross-examinations tend to be extremely brief and may even be waived in cases where a witness's evidence can be adequately challenged on the record as it exists.[4]

4 In one Stockholm Chamber of Commerce arbitration in which I was involved, one week was set aside for the hearing of a $10–20 million case involving geothermal energy contracts. There were nine fact witnesses and four experts. The hearing was actually completed in one and a half days rather than the scheduled week. Cross-examinations were brief and to the point. I was not left with the impression that any point had not adequately been brought to the attention of the tribunal.

With respect to documentary discovery during the arbitration, an extremely disciplined process is usually employed using the *IBA Rules on the Taking of Evidence in International Arbitration* whereby requests can be made for documents that are

1) within narrow and specific categories of documents;
2) reasonably believed to exist;
3) relevant to the case and material to the outcome; and
4) not in the possession, custody, or control of the requesting party and believed to be in the possession, custody, or control of the other party.[5]

These requests are made in a preformatted document (commonly referred to as a "Redfern Schedule") that anticipates, by blank cells, the response of the other side, the reply if any, and the ruling of the tribunal. The process is conducted in a very linear, disciplined manner.

Examinations for discovery or depositions are, for the most part, not requested or allowed, although exceptions are known to occur.

One of the keys to the efficiency of international arbitration is the emphasis on adducing evidence early in the process, and not at the end. However, there are certain aspects peculiar to international arbitration procedure that should, in my view, be further refined for noninternational commercial disputes arbitrated in Canada. For example, the need to exchange two memorials setting out the legal basis of the claims is understandable where the parties may be from jurisdictions with different legal systems employing different legal categories, statutes, concepts, and terminology. In a purely Canadian setting, it is rare for there to be much doubt as to the legal basis on which a claim is put forward in a business dispute. In some cases, where it is unclear, a direction of the tribunal may be sought ordering that some clarification should be provided or that some other procedural relief be granted. But this is rare and does not justify routinely building into

5 International Bar Association, *IBA Rules on the Taking of Evidence in International Arbitration* (London: IBA, 2010) art 3, online: www.ibanet.org/Publications/publications_IBA_guides_and_free_materials.aspx.

the arbitration process two rounds of legal briefs and a double rehashing of the facts. It is normal in noninternational arbitration, especially in larger cases, for counsel to provide an overview of the case shortly before the final hearing, and this may even form part of the formal procedure. In my view, this is more than enough in most commercial cases.

E. COMPARISONS WITH CERTAIN COURT PROCEEDINGS

Initially, when I began to try to implement, with the concurrence of counsel, some of the efficiencies inherent in international arbitration procedure in noninternational cases, I met with resistance based on unfamiliarity and skepticism. Ten years ago, almost all arbitration in Ontario was conducted as private litigation. The only difference was the substitution of an arbitrator for a trial judge when the hearing was reached and, perhaps, the elimination of rights of appeal.[6]

However, I found that I could achieve some traction with counsel by analogizing the international arbitration procedure to the "application procedure" available under the Ontario *Rules of Civil Procedure*.[7] The application procedure offers a more summary method for adjudicating certain types of cases. The applicable rules are interesting because they too contemplate an "evidence first" approach for a limited class of cases.

Using the application procedure under the rules, the applicant delivers a document entitled an "application" that sets out in summary form the nature of the dispute and the relief sought as well as the grounds for seeking the relief.[8] The application is a form of pleading but very much to the point with no requirement for any elaboration as to the facts or evidence. The application is typically accompanied (or followed very shortly) by affidavit evidence and

6 Sadly, this remains true for many noninternational arbitrations today, although the tide is changing.

7 RRO 1990, Reg 194, r 14.05.

8 *Ibid*, r 38.04.

exhibits that constitute the documents relied on by the applicant in making the claim. A respondent is expected to respond with similar material. The parties may request further information and documents from each other and may bring a motion before the court for any disputes in that regard. No examinations for discovery, as such, take place. However, either side may cross-examine on the other side's affidavits or seek to examine a nonparty as a witness on the application. The cross-examinations take place out of court (i.e., not in the presence of a judge), but the transcripts automatically become evidence in the case in their entirety, and not on a selective basis as with examinations for discovery.

The application procedure is limited to certain types of disputes and requests, but some of these are commercial in nature, for example, disputes relating to the interpretation of a contract, disputes relating to land and interests in land, and requests for injunctive or mandatory relief. In theory, the application procedure is also limited to situations in which the facts are not materially in dispute. However, where the facts do prove to be in dispute, the judge hearing the application may direct the trial of an issue, in which case the witnesses may have to testify or be cross-examined in court so that the judge can be in a better position to determine a contentious issue.

As it happens, in Ontario something very akin to the application procedure is also used to determine many important commercial cases relating to matters such as insolvencies and commercial disputes arising in the context of corporate reorganizations. With this type of procedure, these disputes are resolved on a very expeditious timeline, as is required by the obvious exigencies of such cases, despite the fact that the amounts involved may be billions of dollars.

The application procedure provides an ideal model for non-international commercial arbitration. The limitation to situations in which the facts are not in dispute is not applicable in the arbitration context since the arbitrator, unlike the application judge, will be present for the cross-examination of all witnesses and can make determinations of credibility and disputed facts when called upon to do so. Once the "undisputed facts" limitation is removed, the subject matter limitations on the application procedure are also not apposite, although most commercial arbitrations involve as a core issue the interpretation of a contract — which is a typical subject matter for the use of the application procedure in court. Certainly, few commercial arbitrations would exceed in value or complexity the types of proceedings that are dealt with in the commercial courts using a procedure similar to the application procedure for matters relating to insolvency and corporate reorganization. Indeed, if the application procedure were to be made available to parties to commercial disputes in court actions on the same basis as it is made available in arbitration, the two processes would be very similar in terms of procedural efficiency, and other reasons for considering commercial arbitration (which are not the focus of this chapter) would have to be weighed in deciding which process to use. However, in the near term, it seems unlikely that the courts will be able to make sufficient resources available to replicate an arbitration process within the court system for *all* commercial disputes.

The courts have made an attempt to provide a more efficient service by making the summary judgment procedure more readily available and taking a robust view as to the kinds of determinations that can be made, in terms of disputed facts, on a summary judgment motion. Such motions now often incorporate a hearing or minitrial at which witnesses who have provided evidence by affidavit are cross-examined in the presence of the judge hearing the motion.[9] However, while this approach does import into the court system some of the methodology of arbitration, the two remain quite different.

An arbitration hearing is a trial. It is not a hearing to determine whether there is a genuine need for a trial, as is the case on a summary judgment motion. Theoretically, the summary judgment procedure is available to decide clear cases. There is a risk that with the provision of summary judgment as an antidote to

9 See Garry D Watson, QC, & Michael McGowan, *Ontario Civil Practice 2017* (Toronto: Carswell, 2016) at 560–61.

the generally inefficient court process, there will be a tendency to overlook factual or legal nuances in an analysis to justify a final disposition using the more efficient summary judgment process.

Although under some arbitration rules, dispositive motions may be granted, it is rare for such motions to be brought or granted given that they duplicate the effort that is already being expended to bring forward the same evidence on more or less the same timeline.

Generally speaking, an arbitration award is subject to very limited rights of appeal, and usually all rights of appeal have been eliminated by agreement. In the summary judgment process, when judgment is granted, an appeal may be brought as of right with respect to both the judgment on the merits and whether or not the summary judgment rule permitted the matter to be adjudicated at that stage. There is a real risk that the loops will be reactivated.[10]

F. EVIDENCE FIRST ARBITRATION

Included in this chapter, as Appendix 1, is the sample procedural order that I typically use in my arbitrations. As with all procedural rules or orders, there is always an issue as to whether one is looking at the forest or at the trees. On the one hand, it is useful to see whether and how the entire set of rules works together to achieve the desired results of efficiency, fairness, and quality. For example, it is not enough to know when written witness statements will be exchanged; one must also know how they may be used at the final hearing. On the other hand, to focus too much on implementing any overall set of rules risks losing sight of the need for flexibility and creativity in fashioning specific rules for a particular dispute. Both perspectives are vital. For that reason, I emphasize that the sample procedural order included here is a product of the arbitrations I have conducted to date using these rules as a model and that they will be changed by the arbitrations I have yet to conduct. It is

10 For a discussion of loops in court litigation, see Section B(1), above in this chapter.

rare for this or any other set of arbitration rules to not be modified in some way according to the circumstances of a given case.

I should also state unequivocally, in case there is any doubt, that in arbitrations I conduct, the parties are always free to agree upon any other procedure that they wish, even after the arbitration has started. It is a choice that I respect once it is made by agreement of the parties.

Having said the above, I will comment on certain features of my sample procedural order under the section headings below.

1) Preliminary Observations

When an arbitrator is called upon to settle procedural rules, the arbitration is already underway. If the parties have agreed to a set of procedural rules, the arbitrator or tribunal may have little to do after being appointed but await the first procedural dispute or — if all goes well — the final hearing. If the parties have not agreed to a set of procedural rules, the arbitrator may be called upon to settle all of the rules or some aspect of them upon which the parties cannot agree.

My arbitrations invariably begin with a preliminary conference call with counsel in which I determine whether a set of rules has already been agreed upon. If not, I get a sense of what the differences in suggested approach might be. Usually, at the time that the first conference call occurs, the terms of my appointment as arbitrator have not yet been settled, and, indeed, one of the items discussed on the call will be the finalization of those terms so that the terms of appointment can be completed and signed shortly after the call. I make it clear to the parties that I will not make any decisions on contentious issues, including as to procedure, until the terms of appointment have been signed. I encourage them to continue their discussions with regard to procedural rules while the terms of appointment are being finalized. During the conference call, I provide counsel with my sample procedural order by directing them to my website, where it can be found, and I encourage them to consider whether the approach represented in the sample order could work for them. If there are questions regarding the procedure, these are discussed openly and candidly so that the parties will get a good idea of the spirit in which I will implement the sample procedural order if it is adopted.

I have not yet had the experience of parties deciding not to proceed with my appointment as an arbitrator after I have discussed my sample procedural order with them! Perhaps the future holds such an experience. In some instances, counsel discuss the matter among themselves and agree that they will adopt their own procedure, usually one that incorporates the *Rules of Civil Procedure* directly or by analogy. Commonly, when this occurs, the arbitration disappears from my radar screen for months or years — occasionally with brief interludes in which a procedural issue arises. Invariably, on these occasions, one party seeks to enforce the *Rules of Civil Procedure* while the other protests, "But this is arbitration!" My experience is that a hybrid process that uses the *Rules of Civil Procedure* "subject to the discretion of the arbitrator" produces a maximum of confusion, dissatisfaction, and dysfunction in the arbitration.

Introducing my sample procedural order into the discussion, before any agreement on the process has been reached, usually results in one or both parties' seeing the advantages of adopting a procedure that will get to the merits of the case more quickly and efficiently. Counsel then present me with a revised version of the sample procedural order that reflects particular concerns in and circumstances of the case and that sets out an overall timetable with which the parties can live. Usually, this results in an overall schedule that will be completed in six to nine months. I have known many arbitrations using this procedure to be completed in less than two months (some in less than a week!), and some have taken over a year (typically where significant documents are outside the control of either party).

2) Pleadings

Since the procedural order is made after the arbitration has commenced, at a minimum a notice of arbitration (or some similarly titled document) will have already been delivered by the claimant. Usually an answer or response will also have been delivered by the respondent. These documents may contain more or less detail depending on the advocacy style of counsel. However, all that is really necessary for the purposes of the sample procedural order is that the notice of arbitration does the following:

1) identifies the dispute to be resolved in the arbitration
2) identifies the parties to the arbitration
3) states the relief claimed in the arbitration
4) initiates the tribunal formation process, for example, by appointing or nominating an arbitrator

Typically, some factual allegations will be included to support these essential elements. The sufficiency or particularity of these factual allegations is not a critical feature unless the respondent is left in doubt as to one of the four points listed above.

The answer or response to the notice of arbitration is a somewhat more variable document. In addition to stating the respondent's overall position with respect to the dispute and the claims advanced, the respondent should state any objections to the arbitrability of the dispute or the jurisdiction of the arbitrator or tribunal and take the steps required with respect to the formation of the tribunal, for example, by accepting the arbitrator nominated by the claimant or appointing its own arbitrator.[11]

Certainly, if there is any lack of clarity regarding the matters set out in these documents, that can be discussed, and the arbitrator can provide directions as to whether further details should be provided, for example, with respect to the particular agreement under which the claim is made or the time range to which the claim relates. However, much more detail should not be required as the next stage in the arbitration will be the delivery of witness statements and documents and the making of information and document requests. Once this is understood, counsel are usually

11 The *Arbitration Act, 1991*, SO 1991, c 17, s 17(4) provides that participation in the formation of the tribunal does not prevent a party from making an objection to jurisdiction.

comfortable with closing the pleadings based on the formal documents that have been exchanged to initiate the arbitration, and that is what the sample procedural order provides.

3) Witness Statements

The sample procedural order presumes that there is a factual basis for the claim that can be put forward immediately in the form of witness statements and documents. Given that in commercial arbitration we deal with claims arising out of contractual relationships and are concerned with giving effect to the reasonable, contractually based, expectations of the parties, it may be expected that the claimant has a substantial body of information at its disposal upon which to base the claim. Speculative claims are possible in court litigation, but they are discouraged in arbitration, in part, by the use of "evidence first" types of rules.

Since the claimant chooses the moment to begin an arbitration, it can also be expected that in most cases the claimant has already spent some time reviewing the possible claim as well as the evidence that can be brought forward to support it. Particularly because the rules of evidence do not apply in arbitration (other than rules relating to relevance and privilege), there should normally be no difficulty in providing evidence to the tribunal at an early stage. Such evidence lays a foundation for subsequent requests for information and documents not in the possession of the claimant.

In certain types of cases, the claimant may not have all the information that will ultimately be necessary to make a final determination. For example, a claimant advancing a claim involving an alleged breach of a noncompetition agreement or breach of a cost-plus pricing contract may well require information from the respondent. However, such gaps in the claimant's knowledge are understandable and manageable in the arbitration process. There is no need for the claimant to delay putting forward the evidence that it does have to support both the claim and the making of orders for disclosure from the respondent.

The same considerations apply to the respondent. Understandably, the respondent may require more time to put its information forward because it may not have precisely anticipated the timing of the claim or the factual basis upon which it has been asserted. However, this assumption is not always true. For example, in rent renewal or valuation cases there may be no claimant or respondent as such. Each party may have an equal ability and responsibility to put forward evidence supporting the rent or valuation for which it contends. In such cases, the simultaneous exchange of witness statements and documents may be appropriate.

The sample procedural order assumes that expert reports can be delivered on the same schedule as witness statements. However, this can be altered if the case can be made that a party cannot supply its expert with all the information needed for the opinion or that the expert is unable to source the information needed independently until a later date.

In my view, the early exchange of witness statements and documents on which a party relies (with immediate requests for information that is relevant but not in the party's possession) substantially improves the quality of the evidence. Witness statements are put forward much closer to the events described therein, as opposed to evidence given many years after the fact, as occurs at a court trial. Early witness statements are less likely to have been influenced by the litigation or arbitration process itself and by the reconstruction of events that inevitably accompanies any protracted process that will conclude with the attribution of blame or fault.

All processes that use witness statements as a substitute for evidence-in-chief (including some commercial court processes) are subject to the concern that the statements are likely to be written by the lawyers. I suggest that this concern is less valid when the statements are required early in the process, as opposed to just before the hearing. The opportunity to "spin" the evidence and coach the witnesses is much greater later in the proceedings when the actual memories of the witnesses have begun to weaken and when the familiarity of the lawyers with the entire body of evidence has grown. At the early stages, there is a much greater risk that spun evidence will be contradicted by subsequently disclosed information. Therefore, early evidence that conforms most closely to established facts is much more likely to survive, uncontradicted, to the hearing.

The checking of every possible version of events against every possible document that might be produced in the case and the construction of the most plausible version of the facts that supports one's case is less possible when using the evidence first procedure. That is an advantage — and a detriment — experienced by both sides equally.

4) Discovery Requests

Discovery is merely the process by which one learns something that one did not know before. The evidence first procedure makes it clear that a party is not excused from placing in evidence that which it has within its knowledge because there is other information that it still requires to complete its claim or defence. Furthermore, a party is not excused from providing relevant information that it alone has in its possession because it has not yet had an opportunity to review all of the information in its possession that may have some bearing on the dispute.

a) Information and Documents

Under the sample procedural order, either side may, at any time, request in writing information or documents from the other side relevant to the issues raised by the pleadings or the witness statements. In addition to specifying the information sought, requests are to be confined to information and documents not otherwise available to the party making the request. Any unreasonable delay in making a request for information may result in the denial of the request if granting the request would cause unjustified delay in the arbitration schedule.

Note that no distinction is made between requests for information and requests for documents, and there is no specific timetable other than the date beyond which further requests cannot be made without permission from the arbitrator. In my view, the almost exclusive focus on documents and the discouragement of nondocumentary information requests that is evident in many international rules of arbitration[12] is artificial and leads to game playing with respect to the formulation of document requests and answers to document requests.

Whether or not a party is entitled to seek information that is within the possession or control of the other side to complete the proof of its claim or defence is a simple but critical decision that must be made in any dispute resolution process. Many non–common law legal cultures and arbitration rules (especially in the international sphere) manifest ambiguity or agnosticism on this critical point and seek to reduce the number of occasions on which requests for information can be made and to restrict the manner in which such requests must be put forward. Often, this reflects not merely a procedural preference but a fundamental view that parties should not be able to use the dispute resolution process to obtain information from the other party that they would not have been able to obtain in the absence of the dispute.

The sample procedural order is premised on the opposite view — namely, that access to information that is within the possession or control of the other side and that is necessary to the presentation of one's claim or defence is essential to the fairness of any adjudicative result, subject only to questions of relevance and privilege. Once that value judgment is made, an efficient process requires that the participants "cut to the chase" and make relevant information in their possession available without delay. Thus, in the sample procedural order there is no precondition to or rigid schedule for the making of a request for documents or

12 See, for example, International Centre for Dispute Resolution, *International Arbitration Rules* (amended and effective 1 June 2014) art 21(10), online: www.icdr.org/icdr/ShowProperty?nodeId=/UCM/ADRSTAGE2020868&revision=latestreleased: "Depositions, interrogatories, and requests to admit as developed for use in U.S. court procedures generally are not appropriate procedures for obtaining information in an arbitration under these Rules."

information. Such requests may be made at any time during the process until the deadline is reached.

The provision of information in response to specific requests avoids the excuse that a party must find all the information and documents that it might consider relevant before producing any to the other side. It also imposes a discipline that tends to ensure requests are reasonable and pointed because they will be subject to immediate scrutiny by the arbitrator if an objection is raised in that regard. Conversely, the fact that further information requests can be made before the deadline discourages the types of evasive answers that are common when the parties are limited to one or two rounds of requests.

Of course, problems can arise, and in some cases they are insurmountable. For example, in one arbitration, critical documents were in the possession of a third party and could not be provided to the parties to the dispute except through a stringent government security clearance process. We had no choice but to wait for well over a year for the documents to be made available.

A recurring problem is requests involving the production of huge amounts of electronic information — the so-called big data issue. Usually the request is based on a very generalized submission as to relevance. A pragmatic approach is to deconstruct the request by seeking to establish a clearly stated proposition that the request is intended to prove or disprove. Means other than the production of big data may then be considered for verifying or falsifying the proposition. Smaller subsets of the data targeted to specific parameters or time frames may be sufficient for that purpose. Data sampling may be used to establish whether or not an allegation as to a generalized practice is likely to be true. Examination of the data by an objective third-party expert may provide an assurance without requiring the migration of large quantities of data to other secure systems where the data can be examined. This solution may also avoid protracted disputes regarding the access to be given to the data by the opposing side. In extreme cases, the dispute may be bifurcated so that less document-intensive issues (such as contract interpretation) can be determined before more document-intensive issues (such as causation and damages).

But the most important factor in dealing with such disputes is the arbitrator's communication to the parties that tactical requests and objections will not subvert either the determination of the dispute on its merits or the process by which that determination is to take place.

b) Examinations for Discovery or Depositions

The sample procedural order provides that requests for further discovery may include requests to conduct examinations for discovery. However, unless consented to by the other party, requests for examinations for discovery will be granted only if it is demonstrated (1) that there is a specific need for further information before the hearing and (2) that the information requested can be reasonably obtained only in the manner requested. In other words, examinations for discovery will be available only after all other means of exchanging information have been attempted and found wanting. Furthermore, if allowed, examinations for discovery will be confined to the one or more specific issues for which the need was established. There is no conception of being given a time, however short, to do with as one wishes.

Despite the fact that most counsel in my arbitrations come from a litigation rather than an arbitration background and are accustomed to routinely conducting one or more examinations for discovery in the court cases they conduct, I can report that, to the best of my recollection, when the sample procedural order has been used, I have had no more than one or two requests for examinations for discovery.

5) Motions

The sample procedural order makes it clear that when procedural disputes arise, they must be promptly raised for determination. Formal motions to resolve procedural disputes are a last resort and may be brought only with permission of the tribunal. Furthermore, it is made clear that parties should not "sit on" procedural disputes until they begin to affect the schedule. The stockpiling of procedural grievances is a principal cause of arbitration schedules gone awry.

It is important to make it clear that the arbitrator is available and willing to address procedural disputes on very short notice. Typically, a conference call in which the arbitrator hears about the problem and the positions of both sides and then offers one or more solutions is all that is required to resolve the dispute and allow the arbitration to stay on track.

Parties understand without any need for explanation that failure to cooperate with the tribunal that will make the final determination is not a sound strategy. There is almost never any need to mention the possibility of adverse inferences.

It is a rare procedural dispute that requires the expense and delay of a formal motion process. Once the process of using informal consultations to determine procedural disputes has been established, it is readily accepted by counsel. Indeed, my experience is that after one or two such informal consultations, counsel develop a good idea of the approach that the arbitrator is likely to take and require little further assistance.

Making all of this clear in the procedural order itself helps counsel to understand and explain to their clients that they are not taking a less aggressive and less effective approach by seeking early assistance from the arbitrator rather than engaging in an extensive motion practice.

6) The Hearing

The sample procedural order contains a number of provisions to ensure that all of the evidence that each party is relying on to establish its claims or defences is in the record before the hearing, including any information or documents that have been obtained from an opposing party through information requests and documents that will be put to a witness in cross-examination. The element of surprise is virtually eliminated. There may be some room for discussion of whether this is conducive to effective cross-examination of untruthful witnesses. However, it must be remembered that contradictory evidence and documents will already have been put forward in the reply round of evidence exchange when using the sample procedural order. Furthermore, it is open to debate whether a more reliable conclusion as to the facts will be reached if an alleged contradiction in the evidence is raised at the very last moment in a hearing after all opportunities to further explore the factual context have been lost — barring, of course, an adjournment, which would entail additional delay and costs.

In some ways, the downfall of the normal court litigation process is its ambivalence toward the element of surprise. On the one hand, years of convoluted proceedings are justified as avoiding the element of surprise at trial. On the other hand, because only evidence adduced at trial is probative, the element of surprise is unavoidable. The evidence first approach unambiguously eliminates the element of surprise.

G. CONCLUSION

I estimate that I have used the sample procedural order, or some variation of it, in over fifty commercial arbitrations. The amounts in dispute have ranged from under $200,000 to over $100 million. Most disputes have been in the range of $1 to $10 million.

The sample procedural order has worked extremely well. I encourage all counsel and arbitrators to consider using the evidence first approach, and, to the extent that it is helpful, the sample procedural order is included below, as Appendix 1.

APPENDIX 1

Sample Procedural Order

Dates have been preserved to indicate sequence. Note this sample procedural order deals only with the issues addressed in the foregoing chapter.

Pleadings

1) The pleadings shall be limited to the Notice of Arbitration and Answer to Notice of Arbitration, which have already been exchanged.

Exchange of Evidence

2) The evidence of both sides shall be presented in the form of witness statements, which shall be in writing and sworn or affirmed by the witnesses.
3) A party that requires evidence from a witness from whom a witness statement cannot be obtained shall, at or before the time that a witness statement from that witness would have been due, seek directions from the tribunal as to how and when the evidence of the witness in question shall be obtained and submitted to the tribunal.
4) The witness statements submitted by each party shall include all the evidence that party seeks to put forward through its witnesses.
5) The witness statements delivered by each party shall attach or be accompanied by all of the documents on which that party intends to rely at the hearing.
6) Expert reports shall be delivered on the same schedule as witness statements, unless leave is obtained from the tribunal to deliver them on a different schedule. Such leave will not be granted, in the absence of extraordinary circumstances, if it would delay the final hearing.
7) On or before 23 April 20—, the Claimant shall deliver its witness statements, reports, and documents.
8) On or before — May 20—, the Respondent shall deliver its responding witness statements, reports, and documents.

9) On or before 21 May 20—, the Claimant shall deliver its reply witness statements, reports, and documents, if any. The reply witness statements, reports, and documents may include evidence in respect of any information or documents obtained pursuant to the process set out in paragraph 12, below, that the Claimant did not have an opportunity to address in its witness statements, reports, and documents delivered on 23 April 20—.
10) Any witness statement a party needs to file in response to disclosure of documents, or information, or a witness statement from the other side that the party did not have a reasonable opportunity to address, may be filed by agreement of the parties or, failing agreement, pursuant to further direction. No further witness statements shall be delivered prior to the hearing without agreement of the parties or leave of the tribunal.
11) All statements, reports, and documents shall be delivered by sending a copy by email to the other party and the arbitrator, by 5:00 pm Eastern Time of the day in question, with an additional hard copy being delivered to the tribunal within 24 hours.

Discovery Requests

12) Either side may, at any time, request in writing information or documents from the other side relevant to the issues raised by the pleadings or the witness statements. Such requests, in addition to specifying the information sought, should be confined to information and documents not otherwise available to the party making the request. Any unreasonable delay in making a request for information may result in the request being denied, if granting the request would cause unjustified delay in the arbitration schedule.
13) Requests for information or documents shall be responded to promptly as they are received.
14) Any disputes regarding information or document requests, which counsel are unable to resolve after reasonable attempts to do so, shall be raised with the tribunal by email and dealt

with on a conference call, without a formal motion unless so directed by the arbitrator.

15) No issue should be raised with the tribunal before it has been discussed between counsel. All communications with the tribunal shall be copied to the other side. However, it is not necessary to obtain the approval of the other side for the content of any communication to the tribunal.
16) Requests for further discovery may include requests to conduct examinations for discovery. However, unless consented to by the other party, requests for examinations for discovery will only be granted if it is demonstrated that there is a specific need for further information before the hearing and that the information requested can only be reasonably obtained in the manner requested.
17) In the absence of extraordinary circumstances no requests for information, documents, and discovery shall be made after 2 June 20—.
18) By no later than 13 June 20—, each party shall notify the other of the documents, information, or discovery it has obtained from the other side that it intends to use or place in evidence at the hearing.

Prehearing Delivery of Material

19) On or before 27 June 20—, the parties shall provide to the tribunal:
    a) Copies of all witness statements exchanged between the parties;
    b) Copies of expert reports exchanged between the parties;
    c) A joint brief containing all documents produced by both sides, in chronological order, indexed, and tabbed;
    d) Information or discovery from one side that the other side intends to refer to or rely upon at the hearing;
    e) Copies of any key cases or other authorities with important passages highlighted and tabbed; and
    f) A hearing schedule setting out the proposed order of proceeding at the hearing, including the order in which the

witnesses will be examined and the anticipated time required for the examination of each witness.

20) If the parties are unable to agree as to any of the above, one or both of them shall initiate a meeting or conference call with the tribunal to resolve the issue.
21) On or before 10 July 20—, the parties shall deliver any pre-hearing memorial, factum, or other written submissions that a party wishes to submit.

The Hearing

22) The hearing shall take place on weekdays from 14 July to 18 July 20—.
23) The hearing will conclude with oral submissions by both parties. Either party may also submit, or the tribunal may request, written closing submissions at or shortly after the hearing, at such time as can be agreed by the parties or as directed by the tribunal.
24) The hearing may be at any location upon which the parties agree. A transcript of the hearing shall be maintained if it is requested by any party. Costs relating to the hearing facility and transcripts shall be borne equally by the parties, subject to reallocation among the parties in any cost order made by the tribunal.
25) A witness who has provided a statement or report shall be made available for cross-examination at the hearing unless the other side agrees otherwise. If a witness is unavailable for cross-examination, e.g., due to death or disability, the admission into evidence and the weight to be attached to the statement shall be in the discretion of the tribunal.
26) At the evidentiary hearing, witnesses may be briefly examined by the party that submitted their statements or reports, only for the purpose of introducing the witness and highlighting key aspects of the witness's evidence, without adding any new evidence of substance. Such introductory examinations shall not take more than fifteen minutes and shall be followed by a cross-examination of the witness by the other side and re-examination, if required.

27) By agreement of the parties or direction of the tribunal, the cross-examination of any witness or witnesses may take place at a time and place other than the hearing referred to below. However, unless both parties consent, the tribunal shall be present at any such cross-examination.
28) No document may be put to a witness in cross-examination unless it was produced prior to the hearing in accordance with the directions above.

Further Directions

29) Further directions may be sought by either party at any time as the need arises.

chapter seven

Creative Arbitration Design and the First Case Conference

STEPHEN RICHARD MORRISON

A. INTRODUCTION

If asked, most corporate counsel will explain that they routinely include arbitration provisions in many of their commercial agreements because they have been told that arbitration is quicker and cheaper than going to court. The next thing you may hear is that arbitration, unlike the courtroom, is private. The parties to the contract do not need to air their dirty laundry in a courtroom open to the public and media and expose all of their proprietary processes and documents to scrutiny by their customers and competitors. Corporate counsel may also point out the benefits of being able to select a decision maker with specialized knowledge. In the court system, by contrast, parties are stuck with whichever judge is assigned to the case, regardless of their familiarity with the nature of the dispute or the industry from which it arises.

It usually stops there, but the most knowledgeable advocates of arbitration will also identify the most significant advantage of arbitration: the ability of the parties working in conjunction with a skilled and experienced arbitrator to design a procedure most appropriate to the nature of their dispute. The principal advantage of arbitration is that unlike the system of court-based litigation that exists in most jurisdictions, arbitration is flexible and allows the parties to develop efficient and cost-effective practices and procedures that will provide for a just and fair determination of the issues with a minimum of unnecessary procedure.

Yet, in practice, few domestic arbitrations fully embrace the opportunity to custom design a time- and cost-efficient process suitable to the dispute. Far too many arbitrations fall into the trap of becoming ersatz litigation, with prehearing process and procedures modelled on the local court's rules of civil procedure and an evidentiary hearing that is effectively a trial conducted in a boardroom rather than a courtroom. As a result, while the process may be private and while the parties may get to consensually choose a suitable decision maker, the resulting arbitration will not necessarily achieve the goal of being quicker and less expensive than the state-subsidized court system.

Despite its apparent advantages, many users of arbitration, including in-house corporate counsel, are starting to turn away from this process as the preferred method of dispute resolution, in domestic cases in particular. When not properly managed, arbitration can take just as long as litigation and can cost even more because of the need to pay for the arbitrators, the facilities, and a verbatim reporter, all of which are provided at little or no cost in the court system. Fortunately, this situation can be remedied. The balance of this chapter will be devoted to understanding the reasons for the trend away from arbitration and providing pragmatic solutions.

B. THE SOURCE OF THE PROBLEM

For arbitration to achieve its potential advantages, a culture shift is required among counsel, the parties they represent, and, perhaps most importantly, the arbitrators appointed by them. Every aspect of the arbitration process must be looked at from the perspective of ensuring that the procedure is scrupulously fair to all parties, saves time and expense, and ensures that the case will be dealt with in a way that is appropriate to its importance and complexity and the parties' resources.

A core issue is the fundamental failure of practitioners to see arbitration as a completely different sort of animal from litigation. Most counsel who conduct arbitrations are also litigators. The court rules of practice bring with them the comfort of familiarity. Everyone knows what to do and what to do next. Counsel may complain from time to time about the rules' unwieldy nature and the extent to which they cost their clients unnecessary money, but counsel have never seriously contemplated an alternative. Many arbitrators are quite happy to go along with this, and the arbitration then becomes litigation by another name, which captures none of the benefits available to the parties, can take just as long as bringing the case to court, and will cost even more. In fact, where the arbitration tribunal is made up of three members, instead of a sole arbitrator, arbitration can actually take just as long as and cost much more than going to court.

Too often, when compelled by contract or statute to arbitrate, parties and counsel elect, with the concurrence of their arbitrator, to conduct the arbitration exactly as if it were a trial, but a trial conducted in a boardroom instead of a courtroom. One frequently sees consensual provisions in submission to arbitration agreements that state the arbitration will be conducted in accordance with the local court's rules of civil procedure. The parties want affidavits of documents and full rights of discovery. Counsel, perhaps, fear that they will open themselves to allegations of negligence if they do not insist on these steps. And it is not uncommon for the parties to advise that they want the standard rules of evidence to apply to the testimony and introduction of documentary evidence at the hearing itself.

In fairness to the lawyers involved, it is not just them. Running an arbitration just like a trial may also fit better into the comfort zone of many arbitrators for all of the same reasons. Especially if the arbitrator is a retired judge or senior litigation practitioner, replicating the standard adversarial system in an arbitration room will feel like the most time-tested and reliable method of resolving disputes. It is a forum that they are familiar with, and they know the rules and exactly how to conduct the proceedings.

When arbitration is treated like litigation, most of its potential advantages are lost, especially its ability to be more time- and cost-efficient than the courtroom. In arbitration, the losing party usually absorbs 100 percent of the arbitrator's fees and the facility and transcription costs. As far as timeliness is concerned, absent the discipline imposed by a court administration office, status hearings, and the like, getting to an arbitration hearing can drag on and on, and most arbitrators are willing to let the parties set the pace.

C. THE SOLUTION: CREATIVE ARBITRATION PROCESS DESIGN

Creative arbitration process design incorporates procedures that can allow arbitration to fulfill its potential as a quicker, less expensive, more private, and better method of resolving some disputes. Because a state-run court system must be all things to all people and be able to function in the resolution of all manner of disputes, its procedural and evidentiary rules must be highly prescriptive and somewhat bureaucratic. Although the parties, through their counsel and in consultation with the court, can often ameliorate the rigidity of these processes, this rarely happens to the extent that it can and should. The reasons for this are beyond the scope of this book.

The beauty of arbitration is that the parties are able to craft a process capable of securing a fair and just result more expeditiously, less expensively, and more privately than the litigation alternative. Most legislation governing arbitration and, in fact, most institutional arbitration rules provide for all kinds of flexibility. But it does not just happen. The key to success in this regard rests primarily in the hands of the arbitrators themselves.

While very experienced counsel will sometimes work together to develop streamlined procedures for dealing with issues, it will generally take the guidance of a skilled and experienced arbitrator to bring the parties and their counsel around to an understanding of the possible differences between arbitration and litigation and how those differences can be harnessed to advance the parties' objectives. The initial case conference is the first and most important step in achieving this understanding.

D. THE FIRST CASE CONFERENCE

The arbitration process begins with the first case conference or procedural meeting. At its worst, this can be nothing more than a thirty-minute conference call in which a schedule is established for the delivery of pleadings and affidavits of documents, examinations for discovery, prehearing motions, if any, and so on. This kind of pre-arbitration conference generally ensures that the process will become litigation by another name. On the other hand, a proper pre-arbitration case conference will whenever possible be conducted in person with sufficient time to engage in a full discussion of the nature of the case and to explore a variety of alternatives for prehearing procedures and the conduct of the hearing itself. It is also important that the pre-arbitration conference is preceded by a written communication from the arbitrator to counsel outlining all of the issues that will be discussed in a checklist format so that counsel can start thinking about the issues in advance and, where necessary, confer with each other and with their clients.[1]

It is also strongly advised that both parties send a senior representative to the meeting, together with counsel. It is often helpful to have the individuals who will be writing the cheques at the meeting when various time- and cost-saving procedures are being discussed. The parties themselves may be more willing to think outside of the box, under the guidance of a knowledgeable arbitrator, than their lawyers. After all, the parties selected arbitration in their contract in the belief that it would get them a quicker and cheaper resolution of the dispute. They have a vested interest in seeing that occur. Experience demonstrates that when party representatives are in attendance, counsel are far less resistant to adopting common sense processes and procedures recommended by the arbitrator.

1 For a sample letter, see Appendix 1.

A comprehensive case conference will typically consume between two and three hours and follow a format that addresses the questions set out in the sections below.

1) What Is the Case About?

The meeting begins with a general discussion about the case. It is impossible to design an effective dispute resolution process without knowing something about the nature of the dispute itself. While the first case conference is not the place to be arguing the case, it is imperative that the arbitrator learn enough about the case to facilitate the development of an appropriate process for its resolution. The answers to the questions that follow will assist the parties and the arbitrator in determining the nature and extent of prehearing procedures that are required and the time- and cost-saving methods that can be employed in the evidentiary hearing.

a) What Is the Underlying Factual Matrix from Which the Dispute Arises?

For example, is the dispute a fact-intensive one where the decision maker will have to hear lots of competing evidence on the factual matrix and make determinations in that regard? Or does the arbitration principally involve the interpretation of a contractual provision and its application to a given set of agreed-upon facts? Or is it simply a case of establishing fair market value rent for a lease renewal where the principal evidence will be the competing expert testimony of two real estate appraisers. Similarly, a complex construction dispute involving dozens of claims for extra work, owner claims for deficient work, warranty claims, and delay claims going both ways will involve yet a different kind of procedure.

b) Does the Case Primarily Involve Questions of Fact or Issues of Law?

In some cases, whether they concern liability or damages or both, the parties have little common ground with respect to what actually occurred. The facts are highly disputed. The disputes may surround what actually occurred and in what sequence, or, even when the basic facts are not disputed, there may be residual issues of causation. Where claims for damages are involved, the fact of the loss or injury may be in dispute, or merely the value of the loss associated with it. For example, in the case of an insured fire loss, the parties may agree that a business was shut down for six months but disagree on the valuation of the business loss during that period. In these kinds of cases, the arbitrator will be engaged in a significant fact-finding exercise, and this will have an impact on the extent of the prehearing disclosure and discovery processes that may need to be employed and the way that evidence is received at the hearing. Some of these issues are discussed more fully below.

In other cases, the facts are not in dispute at all, or any factual differences are fairly narrow. In these cases, the parties may be concerned primarily with the legal responsibilities or entitlements that flow from a specific series of events. In some cases, the dispute may merely involve the interpretation of a provision in a contract or other document or the application of a contractual provision to a given set of facts. In these cases, where very little is in dispute in a factual sense, there may be little or no need for prehearing disclosure and discovery, and evidence at the hearing may be quite limited or even unnecessary.

c) Does the Dispute Involve One Big Question or Lots of Little Issues, as in the Case of a Multi-issue Construction Dispute?

Many legal disputes involve one major factual issue affecting liability or damages. For example, what was the cause of the roof collapse? or did the CNC machine delivered by the defendant fulfill the requirements set out in the contract? Other types of cases involve many issues, large and small.

A multi-issue dispute arising out of a large construction project can give rise to many independent factual and legal disputes within the context of a single arbitration. Each of these disputes may have nothing to do with the other disputes in the case. For example, the owner may claim that the ceiling lights installed in the meeting rooms fail to meet the contractual requirements for light output and that the recirculating pumps incorporated into the heating system are the wrong size. Each of these issues has nothing to do with the other. At the same time, the contractor may be alleging that the plans and specifications were negligently produced by the owner's architect neccesitating that various aspects of the work be redone at great expense and causing compensable delay. It is not uncommon for construction disputes to involve dozens of separate and unrelated claims. The resolution of each of these claims may involve a separate minitrial and require different witnesses drawn from the ranks of the contractor, subcontractors, and consultants. Some of the disputes may involve many thousands of dollars whereas others may be quite small. Effectively managing the logistics of arbitrations of this kind can be exceedingly demanding and require processes and procedures very different from those required for a single-issue case.

d) Will the Assessment of Credibility Be a Significant Factor in the Outcome?

Even cases that involve significant factual issues do not necessarily require the arbitrator to assess the credibility of witnesses to any significant degree. Of course, in the classic he-said-she-said controversy, the arbitrator will be called upon to ascertain who is telling the truth, and the assessment of the witnesses' credibility will require, among other things, careful observation of their demeanour while the evidence is being given. In many commercial disputes, however, the written correspondence between the parties and other documents often tell the story, and the witnesses merely introduce those documents and may be called upon to explain their contents. The assessment of credibility will often play a much smaller role in the determination of such disputes.

Where credibility is not going to be a significant factor, this may again impact on the extent of prehearing discovery that is required by opposing counsel and the manner in which the evidence can be received at the evidentiary hearing. Where assessing credibility will not play a large role, evidence-in-chief may be received in written form, and in some cases it may be possible to conduct the cross-examinations in advance of the hearing and simply argue the case from the resulting transcripts. Also, where credibility will not be an issue, it may be more feasible to receive the evidence of remote witnesses by teleconference or Internet-based service.

e) Does the Case Involve Only the Interpretation of a Provision in a Contract or Other Document?

Where the dispute is limited to the interpretation of a provision in a contract or other document, the arbitrator can be provided with an agreed statement of facts supplemented by oral or written submissions on each party's interpretation. In these cases, there may be no need for any evidentiary hearing at all, and in some cases the arbitration can be conducted entirely in writing.

f) Will the Case Involve Expert Evidence from One or Both Parties?

Cases requiring expert testimony from witnesses called by one or both parties will require additional consideration. Various measures can be taken to ensure that the evidence of each witness is responsive to that of the other. The parties can agree in advance to provide the same instructions to each of their experts so that both experts will be addressing the same issues. The parties can agree to ask the arbitrator to appoint a mutually acceptable expert and instruct that expert on their behalf, rather than having each party incur the expense of retaining its own expert. And even where each party is calling its own expert witness, the parties can authorize the arbitrator to retain an independent expert to assist the arbitrator in interpreting the evidence of the competing experts. The parties may also want to consider having their experts meet and confer in advance of the hearing to compare their evidence and attempt to narrow the issues to be presented to the arbitrator. Finally, the method of receiving the expert evidence at the evidentiary hearing could involve concurrent expert testimony, sometimes referred to as "hot-tubbing." Some of these issues are discussed more fully below.

g) Are Both Liability and Damages in Dispute?

Many cases involve issues of both liability and damages. In the traditional court system, these issues are addressed in a single trial. Evidence with respect to damages is presented by the plaintiff before knowing whether the issue of liability will be determined in their favour. The evidence presented on damages can, at times, be quite extensive and occupy a good deal of the hearing time. For example, a case may involve three days of evidence on the issue of liability followed by six days of evidence on the issue of the damages suffered. If the court then absolves the defendant of liability, the six days devoted to the issue of damages will have been wasted. During the case conference, understanding what issues are in dispute will help the parties determine whether it makes sense to consider bifurcating the hearing into separate liability and damages phases so that a damages phase of the hearing will occur only if liability is established during the first phase.

Similarly, the necessary prehearing procedures with respect to liability and damages may be very different. Different documentary production and disclosure methods may be appropriate for each aspect of the dispute, and these processes can also be bifurcated in appropriate cases so that documents and other disclosure related solely to damages are produced only after liability is established. Having said that, early disclosure related to liability and damages may facilitate settlement of the dispute through negotiation or mediation, and in such cases delaying damages disclosure may actually hinder early resolution. All of this needs to be understood and discussed at an early stage to facilitate the design of an appropriate process.

2) What Needs to Occur Before the Hearing Can Proceed?

The discussion that follows is intended for general guidance only and is especially applicable to *ad hoc* domestic arbitrations that are not proceeding under the rules of a particular arbitration institution. Where a contract requires that the parties conduct the arbitration pursuant to the rules of a governing institution, careful attention should be paid to those rules, and they should be departed from only with the concurrence of both parties and the arbitrator. Although those rules are commonly less rigid than the court rules of civil procedure in most jurisdictions, they may nonetheless set out specific requirements and times within which steps must be taken. Failure to abide by those rules may have consequences including, in some cases, the loss of the right to have the dispute resolved through arbitration.

Where the parties have not created their own set of rules and where institutional rules are not applicable, the matter will usually be governed by legislation governing the conduct of domestic or international arbitration within the jurisdiction. Usually, as will be discussed below, that legislation tends to be minimally prescriptive and attempts to preserve a high level of flexibility. Nonetheless, the parties should take care to familiarize themselves with the applicable provisions to avoid missteps that can potentially lead to the undoing of the process after the parties have already made a significant investment of time and money.

Whether dealing with the procedural rules set out in the parties' contract, institutional rules, or applicable legislation in the jurisdiction, the parties are, with few exceptions, free to agree, in consultation with the arbitrator, to depart from the rules as the circumstances warrant. Where the parties do not agree to depart from the rules, however, great caution must be taken to adopt procedures that fit within the boundaries of the rules.

a) What Form of Pleadings Is to Be Exchanged and When?

As the initiating phase of the litigation process, traditional pleadings serve a number of purposes. They tell the decision maker what the case is about and identify the issues in dispute. The defending party is informed, with reasonable particularity, of the case that it has to meet, both factually and legally, and the claimant is made aware of the defences that will be raised. Any counterclaims are similarly identified and responded to. In the court system, there is also the possibility of introducing additional parties to the dispute without their consent.

The pleadings not only define the dispute, but also restrict the scope of the pretrial productions and discovery processes, as well as the claims that can be asserted at trial. Except with leave of the court to amend its claim, a party cannot seek relief at trial for something that has not been identified in the pleadings. This would simply be unfair to the responding party.

In arbitration, the rules surrounding pleadings are usually less prescriptive. And since the jurisdiction for the arbitration process is usually the result of a contractual agreement, the addition of parties is rare, because to participate in the arbitration those parties would have to agree to attorn to the jurisdiction of the arbitration tribunal. With these exceptions, however, the original notice to arbitrate, or submission to arbitration, and the arbitration statements exchanged by the parties largely serve the same purpose as pleadings in litigation.

By way of example, the guidance provided in section 25 of the Ontario *Arbitration Act, 1991* with respect to party statements is limited to the following:

> 25(1) An arbitral tribunal may require that the parties submit their statements within a specified period of time.
>
> (2) The parties' statements shall indicate the facts supporting their positions, the points at issue and the relief sought.
>
> (3) The parties may submit with their statements the documents they consider relevant, or may refer to the documents or other evidence they intend to submit.
>
> (4) The parties may amend or supplement their statements during the arbitration; however, the arbitral tribunal may disallow a change that is unduly delayed.
>
> (5) With the arbitral tribunal's permission, the parties may submit their statements orally.[2]

Without the very formalistic provisions in most court rules, this framework affords great flexibility in providing for an exchange of pleadings that is best suited to the nature of the particular dispute.

2 SO 1991, c 17, s 25.

One practice that is encouraged to provide for early disclosure of documentary evidence on which a party is relying is the exchange of arbitration statements in electronic format with embedded hyperlinks to documents referred to in support of factual or legal positions. This is different from the usual litigation rules that discourage the pleading of evidence. In appropriate cases, this is an excellent way to streamline the process and provide early disclosure to the opposing party of the positions being put forward and the documents on which a party will be relying to prove its case. It also forces each party to think carefully about what evidence it will need to prove each element of its case at a very early stage in the process.

b) What Level of Documentary Disclosure Is Required, and How Will It Occur?

In litigation, extensive documentary disclosure has become the default position in most jurisdictions. In theory, this has developed as a means of avoiding trial by ambush and ensuring that both parties have access to all necessary documentary evidence. In cases where there are a significant number of documents, sometimes hundreds of thousands, this has resulted in significant delay in moving the case forward and enormous costs associated with the organization, production, and review of documents by counsel on both sides of the case. Even with the advent of rules invoking the doctrine of proportionality, documentary production in court cases still imposes a substantial burden of time and cost on the parties, thereby reducing access to justice for parties that cannot afford the process.

This situation is not the norm in arbitration. As a general rule, each party is obliged to produce only the documents that it intends to rely on to prove its case. Each party will then have the ability to request additional documents from the opposing party. If the opposing party refuses to produce those additional documents, an application can be made to the tribunal to require production. In addition to section 25(3), reproduced above, which allows the parties to refer to specific documents in their statements, the *Arbitration Act, 1991* includes the following provisions, which are typical:

25(6) The parties and persons claiming through or under them shall, subject to any legal objection, comply with the arbitral tribunal's directions, including directions to,

(a) submit to examination on oath or affirmation with respect to the dispute;

(b) produce records and documents that are in their possession or power.

26(4) The arbitral tribunal shall communicate to the parties any expert reports or other documents on which it may rely in making a decision.

28(2) The arbitral tribunal may require parties to give the expert any relevant information or to allow him or her to inspect property or documents.

29(1) A party may serve a person with a notice, issued by the arbitral tribunal, requiring the person to attend and give evidence at the arbitration at the time and place named in the notice.

(2) The notice has the same effect as a notice in a court proceeding requiring a witness to attend at a hearing or produce documents, and shall be served in the same way.

30 No person shall be compelled to produce information, property or documents or to give evidence in an arbitration that the person could not be compelled to produce or give in a court proceeding.[3]

It will be clear from a review of these brief provisions that the legislation provides broad powers to the arbitral tribunal but little guidance in terms of what must or should be produced and the criteria governing the exercise of those powers.

By contrast, the arbitration rules of the ADR Institute of Canada contain extensive provisions governing the production of documents, which include the requirement that a party produce all documents on which it relies, and the procedures pursuant to which parties may seek to compel the production of additional

3 *Ibid*, ss 25(6), 26(4), 28(2), 29(1), 29(2), and 30.

documents from the opposing party or third parties.[4] Relevance and materiality are the principal grounds on which documents will be ordered to be produced, subject to a number of objections related to privilege, commercial or technical confidentiality, and special political or institutional sensitivity and to considerations of procedural economy, proportionality, fairness, and party equality. Although these grounds for objection are enumerated, the rules contain virtually no guidance regarding their application. All of which is to say that even in the case of highly prescriptive institutional rules, the tribunal usually has significant discretion.

It is clear that the wholesale production of every document touching on the matters in dispute in the possession of each party is not the norm in the world of arbitration. As noted above, in the absence of a specific agreement between the parties to the contrary, the basic rule is that each party will produce only the documents that it needs to prove its case, either with the initiating arbitration statement, as a separate list of documents, or as exhibits to affidavits submitted as evidence-in-chief.[5] A typical protocol would then allow each party to make a formal written request for specific additional documents or classes of documents believed to be in the possession of the opposing party. If the opposing party agrees to produce the requested documents, the arbitrator need not be involved. If the opposing party refuses, however, the arbitrator will hear the objection and decide the issue, usually through an informal hearing process. A timetable for each step in this protocol would be established at the case conference.

At the case conference, it is generally a good idea to discuss whether copies will suffice and agree that original documents will not be required. The parties may also agree to waive the formal proof of documents and any notice provisions governing the introduction of business records, etc. Again, the emphasis should

4 ADR Institute of Canada, *ADRIC Arbitration Rules* (version 2, effective 1 December 2016), online: http://adric.ca/wp-content/uploads/2017/03/ADRIC_Arbitration_Rules_8_5_x_11_2016.pdf.

5 See Section D(3)(c), below in this chapter.

be on streamlining the process and cost saving, provided that fairness and due process are not compromised.

c) How Much and What Kind of Oral Discovery Is Required, and When Will It Occur?

In arbitration, unlike litigation, examinations for discovery and other prehearing forms of discovery are the exception, not the rule. There is generally no provision for an automatic right to examine a party representative or witness in advance of the hearing. Such examinations are typically permitted only by agreement between the parties or upon application to the arbitrator. When such an application is made, the party requesting the examination should be in a position to demonstrate why the examination is necessary for that party to fairly present its case and what issues will form the subject matter of the examination.

The arbitrator may allow oral examination under oath or may restrict the inquiry to written questions on specific issues with the answers given in writing and declared under oath. The arbitrator should also indicate what use may be made of the resulting transcript or written answers at the hearing. Will they be admissible to prove the truth of the statements contained therein or simply used for the purposes of testing credibility in cross-examination?

Despite this being the general approach, counsel will often agree to conduct some form of prehearing oral examinations, and unless presented with an alternative, they will often default to traditional examinations for discovery. That is what they are used to in the court system. The arbitrator may help them to appreciate that not every case requires this step, that it causes delay and adds costs, and that there are other approaches available for consideration. They should be reminded that the stated purposes of prehearing examinations are to allow each party to obtain disclosure of the case that it will have to meet, obtain admissions on factual matters, and have some opportunity to evaluate the demeanour and credibility of one or more witnesses.

There are other more expeditious and less costly ways to achieve these objectives. For example, in situations where there are few factual issues in dispute, there may be no need for any oral discovery. In the alternative, a decision with respect to oral discovery can be deferred until after the parties have produced an agreed statement of facts,[6] and then, if necessary, oral discovery can be restricted to any remaining facts in dispute. Similarly, in cases where affidavits or witness statements will be used to present evidence-in-chief on factual issues,[7] an excellent alternative to conducting examinations for discovery is postponing any oral prehearing examinations until after the written statements have been delivered by each party. Since those statements represent the core evidence on which each party will be relying, examinations for discovery will not be needed for disclosure of each party's case. The statements themselves will need to do that.

Where written statements are used to present evidence-in-chief, a preferred course of action is to allow limited cross-examination before the evidentiary hearing on one or more of the tendered statements for the purposes of testing the evidence, obtaining admissions, and allowing for the evaluation of witnesses. A typical approach would be to allow each party eight hours of cross-examination on one or more of the opposing party's statements conducted without the presence of the arbitrator. Counsel would be free to devote the entire time to one affiant or to divide the time up among several. In either case, the resulting cross-examination transcripts would be admissible as evidence for all purposes at the hearing, in much the same way that they are used in a court application process. Taking some or all of the cross-examinations out of the hearing room can result in a significantly abbreviated and more tightly focused hearing. Cross-examination at the hearing could be limited to those situations where credibility is in issue, and it is necessary for the arbitrator to observe the demeanour of the witnesses.

Another approach is to begin with written interrogatories. After the answers to those questions have been exchanged, each party would be free to apply for an opportunity to cross-examine one or more witnesses in advance of the hearing if the written answers

6 See Section D(3)(a), below in this chapter.

7 See Section D(3)(c), below in this chapter.

can be shown to be inadequate. Knowing that this secondary step is available will encourage most parties to provide more comprehensive written answers with a view to avoiding an oral examination.

Each case will demand a different approach. The important point is that this issue should be carefully canvassed at the initial case conference, when the party representatives are in attendance and can fully appreciate how the method chosen will affect the timeliness and cost of the process. It is also important to remind the parties that if a more expedient and less exhaustive process is chosen and if circumstances later arise requiring more substantial oral examinations, the process can be varied at a later date either on consent or with leave of the arbitrator upon cause being shown.

3) What Else Can Be Done to Streamline the Hearing?

a) Can an Agreed Statement of Facts Be Used to Establish Some, If Not All, of the Relevant Facts?

One of the most useful ways to shorten the hearing and save costs is to require the parties to produce an agreed statement of facts at an early stage in the process. This should be produced shortly after each party has delivered its arbitration statement. In addition to abbreviating the length of the evidentiary hearing, requiring the parties to develop an agreed statement of facts forces them to identify at a very early stage the precise nature of the factual issues in dispute. While in theory pleadings should accomplish this purpose, in practice they rarely do because each party tries to draft its pleading in such a way as to retain the widest ambit of flexibility in the presentation of its case.

The process for getting to an agreed statement of facts can vary, but one useful approach is to have the claimant prepare a detailed statement of facts that it believes the responding party will accept. The claimant should be encouraged to restrict this statement to noncontentious facts and make every attempt to state them in a neutral and objective fashion. This is not intended to be an advocacy document, and terms such as "wrongly," "wilfully," "negligently," and "in breach of" have no place in it. The responding party will then prepare a blackline markup of the claimant's draft excising those portions with which it is not prepared to agree and substituting versions of events that it would be prepared to accept. If the claimant has produced the first draft conscientiously, there should be very few changes, but there may be additional facts that the responding party wishes to have included and that it believes the claimant will accept as factually true.

It is then up to the claimant to do a further markup accepting or rejecting the changes made by the respondent. The final version and all prior drafts should be provided to the arbitrator for future reference. The final version will then be accepted as evidence of the facts contained in it without further proof, and costs sanctions may be imposed on a party that leads excessive evidence concerning matters that have already been dealt with in the agreed statement of facts. Similarly, at the conclusion of the case, either party may ask the arbitrator to consider the opposing party's position when developing the agreed statement of facts in any costs submissions where it can be demonstrated that the opposing party refused to admit facts that were never really disputed but the proof of which unnecessarily prolonged the evidentiary hearing.

The time invested in preparing an agreed statement of facts, when done properly, should be offset by a greater reduction in time spent presenting the evidence-in-chief, whether by way of affidavit or oral testimony. The other principal benefit is that the agreed statement of facts makes the parties focus at a very early stage in the process on precisely which facts are in dispute and then turn their minds to how they will prove their own version of those facts. In other words, a by-product of an agreed statement of facts is the emergence of a clearer understanding of the disputed facts. Whether or not that finds its way into a formal document, it should be of great assistance to the parties in their efforts to prepare for the ultimate hearing.

b) What Tools Are Being Considered to Efficiently Manage the Exchange and Presentation of Documentary Evidence?

It is becoming increasingly common for all documents to be produced in electronic format only. Where the case involves only a few documents, the parties can simply exchange them in PDF format, ideally referenced in each party's arbitration statement or evidentiary affidavits with hyperlinks. Where there will be a large number of documents, however, it is important to discuss which database software will be used, ensuring that it is available to each party and the arbitrator. It is also necessary to establish a uniform protocol for coding documents and, where possible, for the avoidance of unnecessary duplication.

A useful and cost-effective practice is to retain one outside service provider to assemble, code, and, where necessary, scan documents for both parties. The result, whether in electronic or paper format, should be a joint document brief that can be referred to by both parties and the arbitrator. Finally, one or both parties need to take responsibility for ensuring that the venue for the arbitration hearing will be properly equipped to allow for the simultaneous digital presentation of documentary evidence to the parties, counsel, the witnesses, and the arbitrator. Experience demonstrates that this use of technology can shorten the length of a hearing by a very significant extent when a large number of documents are going to be put to the witnesses.

c) Is It an Appropriate Case for Evidence-in-Chief to Be Submitted by Way of Affidavits or Written Witness Statements?

An increasingly common practice in arbitration is for all of the evidence-in-chief on factual issues to be exchanged well in advance of the evidentiary hearing through sworn affidavits or witness statements that will be adopted under oath when the witness is presented for cross-examination. As with the pleadings, documents referred to in those affidavits can be attached as exhibits, and when electronic documents are used, they can be referenced in the witness statements with hyperlinks. When called at the evidentiary hearing, the witness can be asked a few introductory questions to relax him or her before cross-examination by opposing counsel.

There are many advantages to this approach in situations where credibility is not going to be a significant factor. It allows counsel an opportunity to carefully present all of the evidence on which his or her client relies to prove its case in a clear, concise, and comprehensive written format. Because this is generally done early in the process, most of the witness preparation is done at an early stage rather than being left to the last weeks before the hearing, as is often the case with litigation. Counsel is less reliant on the witness's memory and ability to get the evidence on the record. In other words, counsel can carefully lay out their case in-chief through the written statements of one or more witnesses, together with supporting documents. As anyone who has ever elicited evidence-in-chief knows, it can be a laborious and time-consuming process, as counsel attempts to bring forth all of the necessary evidence from the witnesses in a comprehensible form without excessively indulging in leading questions. With a written statement, everything can be neatly laid out in an organized and compelling way. The arbitrator can review each affidavit or witness statement in advance of that witness's testimony, and this can save an enormous amount of time at the hearing.

Pleadings will typically set out the specific facts that each party must prove to make its case. The early preparation of affidavits or witness statements forces counsel to consider how they are going to prove those facts. As a result of adopting this approach, counsel will discover at an early stage what gaps, if any, exist in their ability to prove their client's case. It is generally better to discover these problems early on so that they can be addressed by looking for other sources of evidence, determining what will need to be established through cross-examination of the opposing party's witnesses, or, where necessary, compromising one's position through settlement.

The final, and perhaps most important, benefit of tendering evidence-in-chief in written form is the time that it will save in the evidentiary hearing. The hearing itself is typically the most expensive part of the process since the parties are paying for the time of one or more legal counsel on each side, one or three arbitrators, a hearing room, and a court reporter. To the extent that this part of the process can be abbreviated without impinging on the fairness of the process, everybody gains.

Also, having access to a witness's evidence-in-chief weeks or even months before the evidentiary hearing can allow opposing counsel to develop a shorter and more focused cross-examination. When beginning a cross-examination immediately after hearing oral evidence-in-chief, counsel has been so busy listening to the evidence, taking notes, and trying to absorb what the witness has been saying that there is rarely an opportunity to recast the cross-examination outline prepared before trial. As a general rule, cross-examinations prepared with the benefit of written evidence-in-chief are much tighter, briefer, and more effective than the alternative.

As noted above, adopting written evidence-in-chief is not necessarily the preferred course of action in cases where the observational ability or credibility of one or more witnesses will be challenged in a material way. Where the fundamental truthfulness of a witness is an issue, it will usually be important for the trier of fact to observe the witness's demeanour both in chief and under cross-examination. In such cases, it may be appropriate to have some witnesses provide affidavits or statements and others provide their evidence-in-chief orally.

d) If There Is to Be Expert Testimony, Is It an Appropriate Case for Hot-tubbing the Experts?

The traditional approach to the introduction of expert opinion evidence is for the parties to exchange original and responding expert reports in advance of the trial and then to have each expert testify separately. When this happens, the evidence of the experts may be heard days or even weeks apart, and it can be challenging for the judge or arbitrator to recall what the first expert said when hearing the evidence of the second expert in order to compare and evaluate their testimonies. Also, it is common for each party to have its expert sit in during the testimony of the opposing party's expert. When this occurs, the cost to the parties increases, because each expert has to attend the hearing on two separate occasions.

An approach that is rapidly becoming popular in the world of arbitration is known as concurrent expert testimony, sometimes referred to as "hot-tubbing." When this approach is used, opposing expert reports are exchanged in advance of the hearing and provided to the arbitrator. Both experts attend the hearing on the same day, give their oath or affirmation, and are empanelled to give evidence at the same time. In some cases, the experts may have been asked to meet and confer in private to discuss their opinions and narrow down, if possible, the issues in dispute. The arbitrator will have reviewed their reports before their attendance at the hearing.

While there are many approaches to the receipt of experts' oral testimony, and a full discussion of these is beyond the scope of this chapter, a common approach is to have the parties prepare in advance of the experts' appearance at the hearing a list of questions to be put to the expert panel. The questions should be designed to elicit the necessary evidence on each point of contention. Often, the arbitrator will pose each question and ask each expert to respond in the presence of the other. Each expert may then be given an opportunity to elaborate on their original answer with reference to the evidence of the opposing expert. After both experts have had an opportunity to say everything that they wish to say with respect to a particular question, each counsel will be given an opportunity to examine the witnesses on that question. Since the original answers have been elicited in response to a question from the arbitrator, counsel for each party may be afforded broader latitude in their examination, such that it may take the form of a cross-examination, including the questions put to their own expert. The arbitrator may also ask follow-up questions for clarification.

Aside from the efficiency and cost savings associated with having the experts attend on only one occasion, the principal advantage to this approach is that the decision maker gets to hear both experts' evidence on each point contemporaneously. The arbitrator is less reliant on notes and memory in evaluating the testimony and has the advantage of a far more dynamic process. Counsel are also afforded greater latitude in their own questioning to ensure that all points are fully examined. Finally, it is often the case that the evidence of each expert is more independent and less partisan when it is given in the presence of the opposing expert. Since most experts value the opinion of their peers, they may be less inclined to adopt the mantle of an advocate when they know that their testimony is being observed, evaluated, and may be immediately challenged by someone with expertise equal to their own.

e) Is It a Case Where Some Benefit Would Be Derived from the Arbitrator Retaining a Neutral Expert Instead of or in Addition to the Parties, and If So, What Procedure Will Be Followed to Instruct the Expert and Ensure That Both Parties Are Guaranteed a Fair Opportunity to Explore and Challenge the Findings?

Most arbitration legislation and institutional rules provide the arbitrator with the opportunity to retain a neutral expert. The arbitrator can retain an expert instead of or in addition to each party retaining its own expert. Typically, this would be done with the consent of both parties, although consent is not required. From an efficiency and cost point of view, this approach is more useful when it substitutes for each party calling its own expert.

The usual process is for the parties and their counsel to agree upon the selection of an expert in whom all concerned have confidence. The arbitrator will formally engage the expert and provide background information and a list of issues to be addressed. This document will have been carefully reviewed with and vetted by counsel for each party. The expert will then provide a report setting out an opinion on the issues under review. The expert may also be called as a witness by the arbitrator and subjected to cross-examination by both counsel. Since the expert has been retained by the arbitrator, rather than by either party, this approach can lead to the development of a less partisan and more independent opinion.

f) Is It an Appropriate Case to Consider Bifurcating the Hearing?

As discussed above, most cases involve a determination of legal liability and damages or other relief sought arising from a finding of liability. In the court system, it is common for each party to put forward its case on liability and damages at the same time even though the evidence on damages may become irrelevant if the court determines that the defendant is not liable to the plaintiff. This can be particularly inefficient especially in cases where the evidence on liability is fairly contained and the evidence on damages is extensive. Although the issues of liability and damages can be bifurcated under the court rules of most jurisdictions, this is the exception rather than the rule for a variety of reasons beyond the scope of this chapter.

In the arbitration world, however, bifurcation is much more common. Although bifurcation is not suitable for every case, every case should be examined at an early stage with a view to determining the appropriateness of bifurcation. Where there is a serious issue as to whether liability will be found, it can be useful to separate liability and damages into two separate hearings so that the second evidentiary hearing can be dispensed with if the arbitrator fails to find in favour of the claimant during the first phase of the process. It may also happen that following a finding of liability in favour of the claimant, the parties are able to settle the issue of damages without a second hearing. Bifurcation may also be warranted where the resolution of a single factual or legal issue, such as the applicability of a limitation period or other statutory defence, may be dispositive of the case.

When bifurcation is to be employed, the procedural timetable will need to provide for disclosure both on liability and on damages at the appropriate times in the process. There is no point in having the claimant produce voluminous materials and expert reports on the issue of damages if it cannot succeed in the first phase of the process. Sufficient time should be allowed between the first and second phases for the filing and review of any supplementary materials on the damages issue, but the time should not be so long as to unduly delay the resolution of the case.

g) If There Are Many Individual Issues, Should Both Sides Present Their Evidence on Each Issue Sequentially, or Should the Claimant Present All of Its Evidence on All Issues First, Followed by the Respondent, in the Normal Fashion of a Traditional Trial?

Many cases that go to arbitration are what are sometimes referred to as multi-issue disputes. This is often true of disputes arising out of construction projects, where a contractor may have dozens of separate claims for extra work, the owner may have many individual claims for deficiencies in the quality of the work or under warranties, and both parties may have claims for delay and impact. In some cases, the individual claims and counterclaims will be related to one another, but commonly each claim for extra work or a deficiency will be independent of the other claims. Moreover, the individual claims may be very disproportionate to one another with some involving substantial amounts of money and others involving relatively negligible amounts. Often, the disputes surrounding delay and impact will be related to one or more underlying individual claims.

Following the traditional approach, the claimant presents all of its evidence on all of its claims over the course of several days or weeks, and then the other party presents all of its evidence responding to those claims and asserting its counterclaims. The decision maker is thereby challenged with the task of keeping all of the evidence on each of the claims, with respect to both liability and compensation, organized and compartmentalized over the course of many weeks. This is not necessarily the most efficient way to adjudicate a multi-issue dispute. Aside from the challenges that it poses to the decision maker, it is inefficient in that many witnesses will have to be present or on call throughout the course of the hearing even though each may be testifying on only one or more discrete issues since it will be difficult to know precisely when their evidence will be required.

When, at the prehearing case conference, it appears that the case will involve multiple issues, the arbitrator can help the parties develop a more rational adjudicative process. Consider a hypothetical case (based on an actual arbitration) involving a series of claims by both sides in a construction dispute for extra work, deficiencies, and warranty items. The contractor has many claims for individual bits of extra work, each of which has nothing to do with any other claim. Similarly, the owner has many claims for deficiencies in the work and under various warranties. Again, each of the owner's claims is unrelated to any other claim. In total, there are between fifty and sixty stand-alone claims of this type, some of which are for amounts less than $1,000 and the largest of which is for approximately $85,000. The total of all the claims is a little over $1 million. To complicate matters, many of the contractor's claims are really the claims of its subcontractors or suppliers, and as such each of those claims will require a different cadre of witnesses.

It will be immediately apparent that dealing with these fifty or sixty individual claims in the context of a traditional trial would require fifty or sixty mini-trials within a single proceeding and that the process would consume many weeks or months. The legal costs alone of each side would likely exceed the net payment awarded to the party that succeeded on the greatest number of claims. A better way is needed.

In the context of an arbitration, the parties can retain a knowledgeable and respected construction lawyer to act as an arbitrator. The evidence can be abbreviated on the assumption that the arbitrator will be familiar with industry practices, terminology, and many of the technical issues that would otherwise have to be explained through evidence to a trial judge with a generalist background. In advance of the hearing, the parties can prepare a table setting out all of the issues in dispute listed in descending order from the highest dollar value to the lowest. The table can also set out in successive columns a brief summary of each party's position, the documents on which each party intends to rely, and the witnesses to be called in respect of each individual claim. This table is sometimes referred to as a Scott Schedule. Each party can then prepare binders with all of the documents on which it will be relying with respect to each item under a separate tab numbered to correspond with the table. Even better than binders, documents in electronic format can be hyperlinked to the table. The materials are exchanged well in advance of the hearing date.

The ground rules for the subsequent hearing can be quite simple. The issues will be dealt with in the same order in which they are set out in the table, from the highest dollar value to the lowest. Each side will be allowed a limited amount of time to present its case on each issue. The time allotted to each side may vary in accordance with the amount in dispute in a particular claim. For example, any claim involving more than $50,000 may warrant a presentation time of no more than two hours per side whereas any claim involving $5,000 or less may be restricted to thirty minutes per side. Witnesses could be called on behalf of the claimant or respondent, including representatives of a subcontractor or supplier, but most of the formal rules of evidence may be set aside by agreement, and the arbitrator may be given significant latitude to conduct a more inquisitorial mode of inquiry.

By dealing with the claims in order of magnitude and by imposing a time limit on each claim, the parties can predict with reasonable certainty when each claim will be reached and arrange to have the necessary witnesses present only as required. A knowledgeable arbitrator and careful organization and presentation of the issues and the evidence in support of each party's position coupled with reduced formalities in the presentation of evidence should allow the parties and the arbitrator to move through the list of issues expeditiously. This approach may also incorporate the arbitrator's delivery of decisions at the end of each day with respect to each item covered that day. If the parties agree, time and money can be further saved by not requiring detailed or formal reasons for each decision from the arbitrator.

In the real-life case on which this hypothetical case has been based, because the schedule had been organized in descending dollar value order, when approximately two-thirds of the items were dealt with, more than 85 percent of the dollars in dispute were adjudicated in favour of one party or the other. And at that point, the parties agreed to settle the remaining 15 percent of the amount in dispute by applying the same overall success ratio as had been achieved up to that point to the items remaining. At the end of the process, the owner paid the contractor an amount representing the net difference between their respective successes.

The feedback from both parties was entirely positive. Both had been through litigation before, and they found this process much more satisfying because they had been able to explain their positions in their own words with an absence of formality, achieve a quick result, and not spend a fortune in legal fees to resolve a large number of small disputes. By all accounts, the dispute was resolved in approximately one-third of the time that would have been required to deal with this case in a more traditional fashion. Although there is no way to be sure, there is no reason to believe that the ultimate result was materially different from what would have been achieved through a traditional judicial approach at a much higher cost in terms of money and resources.

h) Is It a Case That Would Benefit from a More Inquisitorial Approach to Dealing with Some or All of the Evidence and Issues in Dispute?

In the adversarial system prevalent in our courts, it is customary for judges to take a fairly passive role, leaving it to the parties and their counsel to present their case as they see fit. Judges rarely intervene during the presentation of the evidence except to ask the occasional clarifying question. Even then, many judges hold their questions until both counsel have completed their examinations of a witness, and then, after asking any questions they may have, judges will invite counsel to re-examine on any of the points that they may have raised.

This form of judicial restraint is consistent with the view that the judge is an impartial referee who will wait patiently for the parties to present whatever evidence they choose. There is a concern that if the judge becomes too actively involved in the questioning, they will appear to have become an advocate for one of the parties, raising concerns of partiality. Moreover, an intervention by the judge may be based on an inaccurate perception of where the party is going with the evidence, and this can do harm to counsel's presentation of the client's case.

This approach is to be contrasted with the more inquisitorial system common in many civil law jurisdictions, where judges actively participate in the fact-finding inquiry by questioning counsel and witnesses. While many arbitrators choose to conduct themselves in accordance with the common law model, especially if they have come out of the common law court system, this non-interventionist approach is not required in arbitration. If the parties retain an arbitrator with specialized knowledge, it may be helpful to have that person ask the questions that are important to him or her in a more active way than would occur in a typical trial situation. Similarly, if witnesses are providing detailed explanations of matters that are already well understood by the arbitrator as a result of their specialized knowledge, it can help to abbreviate the hearing by letting the parties know this.

Having said that, the arbitrator should never take over the role of counsel or adopt the mantle of an advocate for either party. Caution should be exercised with respect to the timing and nature of the questions asked, and counsel should be invited to let the arbitrator know if they are treading in areas that are to be covered later in the evidence. The extent to which the parties wish the arbitrator to play a more inquisitorial role in the hearing is a matter that should be canvassed at an early stage in the case conference process.

i) Can All or a Part of the Case Be Submitted in Writing?

Sometimes a dispute does not involve any controversial facts but merely raises legal issues. A common example is a dispute revolving around the interpretation of a term or clause in a contract or other document. One party says it means one thing, and the other says it means another. In these situations, the arbitration can be determined on the basis of an agreed statement of facts and written arguments submitted by both parties, with or without an opportunity to supplement the written arguments with an attendance before the arbitrator for oral submissions. Similarly, in cases involving something as straightforward as the determination of fair market value under a lease renewal agreement, the report of each party's appraiser can be filed, and time can be scheduled for cross-examination on those reports, followed by written arguments.

j) Is It an Appropriate Case for Baseball Arbitration or Nighttime Baseball Arbitration?

Some kinds of disputes are amenable to a method known as final offer selection, sometimes referred to as baseball arbitration after the way that some salaries are determined in the major leagues: Each party submits its best offer to the other party and the arbitrator, and after hearing the parties' evidence, the arbitrator selects the offer considered to be the most reasonable as a binding award. The arbitrator cannot award an amount between the two offers, so there is no possibility of avoiding a difficult binary choice by "splitting the baby."

This approach forces each party to think long and hard about its final offer since each wants to be seen as the most reasonable in the eyes of the arbitrator. This method has the effect of discouraging unreasonable or inflated offers on both sides, and as one side will leave the arbitration a winner and the other a loser, the method encourages negotiation and compromise and will often produce a settlement rather than a verdict. For example, if the claimant offers to accept $100,000, the defending party offers to pay $50,000, and the arbitrator determines that a fair resolution would require the payment of $82,000, then the claimant will receive $100,000 because its offer was closest to the arbitrator's determination of a fair resolution. If, on the other hand, the arbitrator determines that a fair resolution would require the payment of only $62,000, then the defending party will have to pay only $50,000. As can be readily seen, it is in each party's best interests to present an offer as close as possible to what it perceives the arbitrator will determine to be fair.

This method can be structured in a number of different ways. Ideally, the parties will exchange their final offers shortly before the commencement of the evidentiary hearing. In some cases, the final offers are so close together that the parties will be able to settle the case on some basis and avoid the hearing altogether. A variation on this approach is for the parties to deliver their final offers to each other and the arbitrator after the evidence is in and after they have had an opportunity to evaluate how the case went.

Another variation on this approach is for the parties to exchange final offers but not give them to the arbitrator. The arbitrator then renders a decision independently and without reference to the offers, and the party that is closest to the arbitrator's determination will get the benefit of its offer. This approach is sometimes referred to as nighttime baseball arbitration because the arbitrator is kept in the dark with respect to each party's final offer. It may be advantageous where the parties do not wish the arbitrator to be influenced by their offers in making a determination. Using the above-noted example, if the arbitrator's independent ruling requires the payment of anything between $75,000 and an amount higher than $100,000, then the claimant will receive $100,000. If the arbitrator's ruling requires anything between $0 and $75,000, then the claimant will still receive $50,000.

Under this variation, the two offers also serve as a "cap and a collar" on the potential recovery, thereby removing some of the risk from the process for both sides.

Whichever variation is adopted, the parties should also determine what form of award they will require, but it is quite common in these situations to dispense with detailed reasons for the choice made. Typically, the results of final offer selection arbitrations are final and binding with no rights of appeal. This method can be particularly useful in cases where the issues are straightforward and principally involve the determination of a monetary amount, such as disputes over the determination of fair market value under a lease renewal agreement.

k) Could the Hearing Be More Efficiently Conducted If the Arbitrator Was to Take a View of a Site or Even Conduct the Hearing at the Location Where the Dispute Arose?

In some cases, a lot of time can be saved if the arbitrator has an opportunity to get a first-hand view of a location. For example, where the dispute involves multiple issues arising out of the construction of a water treatment plant, giving the arbitrator a tour of the plant in the company of representatives of both parties can be extremely helpful. Once the arbitrator can visualize and understand the purpose of various aspects of the project, much less time needs to be devoted to putting the arbitrator into the picture through oral testimony. Where a tour is not feasible, the parties can generally prepare a comprehensive video walk-through that may accomplish much the same purpose.

In other cases, a lot of time can be saved if the arbitration hearing, or at least part of it, is held at the location where the dispute arose. For example, where the dispute involves the management of facilities shared by two or more condominium corporations, holding the hearing in a condominium meeting room allows the arbitrator, counsel, the parties, and the witnesses to easily visit various locations to facilitate the giving of evidence and enhance the arbitrator's understanding of the situation from each party's point of view.

4) What Are the Ground Rules?

a) Are All Aspects of the Proceedings to Remain Private and Confidential?

One of the principal benefits of arbitration is the ability to keep the dispute out of the public spotlight. But parties should be made aware that the arbitration legislation in most jurisdictions does not expressly provide for confidentiality, so the parties must typically incorporate this requirement into their agreements. The rules of most arbitration institutions do provide for confidentiality, but those provisions may or may not be adequate for the needs of the parties in any particular case. This is an issue that should be carefully discussed at the first case conference. The parties should also be asked to consider whether they will have the witnesses enter into confidentiality agreements and, if transcripts are to be produced, what safeguards will be employed to ensure that the record remains confidential.

b) Will Witnesses Be Excluded During the Hearing?

Where credibility will be in issue, it is common to exclude witnesses from the hearing while other witnesses are testifying. Instructing party representatives are typically in attendance throughout the hearing, and if they are to testify, their evidence will typically be presented first by each party. The parties should consider at an early stage whether they will be seeking an order to exclude witnesses and any necessary ground rules resulting from that order.

c) What, If Any, Procedural or Evidentiary Rules and Statutory Provisions Are to Be Waived in the Evidentiary Hearing?

How strictly will the rules of evidence be enforced? Will the parties agree to waive formal notice regarding the introduction of business records and other documents under the applicable legislation?

d) What Rights of Appeal Are Contemplated?

One of the identified benefits of arbitration is the finality of the result. Governing legislation in jurisdictions often provides for limited rights of appeal with leave only on questions of law, but some contractual arbitration clauses take away this right. It is useful to discuss what appeal rights, if any, will be provided for in the submission to arbitration agreement. Sometimes parties may wish to reserve rights of appeal only if the monetary value of the judgment exceeds a certain amount. In other cases, parties may mutually wish to reserve limited or broad rights of appeal despite what the legislation or contract may provide for. In these cases, the discussion should include whether the appeal will be to the local court or an appellate arbitration tribunal.

e) How Are Party-and-Party and Arbitration Costs to Be Dealt with in the Award?

The default position under most governing legislation, institutional rules, and contractual arbitration provisions is that costs are to be awarded in the discretion of the arbitration tribunal. Absent an agreement between the parties, it is generally accepted that the ordinary court rules of practice governing the award of costs are not applicable and that arbitrators have wide latitude. Ordinarily, costs will follow the cause, and the unsuccessful party will be required to pay all costs reasonably incurred by the successful party, the fees of the arbitrator, and any facility and transportation costs.

This costs regime, however, need not apply in all cases. The parties are free to agree upon a different approach, and it is advisable to discuss this issue and arrive at an agreement early in the process, when neither party knows how the case will be resolved. For example, to reduce the risk of the process the parties may agree to pay their own legal costs in any event of the cause and to divide the costs of the arbitration equally between themselves. Or they may agree to divide the costs of the arbitration equally but have their party-and-party costs awarded in the cause. If costs are to be awarded in the cause, do the parties want the arbitrator to award all costs reasonably incurred or to use a partial indemnity model similar to that employed by the courts? Finally, what approach do the parties want to employ in the event of a divided result? It is useful to establish clarity around these issues and incorporate any resulting agreement into the submission to arbitration agreement or procedural order.

Where costs are to be awarded by the arbitrator, it is useful to require each party to submit its bill of costs concurrently with its final submissions at the end of the evidentiary hearing, before the outcome is known. Since each party does not know whether it will be paying or receiving a costs award, this approach tends to reduce the likelihood of exaggerated costs submissions being made after the fact. Costs submissions can then be made after the award is issued.

f) Are Settlement Offers to Be Considered in Awarding Costs?

Ordinarily, any settlement offers may be considered by the arbitration tribunal with respect to the costs disposition after the award has been issued. Accordingly, it is advisable to discuss this issue at an early stage and reach agreement between the parties on how offers, if any, will be exchanged, what form they will take, and when they will be brought to the attention of the tribunal. Is it the parties' intention that the costs regime relating to offers set out in the court rules of practice will prevail, or are the parties content to have the arbitrator apply a more flexible approach? Again, whatever is agreed should be incorporated into the submission to arbitration agreement or procedural order.

5) What about the Logistics?

Now attention must be paid to more mundane but nonetheless important aspects of the process if everything is to proceed smoothly. Final decisions on all of the following issues do not necessarily need to be reached at the initial case conference, but all should be discussed and added to the checklist of matters that will need to be addressed well in advance of the hearing date.

a) When Will the Hearing Take Place?

When a realistic timetable for all of the prehearing steps that must be completed is being attempted, it is quite common to establish a date for the commencement of the hearing and then work backwards to develop a schedule for all the preliminary matters. The parties should be asked whether they will be making any organized attempt to settle the dispute through mediation or some other form of facilitation, and, if so, time for this should be made in the schedule, in addition to the procedural steps discussed above. Once a date for the hearing is established, the parties, their counsel, the arbitrator, and all essential witnesses must block this time off in their calendars to ensure that things can proceed on schedule. Moreover, the arbitrator should block some time off in advance of the hearing to review the pleadings, any witness statements or affidavits tendered in advance, and any expert reports so that the hearing can proceed smoothly. The arbitrator should also reserve an appropriate amount of time after the hearing to prepare the award, thereby preventing any undue delay.

b) What Is a Realistic Estimate of the Time Required for the Evidentiary Hearing?

One of the most common errors in hearings of all types relates to estimating the amount of time required to complete the matter. Experience demonstrates that counsel are often prone to seriously underestimate the time required. When the case is not completed within the allotted time, it is often difficult for all the participants to find a mutually available block of time in the near future due to other commitments. When this happens, there may be a long lapse before the hearing can resume, making it more difficult for the arbitrator to have a clear recollection of the previous evidence. Ideally, the hearing should run continuously until concluded. To ensure this, the allotted time reserved by everybody should be extended to allow for underestimation and unforeseen events. And the arbitrator should discuss with the parties whether they are prepared to employ a chess clock approach to the hearing or some other form of time restriction or management to facilitate completing the hearing within the allotted time.

c) Where Will the Hearing Take Place?

The parties must decide where the hearing will take place. In international cases, although the seat of the arbitration may be determined by the agreement between the parties, it is generally acceptable for the hearing to occur in any mutually acceptable jurisdiction. In domestic cases, it is usually just a matter of finding a hearing facility convenient for the parties, counsel, the witnesses, and the arbitrator. Arrangements will need to be made to reserve a hearing room and, if necessary, breakout rooms for the parties and arbitrator, ensuring that the selected facility can accommodate the anticipated numbers and that it can provide any necessary audiovisual equipment and teleconferencing capabilities. Typically, the cost of the facilities will be borne equally by the parties pending the final award and disposition of costs. Counsel for one of the parties should be charged with the responsibility for making the necessary arrangements and communicating them to all concerned.

d) Are the Parties Prepared to Sit Past the Usual Courtroom Hours?

Courts typically begin their sittings at 10:00 am and continue until approximately 4:30 or 5:00 pm with a seventy-five- to ninety-minute lunch break and fifteen-minute coffee breaks in the morning and afternoon, resulting in as little as four and a half hours per day in the courtroom, and even less when the lunch and coffee breaks are allowed to slide. As arbitrators' fees and facility costs are typically paid for by the day, it is more time and cost efficient to sit longer hours. Many arbitrators are prepared to sit a full eight-hour day with a sixty-minute lunch break and two short coffee breaks.

e) Will a Verbatim Reporter and Transcript Be Required?

Since most arbitrations are final and binding with no or limited rights of appeal, a transcript of the evidence and submissions is optional. Many counsel, however, prefer to have a transcript available to them on a daily basis for the purposes of preparing their cross-examinations and final submissions. If a transcript is to be ordered, the arbitrator should ensure that he or she receives a copy, at least in electronic form. If a reporter is required, one or the other counsel should be charged with the responsibility for making the necessary arrangements. An alternative to arranging for a verbatim reporter is simply arranging for an audio or video recording of the proceedings and making copies available to all participants for reference.

f) Will There Be Witnesses from Outside of the Jurisdiction?

If there will be witnesses from outside of the jurisdiction where the hearing will take place, consideration should be given, in the interests of efficiency and cost saving, to whether their evidence can be taken using a teleconference or Internet-based service. Where credibility will be in serious issue, it may be desirable to have the witnesses present in the hearing room, but, in many cases, current technology can provide a very satisfactory alternative, so long as the hearing facility has the necessary capabilities.

g) Will There Be a Need for Any Translation Services?

If any of the witnesses will be unable to testify in the language in which the arbitration is being conducted, consideration needs to be given to what arrangements need to be made for the attendance of translators and which party will be responsible for making those arrangements. Similarly, if any of the documents are in a foreign language, they will likely need to be translated in whole or in part for use at the hearing.

h) What Audiovisual or Computer Equipment Will Be Required?

It is becoming increasingly common for documents to be presented electronically during the course of an arbitration hearing. For this to occur, the facility must be able to provide for the simultaneous projection of documents using mutually acceptable software on monitors for the arbitrator, legal counsel, and witnesses. Many sophisticated arbitration facilities in urban centres are well equipped to handle these requirements.

i) What Are the Catering Requirements?

Ideally, catering for coffee breaks and lunches will be brought in or provided by the facility where the hearing is being held. When participants have to leave the premises, the breaks inevitably become longer, and valuable time is lost.

j) Will Final Arguments Be Oral or in Writing?

Although this can change later in the process, there should be a discussion at an early stage on whether the final submissions will be presented to the arbitrator orally or in writing, or as a combination of both. If there are to be written submissions, the parties should put their minds to how much time they will need to complete those submissions after the evidentiary hearing has finished, and time should be reserved in the timetable to allow for that process.

6) What Are the Financial Arrangements with the Arbitrator?

Where the arbitration is being administered by an institution, the financial arrangements with the arbitrator or arbitration tribunal will largely be managed and administered by that institution. Where, however, it is an ad hoc arbitration process, the arbitrator must discuss and establish the terms of the retainer with the parties directly. This will involve a discussion of the arbitrator's daily and hourly rates of compensation, the payment and administration of deposits, billing frequency, and compensation for the arbitrator if the matter is postponed or settled after a hearing date has been established. Since the arbitrator will typically not have an ongoing relationship with the parties to the dispute, substantial deposits to cover the arbitration costs will typically be required.

It is important for the parties to remember that a significant number of arbitrations are settled before their hearing date. Since the hearing date may be scheduled many months into the future, a late cancellation due to settlement may leave the arbitrator with a significant block of empty time in their schedule that was reserved for the matter and for which he or she will need to be compensated. Each arbitrator will have their own approach to this matter, but generally speaking the size of the cancellation fee will be inversely proportional to how much time the arbitrator will have to fill the reserved time with other work. In other words, if the parties settle the matter thirty days before the scheduled hearing date, they can anticipate paying a substantial cancellation fee. One way to avoid this is to establish the timetable for all of the preliminary steps in the process, but postpone the setting of a hearing date until after the parties have unsuccessfully completed any mediation or other settlement efforts.

E. AFTER THE FIRST CASE CONFERENCE

Once the pre-arbitration conference has occurred, all agreements reached with respect to the process must be incorporated into a memorandum to be reviewed and endorsed by the parties' counsel and the arbitrator. While this task can be delegated to counsel, many arbitrators prefer to prepare the first draft of the memorandum and circulate it to counsel for comment and approval. This memorandum can take the form of a submission to arbitration agreement with a separate retainer agreement, in each case to be executed by the parties or counsel on their behalf. In the case of an institutional arbitration or where the parties have already executed an agreement to arbitrate, the memorandum can take the form of a procedural order issued by the tribunal.

The first pre-arbitration case conference should occur well in advance of the hearing. In appropriate cases, a second shorter conference should be held shortly before the commencement of the hearing to review the checklist and confirm that everything will be ready to proceed on the appointed date, or to deal with any issues that have arisen. The second conference can often be held by conference call if it is not convenient to meet in person.

F. CONCLUSION

As noted at the beginning, a successful arbitration requires significant leadership from a knowledgeable arbitrator. Many counsel, especially if they are inexperienced or have not been involved in many arbitrations, will not even realize what options are available. They may not know what a Scott Schedule is, may have never heard the term "hot-tubbing," and may not be familiar with various forms of final offer arbitration. Counsel may be reluctant to propose initiatives that may appear to be unorthodox or unconventional. Left to their own devices, the parties and their counsel will rarely design a process as efficient as can be achieved with the guidance of a capable and experienced arbitrator. Having said that, the arbitrator must always be extremely mindful of the fact that the parties and their counsel know more about the case than they do, and should be very careful to float many ideas but, ultimately, defer to the judgment of counsel after a thorough discussion has taken place. The parties have selected arbitration as a means to retain greater control over the process, and, in that regard, party autonomy should be respected to the greatest extent possible.

APPENDIX 1

Sample Letter

April 5, 2017

Strictly Private and Confidential By Email

Shmotz, Klotz, & Yotz LLP
764 Prince Street
Toronto, Ontario M7B 4C6

stephen@srmadr.com
file no. 12345-1

Att'n: Sacha Yotz

Tingle, Cringle, & Pringle LLP
42 Polar Road
Toronto, Ontario M5M 8Y5

Att'n: Christopher Cringle

Dear Sirs/Mesdames:

Re: Arbitration between ABC Corp and XYZ Ltd — Pre-arbitration Conference

Thank you for asking me to serve as your arbitrator in the above-noted dispute. It is my practice to conduct a thorough pre-arbitration conference with counsel and client representatives well in advance of the hearing date to ensure that this matter is handled in the most timely, effective, and cost-efficient manner possible, consistent with ensuring a fair determination of the issues. In order to design a process and timeline that accomplishes these objectives, I will need your assistance. In most instances, I find that a face-to-face meeting is most likely to accomplish this, especially if counsel come prepared to address the necessary issues. To that end, I have included, below, a checklist of the issues that we are likely to discuss, so that you can be thinking about these items and, if necessary, confer with your client to obtain any necessary instructions. As you will see, many of the items listed below may not be pertinent to this particular case, but, since my knowledge is limited at this stage, I find it is useful to provide a comprehensive list. I also invite counsel to confer amongst yourselves in advance of the meeting with respect to any of the listed issues, if you believe that to do so would facilitate a more effective meeting.

I confirm that we will have a pre-arbitration conference in my offices on **April 21, 2017** commencing at **2:00 pm**. I would ask that you reserve approximately 2 hours for this meeting. Following the meeting, I will be preparing a memorandum summarizing the agreements reached with respect to all logistical, procedural, and evidentiary issues discussed at the meeting. The areas that I hope to cover are summarized under the following headings:

What is the case about?

1) What is the underlying factual matrix from which the dispute arises?
2) Does the case primarily involve questions of fact or issues of law?
3) Does the dispute involve one big question or lots of little issues, as in the case of a multi-issue construction dispute?
4) Will the assessment of credibility be a significant factor in the outcome?
5) Does the case involve only the interpretation of a provision in a contract or other document?
6) Will the case involve expert evidence from one or both parties?
7) Are both liability and damages in dispute?

What needs to occur before the hearing can proceed?

8) What form of pleadings is to be exchanged and when? Not all disputes require the same kind of pleadings to frame the issues.

9) What level of documentary disclosure is required (i.e., full document production with affidavits of documents, just key documents relied upon by each party, or Redfern schedules), and how will it occur?
10) Timetable for documentary production, follow-up requests, and motions, if necessary.
11) When will documents be disclosed to the Tribunal?
12) How much and what kind of oral discovery is required, and when will it occur?

What else can be done to streamline the hearing?

13) Can the parties agree to an agreed statement of facts with respect to some, if not all, of the relevant facts and documents? In many cases, the process of working out an agreed statement of facts has the effect of identifying and narrowing the real issues in the case. Which party will take the initiative? Timetable for completion.
14) Will there be a significant number of documents, and, if so, what technological tools are being considered to manage them efficiently? Document management tools, such as Summation, can be enormously helpful, especially if the parties ensure that their documents are entered using an agreed-upon protocol that will allow them to mesh the two document sets effectively.
15) Are the parties prepared to present a joint document brief, and can it be presented electronically?
16) If there is to be expert testimony, is it an appropriate case for hot-tubbing the experts? If so, discuss hot-tubbing protocol to be followed. Set delivery dates for reports and reply reports.
17) Is it a case where some benefit would be derived from the arbitrator retaining a neutral expert instead of or in addition to the parties, and, if so, what procedure will be followed to instruct the expert and ensure that both parties are guaranteed a fair opportunity to explore and challenge the findings?

18) Is it an appropriate case to consider bifurcating the hearing? Is there some single issue the determination of which will have a significant impact on the case, such that that issue should be determined first, if possible?
19) Are there any preliminary issues of law or jurisdiction? Set procedure and dates for hearing.
20) Will the parties agree that the Chair of the Tribunal will hear and decide motions?
21) Is it an appropriate case for evidence-in-chief to be submitted by way of affidavits, as is provided for under the simplified procedure? Establish timetable for delivery of original and reply affidavits — concurrent or consecutive exchange?
22) If there are many individual issues, should both sides present their evidence on each issue sequentially, or should the claimant present all of its evidence on all issues first, followed by the respondent, in the normal fashion of a traditional trial?
23) If there are many issues, is it a case that would be assisted by the use of a Scott Schedule?
24) Is it a case that would benefit from a more inquisitorial approach to dealing with some or all of the evidence and issues in dispute? Do you want to set a time to meet with the Tribunal to answer preliminary Tribunal questions?
25) Can all or a part of the case be submitted in writing, such as in the case of a dispute surrounding the interpretation of a contract?
26) Is it an appropriate case for a baseball arbitration or night-time baseball arbitration?

What are the ground rules?

27) Are all aspects of the proceedings to remain private and confidential? Are there confidentiality agreements for witnesses? If so, who will have the right to attend the hearing throughout? If there is to be a transcript, what safeguards will be employed to ensure that the record remains confidential?

28) Will witnesses be excluded during the hearing? Will instructing party representatives testify first?
29) What rights of appeal are contemplated?
30) What, if any, procedural or evidentiary rules and statutory provisions are to be waived in the evidentiary hearing?
31) Are costs to be divided equally or awarded in the cause? If in the cause, are they to be awarded in the discretion of the arbitrator using the substantial indemnity model employed by the courts, or does loser pay all? Is the same principle to be applied to the costs of the arbitration tribunal itself, or does the loser pay these in full? It is useful to have clarity around this issue at the outset.
32) Are settlement offers to be considered in awarding costs? If so, do the standard rules apply?
33) Is interest in issue?

If it is an international arbitration, other issues will need to be canvassed.

34) Where is the seat of the arbitration? Where will the hearing take place? The agreement in the contract may provide for this, but the parties may agree that there is a locale that would be more convenient for the parties, the witnesses, counsel, or even the arbitrator.
35) What is the governing law? Again, the agreement may specify this, but sometimes it does not. Even if it does, the parties may agree that it would be preferable to apply the law of a different jurisdiction.
36) If the parties need to seek the intervention of the courts on either procedural or jurisdictional issues, or for the purposes of appeal, which courts will have jurisdiction? This will usually be determined by the seat of the arbitration, if specified, but it should be clarified and confirmed up front.
37) In what language will the hearing be conducted? In this regard, what translation services will be required? If

there is a court reporter, will the record include only the translation, or will a second court reporter be required to transcribe portions of the hearing in the original language spoken?

38) And, again, given the greater distances usually involved, what technologies can be used to facilitate the taking of evidence of witnesses remotely, in appropriate cases?

What about the logistics?

39) Where and when will the hearing take place?
40) What is a *realistic* estimate of the time required by each party for opening, evidence, and argument? There is nothing worse than breaking up the hearing with lengthy gaps between sessions.
41) Are the parties prepared to sit past the usual courtroom hours?
42) If the hearing is likely to take several weeks, do the parties want to use a four-day workweek?
43) Will a court reporter be required? Will a daily transcript be ordered? Will the Tribunal be provided with a copy?
44) Will there be witnesses from outside of the jurisdiction? In the interests of efficiency and cost saving, can their evidence be taken using Skype or another teleconference service?
45) What audiovisual or computer equipment will be required?
46) Is lunch to be brought in to minimize the length of the lunch breaks?
47) Will final arguments be oral or in writing? Establish timetable for delivery of written briefs and reply briefs, if any.
48) Establish an overall arbitration timetable.
49) Establish arbitrator logistics. Deposits, billing timetable, cancellation and postponement fees, and agreements incorporating no liability provisions. Please review the attached sample submission to arbitration and retainer agreement with respect to standard terms.

What about the award?

50) Is there a proposed time limit for delivery of the award?
51) If there are no rights of appeal, in the interests of expediency and cost saving, do the parties prefer abbreviated reasons?
52) Arbitrators will require payment of fees before delivery of the award.

I am confident that with your assistance we can design a process that will best serve the needs of your respective clients. I look forward to meeting with you.

Yours very truly,

Stephen R. Morrison
Arbitrator

part two

The Middle

Ends and beginnings — there are no such things. There are only middles.

— ROBERT FROST

chapter eight

Advocacy Lessons from the Past*

SHEILA R BLOCK

A. ADVOCACY STYLES ON CROSS

In preparing the 2010 Advocates' Society Charles L Dubin Lecture on Advocacy, I had the good fortune to read a fair bit of advice on advocacy from the legendary lawyers of Charles Dubin's day. There were both lessons in the art of advocacy and cautionary tales for practitioners today. Lawyers like Dubin, John Robinette, Arthur Martin, Arthur Maloney, and John Arnup were frequently in court and had more opportunity than many of us enjoy today to learn by doing.

Dubin was known to be good at all the advocacy skills, both trial and appellate. I am certain this is because he insisted on having such a clear analysis of his case theory. He made choices. They were not always the right ones, but more often than not he was able to persuade the court that his view was the only credible route to judgment. Cross-examination was said to be one of his long suits. So identified was he with this skill that people today who never saw him in action will cite his prowess as a cross-examiner.[1]

* A version of this article was published in (Autumn 2011) 30:2 *Advocates' Journal* 12.

1 See John McLeish, "Cross-examining the Opposing Expert" (2009) 28:3 *Advocates' Journal* 7 at 9.

Robinette, who had many cases with Dubin and was a first-hand witness, describes Dubin's cross-examination this way:

> Charles Dubin was one of the best. I listened to Charles cross-examine. He would put some pretty convoluted questions, the witness would answer, and then Charles would say 'if that is so, this must be so'. The witness would be a little dubious about it, but he would have to admit it and then Charles would take it on to the next step. He had the art. His cross-examinations were long, but he had the art of unfolding and developing a story that fitted his case. He was very good at it.[2]

Attention spans for long, convoluted crosses do not grace the benches in Ontario. We may not regard the cross described by Robinette as an example to be emulated in today's environment. But it is perhaps likely that what Robinette — the master simplifier — describes as "convoluted" and "long" is precisely what we should be going for. As he says, Dubin would unfold and develop a story through cross.

George Finlayson describes both Dubin and Martin as going for the jugular in cross:

> Martin and Dubin, by persistently attacking the accuracy of details in a witness's testimony, by challenging the witness with internal inconsistencies in what he or she said, by confronting the witness with documents and conflicting evidence of other witnesses and pressing their verbal attack without letting up, managed to make the witness look foolish and, most valuable of all, unreliable.[3]

But as Finlayson rightly points out, this is very difficult to accomplish. The full-blown frontal attack raises expectations in both the court and the client. In his view, too many counsel in the present day try to emulate the Martin and Dubin approach "by hurling

2 David Stockwood, "In Conversation: John J. Robinette Part Two" (July 1991) 10:2 *Advocates' Society Journal* 3 at 5.

3 George D Finlayson, *John J. Robinette, Peerless Mentor: An Appreciation* (Toronto: The Osgoode Society, 2003) at 89.

themselves at witnesses and attempting to brow-beat them into submission. This seldom works, but" — and here Finlayson lets us know, in his diplomatic way, what he really thinks — "unfortunately a number of modern trial judges have had so little effective trial experience that they seem impressed by a cross-examination that is in reality little more than a shouting match."[4] A bit harsh, but George was never one to mince words.

Bob Armstrong has described one of Dubin's famous cross-examinations in a fraud case, *R v Kasman*. Pat LeSage was prosecuting. The allegation was that Kasman had forged deposit slips, and the Crown was depending on the evidence of a handwriting expert, Constable Head, to make its case. Armstrong obtained the opinion of the then-leading handwriting expert in the United States, one Ordway Hilton, who had in fact trained all the police handwriting experts then operating in the United States and Canada. The day before the trial, Dubin spent an hour with Hilton to get ready for the cross of the Crown's expert. Armstrong and LeSage agreed: Dubin completely destroyed him. As Armstrong says, "you would think Dubin had spent the last five years training as a handwriting expert. He was just that fast and that good."[5] He stripped the evidence apart "without the witness fully appreciating it . . . . [B]efore the witness knew it, the whole basis of his evidence was destroyed."[6]

Having been cross-examined in the office by Dubin, I can attest to the sinking feeling his victims would have had at the end of his examination. Although I never argued before him in court, my partner, Trish Jackson, had that stimulating experience, and it replicated a vigorous cross-examination. Ian Binnie's Dubin lecture gives a keen portrait of Charlie's *modus operandi* on the bench. He would frame a question according to a working hypothesis and then throw at counsel what Binnie calls "a firestorm of questions which really lit up" to test his analysis of the case. Charlie missed being counsel.

---

4 *Ibid.*

5 Osgoode Society Oral Histories, Interview with Robert Armstrong at 48.

6 *Ibid* at 51.

Robinette describes one of the leaders of the bar in his early days — Colonel Greer — as conducting crosses that were very long: "He would keep on plugging away at a witness until he found some discrepancy on a completely minor point. Then in some magical way he would make the whole case turn on the issue which he had ultimately brought out in cross-examination but which really had not very much to do with the central point of the case. He was very successful."[7] The overbearing style of a Colonel Greer would fail to impress today and is definitely a candidate for the cutting room floor. Cross styles that involve convolution and plugging away at minor discrepancies do not play a very effective role in today's trials, or at least we hope that is the case. Modern trial advocacy training (something that was invented long after these men had been stars) tries to teach students of advocacy that cross-examination is the art of the possible. Pick a point you can make, use closed questions, and then, as Professor Irving Younger inscrutably advised, sit down.[8]

One difference, perhaps coming from the English practice, that can be seen in the older cross-examinations is the liberal use of the open question. Maloney cites one of Martin's opening questions to the pathologist, Dr Simpson, in the Steven Truscott case: "Do you anywhere in this book say that the stomach contents are [a] reliable guide to the time of death?"[9] A totally open question, but safe enough if you know that nowhere in the book does the author say this, but, even so, under modern instruction we would probably urge lawyers to frame it as a closed question.

Maloney in the defence of Gary Staples for murder opened with these classic nonleading questions:

Q: Mrs. Conklin, would you ever tell a lie under oath?

---

7 John Robinette, "An After Dinner Address" (1976) 10 *Law Society Gazette* 21 at 23.

8 Irving Younger, "Ten Commandments of Cross-examination" (St Paul, MN: National Institute for Trial Advocacy, 1975) (videorecording).

9 Arthur Maloney, "Expert Evidence" in *Special Lectures of the Law Society of Upper Canada, 1969: Defending a Case* (Toronto: Richard De Boo, 1969) 77 at 79 and 85.

A: No.
Q: Never?
A: No.
Q: Sure of that?
A: Yes.[10]

We all know how this story is going to end.

In the Evelyn Dick murder case, the Crown, operating in the bad old ambush days, called a surprise witness at the second trial, a nineteen-year-old farmhand named Boehler, who claimed to have heard gun shots, saw the body in the car, and identified the two accused. Robinette was defending. Writing about the trial in his wonderful biography of Robinette, Finlayson describes the scene: "The faces on the Crown's side of the counsel table were smug when Boehler finished his testimony, but in reality they had made a serious tactical mistake. Crown counsel were pressing so hard for a conviction that they did not recognize that this witness's evidence was too good to be true."[11] In a dramatic portion of the cross of Boehler, Robinette asked twenty-one open questions in a series of thirty. Yet he was devastating.

The English style is still to ask quite a few open questions on cross. In September 1990, Tom Heintzman and I participated in an advocacy presentation at the Royal Courts of Justice in London, England, at the annual Canadian Bar Association meeting held there. The idea was to have comparative cross-examinations by two British barristers, two American lawyers (John Shephard and Ralph Lancaster), and the two Canadians. The stylistic differences were pronounced. John Shephard did an American-style jury cross with lots of flamboyance and flourish. The English asked a lot of open questions, and when they got the wrong answer, their stock retort was "So you say," being from the school of thought that the question is more important than the answer.

10 Quoted in W Niels Ortved, "The Defence of Gary Staples" in Franklin R Moskoff, ed, *Advocacy in Court: A Tribute to Arthur Maloney, Q.C.* (Aurora, ON: Canada Law Book, 1986) 1 at 3.

11 Finlayson, above note 3 at 79.

Heintzman and I were good Canadians asking tight, leading questions for which we had an impeaching source to reign in any and all deviations from the predicted response. To be sure, the open question in the hands of a skilled cross-examiner can be very powerful. We have seen that with Linda Rothstein's wonderful examination of Dr Charles Smith at the Goudge Inquiry. Using many open questions, she forcefully asked for his explanation of why he had done what he had done, and there really was no explanation. Displaying that point through open questions was powerful. I and others who have taught a lot of advocacy will, no doubt, still teach the importance of leading questions to maintain control. Dubin and his friends certainly knew how to lead, but the style in their day accommodated more frequent use of the open question on cross.

B. A PRODUCT OF THEIR TIMES

Advocates are always a product of their times. Styles have definitely developed from era to era and will continue to develop to reflect societal changes. Robinette describes Maloney's very emotional jury addresses. He says juries loved Maloney for "his attractive Irish attributes of wit and lucidity."[12] Maloney himself, in an address in 1978, declared florid speech and highly emotional appeals to be passé.[13] Joe Sedgwick was known for his oratory, which was laced with Shakespearian quotations. We do not grow the same kind of barristers as Sedgwick and Maloney in the modern day.

Despite the differences in style, these former leaders of the bar gave many speeches dispensing advice to young counsel in which much resonates positively for today's advocate. They all recommended not wasting time, using beautiful, simple language, and getting to the point. As Arnup put it in the 1978 Goodman lecture, eliminate "interminable questions about non-essentials, cross

12 JJ Robinette, "Foreword" in Moskoff, above note 11.

13 Arthur Maloney, "Advocacy" (1978) 12 *Law Society Gazette* 144.

examining the daylights out of a witness who really gave only damaging answer[s]; arguing a case in an unorganized, rambling or repetitive manner." For emphasis, he quoted Estey J's advice about leave applications: "'be clear, be brief, be gone!'"[14]

C. STYLES OF ORATORY

Arnup spent time in his 1978 lecture documenting the fact that for most of the twentieth century, the old ways of "forensic eloquence" no longer found favour with courts. He cited Sir John Simon's 1921 comments to the effect that Lord Brougham's stirring defence of Queen Caroline would "stupefy a modern jury" and "depress a reader." Instead, what courts wanted, according to Simon, was "forcible and orderly statement far more than rhetorical elaboration which induces belief and effects persuasion."[15] Arnup also quoted Birkett extolling "direct forceful, lucid speech, in all its simplicity."[16] Of course, Arnup was famous for being the antithesis of emotional — he was, as Robinette describes him, "one of the great counsel . . . logical, well-organized, and very persuasive."[17] Arnup himself described his style and Robinette's as one that fit in well with the English style: "analytical, polished, low key," and not oratorical.[18]

Language and communication styles change with the times. The dramatic oratory and "forensic eloquence" of past times referenced by Arnup no longer communicates effectively. Language and speech patterns (not to mention attention spans) continue to be modified as our methods of communication change. The new technologies we use for communicating with and relating to one another electronically — email, Facebook, texting, tweeting, and online shopping and dating — have an effect on language

14 John Arnup, "Advocacy" (1979) 13 *Law Society Gazette* 27 at 39 and 42.

15 Quoted in *ibid* at 32.

16 *Ibid.*

17 Stockwood, above note 2 at 7.

18 Osgoode Society Oral Histories, Interview with John Arnup at 195.

and grammar.[19] What is effective communication will continue to evolve as it always has. We may not sound exactly like Dubin and Robinette or Maloney and Sedgwick, but the fundamentals of persuasion still abide.

D. BEAUTIFUL, SIMPLE LANGUAGE

I question whether we focus enough today on the fundamentals of persuasion. So much of our time as counsel is spent sifting through increasingly complex and voluminous data and documentation that less time is spent on crafting beautiful, simple language. Indeed, we are relieved when we have mastered the massive record and made the tough choices to focus the case and set it out in as straightforward a fashion as we can. Directness and succinctness are the gold standards we strive for today (with varying degrees of success). But beautiful language is something we probably do not spend enough time on.

Language that is direct, simple, and succinct — attributes of the advocacy of Dubin and his friends — is challenge enough. Some of the difficulty arises from overburdened cases with too much data to sift through and the increasing reluctance to make the hard choices. The in-house counsel's job can be on the line in a big case. This tends to favour conservative choices and a reluctance to drop points, witnesses, or arguments. Dubin and Robinette would have told the client how it was to be done — if the client was lucky enough to be told — or they would have just worked up the case as they saw fit, thinking that was their job.

Law school has been cited as the place where we learn how to talk like lawyers and lose our ability to communicate effectively in language that is simple and direct. Consider the following stark contrast. Arnup had the good fortune of being taught real property by Robinette. He declared Robinette "the best lecturer that I

19 See Stanford Professor Seth Lerer's excellent lectures *The History of the English Language* (Chantilly, VA: Teaching Company, 2008) (videorecording & book), where he predicts inevitable changes in syntax and grammar as a result of our changed forms of communication.

ever had, either in law school or at university." Clarity and understandability was the hallmark of his teaching and of his advocacy. There was nothing "ambiguous about any part of his lectures."[20] Fast-forward to January 2010, when Professor James McElhaney of Case Western Reserve University School of Law describes, with his usual good humour, how law teachers ruin students by teaching them to "sound like lawyers."[21]

McElhaney gives some examples of the "confusing verbal clutter" that lawyers who try to "sound like a lawyer" display. Here is one: "'Would you indicate please, for the benefit of the judge and jury, what you did in response to the petitioner's request that you ameliorate the conditions created by your company's failure to make timely delivery of the automatic current interrupters?'"[22] As McElhaney points out, the culprit here is not legal terminology or overcomplicated words. The question is just a tangle. It needs to be broken down and set out clearly. The trouble is, according to McElhaney, that although academics teach their students to think critically and spot all the legal issues in a case, they are not good at expressing difficult ideas simply and understandably, a skill that Dubin and Robinette were justifiably famous for. Law students leave class and practise talking to one another like lawyers — forgetting that explaining the case to clients, jurors, and a judge who knows nothing about it requires a different type of communication. As McGill Faculty of Law Professor Mark Antaki tells his students, "law is a profession of words but it's more fun to say law is a profession of magic words." We can get carried away at times with the magic words and forget the beautiful, simple language that not only communicates but persuades.

Many will remember Morley Torgov's delightful talks and writings. He used humour to make serious points, and in his piece "Anyone Can Be a Lawyer," he pokes fun at our required writing

---

20 Quoted in Finlayson, above note 3 at 34–35.

21 Jim McElhaney, "The Power of Plain Talk" (2010) 96:1 *ABA Journal* at 22.

22 *Ibid.*

style, which he describes as being "as breezy as *Magna Carta*."[23] He gives some examples. Here is one:

> Your opponent has just submitted an unsatisfactory offer to settle on behalf of his client. You could respond thus:
>
> > My client says no to your letter of the 12th.
>
> But when you itemize your services in your bill after the case is settled, one-liners like that will earn you peanuts. Instead, respond thus:
>
> > Yours of the 12th ultimo to hand and acknowledged, and in response thereto my client, the Plaintiff, after due deliberation and in light of circumstances heretofore transpiring, is disposed to reject absolutely and totally the proposal for settlement put forth by your client, the Defendant.[24]

Page limits and time limits have helped counter the tendencies promoted by our law school training and lawyerly pretensions, to make us more succinct. Dubin, Robinette, and Arnup were always masters of that.

According to Robinette, Maloney was an exponent of "controlled and effective emotionalism."[25] Niels Ortved describes Maloney as a student of Shakespeare, GK Chesterton, and other literary giants, with a love of the English language.[26] This attribute may seem a bit old-fashioned to advocates today, but the ability to write a beautiful, powerful, and informative opening paragraph, to just about anything, can stimulate interest and capture attention.

I recently came across this opening paragraph in a biography of Shakespeare by Stephen Greenblatt, *Will in the World*:

---

23 Morley Torgov, "Anyone Can Be a Lawyer" (1977) 25:4 *Chitty's Law Journal* 120 at 120.

24 *Ibid* at 123.

25 Robinette, above note 8.

26 Ortved, above note 11.

> A young man from a small provincial town — a man without independent wealth, without powerful family connections, and without a university education — moves to London in the later 1580s and, in a remarkably short time, becomes the greatest playwright not of his age alone but of all time. His works appeal to the learned and the unlettered, to urban sophisticates and provincial first-time theatergoers. He makes his audiences laugh and cry; he turns politics into poetry; he recklessly mingles vulgar clowning and philosophical subtlety. He grasps with equal penetration the intimate lives of kings and of beggars; he seems at one moment to have studied law, at another theology, at another ancient history, while at the same time he effortlessly mimes the accents of country bumpkins and takes delight in old wives' tales. How is an achievement of this magnitude to be explained? How did Shakespeare become Shakespeare?

In five sentences, Greenblatt sets out his theme, frames the issue, provides essential biographical facts, and whets your interest in the multifaceted dimensions of the man he will describe in detail in the next several hundred pages. Maloney may have talked this way, but we, typically, do not. Maybe we should (within limits).

Another example from a recent reported decision by Quinn J makes the point that you can pack a lot into an opening. His Honour gives Lord Denning a run for his money with this memorable introduction in *Miller v Carley*:

> After a busy day conducting illegal drug transactions, the plaintiff, the defendant and a mutual friend stopped at a corner store where the defendant purchased some "scratch" lottery tickets. One of the tickets proved to be a $5-million winner.
>
> The parties dispute ownership of the winning ticket. If the ticket were a child and the parties vying for custody, I would find them both unfit and bring in Family and Children's Services.
>
> The case is awash in untruths and curiosities. It is a study in good fortune squandered and generosity abused.[27]

27 *Miller v Carley* (2009), 98 OR (3d) 432 at paras 1–3 (SCJ).

E. ADVICE FROM ORWELL

What we should not do is succumb to the pretentious, inflated style identified by George Orwell in his breathtaking 1946 essay "Politics and the English Language."[28] I am fairly certain none of our giants of the previous generation advocated that style. It is characterized, according to Orwell, by dying metaphors, hackneyed phrases, pretentious diction, and meaningless words. This misuse of English, by using vague phrases instead of concrete illustrations, conceals meaning and signals insincerity.

To illustrate his point, Orwell translates a passage of good English into modern English of the worst sort. He chooses a verse from Ecclesiastes: "I returned and saw under the sun, that the race is not to the swift, nor the battle to the strong, neither yet bread to the wise, nor yet riches to men of understanding, nor yet favour to men of skill; but time and change happeneth to them all." The modern English version goes like this: "Objective considerations of contemporary phenomena compel the conclusion that success or failure in competitive activities exhibits no tendency to be commensurate with innate capacity, but that a considerable element of the unpredictable must invariably be taken into account." Orwell notes that the concrete illustrations in the original — "race, battle, bread" — dissolve into vague phrases in the modern version — "success or failure in competitive activities."[29] This, he writes, is part of a tendency in modern prose away from concreteness. Vivid images are replaced by vague phrases, the "gumming together" of "long strips of words," ready-made phrases, and stale metaphors. It may save you mental effort, but, he warns, it leaves your meaning vague for your reader and yourself. Clarity was key for Dubin, Robinette, and friends, and that requires unambiguous expression.

---

28 George Orwell, "Politics and the English Language" in *The Orwell Reader: Fiction, Essays, and Reportage by George Orwell* (New York: Harcourt, Brace & Co, 1956), first published in (1946) 13:76 *Horizon* 252.

29 *Ibid* at 5.

Orwell gives a powerful illustration of the dangers of vagueness in the context of political speech, which he says consists largely of "question-begging and sheer cloudy vagueness," a style to be steadfastly avoided by the advocate. He was of the view that vagueness and euphemism could be used to further political deceit. Here is Orwell's famous quotation from 1946:

> Defenceless villages are bombarded from the air, the inhabitants driven out into the countryside, the cattle machine-gunned, the huts set on fire with incendiary bullets: this is called *pacification* .... Such phraseology is needed if one wants to name things without calling up mental pictures of them. Consider ... some comfortable English professor defending Russian totalitarianism. He cannot say outright, 'I believe in killing off your opponents when you can get good results by doing so.' Probably, therefore, he will say something like this:
>
> > 'While freely conceding that the Soviet regime exhibits certain features which the humanitarian may be inclined to deplore, we must, I think, agree that a certain curtailment of the right to political opposition is an unavoidable concomitant of transitional periods, and that the rigors which the Russian people have been called upon to undergo have been amply justified in the sphere of concrete achievement.'

The great enemy of clear speech, Orwell says, is insincerity. I never saw Dubin exhibit insincerity or unclear expression. In discussing the theory of the case, he would argue his points passionately and complain if you did not accept them, because he would not have put them forward if he did not believe them. He was clear and direct, and he could get to the point because he believed it was the right argument to make on behalf of the client.

Robinette was famous for clarity and succinctness. A dramatic example can be found in the Hamilton Dredging Trial (a bid-rigging case involving harbour-dredging contracts). Lorne Morphy and Charles Scott asked him to take on the appeal from this year-long combines trial. It was a massive case. The factum in the Court of Appeal was 259 pages, a product of collaboration by Morphy, Scott, and Robinette. There were many days of hearing, a new trial was ordered. The Crown applied for leave to appeal to the Supreme Court of Canada, and this time Robinette did the drafting. He submitted a ten-page factum and, by Scott's account, was very forceful at the leave hearing.[30] He told the Court that the Crown's submissions had been "an utter *red herring*" and that the Crown's application for leave was "so devoid of merit that it raised no serious point of law." As Scott said, coming from Robinette, this "carried enormous strength and enormous weight, and the Supreme Court of Canada dismissed the application for leave entirely. So it was a *tour de force*."[31]

F. THE CHALLENGE GOING FORWARD

There is much to be learned from past generations, both attributes to emulate and adapt and attributes to modify or avoid. As complicated, overburdened, and dense as cases have become, our challenge remains — to pick our points and articulate them clearly in beautiful, simple language that persuades.

30 *Canadian Industrial Gas & Oil Ltd v Government of Saskatchewan*, [1978] 2 SCR 545. Another example of Robinette's succinctness pointed out to me by Christine Kates is his factum in the above case, dealing with the constitutionality of taxing at the wellhead in Saskatchewan. His factum was 38 pages. The Court of Appeal judgment was 150 pages, and the Supreme Court's final judgment was 100 pages.

31 Quoted in Finlayson, above note 3 at 342.

chapter nine

Advocacy in Commercial Arbitration

JOHN A M JUDGE

A. INTRODUCTION: LETTING GO OF THE LITIGATION MINDSET

Advocacy is the ability to persuade. Although it is frequently referred to as an art, not a science, the skills of a good advocate can be and are learned. In the past, young lawyers learned by working closely with senior members of the bar. Today, there are a wide variety of advocacy programs available to young lawyers that teach fundamental advocacy skills intended to be honed at a trial in court. However, the dispute landscape has changed significantly in recent years. With the growth of arbitration, particularly in commercial disputes, Canadian litigators bring their litigation strategies, skills, and practices into the arbitral forum, thinking that it is just like a court but private. That is a mistake. While some litigation skills can be translated into the arbitration environment, many cannot. However, the necessary skills for arbitration can be learned.

Good arbitral advocacy requires a sound understanding of arbitral practices and procedures. One of Canada's leading counsel in his day, the late John Sopinka J always said that a good advocate can argue any case in any forum provided that she masters three basics for the case: (1) the procedural rules and practices of the particular forum, (2) the applicable rules of evidence to shape the story, and (3) the narrow issue of substantive law on which the case will turn. Many Canadian litigation counsel assume incorrectly that what works in court will always work in an arbitral forum. They fail to appreciate both fundamental and nuanced differences in arbitration. A good advocate must abandon the litigation mindset and learn the primary arbitral practices to successfully adapt important advocacy skills to the arbitral forum. The intention of this chapter is to assist in that objective and highlight the opportunities for good advocacy in a commercial arbitration, whether domestic or international.

B. THE NATURE OF ARBITRATION

Arbitration is a consensual process intended to provide expeditious, efficient, and cost-effective resolutions of disputes. Parties must agree to arbitrate. This stands in stark contrast to litigation in the courts, which are an integral part of the state-run judicial system. The courts have statutory and inherent jurisdiction. They exercise coercive powers over the parties, the witnesses, and, indeed, counsel appearing before them. Furthermore, the procedural rules of a court are intended to apply to all nature of disputes, from the simplest to the most complex. They are designed to achieve a certain ideal of justice. Moreover, experience has shown that the court rules can be readily used to delay the litigation process, frustrating the timely hearing of a dispute on the merits and rendering the court process oppressively expensive for the parties, quite apart from the delay and costs inherent in the appeal process. Cases settle under the sheer weight of costs in the face of delay. By contrast, arbitration depends on the agreement of the parties that have opted out of this court process in favour of a more efficient and private process. The Supreme Court of Canada has repeatedly recognized that arbitration stands outside of the state's judicial system.

The principle of party autonomy is the foundation of arbitration. In simple terms, this means that the parties have by their agreement to arbitrate taken control of their dispute and submitted it for resolution by a nongovernmental, private decision maker selected by or for the parties, using an impartial adjudicatory process that affords each party an opportunity to present its case before a binding decision is made. As will be discussed below, flexibility of procedure is one of the hallmarks of arbitration. The parties, by committing to arbitrate, can shape the adjudicatory process and procedures for the particular dispute. Therefore, counsel should remain cognizant that when their clients have chosen arbitration, they have rejected the court process and chosen a different, preferred dispute process that affords significant opportunities for and flexibility in the conduct of that dispute process. Both the fact of the agreement to arbitrate and the content of that agreement have a significant impact on the advocacy appropriate for the particular dispute. Therefore, the wholesale adoption of the court rules of civil procedure for use in an arbitration, which is frequently suggested by litigation counsel, not only runs counter to the agreement of the parties but is also an abdication of responsibility and a failure to take advantage of the flexibility offered by arbitration to develop a more expeditious and efficient process within which to advance the clients' case and determine their dispute.

C. THE ARBITRATION CLAUSE

The arbitration clause is often overlooked as being the first opportunity for good arbitral advocacy to shape the process and the presentation of a case. The agreement of the parties to arbitrate is normally set out in an arbitration clause contained in a more comprehensive commercial or transactional agreement. During the negotiation of such an agreement, the parties and their commercial lawyers usually focus on getting the deal done rather than on the specific dispute resolution procedure. Litigation or dispute counsel rarely have any significant input into the arbitration agreement, but they should. Parties are anticipating disputes merely by agreeing to arbitration. Putting careful thought into the arbitration clause can avoid unnecessary delay and costs. Carelessness in drafting the arbitration clause will simply spawn the worst experiences of both arbitration and litigation.

Apart from having a pre-existing arbitration clause in an agreement, parties may also decide to arbitrate after a dispute has arisen by negotiating a formal submission to arbitration agreement, rather than proceeding with court litigation. Reasons for making a submission to arbitration can vary greatly. Often, there is a desire for confidentiality not available in the court process. More frequently of late, counsel have been known to agree to submit to arbitration to avoid a particular trial judge assigned to a case and to ensure that the decision maker has the required expertise. Whether the arbitration agreement is in a specific contractual clause or in a bespoke submission to arbitration, input by counsel is the first opportunity to engage in arbitral advocacy that can significantly influence the arbitration process and hearing.

Much can be written about the arbitration clause.[1] The discussion here will focus on key issues that may affect case presentation, specifically, the scope of arbitrability, number and qualifications of arbitrators, and, finally, applicable procedural rules including the issue of institutional versus ad hoc arbitration.

The scope of arbitrability refers to the types of claims that can be arbitrated. It may be broad or narrow depending on the language used. The Supreme Court of Canada has made it clear that almost any type of claim may, by agreement, be arbitrated, whether based in contract, tort, equity, or statute. Therefore, claims as diverse as copyright infringement, shareholder oppression, and nonpayment of lawyer fees can be arbitrated. However, if more restrictive language is used to limit claims solely to contractual claims arising under the agreement, then a party may be precluded from raising other noncontractual claims. This can complicate the dispute by triggering additional jurisdictional disputes or by allowing some claims to go forward in arbitration while forcing other claims into court proceedings. The better approach is to use

1 See, for example, Chapter 2.

simple, broad language that allows any dispute arising under or relating to the agreement or legal relationship to be arbitrated. This broader language will provide counsel with the greatest flexibility to assert the most appropriate causes of action arising on the facts of the particular case and to avoid having only some of the claims proceed in arbitration.

With respect to arbitrators, the first issue for decision is whether to have one or three arbitrators. There are pros and cons for each alternative; it is not simply a function of cost, with a single arbitrator obviously being less expensive. Each alternative has its own appropriate applications. Smaller dollar-value and less complex cases are well-suited for a single arbitrator. For larger and more complex cases, a tribunal of three arbitrators is usually preferred by corporate users so that each party can appoint a nominee, thereby providing a greater sense of engagement in and ownership of the process. In more complex arbitration agreements, both alternatives may be accommodated through a monetary cut-off: Claims below a certain dollar value will go before a sole arbitrator while claims above that value will be heard by a tribunal of three. Domestically in Canada, a sole arbitrator is used very frequently. In international arbitration, a panel of three is more common, with each party nominating one and the chair being appointed by the party nominees, the parties themselves, or an institution.

The use of a sole arbitrator raises the risk of a rogue decision where the sole arbitrator becomes fixated on one aspect of the case. Therefore, arbitrator selection can become even more important with a single arbitrator. By contrast, a tribunal of three serves as its own court of appeal to more carefully review and test both factual and legal conclusions during the course of deliberations and in writing an award to ensure that all findings are well-founded. The tribunal of three also allows for a combination of different types of expertise, whether legal, commercial, technical, linguistic, or cultural. Where the issues are complex and where significant sums of money are at stake, a tribunal of three inspires in the parties greater confidence that their positions will be understood and fairly considered.

The question of arbitrator qualifications for a case is critical at the time of appointment and is discussed below. However, qualification prerequisites, such as lengthy work experience in a particular industry or field, are often set out in the arbitration clause itself. Usually, these prerequisites are counterproductive once a dispute arises since they unnecessarily limit the flexibility available to match an appropriate arbitrator with the needs of the specific case. While a particular qualification such as specific industry experience can be helpful, it may not be possible to find good qualifying candidates who also have the necessary arbitration experience in the conduct of complex cases and in deciding difficult factual and legal issues for incorporation into an enforceable award. Therefore, care must be taken regarding such qualifications, and the better practice is to avoid them altogether in the clause itself. This will ensure that the advocate has a free hand in selecting the most appropriate arbitrator when the specific dispute is known.

The question of whether to proceed with an institutional or ad hoc arbitration is often debated, but it is a question that each party and counsel must answer when entering into an arbitration agreement. This decision can directly influence the arbitral procedures. For domestic arbitration in Canada, ad hoc arbitration has remained popular, in part because there has been no strong, widely accepted Canadian arbitral institution, though some institutions, such as the ADR Institute of Canada, are making headway with a good set of national arbitral rules. Internationally, institutional arbitration has long been preferred by corporate users and in-house counsel, as confirmed in the 2006 Queen Mary University of London *International Arbitration* survey and subsequent surveys.[2] That trend has remained strong. Indeed, the major international institutions are now making deliberate efforts to promote insti-

2 Queen Mary University of London, Centre for Commercial Law Studies, School of International Arbitration & PricewaterhouseCoopers LLP, *International Arbitration: Corporate Attitudes and Practices 2006* (London: Queen Mary University of London, 2006), online: www.arbitration.qmul.ac.uk/docs/123295.pdf.

tutional arbitration in Canada, even for purely domestic arbitrations, in light of the absence of a strong, nationally recognized Canadian institution. For example, the International Centre for Dispute Resolution (ICDR), the international arm of the American Arbitration Association, has now promulgated a set of Canadian arbitral rules for use in domestic Canadian arbitration.

One of the main advantages of institutional arbitration over ad hoc arbitration is the ability to constitute the tribunal at the outset without delay. If the parties do not select their arbitrator or arbitrators expeditiously, an institution will step in and appoint the arbitrators, thereby avoiding having to go to court, which is the default appointment process in ad hoc arbitration. In ad hoc arbitration, significant delays and costs in the appointment process will arise if recourse must be had to the courts. Furthermore, the courts have limited experience and ability in selecting good, experienced arbitrators. The use of an appointing authority in conjunction with ad hoc arbitration can avoid this delay at the start of an arbitration. However, the use of appointing authorities has not yet achieved common acceptance in Canada. Most arbitral institutions will for a fee act as an appointing authority and appoint arbitrators on a timely basis absent agreement. If ad hoc arbitration is chosen by the parties, counsel are well-advised to name an appointing authority to avoid delay and attendant costs.

Institutional arbitration also offers other procedural advantages over ad hoc arbitration in large part because institutional rules have been frequently modified and revised over the past twenty years to implement and refine more effective arbitral procedures expected by corporate users. By contrast, ad hoc arbitration in Ontario is supported by the domestic *Arbitration Act, 1991*[3] and by the *International Commercial Arbitration Act, 2017*.[4] The former has not been revised in over twenty years, while the latter has recently been updated to reflect the 2006 amendments to the Model Law and also to expressly implement the *New York Convention*.

3 SO 1991, c 17.

4 SO 2017, c 2, Schedule 5.

The use of separate arbitration statutes for domestic and international personal arbitration is common to all provinces save Quebec. The newer, more modern procedures found in institutional rules include expedited appointment and arbitration procedures, emergency arbitrator procedures, and express obligations on arbitrators and counsel to proceed expeditiously and in good faith. Institutionally administered arbitrations also infuse the arbitral process and the final award with enhanced credibility due to the institutional oversight that is provided — to a greater degree (e.g., the International Chamber of Commerce (ICC)) or a lesser degree (e.g., the ICDR and London Court of International Arbitration (LCIA)). This, in turn, eases and facilitates the enforcement of the award in other jurisdictions. That said, sophisticated and experienced corporate users have also opted to use ad hoc arbitration, in part to avoid administrative costs. The general corporate counsel of these sophisticated corporate users, usually large multinational corporations, are generally knowledgeable about arbitration practices. They will, in turn, retain experienced arbitration counsel who are well versed in arbitral procedures and who are able to efficiently and effectively navigate the ad hoc arbitral process. However, experience has shown that in Canada there are few such corporate counsel experienced in arbitration and also few experienced arbitration counsel. Institutional rules for arbitration can provide Canadian practitioners with carefully crafted, well-thought-out rules prepared by experienced arbitration practitioners and grounded in current practices to meet the needs of corporate users. Institutional oversight of the formation of the tribunal through to the conduct of the arbitration can ensure a more expeditious procedure and make institutional arbitration more attractive to the user.

D. PREPARING TO START THE ARBITRATION

In preparing to assert a claim in arbitration, counsel should be ready for a faster, more efficient, and more flexible process than is normally available in court. It is generally accepted that there is an implied obligation on the parties, counsel, and the tribunal to proceed expeditiously in the arbitration. International institutional rules have now been amended to include an express obligation to proceed expeditiously without delay. Counsel should not expect the lengthy delays more common in the court process, where it can take five years or more to get to a hearing on the merits. The speed and efficiency in arbitration will have a direct impact on the advocacy brought to bear on the case. Early preparation is critical.

The preparation should start with a careful review of the arbitration clause in the commercial contract. Ignoring the arbitration clause and instead commencing a court action will simply invite a stay motion that will inevitably be successful, causing unnecessary delay and costs. A careful review of the arbitration clause is not only warranted but necessary for the proper conduct of the arbitration. As noted above, the arbitration clause will identify the applicable procedural rules, whether ad hoc or institutional, to determine where and how to start. The clause will define the scope of arbitrability. Limitations on the scope of arbitral claims will directly affect the formulation of the causes of action to be asserted. It is not uncommon for parties to expressly exclude claims for costs or interest.

The arbitration clause may also establish express jurisdictional or procedural prerequisites to the commencement of the arbitration. Multistep negotiation and mediation clauses can be properly drafted to be enforceable agreements, not just unenforceable agreements to agree. As a result, they may be treated as jurisdictional prerequisites to the commencement of the arbitration that must be respected. Failure to do so may encourage a respondent to seek a stay or adjournment of the arbitration pending the completion of such steps. Motions like these can cause delay and additional costs, or worse. On one such motion, a respondent put before the arbitrators embarrassing settlement discussion correspondence from the claimant to support the motion that the contracted negotiation process was not exhausted, thereby rendering arbitration premature. This also cast the entire claim in a questionable light from the outset. Therefore, counsel should ensure that appropriate evidence is available to prove that any mandated negotiation process has been duly completed.

In addition to setting out the applicable arbitral rules, whether ad hoc or institutional, the arbitration agreement may set out other mandatory procedures to which the parties have agreed. It is not uncommon to find extremely stringent time limits for the conduct of the arbitration and the delivery of the award. For example, in one recent case the agreement stipulated that "an award shall be rendered 30 days after the appointment of the arbitrator." In that case, the parties could not agree on an extension of time, so a hearing had to be scheduled in the third week to allow time to complete an award on time and avoid a loss of jurisdiction. Needless to say, the procedure was significantly streamlined. The style of advocacy was necessarily adjusted, and claims were narrowly focused. Due to the stringent time limits, counsel had to get to the main points of their positions quickly. In that case, the truncated process worked. The parties got exactly what they bargained for. However, counsel should be careful about what their clients wish for and agree to. They may not get the slower-paced court litigation type of hearing process to which they are accustomed. It is imperative for counsel to recognize and respect the jurisdictional time limits mandated by the arbitration clause and adjust accordingly, particularly as agreement on extensions is usually difficult to secure once the dispute has crystallized.

The identification of the proper parties to the arbitration is usually straightforward as they are usually limited to the parties to the arbitration agreement, typically those that signed the main contract containing the arbitration clause. Therefore, the named claimants and respondents will be limited to the contract signatories. The formulation of the cause of action is likewise usually limited to the breach of the contract containing the arbitration clause. Various tort claims such as misrepresentation, fraud, inducing breach of contract, interference with contractual relations, and conspiracy to injure may be asserted but only if the scope of the arbitration clause is sufficiently broad to permit such claims.

Litigation counsel who are not experienced in arbitral procedures are often apt to include multiple causes of action and in doing so name additional parties that are not contract signatories. Such tactics are common in court litigation and are intended to increase risk to more parties and broaden the scope of oral discovery to secure the proof of such creative allegations when evidence to support such claims is unknown and speculative. This fishing expedition is much easier to justify in court litigation. In arbitration, such tactics are fraught with difficulty. The expanded tortious causes of action may well fall outside the scope of arbitrability. But more importantly, the basis for adding nonsignatories as parties is extremely limited. While a nonsignatory such as an assignee may sometimes be allowed to join in the claim as a claimant, it is highly unlikely that a nonsignatory can be rendered liable as a respondent. The initial attempt to add nonsignatories, usually with little likelihood of success, will inevitably lead to a jurisdictional challenge that can be time-consuming and costly. Therefore, good advocacy in arbitration will eschew the common litigation tactic of casting an overbroad net of multiple causes of action in contract and tort against a broad set of targeted actors, many of whom have not signed a contract with an arbitration clause. If the circumstances of the particular case do dictate that a nonsignatory be added at the outset, then the legal and evidentiary grounds for doing so should be carefully and completely developed at the outset in the notice of arbitration. Such grounds may include lifting the corporate veil or alter ego, incorporation of the arbitration clause by reference, assignment, agency, and equitable estoppel. Sufficient grounds for adding a nonsignatory to the arbitration may be made out, for example, where a nonsignatory parent corporation has stripped assets from a subsidiary entity and abused its separate corporate legal existence to frustrate an effective contractual remedy for the claimant's claim.

It is also important to recognize that the nature of the litigation process itself has encouraged the expansive use of tort claims in business disputes, claims in which the mental element of the opposing party is a key element to be proven. The broad discovery process for both oral and documentary discovery in court litigation encourages the assertion of these claims in tort where the claimant has no supporting evidence but simply hopes to obtain that evidence in the discovery process. This tendency of counsel to complicate straightforward contract claims by injecting various tort claims leads to more time-consuming and costly discovery procedures. Counsel rely on protracted examinations for discovery to probe for the evidence to prove the necessary mental element for these additional causes of action. However, in arbitration that approach should be avoided or adopted only with great care and preparation. It is generally recommended that the claimant focus on the main contract claim and not be distracted by collateral or supplementary claims that do not materially add to the case, other than to significantly add to the costs and the time to a hearing. Furthermore, a party will likely be precluded in arbitration from embarking upon a broad-ranging discovery process that indicates a fishing expedition. A basic contract claim requiring proof of the contract term and evidence of the breach and damage does not depend on proof of an ephemeral mental element. A focused contract claim can get the client's case to a hearing on the merits much faster and more efficiently.

Most arbitrations progress much more expeditiously than court litigation. So it is imperative for counsel to recognize the need for early marshalling of the evidence in anticipation of that accelerated progress. When marshalling the evidence, counsel should also be asking themselves what type of hearing will best suit the issues in the case and what is the best way to get the case to that hearing. Written witness statements will usually be delivered as the evidence-in-chief for each party. Therefore, the early collection of detailed witness statements is critical. These are further discussed below. Early document preservation, collection, and review is as necessary in arbitration as in litigation. In addition, the early identification of relevant fields of experts' expertise and retention of the necessary experts is critical as they can play a crucial role in the ongoing preparation of the case. The claimant will have a natural advantage in this regard that simply underscores the importance for the respondent to also advance its preparation as fast as it can once the commencement of the arbitration becomes known.

Before the commencement of any arbitration, counsel must also consider whether there is any need for some interim measures of protection, such as early interim injunctive relief. If so, counsel must consider how that relief will be obtained since a tribunal has not yet been constituted. If the arbitration is ad hoc, then the supervisory court at the seat will be the main alternative to consider. Both the domestic *Arbitration Act, 1991*[5] and the *International Commercial Arbitration Act, 2017*[6] in Ontario contemplate that the court can provide interim relief in aid of the arbitration. Under the latter Act, an Ontario court may also grant interim relief in aid of a foreign arbitration. Courts have been most adept at and experienced in providing such interim relief. By contrast, if the arbitration is being administered by one of the main international institutions, like the ICDR, ICC, or LCIA, procedures will be available under its rules for fast and effective relief within the arbitration. The ICDR pioneered the use of the emergency arbitrator to hear urgent applications at the outset of an arbitration. The ICC has also now implemented an emergency arbitrator procedure. The LCIA had previously instituted a process for the expedited formation of the arbitral tribunal to deal with urgent matters, but more recently it has also implemented an emergency arbitrator procedure in its rules to give parties the ability to obtain urgent relief before the formation of the tribunal. Experience has shown that these emergency arbitrator procedures can be very effective in securing relief to preserve the status quo. In one arbitration in which this author was appointed as an emergency arbitrator under the ICDR rules, a hearing was held within five hours of the appointment even though counsel were located in separate continents. In that case, immediate interim relief was awarded. The emergency arbitrator procedure has worked very

5 Above note 3.

6 Above note 4.

effectively, which is the reason why all major institutions have now adopted it. It should be noted that Ontario has, in the *International Commercial Arbitration Act, 2017*, enacted broader express powers for an arbitral tribunal to grant preliminary interim orders that were included in the revised 2006 *UNCITRAL Model Law*.[7] While these Ontario amendments are certainly welcome, the availability of an emergency arbitrator procedure before the formation of the tribunal remains a distinguishing feature of many institutional sets of rules.

One final issue can be flagged for counsel: Review the applicable rules to ensure the proper commencement of the arbitration. In the ad hoc context, whether under the *Arbitration Act, 1991* or the *International Commercial Arbitration Act, 2017*, service of a notice of arbitration on the respondent is sufficient to validly commence the arbitration. The date of service on the respondent is therefore the critical date for the operation of limitation periods in an ad hoc arbitration. Canadian counsel are generally more familiar with this ad hoc procedure. However, the commencement process is different for arbitration under institutional rules. In institutional arbitration, proper commencement depends on the delivery of a notice of arbitration to the institution.[8] In *Bell Canada v The Plan Group*, the claimant served the notice of arbitration on the respondent but failed to file it with the domestic arbitration institution, the ADR Institute of Canada, in accordance with its rules, though that institution provided minimal, if any, administration.[9] The Ontario Court of Appeal confirmed that the

7 21 June 1985, UN Doc A/40/17, annex 1, with amendments adopted 7 July 2006, UN Doc A/61/17, annex 1, online: www.uncitral.org/pdf/english/texts/arbitration/ml-arb/07-86998_Ebook.pdf.

8 See, for example, ICDR *International Arbitration Rules* (amended and effective 1 June 2014) art 2, online: www.icdr.org/icdr/ShowProperty?nodeId=/UCM/ADRSTAGE2020868&revision=latestreleased; LCIA *Arbitration Rules* (effective 1 October 2014) art 1.1, online: www.lcia.org/Dispute_Resolution_Services/lcia-arbitration-rules-2014.aspx; ICC *Rules of Arbitration* (current as of 1 March 2017) art 4, online: https://iccwbo.org/dispute-resolution-services/arbitration/rules-of-arbitration.

9 (2009), 96 OR (3d) 81 (CA) [*Bell Canada*].

arbitration had not properly been commenced according to the applicable rules since the institution itself had not been served. As a result, a contractual limitation had expired, and the claim could not be advanced. Therefore, a simple warning to counsel: Read the applicable arbitral rules to make sure that the arbitration is commenced strictly in accordance with those rules to avoid limitation issues. It is interesting to note that under the recently revised rules of the ADR Institute of Canada, the *Bell Canada* case has been overruled, and article 2.3 now provides that commencement of the arbitration occurs when the notice of arbitration is delivered to the respondent.[10]

E. SELECTION OF THE ARBITRATOR

Most experienced arbitration practitioners agree that the selection of the arbitrator or arbitrators is the most important decision that counsel and the parties make in the arbitration. The ability to choose the decision maker is one of the most fundamental and distinctive features that sets arbitration apart from court litigation. In any court case, counsel will gather as much information as possible about the judge assigned to the case and use that information to strategically develop the case presentation. In arbitration, the parties have the distinct advantage of being able to choose their decision maker. In international arbitration, counsel undertake considerable due diligence in the identification of potential candidates and the final selection of an arbitrator as their nominee. The international institutions also play a role in arbitrator selection with candidate disclosure requirements, including representations as to conflicts and availability before confirmation. In domestic arbitration, experience has shown that the practices in Canada are perhaps less rigorous and that Canadian counsel do not appear to spend as much time on this important decision. But

10 ADR Institute of Canada, *ADRIC Arbitration Rules* (version 2, effective 1 December 2016) art 2.3, online: http://adric.ca/wp-content/uploads/2017/03/ADRIC_Arbitration_Rules_8_5_x_11_2016.pdf.

they should. The skill to select an appropriate arbitrator for the client's case is another unique feature of good arbitral advocacy.

Regarding the criteria to be considered by counsel in the selection process, mention has already been made of the specific qualifications that may be expressly set out in the arbitration clause.[11] These qualifications should not be so narrowly interpreted as to hamstring the party and counsel's ability to find suitable candidates that satisfy all the necessary criteria for selection. Subject matter experience and knowledge that match key issues in the case are important criteria, whether expressly set out in the clause or not. Reputation in the arbitration community will also be an important factor, not only reputation for legal expertise and experience, but also reputation for fairness in procedure, the conduct of an arbitration, and the treatment of counsel. Often overlooked in the selection equation for domestic arbitration are a candidate's knowledge of arbitral procedures and proactive case management skills and experience. When the procedural schedule for a hearing is tight, parties will want to ensure that procedural disputes can be addressed and resolved promptly to avoid adjournments of the main hearing date. Furthermore, procedural due process issues are the principal grounds for attacks on awards, whether international or domestic, although there may be more expansive grounds to appeal questions of law in domestic awards. Therefore, knowledge and experience in the handling of difficult arbitral procedural disputes will provide greater assurance as to the enforceability of any award that may be rendered. At the same time, the parties will have greater confidence that they will be accorded a fair opportunity to present their case and receive due consideration. Therefore, excellent case management skill is an important criterion in the selection of either a sole arbitrator or the chair of the tribunal.

Regarding the selection of a party nominee for a three-person tribunal, counsel should be mindful of the future working relationship between their party nominee and potential candi-

11 See Section C, above in this chapter.

dates for the chair. Clearly, the ability of a party nominee to work in a collegial manner with and potentially influence the chair is an important factor that counsel and the party must take into account in their selection criteria. Indeed, candidates may well be ruled out because of prior negative experiences working with other arbitrators.

Some counsel or party representatives may naively say that they are looking for an arbitrator who will decide the case in their favour or who will advance their case, suggesting a nominee with a conscious or unconscious bias in favour of the nominating party. Counsel must remember that a party-nominated arbitrator is under a duty to be and remain impartial and independent throughout the arbitration. The party nominee is not an advocate for the nominating party, and the job of that arbitrator is not to advance that party's case. That said, it is generally accepted that the party nominee may, at the very most, ensure that the nominating party's case is given due and fair consideration in deliberations and an award. Some say, quite rightly, that this is of course the duty of all three arbitrators on a three-person tribunal. All three tribunal members should also ensure that the losing party fully understands the reasons why it did not prevail. In terms of the advocacy involved in arbitrator selection, the main point is simply that choosing an arbitrator who will be predisposed to the nominating party and who will act as an advocate is simply short-sighted and bad advocacy. The biased party nominee will be recognized as such by his co-arbitrators, and his views will be discounted or, more likely, ignored altogether.

The confidentiality of arbitration places some limits on the due diligence that counsel can undertake to assess potential candidates. Nevertheless, the usual sources will include references from other counsel, published articles written by candidates, and, in some cases, their awards that have become public. In international arbitration, it has become an accepted norm that potential candidates will be interviewed, sometimes in considerable depth with a party representative present. Guidelines for such interviews have been promulgated by the Chartered Institute of Arbitrators (CIArb), and these are a useful resource for both counsel and arbitrators to consider in identifying the appropriate limits for interviews and clarifying what can and cannot be discussed during the course of such interviews.[12] Topics to be avoided in an interview include the specific facts and circumstances giving rise to the dispute, the positions and arguments of the parties on the merits of the case, and the prospective arbitrator's views on any of these. Permitted topics may include past experience and arbitrations, attitudes on the general conduct of arbitral proceedings, subject matter expertise, availability, potential conflicts, and in ad hoc arbitrations fees and terms of appointment. The International Bar Association has also weighed in on arbitrator interviews in the *IBA Guidelines on Party Representation in International Arbitration*.[13] Concern over the extensive practice of arbitrator interviews was part of a larger concern over the ethical conduct of counsel in international arbitrations. While these IBA guidelines confirm the general rule that there should be no *ex parte* communications between a party and counsel, on the one hand, and any arbitrator, on the other, interviews with potential arbitrators are acknowledged and permitted if they are limited to general matters such as the candidate's experience, expertise, and availability, consistently with the CIArb guidelines. The fact remains that arbitrator interviews continue to be the norm in international arbitration. Canadian counsel in domestic arbitrations have usually been much more reluctant to undertake interviews of arbitral candidates. They are missing out on a valuable opportunity to gather additional information to consider in the selection process. Most arbitrators do not welcome such interviews and will take detailed interview notes as recommended by the CIArb. However, counsel, and perhaps even a party

12 Chartered Institute of Arbitrators, *International Arbitration Practice Guideline: Interviews for Prospective Arbitrators* (London: CIArb, 2016), online: www.ciarb.org/docs/default-source/ciarbdocuments/guidance-and-ethics/practice-guidelines-protocols-and-rules/international-arbitration-guidelines-2015/guideline-on-interviews-for-prospective-arbitrators.pdf?sfvrsn=16.

13 International Bar Association, *IBA Guidelines on Party Representation in International Arbitration* (London: IBA, 2013), online: www.ibanet.org/Publications/publications_IBA_guides_and_free_materials.aspx.

representative, should take advantage of this unique opportunity and interview their case's potential decision maker. General counsel often express the view that interviews give them greater insight into and confidence in the abilities of the candidates. There can be few complaints if care is taken to conduct a proper interview within the prescriptions and limitations set out in the guidelines from the CIArb and IBA.

F. THE IMPORTANCE OF WRITTEN ADVOCACY IN ARBITRATION

Once the tribunal is constituted and a procedural schedule is in place, most of the prehearing work and much, if not all, of the case-in-chief of each party will be in written form. Excellent written advocacy skill is now a critical prerequisite for the commercial arbitration process, perhaps more so than in civil litigation. Substandard written advocacy that fails to articulate a clear persuasive case will create a difficult, perhaps insurmountable, obstacle to effective oral advocacy at the eventual oral hearing. Stirring oral advocacy can rarely overcome a case that does not have a simple, solid foundation in the written record, clearly stating the strengths of your client's case and weaknesses of the opponent's. This is underscored in the more complex and hotly contested cases, particularly if your opponent has in advance of the hearing been quietly using the written record to persuade the tribunal of the merits of its case. Written advocacy is therefore a critical starting point for successfully advancing the client's case in the arbitration. The following brief comments will cover two important aspects of written arbitral advocacy: (1) the development of the case theory and narrative, and (2) specific techniques to apply in the written submissions.

1) The Case Theory and Narrative

The most creative and certainly the most pivotal time in a case is at the outset in the development of the key theory and narrative of the case, based on the careful assessment of the facts and evidence. This development demands a detailed initial investigation and necessary legal analysis that will form the foundation of the case. It is imperative that this be done at the outset before the pace of the arbitration accelerates. This stands in stark contrast to much domestic civil litigation, where the detailed preparation is often left to midstream in the process or even later.

In developing the case theory, counsel should keep in mind the simple questions that will be at the forefront of each tribunal member's mind:

1) What are the key issues?
2) What is the position of each party on each issue?
3) Why is your client right on each issue?

When these questions can be answered in a brief, succinct way, counsel can begin to identify and articulate a more compelling theory to be advanced in the case. In most arbitration cases, the claim is based in contract. In simple terms, the case will require establishing the contractual right to be enforced, breach of that right, and loss caused by that breach. In addition, it is critical to identify and confirm the basis on which the tribunal has the jurisdiction to determine these issues by reference to the arbitration agreement. The respondent's objective is to challenge each of these elements or otherwise raise other substantive contractual defences that arise on the evidence. In developing the theory of either the claim or the defence, counsel must carefully analyze and robustly challenge the evidence on these critical elements to test the strengths and, more importantly, the weaknesses of their case. Consider how the opponent will attack each element and how the tribunal will robustly scrutinize the theory and any weak element of your case. That weakness may be a point of contract interpretation, the evidence of breach, or the causation of the damage claimed. The client must understand that this testing of the case at an early stage is a necessary part of developing a well-organized, coherent case that can withstand detailed scrutiny. Many cases ultimately fall apart because of the failure to do the necessary investigation and then testing of the case to develop a winning theory and strategy for it.

2) Credibility and Techniques of Written Advocacy

The implementation of a well-developed case theory depends on persuasive written advocacy skills and techniques to present that theory to the tribunal long before the oral hearing. The tribunal's willingness to be persuaded will depend on its own assessment of the credibility of the advocate as well as the quality of the written submissions on behalf of the client. The tribunal must perceive the advocate as both credible and reliable in the presentation of the evidence. There are specific techniques that counsel may use to establish credibility and earn the trust of the tribunal in the manner of presenting the case.

Far too often, counsel try to spin the facts to fit a particular legal theory, raising implausible factual arguments to fit the law. In extreme cases, the evidence is misrepresented. However, conclusory statements in the guise of facts do not persuade. The better approach is to present facts in a neutral fashion and in an artful way so that the conclusion naturally emerges from the facts in an obvious, compelling way to support your client's case or undermine your opponent's. Counsel leads the tribunal to draw the clear conclusion dictated by the evidence. In this way, the advocate is seen as presenting a credible case, and earns credibility with and the trust of the tribunal in the process. Arbitrators are generally experienced and sophisticated in separating unsupported conclusory submissions from those rooted in the evidence and facts. However, this task can of course be more difficult and challenging where there are hotly disputed facts. Here, common sense and plausibility are the important tools of the good advocate. An unemotional statement of the important, critical facts, of what was done or what happened and, sometimes more importantly, what was not done, will lead the tribunal to the more plausible findings of fact and then to prefer or accept your client's version of the facts over another. A tribunal prefers to find its own way to a conclusion on the credible evidence pointed out by counsel rather than to be told by counsel what it must find. Overstating the facts or making bold conclusions of fact that are seriously contested or not supported by the evidence can undermine your credibility in the eyes of the tribunal and will fundamentally undermine the strengths of your client's case.

With respect to the submissions of law, it is frequently the findings of fact that will determine which of the competing principles of law will be engaged. However, in terms of the content of the applicable principles, stating them with accuracy is equally critical to establishing and maintaining credibility with the tribunal. This is true not only for domestic arbitrations but also for international arbitrations, where principles of a foreign law may be applicable. Tribunal members are often experienced in applying foreign law, particularly commercial law principles, which engage many common concepts across different legal systems to facilitate international trade. Therefore, legal submissions that misstate or unduly distort the law will, again, seriously undermine your credibility to the detriment of your client's case.

Virtually every case has some weakness, whether on liability or damages. It is generally accepted that good advocacy, whether in litigation or arbitration, demands that appropriate attention be paid to that weakness in the written submissions. Sometimes the weakness can be readily dismissed based on some fact or legal principle, leaving the strengths of the case unaffected and intact. However, some difficult points may carry greater weight and validity with the tribunal, in which case counsel must strive to isolate that weak point and maintain the core strength of the case. To minimize the impact of that point, address it after the development of the main points and before a strong written closing. Be matter of fact in describing the issue and its limited impact without using bold language that overstates the point to be made. Accept that the particular argument may not be your strongest. The candour will further enhance your credibility with the tribunal.

A few suggestions on the structure and language of the written submissions are also appropriate. First and foremost, be direct and concise. In the written submission, state at the outset the main point and conclusion on the facts and law. Enhance that with a short statement of why that conclusion is both warranted and fair, or just. Then proceed with the detailed development of the submission on the facts and the law. In this way, the tribunal will know precisely what the core of your case is and where you are going in the development of that case. The tribunal is ready to be persuaded, not left wondering where you are going. The development of the argument should not be a process of discovery, revealing the main point only at the end. It should be a process of persuasion in favour of the key facts and legal conclusions that have been clearly stated. The tribunal will appreciate knowing exactly where you are going. Once the detailed analysis has been developed, a restatement of the conclusion will be that much more powerful and persuasive, reaffirming the arbitrators' own thought process as they follow the logic of the entire argument. The tribunal will be with you throughout rather than questioning what your purpose may be and where you are going. In this way, the theory of the case will remain front and centre throughout.

In the written submission, use well-defined and logical subheadings that relate to the key factual and legal issues to be determined by the tribunal. This will enhance the logical development of the case. It will also enable the tribunal to come back to certain key sections of the analysis throughout the course of the arbitration as the key points in dispute become more narrowly focused. More complicated factual issues may be simplified by the use of a visual aid, whether a diagram, a table of the chronology of events, or even a short video where appropriate. For example, a complex multiparty transaction can be usefully described in a diagram that accurately identifies the parties, elements of the transaction, and various relationships in the transaction that are critical to understanding the legal issues in the case.

The foregoing general comments on written advocacy in arbitration can be usefully applied to each written stage of the arbitration, including the notice of arbitration, the respondent's answer, the statement of claim or claimant's memorial, the statement of defence or respondent's memorial, and also the short prehearing statement. It is extremely useful to attach the key documents, or material extracts from the key documents, as appendices that can be referenced by the tribunal to more clearly understand the case. In this respect, the written submissions in an arbitration are less like the skeletal pleadings used in court litigation and more like comprehensive narratives encompassing the facts, law, and argument with the supporting documentary evidence for the core of the case. When you describe the detail of the who, what, when, and why of the case using the actual language of the documents attached as appendices, you provide a much more compelling story, with the supporting evidence readily available to be absorbed by the tribunal. This will persuade the tribunal, unlike bold, bald statements made without any supporting evidence that the tribunal may discard as hyperbole without substance.

Persuasive advocacy in the written submissions demands time, attention to detail, and careful editing to simplify and focus the argument. Even though the schedule will be tight, a final careful edit can elevate the work product and significantly enhance its impact on the tribunal. With this short review of certain techniques of written advocacy complete, the focus will now shift to the opportunities for oral advocacy at the critical stages of the arbitration.

G. THE FIRST PROCEDURAL MEETING

Procedural flexibility is one of the hallmarks of arbitration. This flexibility is also one of the major advantages of arbitration over court litigation. The litigation process is governed by detailed procedural rules, both formal and informal, that trigger significant pretrial fighting and jurisprudence, all of which contribute to delay. With arbitration, parties can by agreement shape their own procedure for the particular dispute. Absent agreement, the tribunal exercises a broad discretion to fix the procedure for the conduct of the arbitration, subject only to the requirement to treat the parties fairly and impartially. The procedural framework for the arbitration will be largely established at the first procedural meeting. The importance of this first meeting cannot be overstated. This dictates that counsel thoroughly prepare for the meeting.

To properly prepare, counsel need to know as much as possible about their case — the strengths and weaknesses of the evidence, the key witnesses whose attendance at the main hearing will be necessary, the required areas of expert evidence, and, if possible, the identity of their experts. The claimant will also want to consider the need for any interim measures. Such thorough preparation may be more challenging for the respondent. Given the nature of most contractual disputes, the client will usually be apprised of most of the key issues in dispute through a full documentary record of the business dealings. The respondent must also ensure that any jurisdictional issue is identified and tabled at the first meeting for scheduling of the appropriate motion.

Before the first meeting, counsel should separately put their minds to the timing of the hearing, type of hearing most suitable on the facts of the case, and necessary procedural steps to get to that hearing. Counsel should consider ways and means to streamline the process since the hearing will usually be fixed on a schedule that moves much faster than that of court litigation. The claimant will usually want to avoid delays. Even if the respondent is intent on attempting to delay the process, a dispute tactic commonly played out in litigation, that intent should not become obvious to the tribunal, whose mandate is to proceed efficiently and expeditiously. With thorough preparation, the respondent may identify procedural steps that lend themselves to its view of the case without frustrating a fair and efficient process. For example, in complex cases separate hearings may be arranged in a logical sequence with priority given to threshold legal or factual issues critical for a motion for summary disposition that may resolve all or part of the case. Such threshold issues may include not only jurisdictional issues but also key issues going to the merits of the case. The determination of these issues may shape the course of the procedure even if the dispute is not entirely resolved. Therefore, counsel who are well prepared will be able to identify creative ways to shape the procedural conduct of the case and streamline procedures leading to the hearing in a manner that best fits with their own strategy.

The tribunal will usually expect counsel for the parties to consult with each other and if possible agree on certain procedures to narrow the areas of procedural disagreement. A comprehensive list of the various issues that can be canvassed at the first procedural meeting is found in the *UNCITRAL Notes on Organizing Arbitral Proceedings*.[14] These notes provide a useful list of issues to be discussed by counsel in preparation for the first procedural meeting. Counsel for each party should see this as an opportunity to advance their case and establish credibility with the tribunal by showing an intention to engage and cooperate in the efficient organization of the arbitration to deal with the merits of the dispute. Far too often, Canadian counsel engage in time-consuming and costly procedural fighting of the type that frequently plagues domestic court litigation. Experience has shown that much of such procedural bickering does not materially affect the substantive presentation of the case on the merits and is counterproductive. It must be remembered that the tribunal starts forming impressions of counsel and the case advocated by each at an early stage of the arbitration. Unreasonable positions on procedural matters do nothing to inspire confidence in counsel or establish counsel's credibility in the minds of the arbitrators. While the tribunal will not expect counsel to agree on all procedural issues in advance, it will expect that reasonable efforts and positions will resolve many of the procedural matters to be discussed at the first meeting. And while it is unlikely that counsel will be able to agree on all issues, experienced arbitration counsel will generally be able to agree on many of the prehearing procedures and the procedural schedule.

Proactive case management to ensure that the arbitration progresses in a timely fashion should be expected from a tribunal.

14 United Nations Commission on International Trade Law, *UNCITRAL Notes on Organizing Arbitral Proceedings* (New York: UNCITRAL, 2016), online: www.uncitral.org/pdf/english/texts/arbitration/arb-notes/arb-notes-2016-e.pdf (originally promulgated in 1996 and recently updated and revised in 2016).

This is one of the advantages of arbitration over litigation, and it is a key benefit that counsel should be prepared to use. At the first meeting, the tribunal will ensure that certain basic and necessary issues are not overlooked. Proper appointment and constitution of the tribunal is fundamental, and is a requirement regarding which Canadian counsel can at times be lax. In international arbitration, it is also critical to confirm the seat or legal location of the arbitration to fix the applicable arbitration law. The language of the arbitration must also be determined. While these points are usually identified in the arbitration agreement, if they are not, this can have a significant impact on procedures and costs. Costs for the translation of documents and interpreters for oral evidence can be substantial. Determining the language of the arbitration can result in the allocation of significant costs between the parties. On contentious issues discussed at the meeting, the tribunal will likely try to manoeuvre the parties toward a compromise agreement on procedures and schedule.

At the start of the meeting, the tribunal will look to clarify and confirm the applicable procedural rules for the arbitration. While these are usually clear in the case of institutional arbitration, it will still be important to clarify and confirm the particular version of the arbitral rules that will apply given that many institutions have updated their rules or have created different sets of rules for different types of disputes or industries. Even with ad hoc arbitration, whether domestic or international, the tribunal may look to secure agreement on the application of certain "soft law" or rules such as the *IBA Rules on the Taking of Evidence in International Arbitration*.[15] It is now common for these IBA rules to be adopted outright or to serve as guidelines to be referenced in addressing any procedural issues that may arise in the arbitration. Agreement on the applicable arbitral rules will ensure that counsel and the parties are well aware of the ground rules that will guide their dispute through to the hearing date.

15 International Bar Association, *IBA Rules on the Taking of Evidence in International Arbitration* (London: IBA, 2010), online: www.ibanet.org/Publications/publications_IBA_guides_and_free_materials.aspx [*IBA Evidence Rules*].

Far too often in ad hoc arbitration, civil litigation lawyers will want to use the rules of civil procedure from their provincial court practice as the basis for the governing arbitral procedure. While some of these rules can usefully be applied by way of analogy in the arbitration, it is a fundamental mistake to simply adopt outright the rules of civil procedure. The use of court rules may not only cause delay and significantly increase the costs of the process but may also create a dysfunctional procedural quagmire without the appeal process built in to those rules. Reliance on court rules also shows a complete lack of understanding of the arbitral process and lack of the creativity to use the flexibility of arbitration to tailor the arbitral procedure to the needs of the dispute. Therefore, counsel should expect the tribunal to push back against the wholesale adoption of court rules to govern the arbitral procedure. It must be remembered that under most arbitration rules, the tribunal is entitled to set the rules for the conduct of the arbitration, save only to the extent that the arbitration agreement specifies otherwise.

The tribunal will be bound to accept the procedures set out in the arbitration clause or agreement as the failure to do so can give rise to jurisdictional issues and challenges, whether before or after an award. As for the more informal agreements between counsel on procedures, the tribunal will usually be guided by such agreements, but it is not obliged to be. However, the tribunal will likely raise concerns and seek changes if the timetable and procedures agreed to by counsel appear to unduly delay the process or are unreasonably tight with regard to timing and likely to invite adjournments. To counter a proposed schedule evincing leisurely timing, the tribunal may insist on the attendance of party representatives to ensure that efficiency and proportionality in time, cost, and procedure are reflected in the procedures to be applied to the particular dispute. If the schedule is unreasonably aggressive, again, the tribunal will push back, cautioning counsel that once the hearing date is fixed, an extremely good reason will be required to adjourn that date.

One of the principal objectives of the first procedural meeting is to fix the date for the merits hearing as quickly as possible and then to determine the necessary procedures to advance the case to that hearing. While attempting to balance the schedules of all participants, the tribunal will strive to fix a date that is reasonable for the dispute, taking into account the complexity of the matter and the location and availability of the witnesses as well as any specific requirements of the arbitration agreement. My first international arbitration involved a large complex claim in an ICC arbitration in which counsel for the claimant suggested a hearing of up to three months. The chair was a prominent London-based international arbitrator who simply responded as follows: "I have never had a case go longer than two weeks. We will do the case in two weeks." The schedule proved very tight, but it worked.

Occasionally, the arbitration agreement dictates an unreasonably short time for the completion of the hearing and delivery of an award. While some matters genuinely require such fast-track procedures, these clauses are usually the work product of inexperienced corporate lawyers who failed to consult an arbitration practitioner. An example has already been noted above.[16] Such restrictive time limits will usually deprive the parties of a fair opportunity to prepare their case. Most disputes do not require such tight timelines. Both counsel and parties should be prepared to be flexible in establishing a reasonable schedule for the hearing, given the nature of the dispute and the broader context of the business issues and relationships. Occasionally, the parties cannot agree on alternative timing with the result that the entire dispute process, including preparation time, must be severely truncated to meet the strict timeline set out in the arbitration clause and avoid loss of jurisdiction. Conversely, some counsel regard the date for the hearing as if it were for a court trial, looking to fix a hearing date that is two years or more away and booking many weeks, even months, for the hearing itself. Since arbitration is intended to be more expeditious than court proceedings, experienced arbitrators will resist such lengthy delays. Even the most complex of disputes involving large sums of money can

16 See Section D, above in this chapter.

normally go to a hearing within approximately eighteen months from the first procedural meeting. Most disputes can be scheduled within one year or less, which is far more expeditious than what can be achieved in the cumbersome court process. Indeed, delays still frustrate early trial dates in the court system despite long-standing complaints and attempts to overcome such delays.

Counsel must also carefully consider the length of the merits hearing. An arbitration hearing can usually be concluded more expeditiously than a trial since the case-in-chief of each party is usually delivered in writing in advance of the *viva voce* hearing. At the first procedural meeting, some counsel significantly overestimate the required hearing time, usually basing their estimates on the length of a court trial, which has shorter hearing days and more evidentiary and procedural disputes. The experienced arbitral tribunal will look to conduct the arbitration far more efficiently, often with longer sitting days to ensure completion. Occasionally, counsel may significantly underestimate the length of time required for a hearing, usually due to client pressure to complete the matter. Again, the experienced arbitral tribunal may identify certain issues of evidentiary complexity that will require more hearing time and suggest that additional hearing days be held in reserve to ensure completion during the reserved time. To ensure timely completion, the tribunal may also require that an equal amount of time be allocated at the hearing to each party to complete its evidence and oral submissions. The adoption of a chess clock approach will highlight for counsel the need to consider the timeliness of the conduct of the hearing when preparing cross-examinations. This can be a very effective tool without sacrificing quality.

If at the first procedural meeting, an early motion is requested, whether for interim measures of protection, a jurisdictional challenge, or a summary disposition on a particular point, that motion will generally be scheduled in advance of the merits hearing. Occasionally, a jurisdictional motion is determined with the merits due to the interrelationship of the factual issues. It is usually best to establish parallel procedural tracks for the early motion and for the main merits hearing. In this way, the motion will not unduly delay the procedures leading to the merits hearing of the substantive dispute. The procedural tracks must of course be coordinated, but it is unnecessary to put the entire case on hold while the early motion is addressed and determined. Very often, the early motion can be addressed much more informally, sometimes over an early meeting or phone call, for example, to preserve the status quo while the main dispute proceeds. The flexibility of the arbitral process enables the parties and the tribunal to address these interim issues more informally where appropriate.

Once the dates for the main merits hearing and any urgent motion are fixed, the tribunal will set a detailed schedule with dates for the delivery by the parties of the written statements or memorials, documents relied upon, and witness statements. Much of this prehearing preparation is in written form, and many general comments on this written advocacy have been set out above.[17] However, at the procedural meeting there are a number of important issues for counsel to clarify and confirm since they will have a direct impact on the procedural course of the arbitration and the hearing itself. First, the form of the submissions or memorials and dates for their delivery must be determined. To make the hearing more efficient, the case-in-chief of each party is usually delivered in written form as a full submission on the evidence and law, supported by witness statements, expert reports, and all documents relied upon. These witness statements will largely replace the examinations-in-chief at the hearing, subject to some further comments below. While many counsel seek to use only a skeletal form of pleading of the type typically used in court proceedings, a more comprehensive submission on the law and evidence will ensure that the parties know the case to be met and will ultimately enable the case to proceed on a faster timetable without late surprises that cause delay. A schedule is usually set for the consecutive delivery of the memorials spaced to allow reasonable preparation, though in some instances a concurrent or

17 See Section F, above in this chapter.

simultaneous exchange may be ordered. A reply memorial from the claimant and a rejoinder memorial from the respondent are also frequently built in to the schedule, though counsel may decide to forgo this second round of exchanges.

Once the schedule for the initial memorials is fixed, the tribunal will address the discovery schedule. For an international arbitration, this will usually involve only the exchange of documents since the generally accepted rule is that there is no prehearing oral examination for discovery of witnesses or a representative of the opponent unless the parties themselves expressly agree. The schedule and governing rules for the exchange of documents will be specifically determined at the first procedural meeting. In international arbitration, there is a growing consensus that parties will use the *IBA Evidence Rules*.[18] These are commonly adopted by the parties, frequently at the urging of the tribunal, and confirmed in the procedural order. Even if the parties do not agree on the IBA rules, the tribunal will usually look to those rules for guidance in addressing any issues regarding disputed document requests. Under the *IBA Evidence Rules*, each party is able to make specific requests of the opponent for production of the specified documents. To limit the costly fishing expeditions for documents that are more frequently found in domestic litigation, the IBA rules introduce the test of relevance *and* materiality for a document request. Disputes over document production are usually handled in writing through a schedule, commonly referred to as a Redfern Schedule, that lists in successive columns the particular request, the basis for the request, the objection to produce followed by a short reply, and, finally, the tribunal's decision. This form of schedule facilitates the determination of the disputed document requests in writing.

The approach to witness evidence must also be carefully delineated during the procedural meeting. It is now common for the prehearing exchange of detailed witness statements to be used for the evidence-in-chief of each witness. In international arbi-

18 Above note 15.

tration, these witness statements are included in the memorials together with all documents relied upon. This practice has become more common in domestic arbitration and has also found its way into court practice, particularly in commercial matters. Much of the commercial context of a case can be more effectively set out in witness statements delivered before the hearing. In this way, the key factual issues can be highlighted for the tribunal in advance of the hearing. This procedure serves to significantly shorten the actual hearing, which is devoted principally to cross-examination. Witness statements have been criticized as not reflecting the true evidence of the witnesses. Ways to overcome this problem are discussed in greater detail below.

The dates for the exchange of any expert reports must also be established at this first meeting. The tribunal may first require each party to identify at an early stage the areas of expertise engaged on the facts for which expert evidence will be given, with a brief statement of the issue to be addressed by the expert. The identification and retention of appropriate experts can itself be a time-consuming task. Therefore, the early identification of the areas of expertise will help avoid delays and facilitate the early retention of necessary experts, especially by the respondent. This will ensure that each side's expert will have a fair opportunity to prepare the required report.

The scheduling of the discovery process in a domestic arbitration is usually rendered more complicated where one or both parties insist on conducting an examination for discovery of a representative of the opposite party in a manner consistent with domestic court practice. Indeed, counsel who are less experienced in arbitral practice may seek to conduct all discovery in accordance with court rules of civil procedure. That is a fundamental mistake and is to be discouraged. It must be remembered that the delivery of comprehensive memorials supported by the evidence relied upon ensures that each party knows exactly the case-in-chief of the other that must be met. That alone satisfies one of the principal purposes of oral discovery. Furthermore, the adoption of the court rules of discovery can be an open invitation to permit costly, time-consuming, and abusive discovery tactics that have plagued domestic litigation. The court rules also use procedures that are incompatible with the arbitral process such as motions over refusals to answer questions on a discovery. Experience has shown that bringing such motions, whether before a sole arbitrator or a tribunal of three, can be extremely costly, often outweighing the value and importance of the evidence obtained, while causing delay in the process.

If counsel insist on conducting oral examinations for discovery, it will be important to establish certain ground rules for those examinations during the procedural meeting. Any oral examination should be time limited, to perhaps a half day to one day, to ensure that counsel will get to the important issues quickly. Time limits serve to focus the questioning on what is truly important. An efficient way to handle refusals should also be developed. For example, it may be ordered that the only ground for a refusal to answer is privilege. Then, if there is a dispute over the relevance of a question, it must still be answered subject to its relevance being argued at the hearing before it can be used. Alternatively, where the arbitrator can be reachable by telephone on the day of the examination, the arbitrator may be contacted at a specific time to make an immediate ruling over the phone on any disputed questions. The prospect of such an immediate ruling tends to keep the questioning focused and relevant, thereby discouraging the need for any rulings. A third alternative involves the adaptation of a Redfern Schedule, usually used for document disputes, to list the questions refused with the brief written positions of each party, enabling the motion to be determined in writing. Where parties do insist on oral discoveries, counsel should be creative in designing a process that will be streamlined, efficient, and cost-effective. In terms of scheduling, the timing of any examinations and any motions arising from such examinations must be specified to ensure that they do not cause delays that may disrupt the hearing dates.

Other minor scheduling issues may arise at this first procedural meeting such as the date for the identification of witnesses for cross-examination. Once all memorials, witness statements, and expert reports have been exchanged, counsel will be required to identify those witnesses relied upon by the opponent whose attendance will be required at the hearing for cross-examination. Not all witnesses may be subject to cross-examination, and there is no need for a witness to attend the hearing if she will not be required for cross-examination. Making that decision will require counsel to carefully formulate the hearing strategy well in advance.

At the conclusion of the first procedural meeting, the tribunal will issue a procedural order that sets out the complete set of procedures determined at the first meeting, including a detailed schedule. This order will normally also set a date and time for a case management conference shortly before the hearing to address any last-minute issues. With this order, the parties and counsel will have a complete process and schedule tailored to the needs of their dispute.

H. THE PREHEARING SUBMISSIONS AND CASE MANAGEMENT CONFERENCE

Once the schedule for the arbitration has been set, counsel will undertake the preparation of the mandated written submissions, if they have not started already. Since the tribunal will have endeavoured to establish a reasonable timetable for the dispute, there may be some, but generally little, leeway in the schedule. Ongoing, focused preparation will be required. If difficulties arise with documentary productions or other matters that may jeopardize the schedule, it will be important for counsel to address these difficulties promptly with the tribunal. Motions may have to be brought before the tribunal, frequently on short notice for prompt resolution to maintain the schedule. Most arbitrators and tribunals will strive to respond quickly, sometimes very informally, to resolve issues and ensure a fair process while maintaining the schedule for the hearing.

With respect to the written submissions, general comments have already been provided above on the importance of written advocacy.[19] The discussion and decisions made at the first procedural meeting will have determined the exact form and timing of the written submissions. As noted earlier, in international arbitration the submissions or memorials will normally comprise detailed written submissions of fact, law, and legal argument supported by all witness statements, expert reports, and documents relied upon. These comprehensive submissions, whether exchanged in one or two rounds, will represent the case-in-chief of each party, with the time limited oral hearing devoted mainly to cross-examination. In contrast, some domestic arbitrations proceed as private trials with skeletal pleadings, an exchange of affidavits of documents, and an oral examination for discovery followed by a trial-like hearing involving complete examinations-in-chief and cross-examinations without time limits. However, the trend in domestic arbitration has now clearly shifted. The preferred process involves the prehearing exchange of the case-in-chief of each party in a written record that includes a statement of fact and law, witness statements, expert reports, and the documents relied upon.

To avoid delays and ensure timely completion, the hearing days will usually be fixed with the clear expectation that the case will be finished within the allotted time frame. While the tribunal may be prepared to start early or go late on a given hearing day to complete the evidence, most arbitrators will ensure that the case moves quickly and that the hearing days are productive. The hearing will not proceed at a leisurely pace like some court proceedings. Therefore, in preparing submissions and cross-examinations for the oral hearing, counsel must be mindful of the amount of available time and be prepared to get to the key issues quickly. This is particularly true if hearing time will be allocated equally between the parties using a chess clock approach. As noted earlier, this technique can be very effective without sacrificing the quality of the advocacy. Experience has shown that time limits will

19 See Section F, above in this chapter.

focus counsel's mind on the core preparation of the case to enhance, rather than compromise, the quality of the advocacy.

It is appropriate to provide some comments on the preparation of witness statements. The criticism is often made that witness statements, whether used in court or in arbitration, are of limited value since they are written by lawyers using lawyers' words containing legal argument and other conclusory statements and are not the real evidence of the witnesses. Counsel should heed this criticism. This is a prime example of bad advocacy. A witness statement should use the words, language, and idioms of the witness, not those of the lawyer. A statement that contains conclusory statements in the form of a legal submission instead of factual evidence is of limited or no value to the tribunal. To ensure that the actual words of each witness are captured, counsel should record witness interviews and then use the transcribed recordings as the basis for the eventual statements. In larger, higher dollar-value cases, a reporter may be used, though making a recording may seem less intrusive to the witnesses. Witnesses become comfortable with this process when they are advised and understand that their own words and actual recollections, not just the filtered notes of counsel from the interview, are important. A tribunal can easily determine when a witness statement reflects the recollection and language of the witness and not just the creative writing of the lawyer. Indeed, in the former case the credibility of the witness and counsel is enhanced significantly in the minds of the arbitrators.

A prehearing case management conference shortly before the hearing will provide counsel with a final opportunity to finalize any logistical issues for the hearing and, more importantly, address and resolve any late-breaking procedural or evidentiary disputes. This case conference is useful to identify any issues that could give rise to requests for an adjournment of the hearing. The tribunal will be particularly sensitive to any late attempts to adduce critical evidence that ought to have been produced much earlier in the process. The entire process is structured to avoid this type of surprise and ambush. In managing the case throughout, the tribunal will endeavour to ensure a fair and balanced process with full and proper disclosure by each party of the case relied upon and to be met by the opponent. Any tactical delay in adducing critical evidence may well result in the exclusion of that evidence from the record.

I. THE HEARING

One of the primary benefits of arbitration is that the parties are able to get their case to a hearing much faster than in court litigation. And that is due largely to the proactive case management of each case by the tribunal. Such case management is not consistently available in the court process. This section will provide some comments on certain styles and techniques of advocacy that are appropriate in the hearing.

1) The Opening Statement

Counsel should always take advantage of the opportunity to deliver an opening statement. Some counsel may feel that with detailed written submissions an opening is a waste of time. Not so.

It must be remembered that the case-in-chief of both parties has normally already been delivered to the tribunal well in advance of the oral hearing. The tribunal will have carefully read that material in preparation for the hearing. The arbitration hearing is therefore unlike a court trial. The arbitral opening can be more substantive by focusing on the key legal issues, such as the interpretation of the contract in issue, or on the key factual issues covered by the evidence-in-chief. It can lay the groundwork for the conflict of evidence to be explored in cross-examination. The opening may well be counsel's first opportunity to directly engage with the tribunal on the merits of the case. Because of the detailed preparation undertaken before the start of the hearing, the arbitrators will likely have questions that they want to pose, and these may be asked during the openings. Take advantage of this opportunity to carefully listen to the questions and any comments of the tribunal. It may be necessary to clarify or correct observations or misapprehensions of the tribunal. Do not hesitate to do so, but do so without being argumentative. This is a valuable opportunity to persuade the tribunal of the merits of your case.

Careful preparation of the opening is critical to show your confidence and reliability in the presentation of the evidence, which will, in turn, enhance your credibility with the tribunal. The preparation of a short outline or skeleton of the argument delivered in advance to the tribunal will assist counsel greatly. A short, well-constructed outline of the core argument will serve as a road map for the evidence to follow and may be repeatedly referenced by the tribunal throughout the case. Counsel should firmly state key undisputed facts from the witness statements and reference, even quote, key documents. The tribunal can then draw logical conclusions. The structure of the opening can be basic. Start with an introduction to set the stage and the main theory to be advanced, followed by a factual narrative referencing the key evidence. Then provide a brief, clear review of the applicable legal principles and their application to the key undisputed facts. It is always useful to lightly touch on a brief rebuttal of any key arguments of the opponent that are anticipated. This will convey confidence in the case that you are presenting, particularly if any perceived weakness can be readily neutralized. A brief review of the damages issues may then be followed by the conclusion that you want the tribunal to ultimately make.

2) Examinations and Cross-examinations

As noted earlier, the evidence-in-chief of each witness is normally given by way of a witness statement or in the case of an expert by an expert report, delivered long before the hearing date. In traditional arbitral practice, a witness will be asked to identify the statement or report, confirm its accuracy, and identify any changes or corrections. The witness will then submit to cross-examination.

More recently, a trend has developed to permit a limited and focused examination-in-chief of a witness, of up to thirty minutes or so, to take the witness through the key highlights of the evidence directly before the tribunal. This serves a couple of purposes. First, out of fairness to the witness it enables him to become acclimatized to the hearing setting. Second, it enables the tribunal to see and hear him speak to the key issues in his own voice. Even where the witness statement properly reflects the ideas and words of the witness, as discussed above, this limited examination-in-chief or direct examination allows the tribunal to better assess the witness's credibility in person. Important evidence can have a real impact on the tribunal when heard live from the witness, reinforcing the witness statement or developing a nuance that is not as apparent in the statement. However, this short examination-in-chief is not intended to allow the witness to develop new areas of evidence that could have been but were not provided earlier. That would take the opposing party by surprise. And if that is attempted, objection may be taken, and the tribunal will foreclose that line of questioning. In other respects, the examination of a witness will be similar to the examination in a court proceeding. Witness preparation is essential. The appropriate use of leading and nonleading questions remains important, particularly to reinforce the credibility of the testimony.

With respect to experts, their reports are often lengthy and dense in addressing particular areas of expertise. Furthermore, the areas of dispute in the expert evidence will often have been narrowed by the time of the hearing. Therefore, it is also useful for an expert to be examined in chief for a short period to highlight her expert opinion or, in many cases, simply allow her to provide a presentation for fifteen to twenty minutes on the key expert issues, highlights of her opinion, and underpinnings of that opinion. This can be extremely helpful to the tribunal especially when the expert can simplify complex concepts and the issues of conflict between the competing expert opinions. Finally, after the experts have each given their evidence, it is not uncommon for the tribunal to recall both experts to then give evidence as a panel. This is often called hot tubbing. It allows the tribunal to put differences and competing theories to both experts at the same time to more effectively test their evidence. Counsel frequently do not like this process due to the loss of control that it represents. However, with proper preparation by the tribunal it can be extremely effective. Therefore, counsel should anticipate this and ensure that their expert is properly prepared.

Most of the evidence received at the oral merits hearing will be by way of cross-examination. There are a few important rules of cross-examination usually applied in an arbitration that may differ from the usual court practices. In court, failure to challenge a witness on an evidentiary point will normally constitute acceptance of that evidence. More specifically, under the rule in *Browne v Dunn*, if the credibility of a witness is to be impeached by other evidence or in closing argument, the witness must be confronted with contradictory evidence while giving evidence. In arbitration, as noted earlier, the oral hearing is usually conducted under specific time limits, with an allocation of time between the parties. Given these time limits, it has become a rule of international arbitration that it is no longer necessary for counsel to challenge a witness on every unhelpful statement by him in his witness statement. The witness can still be challenged even if contradictory evidence has not been put to him, and that is true even if the decision has been made not to cross at all. This rule is usually confirmed in a prior procedural order to ensure that all parties are aware of the common ground rules for the conduct of the arbitration.

Another rule of cross-examination that may be confirmed in a procedural order relates to the use of documents to impeach a witness's credibility on cross-examination. In court, documents that have *not* previously been produced in the proceeding may still be used in cross-examination to impeach the credibility of a witness, though they may not be used as substantive evidence at the trial, as proof of the truth of their contents. In an international arbitration, it is usually agreed and confirmed in a procedural order that any document to be used in cross-examination, including for the sole purpose of impeaching credibility, must have been produced in the normal course of the proceeding, failing which it cannot be used. This would be agreed and ordered to avoid surprise and potential delay or adjournment of the hearing. If this approach is to be used in a domestic arbitration, it is best incorporated into a procedural order to ensure that all parties will be playing by the same rules.

Generally, the techniques and advocacy rules for the cross-examination of witnesses in arbitration will be similar to those in court proceedings. However, the decision whether to cross-examine or not will generally be made well before the actual hearing. As noted above, a procedural order will usually require that, following the delivery of all memorials and witness statements, each party will identify those witnesses whose attendance at the hearing will be necessary for cross-examination. This requires clear planning. Otherwise, the decision whether to cross or not is similar in arbitration and court proceedings. Counsel must always have a good answer to the question, why cross-examine this witness at all? It may be to extract useful admissions to support one's case or undermine the opponent's case. It may simply be to undermine the credibility of that witness. However, the purpose of the cross-examination should be clear. Far too often, that purpose is not at all clear to the tribunal listening to the cross. As for winning the case on a cross-examination, that rarely happens. When it does, an extract from the transcript of those questions and answers will usually have found its way into the closing submissions and then into the final award.

The general techniques of and approaches to cross-examination are beyond the scope of this book. Suffice it to say, preparation is critical. Develop a clear plan, but be ready to deviate when necessary. Limit the number of points to be developed. Use simple, plain language in the question formulation, and avoid lengthy compound questions. Leading questions should be used to close the door as much as possible on expansive witness explanations. However, do not be afraid on occasion to use a nonleading but directive question to obtain compelling admissions, particularly from a talkative witness, where it is likely that no harm can be done whatever the answer. Listen to the answers and prepare to follow up to get a direct response. However, avoid arguing with the witness. Instead, save the argument for closing. Above all, be as brief as possible. Some cross-examinations leave the tribunal completely puzzled as to their purpose. The fact is that many cross-examinations simply do not materially add to or detract from the evidence-in-chief adduced by the parties.

It is appropriate to provide a few comments on re-examination or redirect since this is frequently abused. The purpose of re-examination is simply to enable a witness to explain or clarify testimony that may have been obscured, uncertain, or incomplete in the cross-examination or to refute misleading inferences. Re-examination is not an invitation to conduct a further examination-in-chief or provide new facts and evidence on matters not covered in cross-examination. Counsel who are not as familiar with the use of witness statements as evidence-in-chief will frequently attempt to embark on a wide-ranging re-examination and introduce fresh evidence as if it were an examination-in-chief. This will only invite objection not only from opposing counsel but also from the tribunal. Even if an answer is provided by the witness before objection can be made, the evidence will not be relied upon by the tribunal. It is also imperative that leading questions not be used to elicit the critical testimony on re-examination. Unfortunately, in identifying the evidence given on cross-examination that is to be explored on re-examination, some counsel attempt to signal the answer to the witness through leading questions. This is clearly improper. Any witness response to such questions is simply not persuasive. The improper use of a leading question will negate the opportunity to properly elicit clarifying evidence. Any re-examination should be undertaken with great care and only when absolutely necessary. Too often, it can backfire, and damaging testimony is repeated and thereby reinforced and highlighted. It is often said that no re-examination can do no harm. But if done well, the re-examination can save a witness. The best re-examinations are limited to no more than four or five key points.

3) The Closing Submissions

As fatigue starts to set in by the end of the merits hearing, counsel will want to ensure that there is energy in reserve for the closing, the last and probably the most important opportunity to persuade the tribunal. It is essential not to lose sight of this purpose: to assist the tribunal in concluding that your client should win and that the relief sought should be granted, or for the respondent, refused. The closing will be a valuable opportunity to interact with the tribunal and address and alleviate any of its concerns. The question for the advocate is simply, how best to do this?

The form and timing of the closing submissions must be discussed between counsel and agreed to by the tribunal. There may be some differences between the approach taken in international arbitration and in domestic arbitration, largely due to logistical matters and cultural preferences. Counsel from common law jurisdictions with a tradition of oral closings may try to avoid any written closings. That is certainly the case in many Canadian domestic arbitrations. The better practice is to discuss this with the tribunal and determine what will best assist it. To that end, most tribunals will usually table some specific questions about the liability and damages issues in the case to be addressed by counsel at some point during the closings. These questions alone should not dictate the content of the closings, but the answers to these questions should be carefully incorporated into the closings that counsel want to make.

The closing submissions may be entirely written, entirely oral, or a combination of both. In domestic arbitration, there is a growing trend to have a short adjournment after the close of the evidence that permits counsel to prepare and deliver a written closing before reconvening for an oral closing. In many respects, this is the ideal in that it encourages a more developed, thoughtful, and robust interaction at the oral closing between counsel and the tribunal on the key issues to be determined in the award. The challenge with this approach is ensuring that the oral submissions are scheduled soon after the close of evidence without an undue delay. This, of course, is much easier in domestic arbitration where counsel and the tribunal are in the same city. It is more problematic in international arbitration, where counsel and the tribunal members are more likely to be catching planes after the hearing and where it is both difficult and costly to reconvene after a short adjournment. The amounts at stake may well justify this additional cost. If addressed early in the process, a separate date for oral submissions may be easily arranged. However, due to the logistical difficulty of reconvening in international arbitrations, the more common approach is to have a brief oral closing immediately after the last witness, followed by the delivery of written posthearing briefs within a prescribed time.

In organizing the closing submissions, consider using a decision-tree analysis to serve as a roadmap for the critical decisions that must be made, particularly those decisions that may, in turn, render the determination of other issues unnecessary. The logical development of the key issues will enable the tribunal to more readily follow your argument and arrive at the conclusion that you are inviting it to make. Throughout the course of the oral hearing, counsel and the tribunal may overlook or minimize the law due to a focus on the development of the evidence. The use of a decision-tree analysis in closing provides an opportunity to revisit the core legal principles while serving as the framework driving the review and analysis of the material evidence in support of the findings that you are inviting the tribunal to make. The legal submissions must be very specific and clearly supported by the key legal authorities quoted. The number of authorities relied upon should be kept to a bare minimum, focusing only on the most persuasive authorities. There is no reason to cite five or more cases when one or two will do.

The closing should not simply be a rehash of the argument in the memorial or the opening submission. This is the time to focus on and highlight the good points and jettison the weak or bad points. Do not let the weak points detract from the clear strengths in the case. It is important to start with those strengths by stating the important conclusions in direct and emphatic language but without hyperbole. Make it clear that the review of the evidence will amply support those findings, and then ensure that the review does just that. The most relevant documents will have become apparent by the end of the hearing. Focus on those key documents in closing. Take the tribunal to them and quote from them. By the same token, do not waste time on documents of lesser or marginal relevance. In this age of email and texting, the documentary evidence is not just useful but critical in establishing the fundamental narrative for your case. The witness evidence from the statements and the cross-examinations will add important flesh to the skeletal narrative emerging from the documents. In reviewing that witness evidence on disputed issues of fact, you should address the credibility of the key conflicting witnesses and develop the reasons for preferring your own witness to the opponent's. In doing so, you should use the available evidence from the witness statements and transcripts of the cross-examinations. Quoting from those sources directly, particularly critical answers given on cross-examination, can be very persuasive with the tribunal. However, ensure that these quotations are read in their full context as that will enhance the tribunal's perception of your credibility and reliability. Caution and restraint should be exercised in calling a witness a liar or using other excessive language that may alienate the tribunal. It is better to carefully expose the discrepancies in the evidence and lead the tribunal to draw the obvious inference and conclusion. The expert evidence will likewise require a careful review that should expound on the reasons for preferring your own expert over the opponent's, whether relating to qualifications, independence, the scope of material reviewed, the reliability of assumptions made, or the reasonableness of the conclusions.

It will, of course, be important to highlight the weaknesses in the opponent's case. This will be done in part while reviewing the strengths in your own case by weaving appropriate submissions and comments into the argument. You can also then turn specifically to the opponent's case to list and accumulate a series of key weaknesses in that case. This can have a dramatic and persuasive impact on the tribunal.

To finish, come back to the main conclusions on liability and clearly state the specific relief sought in light of the full record. Usually by closing, the nature of the relief is already set in the submissions. However, it can evolve with the benefit of the oral evidence at the hearing. That is particularly true with questions of quantum of damages, which may well be adjusted due to the impact of cross-examination. In deliberations, the tribunal will come back to a clear closing statement of the relief sought.

J. CONCLUSION

Experienced Canadian dispute lawyers generally have excellent advocacy skills developed in court that can be readily adapted and applied to the arbitration context, for both domestic and international arbitration. However, it is important to recognize that arbitration is not court litigation. Adaptation is critical to ensure success in the arbitral forum and avoid procedural practices and mistakes that can undermine the presentation of one's case. It is hoped that the foregoing overview will assist more counsel in this process of adaptation. Counsel and their clients are encouraged to embrace the benefits of a faster, more flexible dispute process. Their commercial disputes, which cannot settle, will get to a hearing on the merits in a far more efficient and effective manner than is normally available in the court process.

chapter ten

Effective Commercial Arbitration: A Conversation with Robert Armstrong, Ian Binnie, and Stephen Goudge

SHANTONA CHAUDHURY

The following is a lightly edited transcript of a conversation I had on 3 October 2016 with three eminent former litigators and appellate judges who are now highly regarded commercial arbitrators. The Hon Robert P Armstrong, QC, retired from the Ontario Court of Appeal in 2013 and is now a resident arbitrator at Arbitration Place. The Hon W Ian C Binnie, CC, QC, retired from the Supreme Court of Canada in 2011 and is now a member arbitrator at Arbitration Place and counsel to Lenczner Slaght Royce Smith Griffin LLP. The Hon Stephen Goudge retired from the Ontario Court of Appeal in 2014 and is now counsel to Paliare Roland Rosenberg Rothstein LLP. These three distinguished arbitrators were kind enough to share their thoughts, experience, and wisdom on a number of topics relating to effective commercial arbitration.

A. ON ARBITRATION AS COMPARED WITH COURT ADJUDICATION

SC: *How does arbitration differ from court adjudication? Is it a more effective form of dispute resolution?*

SG: In my experience, the lawyers who present arbitration cases are a little more interested in getting to a result as effectively and efficiently as they can. And I think that has a whole lot of implications for the system. It means that preliminary objections are probably less frequent than they are in the counterpart commercial trial. It also means that there is often a willingness on the part of the lawyers to have the arbitrator be a little more interventionist. They're more amenable to informal discussion and exploration from the arbitrator about possible outcomes. My instinct because I do a lot of mediating as well is to slip into that mode instead of simply the silent cipher at the front of the room listening and then going away and deciding. So you have the arbitrator helping to do everything from narrowing the issues to helping people move along to a conclusion. And I think that that kind of flexibility is something that makes the arbitration process well worth studying as a kind of model for where the civil justice system needs to go.

SC: *That really puts you in a slightly different place as an arbitrator — like you say, more interventionist. So is arbitration more like a case-managed procedure?*

SG: Absolutely. And one really important point is having the same person carrying the case from start to finish.

RA: Right. Arbitration is very different because in court adjudication, you never see the trial judge until the day you finally get to court. The reverse happens in an arbitration in that the arbitrator is there from the beginning. And the arbitrator and counsel representing each side are in a kind of collegial mode, to get this thing done. You start with setting the hearing date and then work backwards from that date to any interlocutory stuff you want to do, such as pleadings and motions.

I guess the other thing, following on from Steve's point, is that although for many of us one motion is one too many — it's still not very many. You know, the tendency of some lawyers in our jurisdiction is to kind of motion something to death, but that doesn't happen in an arbitration. There are very few motions. And if the lawyers call me and say we need to bring a motion, sometimes I'll simply say "What's the issue?" and then they'll describe the issue, and I'll say "Well, isn't the answer to that either *x* or *y*? Can we not work it out somewhere between *x* and *y*?" And you get it done. From beginning to end, an arbitration is usually under a year.

So I think the role of the arbitrator is different than a trial judge's role in terms of the procedure and the timetable; it's very hands-on. But then when you get to a hearing and you're there hearing the evidence, then you just act how any other adjudicator would act.

The other thing is that there's very little examination-in-chief. The practice is to start a witness with an affidavit, and counsel on the other side simply cross-examine on the affidavit — and I think that really does focus the case. The hearing tends to be a lot more focused than in a trial. You don't get these long rambling cross-examinations which serve no other purpose than to repeat some lengthy examination for discovery two years before. They seem to accept that the parameters of the witness's evidence are the parameters set out in the affidavit, and then they proceed to focus on the cross-examination.

SC: *So do you think that's a good idea for the civil justice system too — i.e., getting rid of the examination-in-chief, starting from written affidavits, and going straight to cross-examination?*

IB: They do that in the Federal Court.

SC: *And in England too — the entire civil justice system, I believe.*

SG: I think it's absolutely the right thing to do. I think the bar has to get used to it, and I think the bench has to get used to it. It's a big challenge for the judge: the notion of having to come into court at ten o'clock in the morning fully familiar with the will-say — as opposed to absorbing it through a day in chief. The first time I ever did it in court was when Dennis O'Connor[1] and I had a trial in

1 The Hon Dennis R O'Connor, OC, QC, former Associate Chief Justice of the Ontario Court of Appeal.

front of Frank Callaghan.[2] It was a fairly major thing, and he wasn't very well, and it nearly killed him. So I think it's a bit of a cultural shift, but I think the system is moving in that direction. As Ian says, the Federal Court does it. And administrative tribunals do too — I mean the Ontario Energy Board has worked that way for ages.

RA: There may be the odd exception. Dennis O'Connor, Doug Cunningham,[3] and I were sitting around this table a month or two ago talking about our experiences with cross-examinations on affidavits. Sometimes when there is no warm-up from the witness at all and all you've done is read the affidavit and then the cross-examination starts maybe in the middle of the affidavit or at the end of the affidavit or on something that is tangential to the affidavit, you're a little bit at sea and almost wish there had been a kind of warm-up. But I think that's really the exception. And good counsel will figure a way to deal with that. I think it's the way to go.

IB: The other point when you're talking about motioning the other side to death is that there is a structural problem in our courts. Scheduling's terrible, apart from the Commercial List. And you can motion somebody to death because you're in front of a different judicial official every time you're at bat. You have to educate them on the case. In the United States, you get the judge, and the judge has a magistrate or junior or master-type official attached to them, and so all those applications go to the same judge or his or her assistant. And I don't think they get into these motion problems.

SG: It's worth spending a little time on the comparison between the domestic court system and the domestic arbitration system because it seems to me that says a lot about the conduct of lawyers and the way results can be produced. It seems to me that arbitration is showing the way in a whole lot of respects. Bob's identified two or three very important distinctions: a single man-

2 The Hon Frank W Callaghan, former Chief Justice, Ontario Court of Justice, General Division.

3 The Hon J Douglas Cunningham, QC, former Associate Chief Justice of the Ontario Superior Court of Justice.

ager of the dispute having it from start to finish; not having evidence-in-chief but rather going on will-say statements. The good thing about arbitration is that what motivates everybody is "let's get to a reasonable result as expeditiously as we can." I'm not sure that's true of every court proceeding.

IB: I think all of the things that have been mentioned are perfectly workable in the court structure. They've been adopted by many courts. It's the reluctance of the Canadian court system to get up to speed (apart from commercial courts) — that's why these problems persist. There's no reason why you can't have a rule to use affidavits as the examination-in-chief, as in the Federal Court. There's no reason why you can't call all of the experts and put them in a box together to fight it out in full view, as in the Federal Court. There's no reason why you can't have the motions go to a single official, whether a prothonotary in the Federal Court or a master or a judge. All of these things, it's true, can be done in arbitration because it's flexible. But it's the fault of the court system for not adapting and adopting common sense reform.

SG: I agree with that. Although it's certainly against my interest as an arbitrator that they should move too quickly!

SC: *Following on from what Bob said earlier about the timeline of an arbitration being under a year from beginning to end and from what Steve said about counsel being in a collegial mode to "get it done" — that's really quite a different mindset than many counsel and parties have in the court system, isn't it? Especially for defendants the strategy often seems to be delay, delay, delay, motion, motion, motion, bleed the other side to death costswise, and it will all eventually go away. So when you walk into an arbitration, you really need two parties who are committed to the same goal, which is getting a result one way or the other, no?*

SG: Often in arbitrations, it's a dispute that is entirely commercial between two parties who have an ongoing or repetitive relationship, so they're interested in getting the dispute behind them and moving on. It's not a one-off situation where there's been a human relationship that has fallen apart with the emotional angst that that creates. So there is likely to be some rationality in the arbitration context that doesn't always exist in the courtroom.

B. ON PRIVATE ARBITRATION VERSUS PUBLIC ARBITRATION

IB: Of course, there's another aspect to this that goes to why commercial entities like arbitration: A huge issue in consumer cases is avoiding class actions, and a lot of companies love putting in arbitration clauses and picking off claimants one at a time and avoiding both the financial exposure and the publicity of a court case. The courts have the potential to play a major public interest role in ventilating things in public; and quite often arbitrating parties have an equal interest, at least on one side, in keeping the whole thing in the closet.

SG: That's something we haven't talked about, but it's really worth emphasizing — the privacy that goes along with a typical arbitration, which is something that often parties have a real incentive to achieve.

RA: I guess my view is that an ordinary business person comes to arbitration not necessarily because of the things we're talking about but because the hearing will be in private and because they get to pick the judge. And that's the big attraction to the lay person who wants their case decided.

IB: Also finality and lack of appeal. You get a result that is enforceable.

SG: That part is quite understandable. But, you know, the first one I did that was entirely cloaked with privacy left me feeling a bit queasy. Having spent my entire adjudicative career in the public domain — you sort of feel like you're part of a little cabal, with a dirty little secret that nobody else will know.

IB: Which is why arbitral processes are increasingly being opened up, whether under NAFTA or some of these arbitrations which on their face are commercial and private but which have a public interest aspect. Bob, that blue box case, which blew apart the confidentiality provisions — the whole attraction of arbitrations!

RA: Well, that was interesting. There was an arbitration between approximately 250 municipalities and Stewardship Ontario, who are the industrial members that contributed to the blue boxes in one way or another. The municipalities were responsible for 50 percent of the cost, and Stewardship Ontario (the people who required the blue box to get rid of their newspapers, cans, bottles, and so on) paid the other 50 percent. There was an arbitration provision developed in 2014, and so I was asked to decide what the annual cost was for 2014. The first issue that was raised by the municipalities was that they wanted the hearing to be public, and Stewardship Ontario said, "No, this is a private arbitration, and private arbitrations are intended to be confidential — intended, in fact, to be private." So I heard a long argument on that and then wrote a decision on it. And I decided that absent an express provision that it was to be in private, the public interest demanded that this kind of arbitration, where public funding was at issue, be public.

SG: Did you then go on to hear the case?

RA: Yes, I did. I said it should be held in public, and it was. The interesting thing was at the time I wrote the judgment, I didn't think there would be a long lineup at the door for the public to get in. And there wasn't. But the fact of the matter was that it was a public arbitration.

SG: Do you think it changed the way counsel conducted it? That would be the worry that I'd have. I have always felt when I'm doing a private arbitration in a commercial dispute that arbitration promotes efficiency because nobody is grandstanding. But if it's going to be open to the public — I mean you had all these municipalities under public scrutiny — did that change the atmosphere?

RA: It didn't in this case. And I think on the whole counsel were not playing for the camera, as it were.

IB: I think what this illustrates, though, is the power of an arbitrator. In this case Bob destroyed one of the three main advantages of arbitration — depressed the market for the rest of us!

SG: What's your instinct about my question, Ian? Do you think a private arbitration tends toward more efficiency than an arbitration that's done in public?

IB: I think probably counsel who argue are more circumspect about what they're prepared to say. But we've all had experience in public inquiries that are televised, and in my experience, as Bob said, you forgot the camera was there. Everybody carried on as they would have done without the camera being present.

SG: It may not be as big an advantage for arbitrations as some of us tend to think it is — that it's usually done in private.

IB: I think if you're dealing with two major companies, it may be important to them that it not be known that they're in this fight. There could be many reasons for confidentiality other than that there's going to be some dirt disclosed. I think that having a confidential process by and large works. But I do think that where the public interest impinges, as in Bob's case or as in these consumer cases, they should be moved into the public forum. It's not in the larger public interest to have them decided behind a closed door.

C. ON ARBITRATION'S EFFECT ON THE DEVELOPMENT OF THE COMMON LAW

SG: In respect of private arbitration, I remember worrying when we were all judges about what happens to the commercial law if you have a plethora of private arbitrations engaging commercial law that nobody knows about.

IB: I'll take a first stab at that. I think it's an absolutely legitimate point that the source of jurisprudence is drying up, but that's the fault of the court system. We've had various evenings at Arbitration Place with general counsel from different companies, and they essentially still have great faith in the Ontario–Canadian court system. They don't feel driven by the inadequacies of the system to arbitration. If the system adjusted itself to address some of the items we've been talking about, it would be very competitive with arbitration. Cases would move at more or less the same speed. Stewardship by one judge or master over the interlocutory proceedings would hasten things. You would get a trial date instead of a court administrator calling you on Friday saying, "I'm sorry. I don't have a judge for you on Monday," and you go to the bottom of the list or whatever. So I think the courts can make themselves attractive. In the Supreme Court of Canada, the Court was actually *looking* for commercial work to take on because it was perceived that the Court was not as present in that area of the law as it should have been and there was precious little coming out of the appellate courts in the provinces.

SC: *Just to push back at that for a second, Ian, in terms of making the court system more relevant, more attractive, more efficient — that's kind of what the Commercial List is trying to do, isn't it?*

IB: Yes, absolutely. I think all of the counsel that I speak to are hugely complimentary about the Commercial List: good judges, knowledgeable judges who aim to move things to a solution as quickly as they can. So the courts can do it, and the courts have made a better job of it in other jurisdictions. And it would, as Steve says, result in a much richer corporate commercial jurisprudence.

SG: They do it, in large part, by emulating arbitration — where a judge will be supervising a case and taking it through the various stages and then trying to get a resolution on a fixed date.

IB: I think that was the system at least in some of the states south of the border long before arbitration acquired its present popularity. But here there is definitely a tension between the courts and arbitration, with each looking to its own turf.

D. ON THE ETHICAL IMPLICATIONS OF THE ENTREPRENEURIAL NATURE OF ARBITRATION

IB: I would like to raise what I think is a big problem in arbitration — which is what I call the entrepreneurial nature of it. People who live by a constant stream of arbitration work are in the same position as lawyers who are always looking for the next case and are insecure about getting it. And I don't know to what extent this applies in Ontario, but the English counsel will say that their clients all keep a very careful record of which arbitrator decides in which way. If the arbitrator to a three-arbitrator panel doesn't bring home the bacon, then certainly the theory in England is that's the end of that arbitrator's stream of work.

And it surely has an impact on the arbitrator, who (unlike a judge, who's functioning on pensionable time) has to earn a living.

RA: I don't know. I mean, I always assumed when I hung up my shingle as an arbitrator that while everybody around might well give me a first run at something, once I started deciding cases and 50 percent of the people before me lost, that 50 percent may well say, "You know, we're not going back to Armstrong." And I couldn't care less!

IB: Well, you couldn't care less because you've got a nice judicial pension! A lot of arbitrators don't have a judicial pension. They're in it as lawyers practising law. Anyhow, the issue is more with a three-person arbitral panel.

SG: Where you have nominees?

IB: Where you have nominees. And where sometimes the expectation of the appointing party is at odds with what should be the protocol.

SG: I think that's true, Ian. I've sat much more as a single arbitrator than as a member of a panel, and it would never occur to me that I might get repeat business.

IB: But I think this is a distinction between the single arbitrator and the panel because clearly inevitably in a single-arbitrator situation there's a winner and a loser. In a three-person arbitration, the client is saying "I appointed Armstrong, and he wasn't able to persuade the chair to his point of view."

SG: Well, apart from the obvious solution of limiting those who can do commercial arbitrations to those on pension, like retired judges, how do you solve that problem?

Maybe that's the solution: the single biggest bane of the existence of commercial arbitration is those who engage in it, without an economic foundation! [laughter]

SC: *Thanks to all of you for taking the (non-pensionable) time to share your wisdom and experience with us.*

chapter eleven

Court Involvement in Commercial Arbitration

J BRIAN CASEY

A. INTRODUCTION

The extent to which the courts in Canada become involved in the arbitral process is now governed expressly by legislation. Historically at common law, the courts had a general supervisory jurisdiction respecting the conduct of arbitrations and a decidedly negative view that any issues of law or legal rights should not be adjudicated outside of a state's judicial regime. The modern view in Canada is that arbitration does not form part of the judicial system of any province[1] but operates as an autonomous dispute resolution regime in which court involvement is generally restricted to the following:[2]

1) requiring parties to honour their obligations under arbitration agreements
2) supervising the conduct of the arbitration and the arbitrators to the extent permitted by legislation
3) providing assistance in the conduct of the arbitration when requested
4) enforcing arbitral awards regardless of where they were made

1 See *Desputeaux v Éditions Chouette (1987) inc*, [2003] 1 SCR 178 at paras 40–41.

2 See, for example, *Arbitration Act*, RSA 2000, c A-43, s 6.

All of the common law provinces make a distinction between domestic and international arbitration. In this chapter, legislation dealing with international arbitration is referred to as the international Act or the *UNCITRAL Model Law*. Legislation dealing with arbitration not covered by the international Act is referred to as the domestic Act.

For international commercial arbitrations, every common law province has adopted the *UNCITRAL Model Law on International Commercial Arbitration*,[3] which provides for very limited court involvement. Most of the common law provinces have also promulgated modern domestic arbitration legislation based on the *UNCITRAL Model Law*. The federal government and Quebec have each passed arbitration legislation based on the *UNCITRAL Model Law* that covers all commercial arbitrations within their jurisdiction. It is thus important when considering whether or not a court can intervene in an arbitration to determine whether the arbitration is considered domestic or international under the appropriate legislation.

Pursuant to the *UNCITRAL Model Law*, an arbitration is international if one of the following is true:

1) The parties to the arbitration agreement have at the time of its conclusion their places of business in different countries.
2) One of the parties has its place of business outside Canada.
3) A substantial part of the obligations of the commercial relationship is to be performed outside Canada.
4) The place of the subject matter of the dispute is most closely connected with a place outside Canada.
5) The parties have agreed that the arbitration is international.[4]

As a further requirement to come within a province's international Act, the arbitration must be considered "commercial." The British Columbia international Act specifically includes a definition of "commercial" in section 1(6):

3 21 June 1985, UN Doc A/40/17, annex 1, online: www.uncitral.org/pdf/english/texts/arbitration/ml-arb/06-54671_Ebook.pdf [*UNCITRAL Model Law*].

4 *Ibid*, art 1.

An arbitration is commercial if it arises out of a relationship of a commercial nature including, but not limited to, the following:

(a) a trade transaction for the supply or exchange of goods or services;
(b) a distribution agreement;
(c) a commercial representation or agency;
(d) an exploitation agreement or concession;
(e) a joint venture or other related form of industrial or business cooperation;
(f) the carriage of goods or passengers by air, sea, rail or road;
(g) the construction of works;
(h) insurance;
(i) licensing;
(j) factoring;
(k) leasing;
(l) consulting;
(m) engineering;
(n) financing;
(o) banking;
(p) investing.[5]

Note that employment is not one of the listed categories. An ordinary employment contract is not sufficiently commercial to engage the international commercial arbitration legislation. In *Patel v Kanbay International Inc*,[6] the Ontario Court of Appeal made particular reference to the analytical commentary contained in a secretary-general report to the General Assembly of the United Nations, which specifically states that labour or employment disputes do not constitute a commercial legal relationship pursuant to the *UNCITRAL Model Law*.[7] The fact that an employment contract is not sufficiently commercial does not mean that the arbitration agreement is void. It simply means that the province's

5 *International Commercial Arbitration Act*, RSBC 1996, c 233, s 1(6).
6 2008 ONCA 867.
7 *International Commercial Arbitration: Analytical Commentary on Draft Text of a Model Law on International Commercial Arbitration — Report of the Secretary-General*, UNCITRAL Docs, 18th Sess, UN Doc A/CN.9/264 (1985) art 1 at para 18.

international commercial arbitration act is not applicable and that any arbitration would be governed by the province's domestic Act.

1) Checklist: Determining the Applicable Act

The first question to ask in determining the extent of court involvement in an arbitration is whether the arbitration is governed by a province's international or domestic Act. The following checklist may assist:

1) Is the place or seat of the arbitration within the province?
2) Does the arbitration agreement specify a particular Act?[8]
3) At the time of signing the arbitration agreement, did at least one party have its place of business outside Canada?
4) Was a substantial part of the contract to be performed outside Canada?
5) Is the subject matter of the dispute most closely connected with a place outside Canada?

If the answer is yes to question 1, yes to any one of questions 3, 4, or 5, and no to question 2, then the arbitration is governed by the province's international Act.[9]

B. APPOINTING ARBITRATORS

All of the domestic and international Acts provide for the court's assistance with the appointment of an arbitrator either if the parties are unable to agree on the process for such appointment or if a process has been agreed but if one of the parties has failed to carry out its obligations thereunder.

---

8 The extent to which parties can specify that a province's domestic Act is to apply to an international arbitration is beyond the scope of this chapter. See the discussion in J Brian Casey, *Arbitration Law of Canada: Practice and Procedure*, 3d ed (Huntington, NY: Juris, 2017) at 477.

9 This analysis is not applicable if the arbitration is in Quebec or in an area of federal jurisdiction because, as stated above, Quebec and the federal government each have one law for all arbitrations.

The *UNCITRAL Model Law* provides as follows in article 11(4):

> Where, under an appointment procedure agreed upon by the parties,
> (a) a party fails to act as required under such procedure, or
> (b) the parties, or two arbitrators, are unable to reach an agreement expected of them under such procedure, or
> (c) a third party, including an institution, fails to perform any function entrusted to it under such procedure,
>
> any party may request the court or other authority specified in article 6 to take the necessary measure, unless the agreement on the appointment procedure provides other means for securing the appointment.[10]

The domestic Acts all have similar provisions. For example, the Ontario domestic Act provides as follows in section 10:

> (1) The court may appoint the arbitral tribunal, on a party's application, if,
> (a) the arbitration agreement provides no procedure for appointing the arbitral tribunal; or
> (b) a person with power to appoint the arbitral tribunal has not done so after a party has given the person seven days notice to do so.[11]

There are no guidelines in the domestic Acts regarding how a court should approach the question of who to appoint. Under the *UNCITRAL Model Law*, in making an appointment, the court is to have due regard to the following:[12]

1) any qualifications required of the arbitrator by the agreement of the parties
2) such considerations as are likely to secure the appointment of an independent and impartial arbitrator

---

10 Above note 3, art 11(4).

11 *Arbitration Act, 1991*, SO 1991, c 17, s 10.

12 Above note 3, art 11(5).

3) where it is a sole or third arbitrator, "the advisability of appointing an arbitrator of a nationality other than those of the parties"

1) Checklist: Court Appointment of an Arbitrator

The application to the court for the appointment of an arbitrator is made under the applicable procedural court rules in force in the province, supported by appropriate affidavit evidence. The supporting material should include the following:

1) a description of the nature of the dispute and amounts involved
2) a list of two or three candidates
3) the current curricula vitae of the proposed arbitrators
4) if appropriate, transcripts of any interviews or questions and answers exchanged with the proposed arbitrators
5) written statements from the proposed arbitrators that they agree to act
6) statements from the proposed arbitrators that they are aware of no circumstances that could give rise to any reasonable apprehension of bias (if under a domestic Act) or to justifiable doubts as to their impartiality or independence (if under the *UNCITRAL Model Law*)

C. CHALLENGE TO AN ARBITRATOR

The fundamental concept in arbitration is that the arbitrator must not only be but also appear to be independent of the parties and impartial respecting both the parties and the nature of the dispute. Of equal importance is the requirement that the arbitrator must at all times treat the parties fairly and equally, giving each a reasonable opportunity to be heard. As stated by Horner J of the Alberta Court of Queen's Bench, "When the principles of natural justice are involved, the mere appearance of unfairness is sufficient to justify the court's supervision."[13]

13 *Flock v Flock*, 2007 ABQB 307 at para 62.

1) Challenge at the Time of Appointment

The *UNCITRAL Model Law* states as follows:

> *Article 12. Grounds for challenge*
> (1) When a person is approached in connection with his possible appointment as an arbitrator, he shall disclose any circumstances likely to give rise to justifiable doubts as to his impartiality or independence. An arbitrator, from the time of his appointment and throughout the arbitral proceedings, shall without delay disclose any such circumstances to the parties unless they have already been informed of them by him.
>
> (2) An arbitrator may be challenged only if circumstances exist that give rise to justifiable doubts as to his impartiality or independence, or if he does not possess qualifications agreed to by the parties. A party may challenge an arbitrator appointed by him, or in whose appointment he has participated, only for reasons of which he becomes aware after the appointment has been made.[14]

The Ontario domestic Act states as follows in section 13:

> (1) A party may challenge an arbitrator only on one of the following grounds:
>
> 1. Circumstances exist that may give rise to a reasonable apprehension of bias.
> 2. The arbitrator does not possess qualifications that the parties have agreed are necessary.
>
> (2) A party who appointed an arbitrator or participated in his or her appointment may challenge the arbitrator only for grounds of which the party was unaware at the time of the appointment.[15]

The domestic Acts speak of "a reasonable apprehension of bias" while the international Acts use the phrase "justifiable doubts as to his impartiality or independence." Ultimately, the test is the same.

14 Above note 3, art 12.

15 Above note 12, s 13.

As stated by the Supreme Court of Canada, "Each party, acting reasonably, is entitled to sustained confidence in the independence of mind of those who are to sit in judgment on him and his affairs."[16]

The New Brunswick Court of Appeal decision in *Rothesay Residents Assn Inc v Rothesay Heritage Preservation & Review Board* sets out the general categories under which a reasonable apprehension of bias may be found:

> The first category involves the decision-maker who has a financial interest in the outcome of the matter being decided. The second is tied to cases in which the decision-maker's impartiality is challenged because of a personal relationship with one or more of the parties or some other person who has a significant role in the case, such as legal counsel or an important witness. The third category consists of cases in which the decision-maker has acquired outside knowledge of or has been involved with the matter in some capacity other than his or her current capacity as a decision-maker. The fourth category is tied to the inappropriate behavior of the decision-maker, whether it comes in the form of words or actions. Cases within this category are sometimes described as "actual bias" cases. Parenthetically, note that the plea of waiver can have no application in cases where the bias allegation is tied to what is said or done during the decision-making process. Finally, the fifth category involves "institutional" arrangements that are said to give rise to a reasonable apprehension of bias. Bias in these cases is generated by the structure or operation of a decision-making body, rather than by the words or actions of an individual decision-maker . . . .[17]

In *Committee for Justice and Liberty v Canada (National Energy Board)*, de Grandpré J sets out the test to be applied in determining an allegation of reasonable apprehension of bias on the part of an adjudicator:

16 *Szilard v Szasz*, [1955] SCR 3 at 7.

17 2006 NBCA 61 at para 14.

> the apprehension of bias must be a reasonable one, held by reasonable and right minded persons, applying themselves to the question and obtaining thereon the required information. In the words of the Court of Appeal, that test is "what would an informed person, viewing the matter realistically and practically — and having thought the matter through — conclude. Would he think that it is more likely than not that [the adjudicator], whether consciously or unconsciously, would not decide fairly."[18]

The mere assertion of bias is not enough, nor will mere suspicion suffice. The burden to rebut the presumption of integrity falls on the party making the allegation. There must be a real likelihood or probability of bias. "'Surmise or conjecture is not enough.'"[19] In *Simcoe Condominium Corporation No 78 v Simcoe Condominium Corporation Nos 50, 52, 53, 56, 59, 63 and 64,* the test is put this way:

> The basic legal principles relating to reasonable apprehension of bias can be summarized as follows. The test of reasonable apprehension of bias applies to arbitrators in the same manner as it applies to courts. The threshold for a finding of real or perceived bias is high because it calls into question both the personal integrity of the adjudicator and the integrity of the administration of justice. The grounds must be substantial and the onus is on the party alleging bias to bring forward the evidence. The inquiry is highly fact-specific. The test for showing reasonable apprehension of bias is an objective test. A real likelihood of bias must be demonstrated; mere suspicion is not enough. The test is "what would an informed person, viewing the matter realistically and practically, and having thought the matter through, conclude:" . . .[20]

---

18 [1978] 1 SCR 369 at 394.

19 *R v Pickersgill* (1970), 14 DLR (3d) 717 at 723 (Man QB). See also *R v Camborne Justices,* [1954] 2 All ER 850; *Metropolitan Properties Co (FGC) Ltd v Lannon,* [1968] 3 All ER 304 at 310.

20 [2006] OJ No 605 at para 57 (SCJ).

The test is whether on the facts a reasonable person would decide that consciously or unconsciously the arbitrator is seized with an attitude of or predilection for bias whereby she must be taken to have prejudged the matter.[21] The inquiry in each case is highly fact specific.[22]

Problems can often arise where the arbitrator is or has been a partner in a large law firm. Few law firms have set up a conflicts system to address the particular obligations of partners who may act as arbitrators.[23] In *Canadian Royalties Inc v Nearctic Nickel Mines Inc*, a decision of the Quebec Superior Court, the sole arbitrator was a partner in a large law firm.[24] Unknown to the respondent, and presumably unknown to the arbitrator, his firm had acted for the Bank of Montreal, which was an underwriter of the securities offerings made by the claimant. In this position, the firm would have been involved in giving opinions on the transactions that were at issue in the arbitration. In setting aside the arbitration award, Pinsonnault J stated as follows:

> What would a person reasonably informed of all those relevant facts have concluded under such circumstances?
>
> It is important to bear in mind that the appearance of conflict of interest is as compelling as the conflict of interest itself.
>
> The Court finds that for the purposes hereof, it is not necessary or even useful to examine in detail if the relationship between Fasken, the Underwriters and CRI actually resulted in a situation of conflict of interest with a member of Fasken acting as sole arbitrator in a bitter dispute between CRI and the Defendants.[25]

---

21 See *R v Pickersgill*, above note 19; *Newfoundland Light & Power Co v Newfoundland (Public Utilities Commission)* (1987), 37 DLR (4th) 35 (Nfld CA), leave to appeal to SCC refused (1987), 65 Nfld & PEIR 270 (note) (SCC).

22 See *R v RDS*, [1997] 3 SCR 484.

23 In particular, arbitrators are to disclose whether their firm has acted for not only a party but also a parent, subsidiary, or affiliate or expert or other witness.

24 2016 QCCS 4828.

25 *Ibid* at paras 126–28.

In *Jacob Securities Inc v Typhoon Capital BV*, the arbitrator was a retired partner of a large law firm.[26] At the time of his appointment, he advised the parties that he had had no previous dealings with the parties or the principals of the corporations involved in the dispute. In providing his answers, he did not undertake a conflict search with his former firm. Unknown to him, his former firm had a relationship with related entities and with a witness in the arbitration. Justice Mew first made a distinction between arbitrators who are still members of a firm and those who have retired. An arbitrator who is a partner of, or otherwise works for, a law firm has a positive duty to investigate any potential conflicts of interest with her law firm to satisfy her disclosure obligations. Justice Mew agreed with the decision in *HSMV Corp v ADI Ltd*,[27] a decision of the US District Court for the Central District of California, that an arbitrator is obligated to conduct a conflict check to see whether she must disclose any circumstances that might cause her impartiality to be questioned.

Where, however, the arbitrator has retired from a firm, Mew J held that different considerations apply. First, he was not persuaded that a former partner of a firm had any duty to conduct a conflict search. Finding the duty of an arbitrator to be the same as a judge, he stated as follows:

> I am aware of no authority which imposes on judges, recently appointed or otherwise, a duty to ask their former firms to conduct conflict searches for the names of all parties to the cases which the judge deals with. Judges will typically know the clients they acted for when they were lawyers as well as other major clients of their former firms. But they cannot possibly know or be expected to know every client that their former firms acted for. I do not see why the position of an arbitrator who is in independent practice and who is no longer associated with a law firm should be any different. As with the judge in *Rando Drugs*, the Arbitrator was unaware of the facts relied upon by the applicant as giving

26 2016 ONSC 604.

27 72 F Supp 2d 1122 (CD Cal 1999).

> rise to a conflict of interest. The notion that a judge or arbitrator must make a concerted effort to search for hitherto unknown conflicts from a firm that he or she no longer works with would be a burdensome exercise and wholly disproportionate response to the duty to disclose.[28]

Further, the judge noted that the arbitrator had not had access to the firm's conflicts system and that law firms owe a duty to their clients not to disclose confidential information to third parties, which would include former partners.

These two cases point out the real dangers that can arise in large law firms with respect to conflicts. Further, unless a sophisticated conflicts system is in place, the arbitrator may not know whether a new matter has been taken on by another office of her firm, yet for conflicts purposes all offices of the firm are treated as one entity, and the arbitrator has a continuing duty to be diligent.

Retired judges also have an obligation of disclosure. Under the guidelines for disclosure established by the International Bar Association, a retired judge is to disclose whether he has within the previous three years heard a significant case involving one of the parties or an affiliate of one of the parties.[29]

2) Removal during the Arbitration

The Ontario domestic Act states as follows in section 15(1):

> The court may remove an arbitrator on a party's application under subsection 13 (6) (challenge), or may do so on a party's application if the arbitrator becomes unable to perform his or her functions, commits a corrupt or fraudulent act, delays unduly in conducting the arbitration or does not conduct it in accordance with section 19 (equality and fairness).[30]

---

28 Above note 27 at para 58.

29 International Bar Association, *IBA Guidelines on Conflicts of Interest in International Arbitration* (London: IBA, 2014), online: www.ibanet.org/Publications/publications_IBA_guides_and_free_materials.aspx.

30 Above note 12, s 15(1).

The *UNCITRAL Model Law* uses different language, but the legal effect is the same:

> If an arbitrator becomes *de jure* or *de facto* unable to perform his functions or for other reasons fails to act without undue delay, his mandate terminates if he withdraws from his office or if the parties agree on the termination. Otherwise, if a controversy remains concerning any of these grounds, any party may request the court or other authority specified in article 6 to decide on the termination of the mandate, which decision shall be subject to no appeal.[31]

The British Columbia domestic Act provides for the removal of an arbitrator who "unduly delays" the proceeding or who has committed an "arbitral error."[32] Arbitral error is defined as corrupt or fraudulent conduct, bias, exceeding the arbitrator's powers, or failing to observe the rules of natural justice.[33]

A reasonable apprehension of a bias may arise where there is no previous involvement with any of the interested parties but where the arbitrator has made statements or expressed opinions that could give rise to a reasonable apprehension of bias or prejudgment of the case.[34] Other examples of misconduct that has given rise to an application to remove an arbitrator include the following situations: where the arbitrator has been given information prejudicial to one party that might otherwise not be admissible in the arbitration,[35] where the arbitrator has had private discussions with one of the parties,[36] and where undue delay has prejudiced a party.[37]

---

31 Above note 3, art 14(1).

32 *Arbitration Act*, RSBC 1996, c 55, s 18(1).

33 *Ibid*, s 1.

34 See *R v Pickersgill*, above note 19.

35 See *Canadian Union of Postal Workers v Canada Post Corporation*, 1998 CanLII 8569 (FCA).

36 See *King-Yonge Properties Ltd v Great-West Life Assurance Co* (1989), 44 BLR 110 (Ont CA).

37 See *Flock v Flock*, above note 14.

In many cases, the parties are quite content with the chosen arbitrator until one of the parties loses. The courts have a healthy suspicion when after having participated in the process without complaint, the losing party then tries to have a final award set aside based on a complaint respecting the impartiality or independence of the arbitrator. In *1513183 Ontario Inc v Pelts*, Lauwers J stated as follows:

> My sense is that the Respondents were so distressed by the draft report of the Arbitrator that they decided not to participate further, and instead decided to do everything they could to bring the arbitration to an end. I find that the challenge was not made in good faith and in accordance with the *Arbitration Act*. It was intended to drop a bomb on the arbitration process in the hope of ending it because the Respondents did not like the results that were signalled by the draft report. This kind of opportunistic tactic by a party to an arbitration is to be discouraged by the court.[38]

Both the *UNCITRAL Model Law* and the domestic Acts provide that a party will be deemed to have waived its right to challenge an arbitrator if the circumstances are known but are not acted on in a timely fashion. The *UNCITRAL Model Law* states as follows:

> *Article 4. Waiver of right to object*
> A party who knows that any provision of this Law from which the parties may derogate or any requirement under the arbitration agreement has not been complied with and yet proceeds with the arbitration without stating his objection to such non-compliance without undue delay or, if a time-limit is provided therefor, within such period of time, shall be deemed to have waived his right to object.[39]

The domestic Acts are to the same effect. For example, the Ontario domestic Act states as follows in section 4(1):

38 2010 ONSC 4863 at para 45.

39 Above note 3, art 4.

> "A party who participates in an arbitration despite being aware of non-compliance with a provision of this Act, except one mentioned in section 3, or with the arbitration agreement, and does not object to the non-compliance within the time limit provided or, if none is provided, within a reasonable time, shall be deemed to have waived the right to object.[40]

The lesson here for both the arbitrator and counsel is to disclose any and all circumstances that might give rise to any challenge at the earliest opportunity and, if necessary, to act on such information in a timely manner.

3) Challenge Procedure

The *UNCITRAL Model Law*[41] and the domestic Acts[42] set out detailed procedures for challenging an arbitrator. The British Columbia domestic Act incorporates the rules of the British Columbia International Commercial Arbitration Centre for the conduct of domestic commercial arbitrations including those with respect to challenging an arbitrator unless the parties agree otherwise.[43]

Where the arbitration is ad hoc under either a domestic Act or the *UNCITRAL Model Law*, a challenge regarding a reasonable apprehension of bias first goes to the tribunal, including the challenged arbitrator, for a decision. Only if the tribunal refuses to remove the arbitrator does the matter go to court. But if the challenge is on the grounds that the arbitrator is unable to perform her functions, has committed a corrupt or fraudulent act, delays unduly in conducting the arbitration, or does not conduct it in accordance with equality and fairness, then the challenge goes directly to court. In all cases, the time limits for bringing a challenge are short. For example, under the Ontario domestic Act a party must send the arbitral tribunal a statement of the grounds

40 Above note 12, s 4(1).

41 Above note 3, art 13 and 15.

42 See, for example, Ontario domestic Act, above note 12, ss 13 and 15.

43 Above note 33, s 22.

for the challenge within fifteen days of becoming aware of them. Then, if the arbitral tribunal does not remove the arbitrator, the party must within ten days of being notified of the tribunal's decision make an application to the court to decide the challenge.[44]

Under the Ontario domestic Act, if the application to remove the arbitrator is based on allegations that he has committed a corrupt or fraudulent act or delayed unduly in conducting the arbitration, the arbitrator has the right to be heard by the court.[45] Under the Alberta, Saskatchewan, and Manitoba domestic Acts, the arbitrator has the right to be heard in any court application seeking his removal.[46] If the court removes the arbitrator for committing a corrupt or fraudulent act or for delaying unduly, it may order that the arbitrator receive no payment for services and that compensation be paid to the parties for all or part of the costs that have been incurred in connection with the arbitration before the arbitrator's removal.[47] Such an order may be appealed to the Court of Appeal with leave of that court.[48] Except for this appeal provision, regarding any penalty imposed on the arbitrator, there is no appeal from a court decision respecting the arbitrator's removal.[49]

The Ontario Divisional Court in *Senjule v Law Society of Upper Canada* has held that where there is an allegation of a denial of natural justice or procedural fairness, the court will review the record and determine whether the applicant has been denied natural justice or procedural fairness on a reasonableness test.[50]

44 Above note 12, s 13. Under the *UNCITRAL Model Law*, above note 3, art 13, a party has thirty days to apply to the court.

45 Above note 12, s 15(2).

46 Alberta domestic Act, above note 2, s 15(2); *The Arbitration Act, 1992*, SS 1992, c A-24.1, s 16(2); *The Arbitration Act*, CCSM c A120, s 15(2).

47 Ontario domestic Act, above note 12, s 15(4).

48 *Ibid*, s 15(5).

49 *Ibid*, s 15(6).

50 2013 ONSC 2817 (Div Ct). See also *Nasjjec Investments Ltd v Nuyork Investments Ltd*, 2015 ONSC 4978.

D. COURT REVIEW OF JURISDICTION

If a party has any objection to the arbitrator's jurisdiction, it is to be raised as soon as possible. By continuing to participate in the arbitration without complaint while knowing of the jurisdictional issue, the party may be taken to have tacitly agreed to give the arbitrator jurisdiction. The question of the arbitrator's jurisdiction is first decided by the arbitrator.

The domestic Acts and the *UNCITRAL Model Law* provide for immediate court review of a tribunal's preliminary decision that it has jurisdiction to conduct the arbitration. For example, the Ontario domestic Act provides as follows in section 17:

> (3) A party who has an objection to the arbitral tribunal's jurisdiction to conduct the arbitration shall make the objection no later than the beginning of the hearing or, if there is no hearing, no later than the first occasion on which the party submits a statement to the tribunal.
>
> (5) A party who has an objection that the arbitral tribunal is exceeding its authority shall make the objection as soon as the matter alleged to be beyond the tribunal's authority is raised during the arbitration. . . .
>
> (7) The arbitral tribunal may rule on an objection as a preliminary question or may deal with it in an award.
>
> (8) If the arbitral tribunal rules on an objection as a preliminary question, a party may, within thirty days after receiving notice of the ruling, make an application to the court to decide the matter.[51]

The objection that "the arbitral tribunal is exceeding its authority" refers to the tribunal's authority to decide the substance or subject matter of the dispute. As stated by Sharpe JA, "The words 'jurisdiction to conduct the arbitration' in s. 17(1) connote jurisdiction over the entire substance or subject matter of the case, not jurisdiction to make interlocutory or procedural orders that do

51 Above note 12, s 17.

not determine the merits of the dispute and that are made along the way to final resolution of the issues."[52]

This review procedure applies only where the tribunal's decision is made as a preliminary award on jurisdiction. If the tribunal does not rule on jurisdiction as a preliminary matter but includes its decision on jurisdiction in the final award, then the appropriate provisions for challenging a final award apply. Challenging a final award is discussed in Chapters 15 and 16.

Under the *UNCITRAL Model Law*, a plea that the tribunal has no jurisdiction to decide the claimant's claims is to be raised no later than the submission of the statement of the respondent. During the hearing, a plea that the tribunal is exceeding the scope of its authority must be raised as soon as the matter alleged to be beyond the scope of its authority is raised during the arbitral proceedings.[53]

As with the domestic Acts, under the *UNCITRAL Model Law* an arbitral tribunal may rule on a plea of exceeding its jurisdiction as a preliminary question or in its award. A party cannot first go to the court. The issue of jurisdiction must be raised and determined at first instance by the arbitral tribunal. If the tribunal rules that it has jurisdiction, any party may request within thirty days after having received notice of the ruling that the court decide the matter. The court's decision is not subject to appeal. While a request to the court is pending, the tribunal may continue the arbitral proceeding and make an award.[54]

1) Standard of Review

There is a question about the standard of review to be employed by the court on a jurisdictional challenge. The domestic Acts and

52 *Inforica Inc v CGI Information Systems and Management Consultants Inc*, 2009 ONCA 642 at para 16. See also *1210558 Ontario Inc v 1464255 Ontario Limited*, 2011 ONSC 5810; *Suncor Energy Inc v Alberta*, 2013 ABQB 728 [*Suncor Energy*].

53 Above note 3, art 16(2). As with the domestic Acts, under the *UNCITRAL Model Law* a tribunal may admit a later plea if it considers the delay justified.

54 *Ibid*, art 16(3).

the *UNCITRAL Model Law* all provide that a party wishing to challenge the arbitrator's jurisdiction may make an application to the court "to decide the matter." This language can be interpreted as permitting the court to hear the matter *de novo*, which would include the right of a party to lead new evidence.

In England, the weight of authority is that the court hears the matter anew, but this practice does not appear to have been followed in Canada. In *Kitt v Voco Developments Inc*, Gallant J of the Alberta Court of Queen's Bench reviewed the applicable legislation and caselaw and stated as follows:

> This is not a standard judicial review provision. Under s. 17(9), the court is empowered [to] decide the matter in question, not just to review it. Based on this language, s. 17(9) could contemplate either a judicial review on a strict standard or something more akin to a hearing *de novo* . . . .
>
> In my opinion, the Act does not clearly describe the process warranted in an application under s. 17(9). When one considers, however, that arbitration proceedings are generally intended to minimize court-based litigation, it appears that a judicial review, rather than a hearing *de novo*, would better accord with that intention. As a result, I find that s. 17(9) contemplates a judicial review process.[55]

But there are also varying degrees of review within the judicial review process. After considering the functional and pragmatic approach and the extent to which deference should be provided to the arbitrator, Gallant J concluded as follows:

> Section 17 reveals that while arbitrators are entitled to make decisions about their jurisdiction, those decisions are not protected from review. Indeed, s. 17(9) specifically states that the court is entitled to "decide the matter". This factor clearly mitigates against deference. In addition, the questions raised in this application revolve around the Arbitrator's jurisdiction, which is an area in which the courts have greater expertise than arbitrators.

55 2005 ABQB 743 at paras 29 and 31.

> Finally, the question of jurisdiction is a question of law, which necessitates a higher standard of review. As a result, while arbitrators are often entitled to a significant degree of deference, in light of the language of s. 17(9) and the nature of the question in issue in this application, I find that the appropriate standard of review is correctness.[56]

In the Supreme Court of Canada decision in *Sattva Capital Corp v Creston Molly Corp*, the Court held that in consensual commercial arbitration, where appeals are restricted to questions of law, the standard of review will be reasonableness unless the question is one that would attract the correctness standard.[57] To date, there has been no decision as to whether a ruling on jurisdiction attracts the reasonableness standard or the correctness standard in light of the *Sattva* decision.

E. CHALLENGE TO INTERIM OR INTERLOCUTORY ORDERS AND DIRECTIONS

None of the domestic Acts nor the *UNCITRAL Model Law* provides for an appeal from or the setting aside of a procedural decision made during the course of arbitration. The Ontario Court of Appeal in *Inforica v CGI Information Systems and Management Consultants Inc* explained as follows:

> A significant feature of the modern approach limiting access to the courts to review decisions of arbitrators is that there are no appeals from procedural or interlocutory orders. In *Environmental Export International of Canada Inc. v. Success International Inc.*, [1995] O.J. No. 453 (Gen. Div.), at para. 14, MacPherson J. held: "There is nothing in the *Arbitration Act* providing for appeals from, or applications to set aside, decisions of arbitrators on procedural points. It would be wrong . . . for the courts to invent such a remedy and inject it into the arbitration process". This principle is reiterated in *Tescor Energy Services Inc. v. Toronto District School Board*, [2002]

56 *Ibid* at para 33.

57 2014 SCC 53 [*Sattva*]. See also *Orgaworld v Ottawa (City)*, 2015 ONSC 318.

> O.J. No. 74 (S.C.), at para. 30, where Lane J. held: "there is nothing in the Act to permit appeals from or the setting aside of decisions of arbitrators on procedural points". This is a deliberate policy, "not a lacuna in our law", to protect the autonomy of the arbitral process. The creation of a power by the courts to intervene on interlocutory rulings by arbitrators "would constitute a most serious reproach to the ability of our system of arbitration to serve the needs of users of the arbitral process": *K/S A/S Biakh v. Hyundai Corp.*, [1988] 1 Lloyd's Rep. 187 (Q.B. Com. Ct.) at p. 189, Steyn J.[58]

Similarly, in the Quebec case of *Endorecherche inc c Université Laval*, the moving party challenged the scope of the documentary production order made by the tribunal, arguing that the order exceeded the scope of the arbitration agreement.[59] The Court of Appeal affirmed the decision that there was no right of review by the court from a procedural order.[60]

F. QUESTIONS OF LAW

Usually it is the role of the arbitral tribunal to determine any question of law that arises during an arbitration.[61] However, in a domestic arbitration, the court may be asked to do so on the application of the arbitral tribunal or a party but only if all parties or the tribunal consent.[62]

G. COURT ASSISTANCE IN COMPELLING DISCOVERY

Under the domestic Acts, the court may enforce any direction of the tribunal to the parties, or those claiming through or under

58 Above note 52 at para 18.

59 2010 QCCA 232.

60 See also *Terrawinds Resources Corp c ABB Inc*, 2009 QCCS 5820; the British Columbia case *Slocan Forest Products Ltd v Skeena Cellulose Inc* (2001), 203 DLR (4th) 216 (BCSC), and the Alberta case *Suncor Energy*, above note 53.

61 See Ontario domestic Act, above note 12, s 8(2); *UNCITRAL Model Law*, above note 3, art 28(1) & (2).

62 See Ontario domestic Act, above note 12, s 8(2).

them, for oral discovery or the production of records and documents in their possession or power.[63] But the matter is not quite as clear if the request for discovery or production affects a nonparty. The domestic Acts speak of discovery and production orders directed to parties or those "claiming through or under them." They have no provision for nonparties.

The court will not enforce an order that the tribunal has no jurisdiction to make, and the tribunal has no jurisdiction to compel discovery from a nonparty. In *Canadian Musical Reproduction Rights Agency Ltd v Canadian Recording Industry Assn*, the arbitrator made an interlocutory order requiring a company that was not a party to the arbitration agreement to answer written interrogatories.[64] Justice Echlin of the Ontario Superior Court of Justice held that the arbitrator did not have the jurisdiction to make such an order.

With respect to the *UNCITRAL Model Law*, in *Jardine Lloyd Thompson Canada Inc v SJO Catlin*, the Alberta Court of Appeal held that article 27 should be read broadly so as to give the court power to order third-party prehearing discovery in appropriate circumstances.[65] Article 27 states, "The arbitral tribunal or a party with the approval of the arbitral tribunal may request from a competent court of this State assistance in taking evidence. The court may execute the request within its competence and according to its rules on taking evidence."[66] Speaking for the Court of Appeal, O'Brien J stated as follows:

> The Model Law is part of the law of Alberta. It must be interpreted in accordance with the ordinary meaning to be given to the terms in their context and in light of its objects and purposes. Article 27 speaks of "assistance in taking evidence". In my view, it is a gloss to add, by implication or otherwise, the words "at the hearing". Those words are not there . . . .

63 See *ibid*, s 25(7).

64 [2005] OJ No 6387 (SCJ).

65 2006 ABCA 18, leave to appeal to SCC refused, [2006] SCCA No 87.

66 Above note 3, art 27.

> The ordinary and plain meaning of evidence includes evidence gathered by way of discovery. In Alberta such evidence may be read in at the trial or otherwise used in pre-trial applications. If the drafters of Article 27 had intended that assistance would only be given for taking evidence at the hearing, they could have expressly said so. This distinction was not made and in the context of an arbitration proceeding conducted in Alberta, the word "evidence" must be given its ordinary meaning which includes all evidence whether pre-hearing or at the hearing itself . . . .
>
> I emphasize that the statute has a number of safeguards. Such requests for examination are not taken at the whim of one of the parties. The tribunal must first be satisfied that the evidence may be useful for purposes of the arbitration before the tribunal can be expected to seek the assistance of the court or to give leave to one of the parties to do so. A tribunal must always weigh the competing relevant interests and value, including the time and expense of the addition[al] discovery, and should be careful in the exercise of its powers.[67]

Courts in England and Hong Kong have come to the opposite conclusion. In *BNP Paribas & Others v Deloitte & Touche LLP*, the court stated, "There is nothing in the Model Law which suggests that the Court should assist with the process of disclosure."[68] And in *Vibroflation AG v Express Builders Co Ltd*, the court likewise interpreted article 27 as providing a means of securing evidence at the hearing and not as a means of obtaining disclosure.[69]

The domestic Acts all have similar provisions providing for the court to make orders respecting the attendance of witnesses and to "make orders and give directions with respect to the taking of evidence for an arbitration as if it were a court proceeding."[70] This is discussed in Section H, below in this chapter. The question

67 Above note 66 at paras 38, 40, and 45.

68 [2003] EWHC 2874 (Comm) at para 13.

69 [1994] 3 HKC 263.

70 Ontario domestic Act, above note 12, s 29(4).

remains whether or not other jurisdictions will follow the lead of the Alberta Court of Appeal and interpret the domestic legislation and the *UNCITRAL Model Law* as giving the court jurisdiction to order nonparties to provide prehearing discovery.

1) Checklist: Court Assistance in Discovery of a Nonparty

To obtain the court's assistance with respect to the prehearing discovery of a nonparty, counsel should demonstrate that the information or documentation to be obtained from the nonparty is truly evidence that will be useful at the hearing and that the exercise is not merely a fishing expedition. Counsel should carefully particularize the request first to the tribunal and then to the court and demonstrate why the information in the possession of the nonparty is relevant to the matters at issue and necessary for a proper adjudication. The test should be at least as stringent as that required for the discovery of a nonparty in a court action:

1) The information is otherwise unobtainable,
2) it would be unfair to the party to proceed to the arbitration hearing without the information, and
3) the examination will not
    a) unduly delay the arbitration,
    b) entail unreasonable expense for the other party to the proceeding, and
    c) result in unfairness to the nonparty.

H. COURT ASSISTANCE IN TAKING EVIDENCE

Under the domestic Acts, on the application of any party or the arbitral tribunal, the court may "make orders and give directions with respect to the taking of evidence for an arbitration as if it were a court proceeding."[71] This includes compelling the attendance of a witness in custody and granting letters of request or letters rogatory.

71 See, for example, Ontario domestic Act, *ibid*, s 29(4).

Under the *UNCITRAL Model Law*, article 27 provides that the arbitral tribunal or a party with the approval of the arbitral tribunal may request from a competent court of the state assistance in taking evidence.[72] This article applies only if the arbitration is taking place within the jurisdiction of the court.[73] The court may execute the request within its competence and according to its rules on taking evidence. This includes issuing a summons to compel a witness to attend from anywhere in Canada and issuing letters of request. Under article 27, a party may only apply to the court with the approval of the arbitral tribunal, and the article gives the court discretion as to whether or not to execute the request.

I. COURT INJUNCTIONS AND PRESERVATION ORDERS

1) Enjoining Arbitration

The power of the court to enjoin arbitration under its general jurisdiction to grant interlocutory relief in an action manifests only in the narrow circumstances where a court action is brought in a matter that is clearly not the subject of an arbitration agreement. For example, if an arbitration agreement deals solely with the valuation of shares under a share purchase agreement and if the validity of the share purchase agreement itself is in issue, the arbitrator's jurisdiction will be too narrow to determine that broader dispute. The question then becomes whether the arbitration should stop until that preliminary dispute has been resolved.

The *UNCITRAL Model Law* states in article 5, "In matters governed by this Law, no court shall intervene except where so provided in this Law."[74] The domestic Acts have similar provisions. The court proceedings in which the injunction is sought must deal with issues that arguably do not even come within the scope of the arbitration agreement. If the subject matter of or the issues in the court proceedings can be said to arguably come within the agree-

72 Above note 3, art 27.

73 See *ibid*, art 1(2).

74 *Ibid*, art 5.

ment to arbitrate, then the court is required to refer the parties to arbitration, except in very limited circumstances.[75] A discussion of the court's obligation to stay its proceedings in the face of a valid arbitration agreement is beyond the scope of this chapter.

In *Deluce Holdings Inc v Air Canada*, in determining whether the court ought to stay an arbitration on the grounds that the court proceedings were in respect of a matter outside the arbitration agreement, Blair J found that there must be a strong *prima facie* case that it would be unfair to permit the arbitration to continue in light of the allegations made in the action.[76] *Deluce Holdings* involved a shareholders' dispute, and the value of the shares upon the termination of the shareholder relationship was to be determined by arbitration. An action was brought claiming that the process by which the plaintiffs were to sell their shares to Air Canada was oppressive and seeking relief under the *Canada Business Corporations Act*. In deciding to stay the arbitration and permit the action to proceed, Blair J found that a stay of the arbitration was proper as the subject matter of the dispute was not a matter that the parties had agreed to submit to arbitration and was one striking at the very underpinning of the contract. The court also found on the evidence that there would be no injustice to Air Canada in imposing a stay because, presumably, if the oppression remedy failed, Air Canada could proceed with the arbitration to fix the value at which the plaintiffs were required to sell their shares. *Deluce Holdings* is an example of the very narrow circumstances where a court can enjoin arbitration under its general jurisdiction to grant interlocutory relief.

75 See *Dell Computer Corp v Union des consommateurs*, [2007] 2 SCR 801; *Seidel v TELUS Communications Inc*, 2011 SCC 15; *Gulf Canada Resources Ltd v Arochem International Ltd* (1992), 66 BCLR (2d) 113 (CA); *Dalimpex Ltd v Janicki* (2003), 64 OR (3d) 737 (CA); *Deluce Holdings Inc v Air Canada* (1992), 12 OR (3d) 131 (Gen Div) [*Deluce Holdings*].

76 *Deluce Holdings, ibid.*

2) Antisuit Injunctions

If the place of an arbitration is in Canada, then the local court has jurisdiction to consider an antisuit injunction where one of the parties to the arbitration agreement brings a court action in a foreign jurisdiction.[77] While such injunctions are rare in Canada, the courts in England have been quite active in protecting arbitrations in their jurisdiction by granting antisuit injunctions preventing parties from continuing court actions in other jurisdictions. As stated by Lord Hoffmann in *West Tankers Inc v RAS Riunione Adriatica di Sicurta SpA & Ors*:

> The Courts of the United Kingdom have for many years exercised the jurisdiction to restrain foreign court proceedings as Colman J did in this case: see *Pena Copper Mines Ltd v Rio Tinto Co Ltd* (1911) 105 LT 846. It is generally regarded as an important and valuable weapon in the hands of a court exercising supervisory jurisdiction over the arbitration. It promotes legal certainty and reduces the possibility of conflict between the arbitration award and the judgment of a national court. As Professor Schlosser also observes, it saves a party to an arbitration agreement from having to keep a watchful eye upon parallel court proceedings in another jurisdiction, trying to steer a course between so much involvement as will amount to a submission to the jurisdiction (which was what eventually happened to the buyers in *The Atlantic Emperor*: see [1992] 1 Lloyd's Rep 624) and so little as to lead to a default judgment. That is just the kind of thing that the parties meant to avoid by having an arbitration agreement.[78]

The Supreme Court of Canada set out the test for antisuit injunctions generally in the case of *Amchem Products Inc v British*

77 See *BG International Ltd v Grynberg Production Corp*, 2009 ABQB 452 [*BG International Ltd*]. As stated above, if a court action is brought in Canada in the face of a valid arbitration agreement, the court is obligated to stay the court proceedings, except in very narrow circumstances: see Casey, above note 9 at 323.

78 [2007] UKHL 4 at para 19.

Columbia (Workers' Compensation Board).[79] That case dealt with competing court actions in more than one jurisdiction, and it has not been decided whether this test should apply to antisuit injunctions to protect the arbitral process. If, however, one was to apply the principles of *Amchem Products* to the situation where a party has commenced a court action in a foreign jurisdiction in the face of an arbitration that is to proceed in Canada, then it is suggested that the test would be as follows:[80]

1) The decision of the foreign court should not be pre-empted, and the court should be given the opportunity to rule on a motion to stay its proceedings unless the moving party can demonstrate why this is not practical or possible.
2) If the foreign court accepts jurisdiction, then the Canadian court if applying the principles of the United Nations *Convention on the Recognition and Enforcement of Foreign Arbitral Awards* (the *New York Convention*)[81] needs to determine whether the foreign court could reasonably have concluded that the arbitration agreement is null and void, inoperative, or incapable of being performed under the law of the arbitration agreement. If so, the Canadian court should respect that decision and dismiss the motion for an antisuit injunction.
3) If the foreign court accepts jurisdiction in a manner that is inconsistent with the principles of the *New York Convention* and Canadian law, then the Canadian court should entertain the antisuit injunction.

In *BG International Limited v Grynberg Production Corporation*, the Alberta Court of Queen's Bench issued an antisuit injunction to protect the integrity of the arbitral process in the following language:

> The Respondents and all persons or bodies corporate controlled by them are enjoined from challenging or raising or pursuing

79 [1993] 1 SCR 897 [*Amchem Products*].

80 See *BG International Ltd*, above note 78.

81 10 June 1958, 330 UNTS 3, online: www.uncitral.org/pdf/english/texts/arbitration/NY-conv/New-York-Convention-E.pdf.

> (or encouraging or assisting any third party to challenge or raise or pursue) any issues or matters related to the Applicants' business or activities in Kazakhstan against BG or any of the other Claimants in any proceedings other than in an Alberta arbitration until such time as an arbitral tribunal is properly constituted in Alberta under the Formal Settlement and has opportunity to either make permanent this injunction or vacate or otherwise vary it.[82]

If the arbitration in Canada is completed and if foreign proceedings are then launched, there is no longer any Canadian arbitration to protect, and an antisuit injunction will not be granted.[83]

3) Interim Preservation Orders

Seeking an interim preservation order from the court is not evidence that a party has abandoned its rights to arbitrate. An interim preservation order from a court is required in situations where nonparties need to be bound by the order or where there is concern that a party may not comply with the order of the tribunal. Also, in urgent situations before the tribunal is constituted the court may be the only recourse. Under section 8(1) of the Ontario domestic Act, for example, the court's powers with respect to the detention, preservation, and inspection of property, interim injunctions, and the appointment of receivers are the same in arbitrations as in court actions.[84] Similarly, the Quebec *Code of Civil Procedure* provides in article 623 that the court on an application may grant provisional measures or safeguard orders before or during arbitration proceedings.[85]

Article 9 of the *UNCITRAL Model Law* permits a party to request from a court an interim measure of protection and the court

82 Unreported (11 June 2008), but see the reference in *BG International Ltd*, above note 78.

83 See *Accentuate Ltd v Asigra Inc*, 2010 ONSC 3364.

84 Above note 12, s 8(1).

85 CQLR c C-25.01, art 623.

to grant such measure.[86] Article 9 is applicable whether or not the place of arbitration is in Canada.[87]

J. COURT-ORDERED CONSOLIDATION

The domestic Acts all provide for court-ordered consolidation of arbitrations but only if all the parties to the arbitrations involved agree. For example, the Ontario domestic Act provides in section 8(4) as follows:

> On the application of all the parties to more than one arbitration the court may order, on such terms as are just,
> (a) that the arbitrations be consolidated;
> (b) that the arbitrations be conducted simultaneously or consecutively; or
> (c) that any of the arbitrations be stayed until any of the others are completed.[88]

This does not necessarily mean that the parties have to consent to the actual terms of the consolidation order. If all of the parties consent to all of the terms for consolidation, there is no need for any court order. The provision is intended to cover those situations in which all the parties have agreed to some form of consolidation but cannot agree on the form that it is to take, the manner in which the arbitrators are to be chosen, or the procedure to be followed. Initial consent to consolidation is, however, a prerequisite, and in many cases it is provided for in the arbitration agreement itself.

In the Ontario case of *Liberty Reinsurance Canada v QBE Insurance and Reinsurance (Europe) Ltd*, a reinsured and a reinsurer entered into two types of reinsurance contracts.[89] Both types had arbitration clauses, but they were not identical. Disputes arose, and one party sought arbitration under both contracts and moved

86 Above note 3, art 9.
87 See *ibid*, art 1(2).
88 Above note 12, s 8(4).
89 (2002), 42 CCLI (3d) 249 (Ont SCJ).

for consolidation. In refusing an order to consolidate, the court held that without consent there was no jurisdiction in the court to make the order. This case has been followed in Alberta in *Western Oil Sands Inc v Allianz Insurance Co of Canada*.[90]

Under the domestic Acts, where the court orders arbitrations to be consolidated, it may appoint the tribunal for the consolidated arbitration.[91]

The *UNCITRAL Model Law* makes no provision for consolidation. However, the provinces have given the courts power to consolidate proceedings under the model law. For example, under section 7 of Saskatchewan's *The International Commercial Arbitration Act*, if all the parties request it, the court can consolidate separate arbitration proceedings.[92] There is no provision in the international Acts for ordering consolidation if all the parties do not agree.

90 2004 ABQB 79.

91 See, for example, Ontario domestic Act, above note 12, s 8(5)

92 SS 1988–89, c I-10.2, s 7.

chapter twelve

Stepping into the Hot Tub: Concurrent Expert Evidence in Commercial Arbitration

DOMINIQUE T HUSSEY & WILL BORTOLIN

A. INTRODUCTION

The presentation of expert evidence in commercial arbitration has generally mirrored that in litigation before the courts: Highly qualified experts appear sequentially before the decision maker, each party hopes that its expert's opinion will be adopted and its opponent's disregarded, and opinions are elicited and tested only through counsel's questions. The result is often that the experts speak at cross-purposes and advocate rather than elucidate. Charisma and craftiness assume the significance of credentials and eclipse the quality of the opinions.

Many litigants are dissatisfied with the traditional method of adducing expert evidence. The common complaints are that (1) the other party's expert witness evidence suffers from bias, (2) adjudicators lacking subject matter expertise struggle to resolve contradictory opinions, and (3) the process is tedious, time-consuming, and costly.

Concurrent expert evidence, also known as hot tubbing or expert panels, is an alternative method of presenting expert evidence to a tribunal. The core feature is that experts having contradictory views are sworn in at the same time and invited to engage in a direct dialogue with a view to explaining, exploring, and potentially resolving their differences. This method first rose to prominence in Australia and has since drawn keen interest from the judicial systems in the United Kingdom, the United States, and Canada. There are also anecdotal reports of its use in private arbitrations.[1]

As the method has made its way to the Canadian courts and appears to be here to stay, its use in commercial arbitration will naturally follow. Canadian legal practitioners should therefore understand the advantages and pitfalls of "hot tubbing." This chapter discusses the function of expert evidence and its associated problems. It then evaluates the purported advantages of hot tubbing in addressing these problems as experienced in several jurisdictions and concludes with a suggested framework for assessing whether hot tubbing would be appropriate in a particular commercial arbitration.

B. THE FUNCTION OF EXPERT EVIDENCE IN RESOLVING DISPUTES

Expert evidence serves two distinguishable functions. The first is informational. In a dispute that involves sophisticated subject matter, as commercial arbitration often does, the adjudicator may need help understanding basic principles or background facts necessary to resolve the dispute. The expert's "opinion" here functions as factual evidence, which feeds into the legal tests that the adjudicator will apply. In a patent infringement case, for example, experts are often called upon to opine on what a "person of ordinary skill" in a particular field would have known or believed as of a historical date. With the benefit of that information, the adjudicator can determine how the patent should be interpreted, whether it has been infringed, or whether the patented subject matter was indeed inventive and therefore validly granted as of the relevant date.

1 See Doug Jones, "Recent Developments in International Commercial Arbitration" (2008) 11 *International Trade and Business Law Review* 83 at 104–5.

The second function of expert evidence is to provide ready-made inferences. The expert applies expertise to the facts at hand and opines on the conclusion that the adjudicator should draw from those facts. Opinion evidence going to an ultimate issue in a dispute is subject to special scrutiny as it risks usurping the adjudicator's function.[2] Opinions on ultimate issues are nevertheless common and often useful. This is because even if the adjudicator does not adopt an expert's opinion on an ultimate issue, it may be helpful to observe how the expert applies expertise to the issue. For example, in shareholder disputes experts are often called upon to give a valuation estimate of a company. An expert who shows how her valuation methodology applies to the facts may be far more helpful than one who provides a textbook description of a valuation methodology but with the input variables left blank. In the medical context, an expert who interprets radiological images (generally very difficult to do without practice and training) is more helpful than one who teaches a judge how to interpret them. Yet the interpretation may be the ultimate issue in a malpractice case.

1) The Trouble with the Traditional Presentation

When expert evidence is prepared and presented in the traditional way, three principal issues may arise: untrustworthiness, inefficiency, and incomprehensibility.

a) The Untrustworthiness Problem

The adversarial system is relied upon to expose the flaws in a party's evidence and reveal the truth. Courts, wary of the expert's allure, take measures to prevent unreliable or unnecessary expert evidence from ever being heard. This gatekeeping function involves assessing the qualifications of experts, their independence, and the relevance and necessity of their opinions. Expert evidence that clears this gatekeeping threshold is, ostensibly, trustworthy.

---

2 See *R v Mohan*, [1994] 2 SCR 9.

Expert evidence that does not clear this threshold is effectively deemed to be more trouble than it is worth and excluded.[3]

But gatekeeping may not be enough. The act of receiving expert evidence is a marked departure from weighing the evidence and assessing the credibility of a percipient fact witness. Expert evidence is generally admissible only where the adjudicator lacks the expert's expertise and needs assistance to resolve an issue. Starting with a knowledge deficit, an adjudicator may be ill positioned to second-guess an expert with apparently impressive credentials opining on complex subject matter. This leaves the adjudicator vulnerable to being led astray by flaws in the evidence that may go undetected.

Expert evidence may be flawed or unreliable and therefore untrustworthy for many reasons, but most commonly this is because the expert evidence is tainted by bias (conscious or unconscious) or mistake. The bias may be one or more of the following:

1) *Selection bias*: An expert may have been selected by a party because of espoused views that are favourable to that party but that are not necessarily reflective of mainstream views in the field.
2) *Affiliation bias*: An expert who is paid by, receives instructions from, has preparation sessions with, and travels to court with one party may develop the mentality of being "part of the team" and, consciously or unconsciously, slant evidence accordingly.
3) *Economic bias*: An expert with aspirations of being retained again may strive to be helpful to preserve future consulting prospects, or he may be motivated to deliver the desired result to justify a big pay cheque.[4]

---

3 See *White Burgess Langille Inman v Abbott and Haliburton Co*, 2015 SCC 23.

4 See, generally, David Sonenshein & Charles Fitzpatrick, "The Problem of Partisan Experts and the Potential for Reform through Concurrent Evidence" (2013) 32 *Review of Litigation* 1 at 3–20; Jennifer L Mnookin, "Expert Evidence, Partisanship and Epistemic Competence" (2008) 73:3 *Brooklyn Law Review* 1009; Megan A Yarnall, "Dueling Scientific Experts: Is Australia's Hot Tub Method a Viable Solution for the American Judiciary?" (2009) 88:1 *Oregon Law Review* 311 at 317–21.

An expert may also make a mistake due to a lack of sufficient experience or qualifications in the subject area or because the opinion relies on a faulty factual foundation or false assumption.

These concerns about trustworthiness have loomed large in criminal proceedings.[5] In the civil context, there is an equal concern about the trustworthiness of expert evidence, but it is secondary to concerns about the delay and cost associated with untrustworthy (and therefore unhelpful) expert evidence. The 2007 *Osborne Report* in Ontario resulted in sweeping changes to Ontario's *Rules of Civil Procedure*[6] with respect to the handling of expert evidence.[7] The report acknowledged the issue of "hired guns" and recommended imposing an explicit overriding duty of independence and impartiality on experts. The issues of delay and cost are linked to untrustworthiness because biased or partisan expert evidence tends to complicate and prolong proceedings, with partisan experts assuming polarized positions and refusing to make reasonable and appropriate concessions.

b) The Inefficiency Problem

Expert evidence is notoriously time-consuming and costly. Each expert prepares a written report before the hearing and is then examined and cross-examined at the hearing. Experts are often heard days or weeks apart from one another. Lawyers, tending to be cautious, often canvass every conceivably relevant issue with their own experts, and they are equally thorough in their scrutiny of the other party's experts on cross-examination to try to expose all mistakes. Experts may be recalled to the stand for rebuttal or to address new issues raised after their initial testimony. Lawyers may wait until closing arguments before committing themselves

5 For example, dubious convictions have been entered on the back of junk science espoused by overconfident experts.

6 RRO 1990, Reg 194.

7 Coulter A Osborne, *Summary of Findings and Recommendations of the Civil Justice Reform Project* (Toronto: Ontario Ministry of the Attorney General, 2007) Recommendation 9 "Expert Evidence," online: www.attorneygeneral.jus.gov.on.ca/english/about/pubs/cjrp/110_expert.php [*Osborne Report*].

to a narrower set of key issues and arguments as to why one expert's evidence should be preferred over the other's. As a result, significant time may have been expended canvassing ultimately irrelevant issues.

c) The Incomprehensibility Problem

It can be difficult for adjudicators to digest expert testimony, particularly where two knowledgeable experts present competing views. Inherent in the necessity of expert evidence is that the adjudicator does not possess the same specialized knowledge as the witness. The adjudicator must learn from the expert what she needs to know to resolve the case. But despite this being the essential purpose of expert evidence, the evidence may be presented in a way that is challenging for the adjudicator to understand. Adjudicators may lack a concrete sense of which facts and issues are important to understand and explore and therefore what questions need to be asked (i.e., they may not know what they do not know).

We lawyers shoulder much of the blame. While adjudicators have some latitude to interject with their own questions, the lawyers' lines of questioning generally confine the evidence. The questioning is conducted by lawyers motivated to de-emphasize or obscure any aspect of the subject matter that is not favourable to their case. Examinations by lawyers may fail to focus on key issues so that the expert issues become lost in a maze of detail.[8]

Part of the problem, however, comes from the limitations of the process itself. Experts from each party usually testify days if not weeks apart, straining the memory of the adjudicator and making it more difficult to identify and understand the areas of dispute. By the time that the essence of the dispute has been distilled, the experts are no longer available to answer the adjudicator's questions.

Even if the experts are available to answer questions and even if the adjudicator's memory is flawless, it still falls to the adjudicator to resolve any conflict between the experts. One Australian

8 See Steven Rares, "Using the 'Hot Tub' — How Concurrent Expert Evidence Aids Understanding Issues" (2012) 31:1 *Civil Justice Quarterly* 30 at 30–31.

judge described the issue as follows: A "good deal [of scientific and technical evidence] is quite beyond the capacity of most judges to understand. And in many cases in which a judge has some capacity to understand the evidence he or she will lack an expert's capacity to decide between competing opinions."[9] In these circumstances, personality characteristics and an air of gravitas or confidence rather than correctness may win the day.

The best-case scenario for an adjudicator is that the experts will make concessions that resolve the dispute. The adjudicator will then be able to proceed based on consensus. The worst-case scenario for an adjudicator is that there will be a disagreement between the experts that has no definitive resolution, and the opinions of the experts will be irreconcilable. For example, in *Warner v Smith & Nephew Inc*, a proposed class action in Alberta, the plaintiffs alleged that hip implants manufactured by the defendant had deleterious health effects.[10] On an appeal of the certification decision, Slatter J held (in dissent) that certification should be denied because the putative class members' success depended upon the answer to a "scientific mystery" that the court could not solve:

> The evidence on this record is uncontradicted: no one knows what the long term effects are, or whether the ions are harmful, or harmful enough to worry about . . . .
>
> If the scientists and doctors have not been able to resolve this issue using the usual scientific methods (lab experiments, long term blind studies, etc.) how is it realistic to think that a trial judge is going to find the answer in a civil trial? A trial judge has no laboratory. A trial judge has no ability to follow patients in the long term, alongside a control group, to try to find the answer. All that will happen (as far as this record shows) is that a series of experts might testify that "no one really knows".[11]

---

9 Geoffrey L Davies, "The Changing Face of Litigation" (1997) 6 *Journal of Judicial Administration* 179 at 188, cited in Yarnall, above note 4 at 314.

10 2016 ABCA 223.

11 *Ibid* at paras 111 & 112. The majority of the court certified the class action on the basis that it was not appropriate at the certification stage to weigh evidence going to the merits.

Between these extremes is the typical case, where the experts' opinions appear irreconcilable on the surface but can be brought into alignment by stripping away hyperbole and exposing undisclosed qualifications to the experts' opinions, exposing differences in the factual assumptions made by the experts and assessing the validity of the assumptions, exposing errors or logical fallacies in the analysis of one of the experts (e.g., ignoring relevant data, applying tautological reasoning, or applying a principle inconsistently), or demonstrating that one of the experts has applied an approach that has been discredited or widely rejected in the broader expert community.

One way to resolve conflicting expert opinions would be for the parties in an action or arbitration to retain a joint expert. Experts are, in theory, independent, so the concept is not far-fetched. Some jurisdictions in Canada have a procedural rule expressly permitting the appointment of joint experts,[12] and even those that do not would still likely be open to the approach.[13] Yet parties virtually always retain their own experts because lawyers, understandably, want to be able to control the evidence.

Accordingly, using individual, sequentially appearing experts raises intractable issues. Retaining a joint expert is often unpalatable. The solution — maybe a warm bath?

C. INTERNATIONAL ACCEPTANCE OF THE CONCURRENT EVIDENCE FORMAT

Against the backdrop of dissatisfaction with the traditional presentation of expert evidence, the concept of hot tubbing has taken hold in several common law jurisdictions, with Australia leading the charge and the United Kingdom, the United States, and Canada following suit. The experiences in each region illuminate the benefits and disadvantages of the hot tub format.

12 See, for example, *Federal Courts Rules*, SOR/98-106, r 52.1(2); *Supreme Court Civil Rules*, BC Reg 168/2009, r 11-3; *Code of Civil Procedure*, CQLR c C-25.01, art 158, 233, and 540.

13 See, for example, *Mowers v Acland*, 2015 ONSC 1313 at para 19.

1) Australia Takes Up the Hot Tub Habit

Justice Peter Heerey, of the Federal Court of Australia, has been among the most vocal proponents of hot tubbing. In an influential 2004 journal article, he described the hot tubbing procedure then being "widely used" in Federal Court of Australia trials as follows:

> The procedure involves the parties' experts giving evidence in the presence of each other after all the lay evidence on both sides has been given. The experts are sworn in and sit in the witness box or a suitably large table . . . . In the box the plaintiff's expert will give a brief oral exposition typically for ten minutes or so. Then the defendant's expert will ask the plaintiff's expert questions, that is to say directly, without the intervention of counsel. Then the process is reversed. In effect a brief colloquium takes place. Finally each expert gives a brief summary. When all this is complete, counsel cross-examine and re-examine in the conventional way.[14]

Justice Heerey perceives this procedure as having several benefits including that:

- the removal of the witness "from his party's camp" and placement in the proximity of "a (usually) respected" professional colleague tends to reduce the level of partisanship (thereby addressing the untrustworthiness problem),
- the procedure can save a lot of time (thereby addressing the inefficiency problem), and
- the "judge does not have to compare a witness giving evidence now with the half remembered evidence of another expert given perhaps some weeks previously and based on assumptions which may have been destroyed or substantially qualified in the meantime" (thereby addressing the incomprehensibility problem).[15]

---

14 Peter Heerey, "Recent Australian Developments" (2004) 23 *Civil Justice Quarterly* 386 at 390–91.

15 *Ibid* at 391.

Justice Geoffrey Davies, of the Queensland Court of Appeal, has espoused the contrary view that hot tubbing is "widely perceived as unduly adversarial and expensive" and noted that experts go into the hot tub after having been "subjected to subtle pressure to shade views, conceal doubt, overstate nuance, and downplay the weak points of the client's case . . . . We should not delude ourselves that this does not occur."[16] Justice Davies predicts that one of two possible consequences is likely to occur after concurrent evidence has been presented:

> The first is that the judge will be left with two opposed but apparently convincing opinions by equally well-qualified experts, neither of them has been shaken in the process. The second, and unfortunately more likely, consequence is that the judge will be unwittingly convinced by the more articulate and apparently authoritative personality. The likelihood of this latter consequence increases as the complexity of the question in issue increases.[17]

In subsequent years, enthusiasm for the concurrent expert evidence method among Australian judges has remained strong, and voices of dissent have been the exception. Anecdotal reports from judges have generally been positive: The procedure saves time, and it is perceived as an effective way of exposing flaws in experts' evidence.[18] One survey of Australian judges found that 94.9 percent were satisfied with the procedure.[19]

The following are other advantages of hot tubbing, generally addressed to efficiency, cited by proponents of the method:[20]

---

16 Geoffrey L Davies, "Recent Australian Developments: A Response to Peter Heerey" (2004) 23 *Civil Justice Quarterly* 396 at 398.

17 *Ibid* at 398–99.

18 See, for example, Rares, above note 8; Rupert Jackson, "Concurrent Expert Evidence — A Gift from Australia" (Lecture delivered at The London 2016 International Commercial Law Conference of The Commercial Bar Association of Victoria, 29 June 2016) at 1 and 3, online: www.judiciary.gov.uk/wp-content/uploads/2016/06/lj-jackson-concurrent-expert-evidence.pdf.

19 See Sonenshein & Fitzpatrick, above note 4 at 61–62.

20 See, generally, Rares, above note 8; Lisa C Wood, "Experts in the Tub" (2007) 21:3 *Anti-Trust* 95 at 96; Gary Edmond, "Merton and the Hot Tub: Scientific

- It can help focus the dispute on its essence by stripping away areas of agreement.
- Experts are able to more freely explain their opinion when not constrained by narrow questions.
- It can save time by avoiding having to call an expert back to clarify or respond to something raised by another party's expert.
- Because the dispute between the experts crystallizes while the experts are both on the stand, less time is wasted dealing with issues that ultimately prove not to be controversial.
- It tempers the tendency toward partisanship and bias by placing the experts on the same side of the table and removing lawyers' direct influence.
- It keeps experts accountable by putting them opposite another expert who can expose any inappropriate answer immediately.
- Its conversational nature more closely mirrors what experts are comfortable with in their professional sphere.

The enthusiasm among lawyers for concurrent expert evidence procedures has failed to match the near-universal support among judges.[21] Reviewing survey evidence, one lawyer observes the following: "On average, lawyers tend to dislike the concurrent-evidence procedures, especially the idiosyncratic ways in which they are implemented by the various institutions and individual judges." "Concurrent evidence is . . . a bit like communism, good in theory but it doesn't work in practice."[22] Acknowledging this resistance from lawyers, Steven Rares J, of the Federal Court of Australia, an avid proponent of concurrent evidence states, "Initially, and my own experience is to this effect, uninitiated counsel are highly suspicious of concurrent evidence. That suspicion evaporates once

Conventions and Expert Evidence in Australian Civil Procedure" (2009) 72 *Law and Contemporary Problems* 159 at 167–69.

21 See Jackson, above note 18 at 3.

22 Edmond, above note 20 at 183–86 and 183.

they participate. Why is this so? It is because of the efficiency and discipline which the process brings to bear."[23]

It bears noting that the Federal Court of Australia routinely requires experts to confer together before trial and prepare a joint report on the matters that they agree and disagree about, which helps focus the agenda of the expert panel.[24]

2) The United Kingdom Wades In

In England and Wales, the availability of concurrent expert evidence was formalized by a practice direction in April 2013, which expressly provides judges with the discretion to direct that some or all experts in a case from similar disciplines give their oral evidence concurrently.[25] The practice direction approximately follows the Australian procedure, allowing the judge to "initiate the discussion by asking the experts, in turn, for their views. Once an expert has expressed a view the judge may ask questions about it. At one or more appropriate stages when questioning a particular expert, the judge may invite the other expert to comment or to ask that expert's own questions of the first expert."[26] The questions that counsel is subsequently permitted to ask, however, "should not cover ground which has been fully explored already. In general, a full cross-examination or re-examination is neither necessary nor appropriate."[27] The cross-examiner's role is thus curtailed. Following testimony, "the judge may summarise the experts' different positions on the issue and ask them to confirm or correct that summary."[28]

23 Rares, above note 8 at 35.

24 See *ibid* at 35–36.

25 Ministry of Justice, United Kingdom, Practice Direction 35 "Experts and Assessors" (updated 30 January 2017) at para 11, online: www.justice.gov.uk/courts/procedure-rules/civil/rules/part35/pd_part35#11.1.

26 *Ibid* at para 11.4.

27 *Ibid.*

28 *Ibid.*

This practice direction followed on the heels of a concurrent expert evidence pilot project.[29] Only three of fifteen cases assigned to the pilot project had made it to trial, but hot tubbing was viewed as a success, particularly by judges and the experts who had testified.[30] However, there was a clear difference in perception regarding the rigour of the process in one case: While the judge and the claimant's solicitor felt that the process had been more rigorous than the conventional approach to expert evidence, both barristers and the defendant's solicitor felt that the process had been less rigorous than sequential evidence and cross-examination.[31]

In 2016, Lord Justice Jackson gave a speech reflecting on England and Wales's experience with hot tubbing.[32] Reporting on his discussions with several judges and practitioners, he found that the majority were supportive and that judges were consistently of the view that the procedure saved time. As in Australia, the response from practitioners was mixed. Of fifteen who were straw polled, "three were hostile." Lord Justice Jackson observed, however, that "the majority of those who are hostile to the procedure are judges or practitioners who have never used it."[33]

3) The United States Tests the Water

The US judicial system differs from that of Australia, England, and Canada in that civil proceedings are routinely decided by juries rather than judges. The practical inability to have a whole panel of jurors participate in hot tubbing renders impractical one

29 See The Right Honourable Lord Justice Jackson, *Review of Civil Litigation Costs: Final Report* (London: United Kingdom Ministry of Justice, 2010) at 381, online: www.judiciary.gov.uk/wp-content/uploads/JCO/Documents/Reports/jackson-final-report-140110.pdf.

30 See Jackson, above note 18, Appendix A.

31 See Hazel Genn, *Manchester Concurrent Evidence Pilot: Interim Report* (London: University College London Judicial Institute, 2012) at 4, online: www.judiciary.gov.uk/wp-content/uploads/JCO/Documents/Reports/concurrent-evidence-interim-report.pdf.

32 Jackson, above note 18.

33 *Ibid* at 5 & 6.

of the key elements of hot tubbing: the decision maker's participation in the discussion.[34]

One commenter has advocated for exploring the use of concurrent expert evidence even in jury trials, notwithstanding the practical hurdles, reasoning that "if hot tubbing can enhance judges' understanding of complex issues, it may have a greater benefit for lay jurors."[35] Others have predicted that having up to twelve individuals ask questions of two or more experts about complex evidence "could easily slide into pandemonium."[36]

The use of hot tubbing has been recommended in nonjury trials,[37] and a small number of judges have enthusiastically adopted it. Hot tubbing is not integrated into US procedural rules, but it has still been imposed by some judges on an ad hoc basis as being within their broad discretion over courtroom procedure.[38] Adopters speak highly of its benefits but have noted that it is not appropriate in every case.[39] Some judges implement the practice *after* expert evidence has been given in the traditional way, which differs from the standard Australian procedure. Hot tubbing is demonstrably effective at getting experts to respond directly to each other's points; otherwise they may pass like two ships in the night. Also notable is the "remarkably quiet" spectators' role played by counsel in these exchanges, with the judge completely assuming the interrogator's role.[40]

4) Canada Soaks It Up

In direct response to the growing popularity of concurrent expert evidence in Australia, Canadian lawmakers have developed

34 See Yarnall, above note 4 at 335–36.

35 Edie Greene & Natalie Gordon, "Can the 'Hot Tub' Enhance Jurors' Understanding and Use of Expert Testimony?" (2016) 16:2 *Wyoming Law Review* 359 at 383–85.

36 Yarnall, above note 4 at 336.

37 See *ibid* at 389.

38 See Wood, above note 20.

39 See *ibid* at 97.

40 *Ibid* at 101.

a keen interest in the hot tubbing procedure. In 2006, the rules of procedure for the Competition Tribunal (an administrative body for prosecuting civil violations under the *Competition Act*) were amended to provide simply that "[t]he Tribunal may require that some or all of the witnesses testify as a panel."[41] In Ontario, a procedure sometimes referred to as "pretrial hot tubbing" is contemplated by the *Rules of Civil Procedure* and has been ordered in some cases, but it is fundamentally different from the procedure described in this chapter.[42] In 2010, the *Federal Courts Rules* were amended to provide for concurrent expert evidence:

> *Expert witness panel*
> 282.1 The Court may require that some or all of the expert witnesses testify as a panel after the completion of the testimony of the non-expert witnesses of each party or at any other time that the Court may determine.
>
> *Testimony of panel members*
> 282.2(1) Expert witnesses shall give their views and may be directed to comment on the views of other panel members and to make concluding statements. With leave of the Court, they may pose questions to other panel members.
>
> *Examination of panel members*
> (2) On completion of the testimony of the panel, the panel members may be cross-examined and re-examined in the sequence directed by Court.[43]

Provincial civil courts have yet to codify the option of concurrent expert evidence, but it is likely that judges will be receptive to the option if counsel for both parties consent to it.

41 *Competition Tribunal Rules*, SOR/2008-141, rr 75–76.

42 It is a without prejudice meeting to narrow the dispute between the experts: *Rules of Civil Procedure*, above note 6, rr 20.05(2)(k) and 50.07(1)(c). See Paul Michell, "Pre-hearing Expert Conferences: Canadian Developments" (2011) 30:1 *Civil Justice Quarterly* 93. See, for example, *Paul v Oliver Fuels Ltd*, 2012 ONSC 978 at para 46; *Karrys Bros Ltd v Ruffa*, 2014 ONSC 713 at para 19.

43 *Federal Courts Rules*, above note 12, rr 282.1–282.2.

Judges in Canada have pushed for the implementation of concurrent evidence procedures. Former Supreme Court of Canada justice Ian Binnie has written that "a court should be able to require opposing experts to testify on the same panel and be subject to questioning in the presence of each other, with the right to question each other in the presence of the trier of fact."[44] Also, judges have from time to time suggested in retrospect that hot tubbing would have been of assistance.[45]

But the uptake by litigants has been unenthusiastic. And because lawyers ultimately control the process, concurrent expert evidence remains an uncommon practice in Canadian judicial proceedings.

D. THE HOT TUBBING TRADE-OFF

The beginning of this chapter reviewed three significant problems with expert evidence: untrustworthiness, inefficiency, and incomprehensibility. Australia, the United Kingdom, the United States, and Canada have acknowledged that hot tubbing has significant potential to make expert evidence more comprehensible and to reduce the time it takes for the decision maker to hear and resolve disputes between experts.

However, hot tubbing's potential to make expert evidence more trustworthy is more doubtful. Expert witnesses in a hot tub are just as likely to suffer from selection or economic bias, lack qualifications, or make a mistake. Even affiliation bias would not be eliminated. Accordingly, hot tubbing may not significantly reduce the risk of flawed expert evidence. To the contrary, it may in some circumstances reduce the chances that flaws will be de-

44 Ian Binnie, "The Changing Role of the Expert Witness" (2010) 49 *Supreme Court Law Review* (2d) 179 at 191, cited in Peter EJ Wells & Samantha Gordon, "Issues in the Preparation and Presentation of Expert Evidence" (2015) 45:1 *Advocates' Quarterly* 1 at 10.

45 See, for example, *Eli Lily and Co v Apotex Inc*, 2009 FC 991 at para 578, n 234: "I truly believe that the use of hot tubbing would have been particularly useful here."

tected. This is because the efficiency gained by concurrent evidence procedures comes at the expense of procedural safeguards designed to expose flaws in expert evidence.

The premise underlying the view that concurrent expert evidence is more reliable than conventional expert evidence is that lawyers are to blame for the trustworthiness issue. There is some truth to this sentiment. Lawyers do shape the content of expert reports and guide expert witness questioning to serve partisan objectives that may distort the experts' evidence. To the extent that hot tubbing procedures take lawyers out of the picture, those procedures remove this hazard. But opposing counsel also plays an important role in exposing flaws and bias in expert evidence through the fundamentally important truth-seeking tool of cross-examination. As a result, lawyers are a much bigger part of the solution. Indeed, it may be that concurrently presented expert evidence is perceived to be less biased as the very consequence of forgoing thorough cross-examination and thereby shielding the flaws in the expert evidence from exposure.

It is not a foregone conclusion that hot tubbing will eliminate cross-examination by counsel. Where cross-examination by counsel is permitted, experts could face even greater scrutiny in the hot tub from the combination of the opposing party's lawyer *and* the opposing party's expert, *and* the adjudicator. But the benefits are likely illusory. Additional, rigorous examinations by lawyers would come at the expense of efficiency unless they are limited to issues that were not previously explored or to clarifying error. And if limited to these areas, coherent and surgical cross-examination would require uncommon skill to achieve. The narrative of the experts' evidence and of the dispute between them will have already been cast, and examinations following an expert panel would usually be significantly impaired.

Accordingly, even if a concurrent evidence procedure includes an opportunity for cross-examination, the parties should not anticipate having the ability to comprehensively cross-examine the other party's expert or expect to have control over the narrative of the dispute. More likely, the adjudicator will decide the issues based on the discussion between the experts and based on how they respond to her questions. Counsel's role in the procedure may amount to a footnote.

This may not be entirely a bad thing. Experts can be very effective at scrutinizing each other's evidence. Unlike ordinary fact witnesses, they are masters of the subject matter. Recollection is not a key concern. Experts are uniquely qualified to understand which facts are relevant, which facts weaken a conclusion, and what questions need to be asked to test the validity of a conclusion. Scientific experts tend to have extensive experience with the process of peer review, which requires justifying and defending their own conclusions as well as scrutinizing and criticizing the conclusions of their peers. These skills may translate well to the concurrent evidence format.

But hot tubbing should not rule the day in those situations in which the well-prepared lawyer will inevitably outperform the expert and the adjudicator in testing the opposing expert's evidence and presenting the case.

E. SHOULD YOU USE THE HOT TUB IN YOUR COMMERCIAL ARBITRATION?

Hot tubbing does not present an answer to all of the problems associated with the traditional presentation of expert evidence. Accordingly, not every dispute will be suitable for concurrent expert evidence. However, it is a viable option that offers meaningful advantages when used in the right circumstances and in the right way.

Hot tubbing may be particularly well-suited to commercial arbitration as compared with court litigation. Some litigants select commercial arbitration because of its relative speed from initiation to decision. The efficiency of the hot tub format would therefore be appropriate and appealing. While judges can never be chosen, parties to commercial arbitration can choose the arbitrator or a blue-ribbon panel of decision makers and can therefore select for knowledge of and experience in the subject matter of the dispute. This allows the parties to a commercial arbitration to capitalize on the benefits of efficiency and comprehensibility while minimizing the inherent risk of untrustworthiness arising from a knowledge disparity between expert and decision maker. Further, the private and confidential nature of arbitration proceedings may encourage experts to be more forthright and willing to make concessions.

Nevertheless, it would be risky to agree to concurrent expert evidence as a blanket rule, for example, when negotiating a dispute resolution clause in a commercial agreement. The best time to determine whether concurrent evidence is appropriate is after the experts' written reports have been exchanged and, if applicable, after any prehearing cross-examination of the experts. In evaluating whether your case is appropriate for concurrent expert evidence, consider the following factors:

1) the nature of the disagreement between the experts
2) the personalities of the experts
3) the sophistication of the adjudicator in the subject area

1) The Nature of the Disagreement

Give careful thought to exactly what is the disagreement between the experts and what is the likely outcome of a conversation between the experts about the issue.

a) Is the Central Issue a Matter of Right and Wrong or a Function of Preferred Approach?

Hot tubbing is best suited to relatively black-and-white disputes where each expert needs to explain to the adjudicator why he is right and the other expert is wrong. The hot tub is an efficient format for this as it brings the dispute into focus for the adjudicator and allows the experts to exchange and respond to criticisms directly and immediately.

Hot tubbing is not ideal for resolving disputes involving competing approaches to the same question where both approaches are credible and valid. This issue arises where, for example, each expert applies a different method for valuing a corporation in a shareholder dispute or a different theory of psychology in a dispute involving a claim of psychiatric harm. The dispute in these types of cases is not about uncovering an objective truth but rather about which expert's methodology is more appropriate in the circumstances of the case and in the context of the applicable legal test. This presents an advocacy challenge that is usually better left to the lawyers.

Similarly, concurrent expert evidence may not be suitable where the disagreement between the experts relates only to their conclusion on the ultimate issue before the tribunal, that is, where the experts agree on the basic principles and theories relevant to determining the issue (the questions of right and wrong) but disagree on how those principles and theories apply to the facts of the case. It is the adjudicator's province to exercise her own judgment on the facts of the case and counsel's province to argue how the adjudicator should exercise that judgment. If a dispute over the ultimate issue becomes a battle between the experts, counsel will have surrendered the responsibility for framing and arguing the ultimate issue. This loss of control presents uncertainty and risk for both parties.

b) Which Is More Important to Your Case — the Nuance or the Big Picture?

Concurrent expert evidence will tend to focus and simplify a dispute. It is designed to put pressure on the experts to summarize the big picture and distill what the dispute is *really* about. This will usually improve the efficiency of the proceedings and simplify the task of the adjudicator, particularly where the experts disagree on minor points that are distracting rather than dispositive.

As lawyers tend to be overinclusive in selecting the issues to be canvassed by their experts to preserve flexibility, once the dispute has crystallized and once the parties have developed their theories of the case, it may be possible to "strip away peripheral areas of agreement."[46] Concurrent expert evidence is an efficient format for this because the experts can in real time agree on which issues are unimportant or which issues there is no disagreement about and simply skip addressing those issues.

Sometimes, however, a party's position hinges on an argument that is nuanced or technical from a legal perspective and that the expert may not appreciate because, for example, it revolves around the requirements of a peculiar test. In such a case, the big picture may represent a dangerous oversimplification where the case could benefit from expert evidence that is laid out precisely and methodically under focused questioning from the party's lawyer. If the expert were left to his own devices in the conversational context of the hot tub, there would be a risk that he, in the spirit of being agreeable, overlook the critical nuance or accept or articulate a harmful generalization.

2) The Personalities of the Experts

An expert's personality does not have any direct bearing on the rightness or wrongness of her opinion. But where the adjudicator is having difficulty discerning which expert is right, secondary factors such as the experts' relative qualifications and experience or the clarity and confidence with which they present their opinions may be what tips the scales.[47] This is an important consideration when deciding whether to engage in hot tubbing as the change in format affects how experts are likely to be perceived by the adjudicator.

46 Yarnall, above note 4 at 326.

47 See Davies, above note 16 at 398–99; Mnookin, above note 4 at 1012–13; Sonenshein & Fitzpatrick, above note 4 at 14–15: "The qualities in a witness which fact-finders find most convincing such as verbal fluency, ease of manner, the appearance of humility, and stellar credentials, have little relation to the truth."

a) Is Your Expert Confident and Charismatic?

If the parties' experts are equally objective and reasonable and equally willing to challenge and criticize each other, then neither party gains an advantage by removing lawyers from the process. The unstructured environment of the hot tub allows for experts' individual personalities to emerge more than they might under focused questioning by a lawyer. Adjudicators tend to loathe the hired gun, but if one party puts forward a hired gun loaded with equal parts bluster and charisma and if the other puts forward a humble, modest, or awkward expert, the party with the hired gun may nevertheless enjoy an advantage by conveying confidence and qualification. While the same risk exists when evidence is given through the traditional process of examination and cross-examination, it is amplified in the hot tub because the adjudicator observes the experts simultaneously, side by side, rather than in separate examinations scheduled days or weeks apart. This is a side effect of diminishing the role of cross-examination, which is otherwise a tool that can be used to stamp out hyperbole and drill down to the substance beneath a hired gun's shiny veneer.

In the concurrent expert evidence format, each expert has the opportunity to attack the other's evidence, but a relatively modest and understated expert may not take that opportunity. The experts have no vested interest in the outcome of the case and may soften or withhold their criticisms out of respect or professional courtesy. Lawyers who are cross-examining have no such qualms. In the standard format, a modest and understated expert will often look much better after cross-examination than one who is bombastic and hyperbole-prone.

b) Will Your Expert Look Less Authoritative?

If an expert is qualified, it should not in theory matter whether five or forty-five years of experience support the qualification. But the contrast in appearance between a jittery prodigy and a steely veteran of the field cannot be overlooked by the adjudicator, and that contrast will be sharpened if the experts give evidence concurrently. If the elder expert has been well coached by his party's lawyers, he will naturally make repeated reference to his decades of experience as he answers questions. The conversational format of the hot tub may make this even easier.

3) The Sophistication of the Adjudicator

Concurrent expert evidence functions best where the adjudicator is relatively sophisticated in the subject area being addressed by the experts. With the parties' lawyers taking a back seat, the adjudicator needs to take control. Reports on the English experience with concurrent expert evidence have highlighted that it requires the judge "to be completely on top of the expert issues before trial, otherwise this process of a structured dialogue—which is judge-led—will not work."[48] The sophisticated adjudicator can detect hyperbole without assistance. The risk of the adjudicator's relying on secondary factors like personality and appearance to pick the winning expert opinion will be diminished if the adjudicator has the capacity to fully understand the disputed issue and determine with confidence which opinion (if either) is correct.

Concurrent expert evidence can still be used when dealing with complex subject matter well beyond the adjudicator's existing knowledge, but it involves a trade-off. On one hand, the concurrent evidence format generally makes it easier for the adjudicator to understand and resolve complex issues justly and efficiently. On the other hand, an adjudicator who relies heavily on the experts to understand the issues is likely going to be less effective in scrutinizing the experts' testimony and therefore more vulnerable to undue influence by a charismatic hired gun. A party should agree to concurrent expert evidence only if it is confident in the adjudicator's knowledge and in its expert's ability to identify and clearly explain any flaws in the evidence of the other party.

48 Jackson, above note 18 at 5 and 8.

F. HOW TO PREPARE FOR THE HOT TUB

If you decide to pursue the hot tub option, give thorough thought to how to proceed. You may wish to consider the following practices:

1) Determine a detailed protocol for the format of the expert panel, considering the following:
   - whether to negotiate a predetermined list of issues that will be addressed by both experts
   - whether concessions can be secured (or granted) in advance of the hearing that will narrow the issues to be addressed by the experts
   - whether the experts on the panel should provide a joint tutorial on the subject matter at issue or whether the parties may agree on a different joint expert for this role in advance of the hot tub round
   - whether the experts should make opening statements and, if so, how long they should be and whether they can be led by counsel to address specific subjects
   - who among the adjudicator, counsel, and the other expert will be allowed to ask questions and when (for example, a panel could begin with opening statements, proceed to a period of questioning between the experts, either with or without intervention from the adjudicator, and then proceed to questioning by counsel.)
   - whether a traditional cross-examination of each expert individually should follow the expert panel and, if so, whether it needs to be confined to the specific points already raised during the expert panel
2) Prepare the expert you retained in the following ways:
   - Give the expert context about the key issues on which the case turns and how the evidence fits into those issues. This will allow the expert to understand what the testimony should be focused on and to avoid trailing off into irrelevant tangents that will not advance the case. This can be more difficult to achieve outside of the structured context of direct examination and cross-examination.

- Simulate the hot tub environment for your expert by advancing the opinions held and criticisms levelled by the opposing expert, and see how your expert responds. Consider engaging another expert to rehearse, understanding that on the day, the evidence will be far more improvised than scripted.
- Coach your expert to be respectful and direct and to acknowledge when the opposing expert is expressing a valid alternative view. Explain that condescension, dismissiveness, or anger in the face of criticism will cause the expert to lose credibility with the adjudicator.
- Instruct your expert not to answer questions that lead outside of her area of expertise or that would require more information, analysis, or research to answer reliably. The conversational flow of the hot tub may make this discipline more difficult.
- Remind the expert that her key role is to assist the adjudicator in understanding the subject matter in which the expert has expertise in an unbiased way. The hot tub format does not change this but may require extra vigilance on the part of the expert to ensure that the opinion is articulated and understood clearly, decisively, and completely notwithstanding the conversational nature of the format.

G. CONCLUSION

The concurrent expert evidence format is an interesting option for presenting expert evidence more efficiently and effectively. It undoubtedly has value, but it is not right for every case and needs to be approached with caution. The clearest benefit is efficiency. But this comes at a price. With fewer questions being asked of experts and a less formal structure confining their testimony, there is a greater risk that flaws in the evidence will go undetected and that the experts' advocacy skills rather than their expertise will decide the dispute. Concurrent expert evidence should be reserved for cases where this risk is minimized, cases that can generally be identified by the following indicia:

- The dispute goes to black and white questions of right and wrong rather than debatable matters of advocacy that are better left to professional advocates.
- The governing legal test is straightforward enough that the experts can understand how their evidence fits within it rather than get lost in irrelevant tangents or inadvertently brush over an important nuance.
- Either expert (but particularly your expert) would not be at a significant disadvantage if the dispute ultimately came down to a personality contest.
- The adjudicator is either studious enough or sophisticated enough in the subject area to guarantee active and meaningful participation in the expert panel.

Adjudicators have showered the concurrent expert evidence procedure with almost unanimous praise. This cannot be ignored. But adjudicators may be predisposed to being satisfied with the concurrent evidence procedure because it puts them in the driver's seat, allowing them to run the show and ask all the questions they want to ask. And adjudicators are not the ones whose cases are on trial. It is more important that the *parties* are satisfied with the procedure and see justice as having been done.

Ultimately, the parties and their counsel need to determine which procedure is in their own best interests and—win or lose—which will give them the greatest confidence that a right result has been achieved. Keep the hot tubbing option in mind; you may find that you warm up to it.

chapter thirteen

The Use of Experts and the Assessment of Economic Damages in Commercial Arbitration

NEAL MIZRAHI*

A. INTRODUCTION

Experts are generally retained to provide an independent and objective opinion to assist the tribunal to form a conclusion in areas that require expertise. While this role is generally well-known, experts have been criticized for being advocates for their client.

The first part of this chapter outlines the role of the expert and the various ways that bias may impact the expert's evidence. The second part outlines some best practices that counsel and the expert may employ to increase the efficiency of the expert engagement and improve the quality of the expert evidence in the arbitration. The third part discusses the collaboration of expert witnesses in arbitration in prehearing meetings, joint statements, and expert witness conferencing (or hot tubbing). The fourth and final part of this chapter provides a primer on business valuation methodologies and discusses the challenges that an expert may face in a commonly encountered scenario: the valuation of a business or project in an early stage of its economic life. This discussion is useful in

* The techniques and examples herein are illustrative. Their applicability will depend on case factors (i.e. constraints, instructions) and the expert's professional judgment.

demonstrating the type of complexities that valuation experts commonly face and judgment that they commonly exercise.

While the discussion in this chapter is generally applicable to all experts, its focus is on business valuation and damages quantification experts. The discussion centres on the use of party-appointed, as opposed to tribunal-appointed, experts primarily in Canadian and international commercial arbitration.

B. THE ROLE OF THE EXPERT

1) To Assist the Tribunal

Generally, in the context of both litigation and arbitration a party-appointed expert is to be independent and objective, possess the expertise to provide an opinion on a matter, and assist the judge or tribunal in areas that require expertise. The expert's general duty is perhaps most comprehensively defined in the *Federal Courts Rules*:

> 1 An expert witness named to provide a report for use as evidence, or to testify in a proceeding, has an overriding duty to assist the Court impartially on matters relevant to his or her area of expertise.
>
> 2 This duty overrides any duty to a party to the proceeding, including the person retaining the expert witness. An expert is to be independent and objective. An expert is not an advocate for a party.[1]

While this definition is applicable to Canadian litigation, the expert's role in litigation is generally consistent with the expert's role in arbitration, and this definition is useful to set the stage for describing that role.

Before proceeding with this discussion, I note that for an expert to give evidence in a Canadian court, he or she must undergo a qualification process under oath. This process generally involves a presentation of the expert's credentials and experience, which may be tested through cross-examination. Such a qualification process is not generally found in practice in arbitration, as will be explained below.

---

1 SOR/98-106, Schedule (Rule 52.2).

Expert evidence is governed by a set of rules specific to each arbitral institution and the standardized rules that the parties may choose to accompany the institutional rules, such as those formulated by the International Bar Association (IBA), United Nations Commission on International Trade Law (UNCITRAL), and Chartered Institute of Arbitrators (CIArb). While these rules do not explicitly address the role of expert witnesses and the standards that apply to the admissibility of their evidence, a common theme across institutional and standardized rules is the requirement of independence, generally provided in the form of a declaration from the expert.

While not addressing independence explicitly, the International Centre for Settlement of Investment Disputes rules require experts to make a declaration regarding their opinion in the following form: "I solemnly declare upon my honour and conscience that my statement will be in accordance with my sincere belief."[2] The *IBA Rules on the Taking of Evidence in International Arbitration* require an expert's report to contain, among other things, the following: "a statement of his or her independence from the Parties, their legal advisors and the Arbitral Tribunal; . . . an affirmation of his or her genuine belief in the opinions expressed in the Expert Report."[3] The CIArb *Protocol for the Use of Party-Appointed Expert Witnesses in International Arbitration* requires similar, perhaps expanded, declarations including the following:

> (a) I understand that my duty in giving evidence in this arbitration is to assist the arbitral tribunal [to] decide the issues in respect of which expert evidence is adduced. I have complied with, and will continue to comply with, that duty.
> (b) I confirm that this is my own, impartial, objective, unbiased opinion which has not been influenced by the pressures of the dispute resolution process or by any party to the arbitration.

2 International Centre for Settlement of Investment Disputes, *Rules of Procedure for Arbitration Proceedings* (April 2006), applicable to proceedings under the ICSID *Convention on the Settlement of Investment Disputes between States and Nationals of Other States*, r 35(3), online: http://icsidfiles.worldbank.org/icsid/icsid/StaticFiles/basicdoc/partF.htm.

3 International Bar Association, *IBA Rules on the Taking of Evidence in International Arbitration* (London: IBA, 2010) art 5, online: www.ibanet.org/Publications/publications_IBA_guides_and_free_materials.aspx [*IBA Evidence Rules*].

(c) I confirm that all matters upon which I have expressed an opinion are within my area of expertise.[4]

Thus, the concept that experts' duty is first and foremost to the tribunal and that they are to provide an opinion that either reflects their belief or is independent is pervasive both in Canadian courts and in arbitration. Since arbitration proceedings are flexible, they rely on the tribunal performing its gatekeeping function to direct, for example, the manner in which written and oral testimony is presented and the collaboration of experts. And in a case where an expert's testimony is perceived to be biased, the tribunal may decide to disregard, in whole or in part, that expert's opinion.

2) The Impact of Bias on Expert Evidence

The assessment of economic damages is a complex process that generally requires the application of professional judgment and principles that draw from a number of disciplines, including accounting, finance, and economics.

Despite the requirement that experts assist the tribunal and remain independent, they are frequently criticized for advocating their client's position. I believe that most qualified experts understand their role but that other forces (e.g., financial incentives and client influence) affect their objectivity. There are three main areas where bias is seen in expert evidence: the underlying analysis and assumptions, written evidence, and oral testimony:

1) *Analysis and assumptions*: In the course of their analyses, biased experts may "cherry pick" information that is beneficial to their client's case while disregarding facts that do not support it. Biased experts may use assumptions that are unrealistic

4 Chartered Institute of Arbitrators, *Protocol for the Use of Party-Appointed Expert Witnesses in International Arbitration* (London: CIArb, 2007) art 8, online: www.ciarb.org/docs/default-source/ciarbdocuments/international-arbitration-protocols/partyappointedexpertsinternationalarbitration.pdf?sfvrsn=8 [*CIArb Protocol*].

and unsupported, and they may be inconsistent in their use of methodologies from one case to another, depending on the side that retains them in the arbitration.

2) *Written evidence*: The reports of biased experts may contain language that is aggressive or unduly critical of the opposing expert, legal argument, or findings on factual matters. Additionally, such reports may be intentionally lengthy or complex or contain calculations that are not transparent, which hinder a meaningful peer review. Some experts may author reply reports that only criticize in cases where they are able to offer the tribunal an alternative quantification of damages.
3) *Oral testimony*: At the arbitral hearing, biased experts may be evasive or nonresponsive to reasonable questioning. They may advocate a position and defend their analysis unreasonably, they may fail to admit errors, or they may stray outside of what is in their written evidence to advocate their client's position. Lastly, they may be disrespectful to counsel, the tribunal, or the opposing expert.

Clearly, an expert who allows bias to permeate her evidence circumvents her duty to the tribunal and, in doing so, severely limits the usefulness of her written evidence and oral testimony. An expert who discharges her duty to the tribunal is independent in fact and appearance. She understands that her role is to assist the tribunal, and in doing so, she provides an analysis that is balanced, with consideration of all relevant factors. An effective expert also discharges her duty to the tribunal by being an effective communicator. She explains complex concepts clearly and concisely and can think on her feet during the arbitral hearing in responding to questions from counsel and the tribunal.

C. BEST PRACTICES IN DEALING WITH EXPERT WITNESSES

This section discusses best practices that counsel and experts can utilize to maximize the efficiency and benefit of experts and their written and oral evidence. While a comprehensive discussion of best practices for counsel and experts is beyond the scope of this chapter, the following discussion highlights best practices pertaining to the timing of the expert's retainer, the expert's access to documents, counsel's role in providing comments on expert reports, and matters leading up to and at the hearing.

1) Timing of Retainer

It is beneficial if an expert is engaged as early in the arbitration process as possible. This affords the expert sufficient time to formulate an approach to damages based on the factual background and counsel's legal framing of the case. Not only is the engagement of an expert at an early stage useful in managing the expectations of the client, but it also allows the expert to make requests for documents necessary to support his opinion of damages. This also leaves enough time for gaps in the documentary evidence to potentially be filled by fact witness evidence or witness statements. While there are obvious fee implications associated with retaining an expert early, more often than not the efficiencies gained in subsequent stages of the expert's work will offset this cost.

2) Access to Documents

In formulating an opinion of damages, an effective expert reviews all relevant information produced by the parties in the arbitration. It is common practice for counsel to provide experts with documents that counsel believe are relevant to economic damages. While this may be sufficient in most cases, a more effective approach is for counsel to provide the expert with access to all information produced in the arbitration, where it is practical to do so. This allows the expert to identify factors — both helpful and detrimental to her client's position — that bear on the assessment of damages. Then, if the expert is able to consider, and if necessary, address those factors in her written evidence, it allows her to provide a balanced, supported opinion of economic damages.

3) Counsel's Input on Expert Reports

Generally, an expert will draft his report and provide it to counsel (on behalf of the client) before finalizing it. It is commonplace for counsel to review and provide input on the expert's draft report. This type of input is most beneficial to the expert when it relates to the identification of factual inaccuracies and, in cases where the subject matter is technical or complex, portions of the report that may benefit from further clarification. While counsel's input is generally useful, during this process experts may face pressure to modify their conclusions to further their client's position or to include aggressive language or legal argument. Effective experts are able to consider comments but ultimately remain true to their role — that is, to assist the tribunal.

4) The Arbitral Hearing

In contrast with court cases, arbitrations are generally conducted under a short time frame. This has two implications for experts. First, a short time frame means that less time is allocated to expert evidence. Second, to efficiently conduct the arbitration, tribunals are generally familiar with the written evidence, and during the hearing they are active in the questioning of experts. Taking these factors into account, effective experts in the arbitration setting are those who clearly and concisely communicate their opinion while being able to think on their feet.

There are a number of things that counsel and the expert can do leading up to the hearing to maximize the utility of expert evidence. First, preparation leading up to the arbitral hearing is critical to the effectiveness of the expert's testimony. Effective experts have deep knowledge of their reports, the opposing expert's reports, and key documents. Similarly, well-prepared counsel will be more alert to potential areas of re-examination of their expert and better equipped to cross-examine the opposing expert. In cases that involve expert witness conferencing (discussed in Section D(2), below), prepared counsel can be more reactive to the concurrent testimony of the experts, asking pointed questions and regaining some of the control that is thought to be lost in this process.

Next, in my experience, a brief presentation by the expert at the hearing is generally useful to the tribunal. In lieu of direct examination, it is common for expert evidence to be submitted through affidavits or witness statements, which will then be tested through cross-examination at the hearing. However, since expert testimony generally deals with complex and technical subject matter, it is beneficial to the tribunal if the expert provides a brief (i.e., half hour to one hour) presentation outlining her opinions, methodologies, and key assumptions and, if applicable, the key areas where she agrees and disagrees with the opposing expert (not just rehashing the reports). This type of presentation clarifies matters raised in the experts' reports and generally serves to focus the discussion on quantum issues.

Finally, before the arbitral hearing it is common for the expert and counsel to meet. Such meetings may be useful for familiarizing counsel with the expert's testifying style or providing counsel with the comfort that their expert has considered possible criticisms of her report. While mock cross-examinations are prohibited in some jurisdictions, most arbitration rules permit communications between counsel and experts for the preparation of reports and witness testimony with the provision that the experts' opinions represent their own.

D. THE COLLABORATION OF EXPERTS IN ARBITRATION

1) Expert Meetings and Joint Reports

Collaboration between opposing experts before the hearing may narrow the issues between them and alleviate the adversarial nature of the evidentiary process. Typically, such discussions exclude counsel and occur on a without prejudice basis. In most instances, the discussions culminate in a joint statement prepared by both experts on issues that they have been asked to address.

The concept of expert collaboration is acknowledged by the *Federal Courts Rules*, which provide that courts may order expert witnesses to confer before the hearing with a view to narrowing the issues between them and identifying areas where they differ.[5] Additionally, the rules permit experts to prepare a joint statement setting out these issues following their discussion.[6]

Most sets of arbitral rules allow the tribunal to order witnesses to confer before the hearing. For example, the *IBA Evidence Rules* state as follows:

> The Arbitral Tribunal in its discretion may order that any Party-Appointed Experts who will submit or who have submitted Expert Reports on the same or related issues meet and confer on such issues. At such meeting, the Party-Appointed Experts shall attempt to reach agreement on the issues within the scope of their Expert Reports, and they shall record in writing any such issues on which they reach agreement, any remaining areas of disagreement and the reasons therefore.[7]

In my experience, prehearing collaboration and the issuance of joint statements are common in arbitration. However, in practice, collaboration between experts generally occurs after each has authored his initial and reply reports. As a result, each expert may be reluctant to waiver from the opinions set out in their reports. In such cases, a joint statement simply summarizes the areas of agreement and disagreement in the experts' reports, which in any event may serve as a useful road map for the tribunal at the hearing.

In my view, collaboration of the experts earlier on in the arbitral process may lead to expert evidence that is more focused, objective, and relevant to the issues in the arbitration. The *CIArb Protocol* sets out a process that encourages earlier collaboration, which is summarized below:[8]

---

5 Above note 1, r 52.6(1).
6 *Ibid*, r 52.6(4).
7 Above note 3, art 5(4).
8 Above note 4, art 6.

1) The experts hold an initial discussion for the purposes of identifying issues and tests or analyses that are to be conducted and, where possible, reaching agreement on those issues and tests or analyses. Experts may prepare and exchange draft outline opinions for the purposes of these meetings (without prejudice).
2) A joint statement outlining the findings of the discussion is circulated to the parties and tribunal.
3) Each expert prepares a report outlining her opinion on the agreed-upon issues, and such opinions are exchanged simultaneously.
4) Each expert is entitled to provide a further written opinion dealing only with issues in the written opinion of the other expert, and such opinions are also exchanged simultaneously.

While much can be done to increase the collaboration of experts before the arbitral hearing, the guidance in the *CIArb Protocol* is a step in the right direction. The initial discussion to define the issues forces collaboration (and potential agreement on issues) early, before the authoring of the initial round of expert reports. The narrowing of issues in the joint statement clearly specifies which issues are to be addressed by the experts. However, while this may make the expert reports more focused, it may also be unduly restrictive as quantifying economic damages is a dynamic process that may change course as new issues are discovered, for example, during document review or industry research. Nevertheless, the flexibility to address new issues can easily be dealt with in the joint statement. Additionally, the *CIArb Protocol* calls for the simultaneous exchange of expert reports, which is beneficial as it may serve to mitigate the effects of the usual, more adversarial process whereby an expert replies to the report of the opposing expert, and she replies in turn.

2) Expert Witness Conferencing

The traditional evidentiary process of direct examination, cross-examination, and re-examination does not always allow experts to adequately communicate their findings to the tribunal. Often, the consequence is that the tribunal is not able to reach an informed conclusion on an issue requiring expertise. Many tribunals have expressed frustration with the adversarial nature of expert evidence's presentation.

Most sets of arbitral rules allow the tribunal to direct expert evidence in a manner that is best suited to the case. Expert witness conferencing, often referred to as hot tubbing, is a flexible evidentiary process that typically involves the simultaneous testimony of the experts during the hearing. This may be in place of or an accompaniment to the traditional cross-examination of each expert. Additionally, if the experts are separately cross-examined, witness conferencing may occur before or after that.

Expert witness conferencing generally has several benefits. First, the process is efficient in that both experts, at times with opposing views on one or more issues, are able to address points raised by the other. As experts are likely to be more conversant with technical issues than counsel, they are able to expose any weaknesses in the opposing expert's analysis, which may be addressed by that expert in real time. Thus, as the process repeats itself, the experts may resolve differences or, at a minimum, clarify their positions for the benefit of the tribunal. Second, expert witness conferencing may keep experts more intellectually honest as expert witnesses generally find it difficult to make incorrect statements in front of another expert witness. Finally, expert witness conferencing can be a very effective tool in highlighting the quality and objectivity of an expert's opinion or in exposing a biased analysis.

The free-flowing nature of expert witness conferencing means that the tribunal and counsel may pose questions to either expert. Thus, a common concern of counsel is that they will lose control of the process. However, because of its obvious benefits, tribunals are increasingly requesting expert witness conferencing at the hearing, and tribunals are well-prepared to guide the flow of the discussion to maximize the benefits of the confrontation.

Expert witness conferencing raises the bar for experts' capabilities. Even more than with the traditional evidentiary process, a properly qualified expert must have a solid delivery and the ability to explain clearly and react to unexpected questions from counsel, the tribunal, and the opposing expert. Additionally, expert witness conferencing places more importance on an objective, rigorous analysis that makes sense from a big picture perspective as the opposing expert will expose any glaring weaknesses.

E. BUSINESS VALUATION TECHNIQUES AND THE VALUATION OF EARLY-STAGE BUSINESSES

1) Quantification of Economic Damages in Arbitration

Depending on the nature of the alleged wrongful act, economic damages may be measured on the basis of lost profits, the fair market value of a business interest, or both. Fair market value is defined as "the price, expressed in terms of cash equivalents, at which property would change hands between a hypothetical willing and able buyer and a hypothetical willing and able seller, acting at arms-length in an open and unrestricted market, when neither is under compulsion to buy or sell and when both have reasonable knowledge of the relevant facts."[9] Thus, in the absence of an actual transaction, in assessing fair market value, the expert must construct a notional transaction that meets the above definition. The following is a discussion of the considerations involved in doing so.

An analysis of the aspects of the business environment — such as those related to the economy, the industry, and the business itself — is critical in determining the fair market value of a business. On the basis of that analysis, an expert will be able to assess the appropriate valuation methodology. Generally, for a business that is expected to continue to operate as a going concern (i.e., in the absence of some wrongful act), there are three valuation approaches that an expert valuator would consider:

9 The Canadian Institute of Chartered Business Valuators, "Practice Bulletin No. 2: International Glossary of Business Valuation Terms" at 4, online: https://cicbv.ca/wp-content/uploads/2010/10/Practice-Bulletin-No-2-E-2001.pdf.

1) *Income-based approach*: This is based on the present value of future expected cash flows. The most popular and widely applied income-based approach is the discounted cash flow (DCF) methodology. In applying the DCF methodology, one would forecast future cash flows, typically on an annual basis, and then determine the present value that is based on a discount rate reflective of the risks of realizing or achieving such cash flows. The DCF methodology is the most appropriate in cases where future cash flows can be reasonably estimated and where a proxy for an appropriate discount rate is available. The strength of this approach lies in its theoretical and practical soundness in that its basis is the economic theory that the value of an asset is a function of its future economic benefits. However, given that it is forward looking in nature, the approach requires assumptions that relate to future revenues and costs, among other things. To the extent that key assumptions are not well reasoned and properly supported, a DCF analysis may result in an unreliable conclusion as to value.
2) *Market-based approach*: This is based on one or more references to valuation metrics observed in comparable publicly traded companies and open market transactions. The strengths of this approach are that it is relatively straightforward to apply and understand and that its conclusions are driven by valuation metrics that are observable in the marketplace. The main downside to this approach is the inherent difficulty of finding a company that is truly comparable to the subject company as no two businesses or projects are identical. Often compounding this is the general lack of sufficient detail regarding transactions to completely analyze and understand the underlying data.
3) *Asset-based approach*: This is based on the value of each of the underlying tangible and intangible assets of the business. An example of such an approach is the adjusted book value (ABV)

Note that in Canada the term "price" should be replaced with the term "highest price."

methodology, whereby the book value of equity is taken as a starting point and is then adjusted to reflect the fair market value of specific assets and liabilities. This approach is useful as it compartmentalizes value based on each asset and liability. However, there may be some difficulty in separately valuing each asset and liability, for example, in the case of a business unit with productive assets that operate as a group. Additionally, since the income- and market-based approaches account for the value of both tangible and intangible assets and liabilities, the ABV approach may not be necessary. Generally, the asset-based approach is not used as the primary valuation approach for an operating business deemed to be a going concern unless it is commonly used by buyers and sellers in the particular industry.

While the selection of an appropriate valuation approach is important, the fair market value of a business should be the same or similar regardless of the methodology applied, as fair market value is a universal term. Additionally, to bolster a conclusion of value, it is often useful to apply multiple valuation approaches, where possible. Generally, but not in all cases, when sufficiently reliable information is available, the income-based approach is applied as the primary methodology with the market- or asset-based approach applied as the secondary methodology.

While a comprehensive discussion of each valuation approach is beyond the scope of this chapter, the following section is relevant to a commonly encountered issue in the quantification of economic damages: the valuation of an early-stage business or project.

2) The Valuation of Early-Stage Businesses and Projects

One of the more difficult valuation exercises involves the valuation of an early-stage business or project. Early-stage businesses and projects are typically characterized by a lack of track record of positive earnings or as requiring investment to progress from a period of little or no earnings to one of growth and maturity. That progression is often plagued with uncertainty regarding the timing and quantum of cash flows. Additionally, as is the case with any start-up, there is a risk that the business or project will not progress and never experience growth and maturity. For these reasons, it may be difficult to formulate assumptions regarding a counterfactual or "but for" world.

In the valuation of a mature business, an expert will typically consider historical results in order to form a baseline expectation of the business's cash flows. Following that, the expert will consider how expectations regarding the relevant business, industry, and economic factors may impact future cash flows. Based on this review of historical performance and information about the future, the expert will formulate an expectation with respect to future cash flows. In the case of a business in its early stage, such an analysis may not be meaningful as historical cash flows may be nominal and bear little resemblance to expected future cash flows. This difficulty is compounded if the industry is also in its infancy as available research on and analysis of the industry may be sparse.

Experts may take steps to mitigate the challenges associated with valuing an early-stage business. For example, they may base their analyses (in whole or in part) on business plans or forecasts that have been prepared at or around the valuation date. Operating under the assumption that proper diligence has been exercised in their preparation, experts may view such forecasts as management's best estimate of the future prospects of the business or project. If relying on such documents, experts should independently evaluate whether the business plans or forecasts are reasonable in light of all relevant factors as at the valuation date.

In addition or as an alternative to the use of forecasts, the quantum expert may consider analyses produced by independent industry experts. Industry experts may be useful in, for example, analyzing relevant industry trends, forecasting drivers of revenues and expenses, providing fair market values of tangible assets, and identifying comparable assets in the market. This expertise is particularly useful in specialized industries such as energy and mining. An industry expert may mitigate the uncertainty associated with utilizing a DCF (or lost profits) methodology to value an early-stage business.

For the reasons outlined above, and given the inherent subjectivity involved, opposing experts will often disagree on the appropriate manner to value an early-stage business or project. Frequently, the expert acting for the claimant will advocate the use of a cash flow–based approach while the expert acting for the respondent will characterize the former's application of the approach as speculative or unsupported. Unfortunately, there is no one-size-fits-all solution. The appropriateness and credibility of a value conclusion will ultimately depend on the specific circumstances, nature of the information available, judgment of the expert, and characteristics of the market in which the subject assets are traded.

F. CONCLUSION

The role of the expert is to be independent and objective in assisting the tribunal to reach a conclusion in areas that require expertise. Despite the fact that this role is well-known, experts are increasingly criticized for advocating a position for their client. However, best practices in dealing with experts and increased collaboration of experts before and during the arbitral hearing may serve to increase the objectivity and rigour of expert analyses.

As demonstrated in the technical discussion above of valuation techniques and in particular those that apply to the valuation of an early-stage business or project, the expert's task involves a great deal of expertise and judgment. Thus, while disagreement between experts will no doubt continue into the foreseeable future, I believe that the collaboration of experts, the increasing sophistication of tribunals in the area of damages and valuation, and the higher standards that the market will set for qualified experts are all encouraging for the future of expert evidence.

part three

The End

The problem with books is that they end.

—CAROLINE KEPNES, *You*

chapter fourteen

Med-Arb: Crossing the Line

LESLIE DIZGUN

A. OVERVIEW

This chapter reviews the advantages and disadvantages of Med-Arb and generally takes the position that Med-Arb is a useful and cost-effective dispute resolution mechanism in light of the alternatives.

B. MED-ARB DEFINED

Med-Arb can be defined simply as an alternative dispute resolution process that allows the same selected person to both mediate and, if the mediation fails, arbitrate the dispute. This can also be referred to as using the same neutral for the entire process, as opposed to choosing a mediator to mediate the dispute and a different person to arbitrate the dispute. The advantages and disadvantages of Med-Arb are inherent in the engagement of the same person to perform both functions.

C. THE *ARBITRATION ACT*

The initial hurdle to employing the same person to mediate and arbitrate is an express prohibition set out in section 35 of the

Ontario *Arbitration Act, 1991*: "The members of an arbitral tribunal shall not conduct any part of the arbitration as a mediation or conciliation process or other similar process that might compromise or appear to compromise the arbitral tribunal's ability to decide the dispute impartially."[1]

Section 3 of the Act permits the parties to contract out of any provision of the Act except those listed in section 3. Accordingly, it is permissible for the parties to an arbitration to contract out of section 35 of the Act and allow the same person to mediate and arbitrate the dispute. The following is an example of such a provision:

> Upon the written consent of the parties, the Arbitrator may resolve or attempt to resolve the issues raised in the Arbitration by Mediation. The parties recognize that the Arbitrator/Mediator will receive relevant information while acting as Mediator during private caucuses and otherwise and agree that these activities will not impair the ability, status or jurisdiction of the Mediator/Arbitrator to decide as Arbitrator if the dispute is not settled by Mediation. The Mediation phase in the Arbitration will terminate if the parties reach a settlement of all outstanding issues or if the Mediator/Arbitrator determines that the Mediation process should be terminated and that the Mediator/Arbitrator should prepare to decide the issues. If the Mediation is terminated, the Arbitration process will begin or continue. The Arbitrator, after hearing from the parties, will decide in his sole and absolute discretion what, if any, information that was received in the Mediation process should be accepted and relied on in the Arbitration.

D. THE BACKGROUND DILEMMA

The current circumstances of the civil justice system provide a strong incentive to find fair, efficient, and cost-effective alternatives to litigation. It is evident from the "vanishing trial" phe-

1 SO 1991, c 17, s 35.

nomenon that many litigants cannot afford to take a dispute to trial and may accept less than optimal, or even at times acceptable, settlements.[2]

The simplified procedure under the Ontario *Rules of Civil Procedure* is one example of the attempts made by the civil justice system to rationalize litigation expenditures with respect to the quantum of a claim.[3] Assuming that the *Rules of Civil Procedure* provide for the fairest process to resolve disputes, the courts are choosing to favour early resolution over fairness by restricting the scope of the rules where certain criteria, for example, relating to the quantum of a claim, are met. These restrictions are intended to provide for more expeditious and less costly dispute resolution. Another example is the Ontario *Family Law Rules* requirements for leave to cross-examine deponents on affidavits in motions in the Superior Court and for a conference before the motion proceeds.[4]

These are all attempts to reduce costs to litigants so that disputes may be dealt with in the court system without litigants being crippled by court costs. The search for alternatives to the civil justice system is in many respects a search for certainty and reduced costs rather than for ideal notions of a just outcome. I suggest that to resolve disputes effectively, we must also reconsider our ideal notions of procedural justice and determine procedural justice contextually, in light of the dispute.

E. MEDIATION

Much of the debate concerning the promotion of mediation in the court system or otherwise is relevant to the controversies concerning Med-Arb. In my view, the primary advantages of mediating a dispute are the following:

2 See The Honourable Chief Justice Warren K Winkler, "The Vanishing Trial" (2008) 27:2 *Advocates' Society Journal* 3.

3 RRO 1990, Reg 194, rr 1.04(1.1) and 76.

4 O Reg 114/99,rr 14(4), 20(5), and 20(7).

- The clients participate in the decision making and thereby maintain control over the dispute and their choice to resolve it or not.
- The dispute may frequently be put on a business decision making platform as opposed to a legal platform.
- The mediator may be privy to more information than would be available to an adjudicator and therefore be more effective in assisting the parties to resolve their dispute.

The classic disadvantages of mediation are no different from those that are put forward against Med-Arb. Critiques of mediation ask whether the mediation process is fair and whether it leads to just results, often with reference to what a trial outcome would be if the matter proceeded to trial.

F. ARBITRATION

The main current critique of arbitration is that it simply replicates the litigation process and is, therefore, equally expensive, complex, alienating for the clients, and adversarial in design and conduct. There is a growing literature, especially in the United States, that is highly critical of arbitration for these reasons.[5]

Arbitration can work only when it is streamlined and, therefore, does not necessarily comply entirely with the *Rules of Civil Procedure*, in other words, when the arbitration procedures are designed to permit more efficiency, allowing issues to be narrowed and hearing time to be reduced. When arbitration does not reflect these characteristics, there is no particular justification for utilizing it rather than the court system.

Accordingly, when we talk about Med-Arb, we should be talking about a process for mediation and arbitration that is streamlined and adapted directly to the client's dispute. In my view, the

5 Thomas J Stipanowich, ed, *Protocols For Expeditious, Cost Effective Arbitration* (Austin, TX: College of Commercial Arbitrators, 2010), Christopher R Drahozal & Quentin R Wittrock, "Is There a Flight from Arbitration?" (2008) 37 *Hofstra Law Review* 71.

general efficiency of arbitration is enhanced by the use of the same person as mediator and arbitrator.

G. FINALITY AND JUSTICE

There are a number of issues that need to be raised and debated to assess the merits of Med-Arb, and this will require a brief discussion of the justice system in the context of commercial cases.

Unlike in the criminal justice system, in the civil or "commercial" justice system (the system that adjudicates contractual, employment-related, and commercial matters) fairness to the parties needs to be weighed against the finality of the dispute between the parties. Corporations and businesses are in the business of doing business, not litigating their disputes. We as lawyers all know that. Therefore, a major component of commercial justice is achieving finality in a dispute — and closure. Whether it removes contingent liabilities from the books of a company or permits key players in a business to continue to focus on the business, finality is a significant component of any civil justice system. The focus of current attempts to improve the commercial justice system is on achieving finality (and just outcomes) in a timely and cost-effective fashion.

The introduction of proportionality as a general principle in the litigation of disputes has now enshrined the notion that, in ideal terms, costs expended on a dispute and the nature of the procedures applied to the dispute should be proportionate to the dispute and, often, the money at issue in the dispute. In the context of Med-Arb, the question to ask is, what procedures remain necessary in light of proportionality to advance your client's case to resolution? Most often, answering this requires being attentive to ways to streamline the arbitration component.

Med-Arb should be viewed in terms of a proportionate balancing of finality against the principles that we as lawyers generally believe are important including fair process, full disclosure, knowing the case that one has to meet, and having a hearing before an adjudicator with all the attributes that we have become accustomed to in the court system. In my view, it is now necessary to assess every dispute in light of proportionality and to assess, among other things, the relative importance of finality against the overall fairness content of any procedures applied to the resolution of a dispute. We can no longer afford, nor is it necessarily appropriate, to employ all the mechanisms of the commercial justice system in each and every commercial dispute.

Med-Arb can be a very effective way to achieve finality, with procedural justice tailored to the nature of the dispute between the parties.

H. BENEFITS OF MED-ARB IN COMMERCIAL CASES

Med-Arb has several important benefits for commercial cases. First, in Med-Arb the same person both mediates and, if the mediation fails, adjudicates the dispute between the parties. Implicit in this structure is that the mediator may have a significant influence on the outcome because the parties are aware that the mediator will be the adjudicator. In part, the power of Med-Arb is in its design.

Understand that when you choose the mediator, the person you choose may have that kind of influence on the mediation. I fail to see how this is different from choosing an evaluative mediator, something that lawyers tend to do more frequently than not in court-mandated mediations. Often, such a mediator is chosen because the lawyers want the mediator to exercise some influence and indicate her opinion as to the merits. Ironically, we then conclude that where the mediator will also be the adjudicator, there should be no evaluation. However, if the mediator provides a thorough risk analysis to the parties and points out both strengths and weaknesses in their positions and if her efforts are aimed at achieving a settlement between them and not at adjudicating the merits of the dispute, then providing an opinion is not necessary. In my view, such an approach, which has evaluative components, should not cause concerns to counsel or their clients.

If the mediator is also the chosen arbitrator, that mediator has now gained a significant insight into the dispute and may be able to assist the parties in narrowing the issues or framing a more efficient procedure for the arbitration. The arbitrator who has mediated the dispute also requires considerably less education about the dispute at the hearing of the arbitration, should the mediation fail.

Med-Arb is frequently used in the labour relations field, and is de facto used frequently in grievance arbitration in particular, usually because the employer and union have sufficient confidence in the arbitrator to invite the arbitrator to mediate before the actual arbitration. This often avoids the costs of an arbitration.

As both a mediator and an arbitrator, I see a sharp distinction between mediation and arbitration. Evaluation in mediation is aimed at bringing the parties closer to a mutually acceptable settlement by getting them into a settlement range while evaluation in arbitration is aimed at the application of the law to the facts. An arbitrator can decide the matter based only on the evidence provided at the arbitration and not on other information provided or conversation that occurred at the mediation.

Med-Arb puts the arbitrator in a uniquely advantageous position to assist the parties in resolving their dispute or in continuing their dispute in an efficient and cost-effective manner.

I. CRITIQUES OF MED-ARB

Critiques of Med-Arb are perhaps strongest in the commercial context. Commercial litigation practitioners, unlike labour or family law practitioners, are quite entrenched in their concerns about neutrality, impartiality, and implicit bias where the arbitrator is also the mediator.

The first thing to say about the concepts of neutrality and impartiality is that they are recognized as foundational in our justice system. But the particularity of the procedural rules in the *Rules of Civil Procedure* aimed at guaranteeing these concepts may not always be necessary for every dispute. Can we achieve sufficient neutrality and impartiality while limiting the scope of particular procedures that are intended to ensure fairness in the system? Such limitations have already formed a significant part of the attempts to improve the civil and commercial justice system, as evidenced by, among other things, simplified procedure and summary trials.

One study in the labour relations context examined the Ontario Grievance Settlement Board and concluded that criticisms of Med-Arb were actually directed against the specific abilities of the person chosen to conduct the Med-Arb rather than the process. Evidence from experienced med-arbitrators indicated that they were able to move easily between roles and not be affected by information learned during the mediation.[6]

In my experience, it is very possible to step between mediator and arbitrator roles. Adjudication is necessarily based only on the evidence put before the adjudicator and, in my experience, may result in an outcome that is quite different from that achieved in a negotiated settlement between the parties to a mediation. In addition, lawyers are well trained in distinguishing between conversation at a mediation and admissible evidence at an arbitration. Martin Teplitsky has noted this in comments made on the case of *McClintock v Karam*.[7]

Critics have also raised the matter of implicit bias.[8] I assume that by implicit bias, critics mean that having mediated the dispute, the arbitrator may have developed a view of one or other of the parties, or somehow become more or less sympathetic to one or other of the parties. I see this as being no different from the situation of an arbitrator who observing the parties and their counsel at the arbitration, may develop a certain implicit view of the parties' character or personality or of their past motivations.

6 See Megan Elizabeth Telford, *Med-Arb: A Viable Dispute Resolution Alternative*, Current Issues Series (Kingston, ON: Industrial Relations Centre Press, 2000), online: http://irc.queensu.ca/sites/default/files/articles/med-arb-a-viable-dispute-resolution-alternative.pdf.

7 2015 ONSC 1024; Martin Teplitsky, "Mediation/Arbitration in Commercial Cases: A Remedy for Litigants Who Have Run Out of Patience and Cash" (2015) 34:2 *Advocates' Journal* 12.

8 See Brian A Pappas, "Med-Arb and the Legalization of Alternative Dispute Resolution" (2015) 20 *Harvard Negotiation Law Review* 157.

The only thing that the mediation will do is provide the arbitrator with more opportunity to make these assessments and, arguably, develop a fuller and more balanced view of the parties. I am skeptical of how far these kinds of assessments enter into any decision making in an arbitration, but I nevertheless see no disadvantage in the context of Med-Arb as opposed to in the hearing of an arbitration by an adjudicator who has not conducted a mediation between the parties.

Neutrality, another important fairness principle, is quite contentious in the context of mediation. Many mediators do not find it a particularly useful concept in the context of mediating a dispute. To the extent that it means treating the parties even-handedly, there is no difference between the neutrality of Med-Arb and the neutrality where the person chosen to conduct the mediation is different from the one chosen to conduct the arbitration. Mediators quite often challenge each party's case, and in that sense they are not what we think of as neutral. To properly engage with the facts and issues, a mediator may not be neutral as we commonly understand the term. The neutrality of an arbitrator really rests on the fact that the arbitrator determines the result based on the evidence put before him and the application of the law to that evidence.

In many ways, Med-Arb's advantages may be viewed as its disadvantages depending on your point of view. The additional knowledge of the parties' dispute and the parties themselves gained by the mediator is an advantage. But to critics, it remains a disadvantage suggesting that there may be implicit bias.

J. THE CHARACTER OF THE MED-ARBITRATOR

Ultimately, a positive experience with Med-Arb depends on the quality of the person who conducts the mediation and then, if the mediation fails, the arbitration. Counsel and the parties must have sufficient confidence in that person to believe that she will deal fairly with them should the mediation fail. An experienced mediator and arbitrator will have sufficient expertise to be able to move comfortably from the role of mediator to that of arbitrator.

A Med-Arb regime is essentially an evaluative dispute resolution tool where the arbitrator is likely to have subject matter expertise and, accordingly, the necessary skills to apply to the mediation in the shadow of arbitration. Often, however, the arbitrator will conduct a facilitative mediation rather than one with an evaluative component for fear of provoking an allegation of bias later. In my view, this defeats the purpose of the Med-Arb regime. Med-Arb is a powerful tool to resolve your clients' cases early, with finality, and in a cost-effective fashion.

K. FACTORS TO CONSIDER BEFORE CHOOSING MED-ARB

1) *Complexity of dispute*: Disputes that are not complex and in which the law is fairly straightforward are quite amenable to Med-Arb.
2) *Type of dispute*: Med-Arb may lend itself to certain kinds of disputes more than others. For example, employment or wrongful dismissal disputes where cause is not alleged and where the issues are about the reasonable notice period and the quantum of damages may be more suited to the Med-Arb regime, rather than disputes involving nonsolicitation or noncompetition, which are usually factually complex.
3) *Trustworthiness of the neutral*: It is imperative that you choose someone that both counsel and their clients can trust as a fair and reasonable neutral with the requisite experience. In addition, you should choose someone with subject matter expertise relevant to the dispute. For example, the mediator-arbitrator in an employment law dispute should be very familiar with employment law concepts and the current law.
4) *Quantum of the claim*: Disputes in which the amount claimed is under a fixed sum of money such as simplified procedure disputes (under $100,000) should be med-arbed as the cost of counsel cannot be justified in light of the money at issue.

Med-Arb can be a very effective dispute resolution tool in commercial cases, reflecting the parties' desire for finality and a fair process.

chapter fifteen

Arbitral Awards: Appeals, Setting Aside, and Enforcement

HARVIN PITCH & LUCAS KITTMER

A. INTRODUCTION

This chapter is about conducting domestic and international arbitration. A domestic arbitration is one where the parties to the dispute reside or carry on business in Canada. An international arbitration is one where the parties reside or carry on business in different countries. While there are many principles of law that apply to both domestic and international arbitration, they are governed by separate statutes.

This chapter will concentrate mainly on the law as it applies in the province of Ontario. However, subject to certain statutory exceptions, the law is applied similarly across the common law provinces.[1]

1 For a discussion of the federal and provincial laws applying to domestic and international arbitration in Canada, see J Brian Casey, *Arbitration Law of Canada: Practice and Procedure*, 2d ed (Huntington, NY: Juris, 2011) ch 2; Babak Barin, Andrew D Little, & Randy A Pepper, *The Osler Guide to Commercial Arbitration in Canada: A Practical Introduction to Domestic and International Commercial Arbitration* (The Hague: Kluwer Law International, 2006) ch 4.

B. HISTORY OF THE LEGISLATION

Until the 1990s, litigation was carried on primarily in the courts. While arbitration existed, our courts were slow to recognize that arbitration was an effective substitute for the courts, and the provinces were slow to recognize the distinction between domestic and international arbitration.[2]

This all began to change in 1986 when Canada signed the United Nations *Convention on the Recognition and Enforcement of Foreign Arbitral Awards* (the *New York Convention*)[3] and adopted the *UNCITRAL Model Law on International Commercial Arbitration*.[4] The *New York Convention* was quickly ratified at the federal level, making Canada the first country to adopt legislation based on the *New York Convention*.[5] Before long, the model law was implemented in provincial legislation across Canada.

Contrary to what one might expect from such a rapid, matter-of-fact adoption of United Nations legislation, the ratification of the *UNCITRAL Model Law* was an incredibly significant watershed moment for Canada's approach to arbitration conducted both at home and abroad. The overarching policy objective of the *New York Convention* and the *UNCITRAL Model Law* is to strengthen the certainty and enforceability of international commercial arbitration as a dispute resolution mechanism. As a result, the *UNCITRAL Model Law* promotes a high degree of deference to arbitration awards made in compliance with basic principles of fairness. Canadian courts' traditional skepticism of foreign arbitral awards, particularly the further one got from traditional Western-style democracies, gave way to a robust paradigm of respect for arbitration agreements so long

2 See Casey, above note 1 at 2–3.

3 10 June 1958, 330 UNTS 3, online: www.uncitral.org/pdf/english/texts/arbitration/NY-conv/New-York-Convention-E.pdf.

4 21 June 1985, UN Doc A/40/17, annex 1, with amendments adopted 7 July 2006, UN Doc A/61/17, annex 1, online: www.uncitral.org/pdf/english/texts/arbitration/ml-arb/07-86998_Ebook.pdf [*UNCITRAL Model Law*].

5 See Randy A Pepper, "Why Arbitrate?: Ontario's Recent Experience with Commercial Arbitration" (1988) 36:4 *Osgoode Hall Law Journal* 807.

as they met the most fundamental requirements of justice under the UNCITRAL rules.

The *New York Convention* deals with the enforcement of foreign international arbitration awards that are sought to be enforced in the local province. The *UNCITRAL Model Law* deals with the conduct of international commercial arbitration in the local province. It also provides for the setting aside of international arbitration awards. The *New York Convention* has been adopted as special legislation in most of the provinces. In Ontario, the *New York Convention* is contained in the *International Commercial Arbitration Act, 2017*.[6] The *UNCITRAL Model Law* has been incorporated into that Act.

The provinces were concerned that the *UNCITRAL Model Law* would have to be amended to deal with the circumstances of pure domestic arbitration to give the court more flexibility to intervene. For example, under the *UNCITRAL Model Law* there is no right of appeal, and a right of appeal is included under the domestic legislation. There are, therefore, some differences between the domestic acts and the *UNCITRAL Model Law*. The model law is nevertheless the basis for the provincial legislation, including the Ontario *Arbitration Act, 1991*.[7]

C. FURTHER COMMENTS

The policy underlying the *UNCITRAL Model Law* and therefore the policy underlying both the *ICAA* and the *Arbitration Act* is the recognition of parties' autonomy to agree upon and implement their own dispute resolution mechanisms outside of the court process.[8]

The courts are now generally inclined to enforce parties' express agreements to defer disputes to arbitration and to enforce

6 SO 2017, c 2, Schedule 5 [*ICAA*].

7 SO 1991, c 17 [*Arbitration Act*].

8 See Colin P Stevenson, "Arbitral Awards: Appeals, Setting Aside and Enforcement" (Delivered at the Law Society of Upper Canada program A Primer on Arbitration: For Litigators, Toronto, 5 April 2016) at 2, online: www.swlawyers.ca/docs/Arbitral-Awards-Appeals-Setting-Aside-and-Enforcement_-_Colin-Stevenson.pdf.

arbitral awards; they give arbitration agreements a liberal interpretation, and arbitration awards are readily enforced.[9] Basically, the Ontario courts lean toward any contractual interpretation that favours arbitration.[10]

Both the *ICAA* and the *Arbitration Act* require that before an award can be enforced, there needs to be court intervention. A court order must be secured to enforce the arbitration award. Also, it should be pointed out that the basic theme governing arbitration is that the arbitration procedure and the arbitration itself must incorporate basic principles of fairness and provide both sides the opportunity of fully participating in the arbitration. This theme governs motions to enforce arbitration awards, whether foreign or domestic, and motions to set aside arbitration awards, whether foreign or domestic.

D. DOMESTIC ARBITRATION

1) Introduction

Ontario has now fully adopted a deferential approach to arbitrators. Arbitration agreements are given a liberal interpretation and readily enforced while arbitrators are afforded the authority to rule first on their own jurisdiction.[11] In Ontario, section 6 of the *Arbitration Act* prohibits any court intervention in arbitration outside of four specific exceptions:

1. To assist the conducting of arbitrations.
2. To ensure that arbitrations are conducted in accordance with arbitration agreements.
3. To prevent unequal or unfair treatment of parties to arbitration agreements.

9 See *Dalimpex Ltd v Janicki* (2003), 64 OR (3d) 737 at paras 21–22 (CA) [*Dalimpex*]; *Ontario Medical Assn v Willis Canada Inc*, 2013 ONCA 745 at para 20; *Dell Computer Corp v Union des consommateurs*, 2007 SCC 34 at paras 84–85; *GreCon Dimter Inc v JR Normand Inc*, 2005 SCC 46 at para 38.

10 See *Canadian National Railway Co v Lovat Tunnel Equipment Inc* (1999), 174 DLR (4th) 385 (Ont CA).

11 See *Dalimpex*, above note 9.

4. To enforce awards.[12]

To facilitate arbitral tribunals' broad authority outside of these exceptions, the *Arbitration Act* permits arbitral tribunals to make interim or final awards, including orders for specific performance, injunctions, and other equitable remedies.[13] However, parties are free to contract out of these remedies if they so wish. In fact, parties may contract out of the majority of *Arbitration Act* provisions. Other than family arbitration (which has its own set of rules), parties may contract out of anything *except* for the following:[14]

1) contractual provisions requiring arbitration as a prerequisite to an application to the court
2) the equality and fairness guarantee
3) the extension of time limits
4) the setting aside of an award
5) a declaration of invalidity of an arbitration
6) the enforcement of an award

Combined with the high degree of deference given to arbitral tribunals, this expansive freedom to contract out of *Arbitration Act* provisions gives parties an unprecedented level of control in constructing custom arbitration agreements to suit their specific needs.

2) Right of Appeal

In Ontario, the parties to an arbitration agreement can contract to remove the right of appeal or provide for an appeal on any basis, such as law, fact, or mixed fact and law. If the agreement is silent, however, section 45 of the *Arbitration Act* applies. That section provides as follows:[15]

- An appeal is only available with leave.
- An appeal is only available on a question of law.

12 Above note 7, s 6.

13 *Ibid*, s 31.

14 *Ibid*, ss 5(4), 19, 39, 46, 48, and 50.

15 *Ibid*, s 45.

- And even if the matter is a question of law, the court must be satisfied that the importance to the parties of the matters at stake in the arbitration justifies an appeal and that the determination of the question of law at issue will significantly affect the rights of the parties.

Traditionally, this was a relatively low hurdle in Canadian courts since determining the legal rights and obligations of parties under a written contract was considered a pure question of law.[16] However, in its recent decision in *Sattva Capital Corp v Creston Moly Corp*, the Supreme Court of Canada held that the interpretation of a contract is now a matter of fact and law.[17] Matters of fact and law are subject to the "palpable error" standard of review, which is almost impossible to meet.[18] The Court in *Sattva* held that a question of law might still be available in a contract case if there was a defined, extricable legal issue to be determined by the court, but this is a very difficult standard to meet.[19]

3) Standard of Review

In keeping with the Supreme Court of Canada's restrictive approach to arbitration appeals and the general train of Canadian jurisprudence promoting deference to arbitrators and the contractual autonomy of parties, the standard of review for most commercial arbitration appeals is the standard of reasonableness, which is a relatively easy standard for a responding party to meet. The standard of correctness will apply only if the question is a constitutional one or a question of law that is of central importance to the legal system as a whole and outside of the ad-

16 See Kim Lewison, *The Interpretation of Contracts*, 5th ed & 1st supp (London: Sweet & Maxwell, 2011 & 2013) at 173–76; Geoff Robert Hall, *Canadian Contractual Interpretation Law*, 2d ed (Markham, ON: LexisNexis, 2012) at 125–26.

17 2014 SCC 53 [*Sattva*].

18 *Ibid* at para 47.

19 See, for example, the recent decision *Ottawa (City) Coliseum Inc*, 2016 ONCA 363.

judicator's expertise.[20] The Ontario Court of Appeal in its recent decision in *Popack v Lipszyc* held that in applying the reasonableness standard, the court should be deferential toward the decision of the arbitrator.[21]

It is important to consider this standard of review in the context of other remedies available to parties under the *Arbitration Act*. Parties could have an agreement set aside under section 46 if there has been a breach of fundamental rules of justice and procedural fairness.[22] So any ground sufficient to convince an appeals judge that an arbitration award fails to meet a reasonableness standard would likely persuade the Superior Court, with considerably less time and expense, to grant a section 46 application. There is little doubt that for all but the most generally applicable questions of law, appeals are a tenuous strategy for commercial arbitration disputes.

An appeal must be brought within thirty days after the award is made unless the applicant alleges corruption or fraud.[23] This same time limit applies to an application to set aside an award. The time limit cannot be extended by the court.[24]

4) Setting Aside Awards

If parties are unable or unwilling to attempt to bring an appeal, they may instead attempt to challenge an arbitral decision by making an application to set aside the award under section 46 of the *Arbitration Act*.[25] Even where parties have expressly contracted out of appeal rights, the grounds in section 46(1) permit setting aside an arbitral award if basic standards of fairness have not been met.

20 See *Sattva*, above note 17 at para 106.

21 2016 ONCA 135 at para 26, an appeal from the motion judge's decision at 2015 ONSC 3460.

22 Above note 7, s 46.

23 *Ibid*, s 47.

24 See *R & G Draper Farms (Keswick) Ltd v 1758691 Ontario Inc (cob ATV Farms)*, 2014 ONCA 278 at paras 16–21 [*R & G Draper*].

25 Above note 7, s 46.

An arbitral award may be set aside only on the grounds laid out in section 46(1):

1. A party entered into the arbitration agreement while under a legal incapacity.
2. The arbitration agreement is invalid or has ceased to exist.
3. The award deals with a dispute that the arbitration agreement does not cover or contains a decision on a matter that is beyond the scope of the agreement.
4. The composition of the arbitral tribunal was not in accordance with the arbitration agreement or, if the agreement did not deal with that matter, was not in accordance with this Act.
5. The subject-matter of the dispute is not capable of being the subject of arbitration under Ontario law.
6. The applicant was not treated equally and fairly, was not given an opportunity to present a case or to respond to another party's case, or was not given proper notice of the arbitration or of the appointment of an arbitrator.
7. The procedures followed in the arbitration did not comply with this Act.
8. An arbitrator has committed a corrupt or fraudulent act or there is a reasonable apprehension of bias.
9. The award was obtained by fraud.
10. The award is a family arbitration award that is not enforceable under the *Family Law Act*.[26]

Generally speaking, these grounds are limited to flagrant breaches of procedural justice or objectivity, and applications should thus be made sparingly. This is not the venue to debate terms of construction or the interpretation of agreements. Moreover, the *Arbitration Act* includes safeguards to prevent a party from sitting back and waiting to see how an arbitral tribunal rules before deciding to take action. Under restrictions in sections 46(3) to (6), a court must not set aside an award if the party to the arbitration has had an opportunity to challenge the arbitrator on

26 *Ibid.*

any of the grounds in section 46(1) and has chosen not to do so.[27] This is unsurprising. A party that intentionally includes express provisions waiving appeal rights in an arbitration agreement and then attempts to set aside an unfavourable award after the fact goes against the core intent of the *UNCITRAL Model Law*. Letting the most prudent and cost-efficient time for a challenge pass to see what happens will lead the court to conclude that the party has waived its right to object on that particular ground for an application to set aside the award.[28]

5) Discretion

Section 46(1) of the *Arbitration Act* provides that the court "may" set aside a domestic arbitration award. This allows the court, having found that grounds to set aside exist, discretion as to whether it should set aside the award.[29] This section is similar to provisions of the *ICAA* discussed in Section E(4), below.

As stated above, a party must move to set aside an award within thirty days after the award is made unless the applicant alleges corruption or fraud.[30] This time limit cannot be extended by the court.[31]

6) Recognition and Enforcement of Awards

Any party that seeks to enforce its domestic arbitral award, whether interim or final, must apply to the court for recognition and enforcement of the award pursuant to section 50 of the *Arbitration Act*.[32] Since arbitrators have no power over third parties, the court's intervention is necessary to actuate enforcement mechanisms against any of the defendant's funds or assets. Fortunately for

27 *Ibid*, ss 46(3)–(6).

28 *Ibid*, s 46(5).

29 *Ibid*, s 46.

30 *Ibid*, s 47.

31 See *R & G Draper*, above note 24 at paras 16–21.

32 Above note 7, s 50.

parties, section 50 states that a court shall recognize and enforce an arbitral award made in Ontario and put before it unless one of four special circumstances exists:

(a) the thirty-day period for commencing an appeal or an application to set the award aside has not yet elapsed;
(b) there is a pending appeal, application to set the award aside or application for a declaration of invalidity;
(c) the award has been set aside or the arbitration is the subject of a declaration of invalidity; or
(d) the award is a family arbitration award.[33]

As a result, the courts will usually issue orders for things like *Mareva* injunctions as a matter of course so long as the standard common law tests are met.[34]

An arbitral award made elsewhere in Canada that has not been set aside in the province or territory in which it was made is eligible for an application under section 50 unless its subject matter is not capable of being the subject of arbitration under Ontario law, there is a pending appeal, or the time limit for commencing an appeal has not yet elapsed.[35] An arbitral award is not a judgment or a court order for the payment of money and is therefore subject to the two-year limitation period under the Ontario *Limitations Act, 2002*.[36] All the usual court enforcement mechanisms apply to a court order for recognition and enforcement of an arbitral award.[37]

The oppression remedy available under section 248 of the Ontario *Business Corporations Act* can also be used to enforce an arbitration award.[38]

---

33 *Ibid*, s 50(3).

34 See *Farah v Sauvageau Holdings Inc*, 2011 ONSC 1819.

35 Above note 7, s 50(4).

36 RSA 2000, c L-12. See *Yugraneft Corp v Rexx Management Corp*, 2010 SCC 19. The two-year period is, of course, subject to the rules of discoverability.

37 See *Rules of Civil Procedure*, RRO 1990, Reg 194, r 60; *Execution Act*, RSO 1990, c E.24.

38 RSO 1990, c B.16. See *T Films SA Future Films (3) Ltd v Cinemavault Releasing International Inc*, 2015 ONSC 6608.

E. INTERNATIONAL COMMERCIAL ARBITRATION

1) Introduction

There are a number of similarities between Ontario's domestic *Arbitration Act* and the *ICAA*, under which courts are able to provide interlocutory relief pursuant to article 9,[39] they are once again required to provide recognition and enforcement except in a handful of limited circumstances, and there is a similar procedure for getting arbitral awards set aside when they breach fundamental principles of fairness. However, there are also a number of key differences. Most significantly, there are no appeals from an award under the *ICAA*. The only way to challenge a foreign arbitral award is to seek to set it aside under article 34 of the *ICAA*.[40]

International commercial arbitration thus places greater restrictions on court intervention than domestic arbitration regimes. Parties that seek to enforce an arbitration award in a foreign jurisdiction must bring an application for recognition and enforcement of that award in the jurisdiction where they want to have the award enforced.

2) Right of Appeal

The *UNCITRAL Model Law* as incorporated into provincial legislation, including the Ontario *ISAA*, contains no right of appeal.

3) Setting Aside Awards

The only means of challenging an arbitral award under the *ISAA* is by an application to the court to set aside the award under article 34 of the *UNCITRAL Model Law*, which is incorporated into

---

39 Above note 6, Schedule 2, art 9.

40 *Ibid*, Schedule 2, art 34.

the *ISAA* and applies to setting aside any arbitral award whether made in Ontario or elsewhere.[41]

Popack v Lipszyc, which is discussed in detail in Section E(4), below, provides considerable insight into the factors that come into play in an application to set aside an award under the *ISAA*.[42] In that case, one of the parties to an award made by a rabbinical court in New York state launched an application in Ontario to set aside that award pursuant to the provisions of the *UNCITRAL Model Law* dealing with setting aside international awards that are incorporated into the *ICAA*.

Article 34(2) of the *UNCITRAL Model Law* (which is incorporated into the *ICAA*) states that an arbitral award may be set aside by the court (in this case, the Ontario Superior Court) only if

> (a) the party making the application furnishes proof that:
>
> (i) a party to the arbitration agreement referred to in article 7 was under some incapacity; or the said agreement is not valid under the law to which the parties have subjected it or, failing any indication thereon, under the law of this State; or
>
> (ii) the party making the application was not given proper notice of the appointment of an arbitrator or of the arbitral proceedings or was otherwise unable to present his case; or
>
> (iii) the award deals with a dispute not contemplated by or not falling within the terms of the submission to arbitration, or contains decisions on matters beyond the scope of the submission to arbitration, provided that, if the decisions on matters submitted to arbitration can be separated from those not so submitted, only that part of the award which contains decisions on matters not submitted to arbitration may be set aside; or

41 *Ibid.* For a precedent notice of application to set aside an arbitration award under article 34 of the *UNCITRAL Model Law*, see Appendix 1, at the end of this chapter.

42 Above note 21 (ONCA).

(iv) the composition of the arbitral tribunal or the arbitral procedure was not in accordance with the agreement of the parties, unless such agreement was in conflict with a provision of this Law from which the parties cannot derogate, or, failing such agreement, was not in accordance with this Law; or

(b) the court finds that:

(i) the subject-matter of the dispute is not capable of settlement by arbitration under the law of this State; or

(ii) the award is in conflict with the public policy of this State.[43]

Furthermore, articles 34(3) and (4) provide as follows:

> (3) An application for setting aside may not be made after three months have elapsed from the date on which the party making that application had received the award or, if a request had been made under article 33 [correction and interpretation of an award], from the date on which that request had been disposed of by the arbitral tribunal.
>
> (4) The court, when asked to set aside an award, may, where appropriate and so requested by a party, suspend the setting aside proceedings for a period of time determined by it in order to give the arbitral tribunal an opportunity to resume the arbitral proceedings or to take such other action as in the arbitral tribunal's opinion will eliminate the grounds for setting aside.[44]

It is important to note that even if the grounds to set aside an arbitral award exist, the court "may" do so — that is, the court has discretion. Similarly, on the issue of enforcement (dealt with in Section E(5), below) the court also has discretion to decide whether or not to refuse to enforce a foreign award even if the grounds for refusal have been met. The discretionary test that applies in the case of motions to set aside arbitral awards is the same that applies to the discretion as to whether or not to refuse to enforce an award.

---

43 Above note 6, Schedule 2, art 34(2).

44 *Ibid*, Schedule 2, art 34(3)–(4).

4) Discretion

The case of *Popack v Lipszyc* deals with the discretion that the court has to set aside an arbitral award where one of the grounds for doing so has been met.[45] This recent case is worth exploring as it addresses the types of facts that will and will not motivate the court to exercise its discretion and the test to be used by the court in determining whether to exercise its discretion.

The facts in *Popack v Lipszyc* are essentially as follows:

- The parties conducted an arbitration before a rabbinical court in New York state. This was the second arbitration that was held.
- The arbitration agreement provided that both parties would be informed of hearings.
- During the arbitration, one side suggested to the panel that the panel speak to the individual who had been the first arbitrator. The other side raised no objection.
- Without notice to either party, the panel met with the first arbitrator.
- When the party who had raised no objection heard about the meeting, he wrote to the panel (without notice to the other side) setting out his version of events at the first arbitration and requested a full hearing of the panel if the panel intended to rely on the first arbitrator's evidence.
- The panel, however, decided not to hold a new hearing. It came to its decision and wrote to both parties saying that the evidence of the first arbitrator had had no effect on its decision.
- The party who was unsuccessful in the arbitration and who had written the letter to the panel requesting a further hearing applied to the Ontario court under the *ICAA* to set aside the award pursuant to article 34(2) of the *UNCITRAL Model Law* incorporated into the *ICAA*. The applicant's opposition was that the arbitration had not been held in ac-

45 Above note 21.

cordance with the provisions of the arbitration agreement because both sides were to be informed of hearings, and by having held an *ex parte* hearing to meet with the first arbitrator, the panel had breached the arbitration agreement. This is one of the grounds for setting aside an arbitration award.

The motion judge refused to set aside the award. She considered the following factors in exercising her discretion:

- How serious is the breach?
- What potential impact does the breach have on the award?
- Will setting aside the award cause prejudice to the arbitration process?
- What was the conduct of the complaining party once he became aware of the error?

The motion judge refused to set aside the award on the grounds that when the complaining party had heard about the meeting with the first arbitrator, he had not *demanded* (but merely suggested) a rehearing and that if the arbitration award were to be set aside, the arbitration process would be prejudiced both because there would be the additional cost of the new arbitration and, more importantly, because a key witness had since died, and his evidence would not be available.

The Court of Appeal affirmed the decision, holding that the motion judge had exercised her discretion properly and reasonably. It gave deference to the award.[46] The court noted that the scope of discretion under article 34(2) of the *UNCITRAL Model Law* is significantly affected by the ground on which the award could be set aside. For example, if the arbitration agreement were invalid, the court would have less discretion to uphold the award. Where the ground on which the award could be set aside is simply a matter of procedure, the court will be more likely to uphold the award.[47] The Court of Appeal held that the key test was, how

46 *Ibid* at para 26.

47 *Ibid* at para 30.

far had the breach of procedure undermined the appearance of fairness, and what was the effect of that breach on the award?[48] The court looked at what other courts in other jurisdictions had done when confronted with procedural irregularities[49] and held that in the circumstances the private meeting with the arbitrator had not been serious enough to warrant setting aside the award.

5) Recognition and Enforcement of Awards

Articles 35 and 36 of the *UNCITRAL Model Law* provide as follows:

> *Article 35. Recognition and enforcement*
> (1) An arbitral award, irrespective of the country in which it was made, shall be recognized as binding and, upon application in writing to the competent court, shall be enforced subject to the provisions of this article and of article 36.
> (2) The party relying on an award or applying for its enforcement shall supply the original award or a copy thereof. If the award is not made in an official language of this State, the court may request the party to supply a translation thereof into such language.
>
> *Article 36. Grounds for refusing recognition or enforcement*
> (1) Recognition or enforcement of an arbitral award, irrespective of the country in which it was made, may be refused only:
> (a) at the request of the party against whom it is invoked, if that party furnishes to the competent court where recognition or enforcement is sought proof that:
> (i) a party to the arbitration agreement referred to in article 7 was under some incapacity; or the said agreement is not valid under the law to which the parties have subjected it or, failing any indication thereon, under the law of the country where the award was made; or
> (ii) the party against whom the award is invoked was not given proper notice of the appointment of an arbitrator

48 *Ibid* at paras 31 and 36.
49 For some examples, see *ibid* at paras 32 and 35.

or of the arbitral proceedings or was otherwise unable to present his case; or

(iii) the award deals with a dispute not contemplated by or not falling within the terms of the submission to arbitration, or it contains decisions on matters beyond the scope of the submission to arbitration, provided that, if the decisions on matters submitted to arbitration can be separated from those not so submitted, that part of the award which contains decisions on matters submitted to arbitration may be recognized and enforced; or

(iv) the composition of the arbitral tribunal or the arbitral procedure was not in accordance with the agreement of the parties or, failing such agreement, was not in accordance with the law of the country where the arbitration took place; or

(v) the award has not yet become binding on the parties or has been set aside or suspended by a court of the country in which, or under the law of which, that award was made; or

(b) if the court finds that:

(i) the subject-matter of the dispute is not capable of settlement by arbitration under the law of this State; or

(ii) the recognition or enforcement of the award would be contrary to the public policy of this State.

(2) If an application for setting aside or suspension of an award has been made to a court referred to in paragraph (1)(a)(v) of this article, the court where recognition or enforcement is sought may, if it considers it proper, adjourn its decision and may also, on the application of the party claiming recognition or enforcement of the award, order the other party to provide appropriate security.[50]

50 Above note 6, Schedule 2, art 35–36. For a precedent notice of application for enforcement of an arbitration award under article 35 of the *UNCITRAL Model Law*, see Appendix 2, at the end of this chapter.

As stated above, the court has discretion as to whether or not to refuse to enforce an award and will exercise that discretion on the same basis as it exercises its discretion to set aside an award.

Despite the implication of article 36(1)(b), Canadian courts have been clear that they will refuse to enforce an award that has been enforced in a foreign jurisdiction only in the most egregious circumstances. In *Schreter v Gasmac Inc*, the Ontario court suggested that to do otherwise would undermine the intent of the *UNCITRAL Model Law*:

> Nothing in those articles suggests that if an award has been confirmed by a court order or judgment in the jurisdiction where the award was made, it will not then be enforced in Ontario.
>
> It is clear that any such bar to enforcement would create a gaping hole in the scope of the Act and in the assistance and encouragement it is able to offer to those who wish to use the mechanism of international commercial arbitration with relative ease and with confidence in the enforcement procedure . . . .
>
> The concept of imposing our public policy on foreign awards is to guard against enforcement of an award which offends our local principles of justice and fairness in a fundamental way, and in a way which the parties could attribute to the fact that the award was made in another jurisdiction where the procedural or substantive rules diverge markedly from our own, or where there was ignorance or corruption on the part of the tribunal which could not be seen to be tolerated or condoned by our courts.[51]

The court went on to enforce the arbitration agreement at issue despite the fact that the arbitrator had not provided reasons for her decision and that the award included a sum representing damages not contemplated by the parties at the time the agreement had been signed. In rejecting the respondent's public policy arguments on these points, the court stated that refusing to enforce an award for anything less than serious misconduct would undermine the *UNCITRAL Model Law*'s enforcement mechanisms and leave uncer-

51 [1992] OJ No 257 at paras 29–30 and 50 (Gen Div) [*Schreter v Gasmac*].

tainty for future parties about whether the province would be willing to acquiesce to the strong party-autonomy intent of the *ICAA*. Indeed, concerns over inconsistency in enforcement across jurisdictions have already been the subject of considerable academic discussion.[52] The court's approach in *Schreter v Gasmac* has been followed by a number of recent Canadian cases,[53] and the case is generally regarded as the leading case on the tendency of Canadian courts to recognize and enforce foreign arbitral awards.[54]

6) Appropriate Procedure

The appropriate procedure to enforce an international arbitral award in Ontario is to make an application to recognize the foreign arbitral award, not an application to recognize any foreign judgment recognizing that award in any other jurisdiction.[55] It does not matter that a foreign arbitral award has been recognized (or domesticated) by an order of a foreign court.

F. CONFLICTS OF LAW ACROSS JURISDICTIONS

It is important to give some context to the broad statements made by the court in *Schreter v Gasmac* about the necessity of enforcing foreign arbitral awards in most circumstances and the application of article 36(1)(b).[56]

The courts have been clear that where an arbitration award would go against a substantive rule of the local jurisdiction (relating

52 See Frank Spoorenberg & Jorge E Viñuales, "Conflicting Decisions in International Arbitration" (2009) 8:1 *Law and Practice of International Courts and Tribunals* 91.

53 See *CE International Resources Holdings LLC v Yeap Soon Sit*, 2013 BCSC 1804; *Depo Traffic Facilities (Kunshan) Co v Vikeda International Logistics and Automotive Supply Ltd*, 2015 ONSC 999; *Belokon v Kyrgyz Republic*, 2015 ONSC 5918.

54 See Claude R Thomson & Annie MK Finn, "International Commercial Arbitration: A Canadian Perspective" (2002) 18:2 *Arbitration International* 205, online: https://doi.org/10.1023/A:1015760204767.

55 *Activ Financial v Systems Inc v Orbixa Management Services Inc*, 2011 ONSC 7286 [*Activ Financial*].

56 *Schreter v Gasmac*, above note 51; *ICAA*, above note 6, Schedule 2, art 36(1)(b).

to, for example, an unlawful penalty clause or a restriction against arbitration in certain family law proceedings), the court will refuse to enforce the agreement under article 36(1)(b), regardless of whether it has already been enforced in a foreign jurisdiction. In *Activ Financial Systems Inc v Orbixa Management Services Inc*, Perell J went as far as saying that it is irrelevant to a court's analysis under article 36 that an award may already have been recognized in a foreign jurisdiction:

> As I will explain later, it is my opinion, that the International Commercial Arbitration Act is the exclusive means to enforce a foreign arbitral award, but I reach that decision without relying on *Schreter v. Gasmac Inc*. Because I see the *Model Law* as being the exclusive means to enforce the foreign arbitral award, I agree with Orbixa that an application under the *Model Law* is not influenced by the fact that another jurisdiction may have covered the arbitral award with a court judgment; that circumstance is neutral to the enforcement under the *Model Law*.[57]

That said, Perell J went on to follow *Schreter v Gasmac* on the issue of an arbitrator's not providing reasons and on the law of liquidated damages and penalties,[58] and he ultimately enforced the New York arbitration agreement at issue in the case.

Nevertheless, *Activ Financial* illustrates that significant misconduct in the form of corruption or ignorance is not the only factor that will cause a Canadian court to rely on article 36(1)(b). Courts will also refuse to enforce arbitration agreements that break fundamental Canadian common law principles, despite what the impact may be on the perceived strength of the *UNCITRAL Model Law*'s enforcement procedures. While this remains a point of concern for those who are worried about inconsistency in international commercial arbitration, occasional disparities in enforcement where foreign arbitral awards go against core principles of a nation's common law are unavoidable without sacrificing judicial sovereignty.

57 *Activ Financial*, above note 55 at para 45.

58 *Ibid* at para 47.

G. LIMITATION PERIODS[59]

The Supreme Court of Canada in *Yugraneft Corp v Rexx Management Corp* had to determine the enforceability of a Russian arbitral award in favour of Yugraneft against an Alberta company, Rexx, for US$952,614.[60] More than three years after the Russian arbitral award, Yugraneft applied for an order recognizing and enforcing the award in Alberta pursuant to Alberta's *International Commercial Arbitration Act*. The Supreme Court in *Yugraneft* confirmed that a foreign arbitral award is not equivalent to a domestic judgment and therefore requires a recognition order (or homologation) before it can be the subject of enforcement measures. The Court concluded that Alberta's two-year limitation period applied to foreign arbitral awards with the result that Yugraneft's action was barred by Alberta's limitations statute.

It is worth noting, however, that the commencement of any limitation period is subject to the discoverability rules. Thus, if an applicant seeking to enforce an arbitral award did not reasonably anticipate that the respondent had assets within a particular jurisdiction until a later time, the applicant does not need to worry about the limitation period starting until that specific, later, time.

Furthermore, the limitation clock does not start ticking until the three-month time limit to apply to the local court to have an award set aside under the *UNCITRAL Model Law* has run its course.[61]

59 I am indebted to Stevenson, above note 8 at 16–17, for his discussion of the limitation period issue.

60 Above note 36.

61 Stevenson, above note 8 at 17, n 34, points out, "One can assume Ontario's limitation period and discoverability rules apply to the enforcement of foreign arbitral awards notwithstanding s. 16 of the *Limitations Act, 2002* which removes any limitation period for judgments." See also *Commission de la Construction du Québec v Access Rigging Services Inc*, 2010 ONSC 5897; *PT ATPK Resources TBK (Indonesia) v Diversified Energy and Resource Corp*, 2013 ONSC 5913. Note that Ontario's *Limitations Act, 2002*, SO 2002, c 24, Schedule B, omits any reference to the *ICAA*, above note 6, and the *ICAA*, s 11(1) provides that an arbitral award recognized by the court is enforceable in the same manner as a judgment or order of the court. See also *R & G Draper*, above note 24; *Edmonton (City) v Lafarge Canada Inc*, 2015 ABQB 56. See limitation provisions in s 10 of the *International Commercial Arbitration Act, 2017*, above note 6.

APPENDIX 1

Precedent Notice of Application to Set Aside an Arbitration Award

Court File No. ____________________

ONTARIO

SUPERIOR COURT OF JUSTICE

APPLICATION UNDER THE *International Commercial Arbitration Act*, R.S.O. 1990, c. I.9, Articles 18 and 34, and Rule 14.05(2) and (3)(d) and (h) of the *Rules of Civil Procedure*, R.R.O. 1990, Reg. 194

B E T W E E N :

JOSEPH POPACK,
UNITED BURLINGTON RETAIL PORTFOLIO INC., and
UNITED NORTHEASTERN RETAIL PORTFOLIO INC.

Applicants

- and -

MOSHE LIPSZYC and SARA LIPSZYC

Respondents

NOTICE OF APPLICATION

TO THE RESPONDENTS:

A LEGAL PROCEEDING HAS BEEN COMMENCED by the Applicants. The claim made by the Applicants appears on the following page.

THIS APPLICATION will come on for a hearing on ______________, 2013 at 10:00 a.m. at 393 University Avenue, 10th Floor, Toronto, Ontario.

IF YOU WISH TO OPPOSE THIS APPLICATION, to receive notice of any step in the application, or to be served with any documents in the application, you or an Ontario lawyer acting for you must forthwith prepare a notice of appearance in Form 38A prescribed by the *Rules of Civil Procedure*, serve it on the Applicants' lawyer or, where the Applicants do not have a lawyer, serve it on the Applicants, and file it, with proof of service, in this court office, and you or your lawyer must appear at the hearing.

IF YOU WISH TO PRESENT AFFIDAVIT OR OTHER DOCUMENTARY EVIDENCE TO THE COURT OR TO EXAMINE OR CROSS-EXAMINE WITNESSES ON THE APPLICATION, you or your lawyer must, in addition to serving your notice of appearance, serve a copy of the evidence on the Applicants' lawyer or, where the Applicants do not have a lawyer, serve it on the Applicants, and file it, with proof of service, in the court office where the application is to be heard as soon as possible, but at least four days before the hearing.

IF YOU FAIL TO APPEAR AT THE HEARING, JUDGMENT MAY BE GIVEN IN YOUR ABSENCE AND WITHOUT FURTHER NOTICE TO YOU. IF YOU WISH TO OPPOSE THIS APPLICATION BUT ARE UNABLE TO PAY LEGAL FEES, LEGAL AID MAY BE AVAILABLE TO YOU BY CONTACTING A LOCAL LEGAL AID OFFICE.

Date: ____________________

Issued by: ____________________
Registrar

Address of Court Office:
393 University Avenue
10th Floor
Toronto, ON M5G 1E6

TO: Moshe and Sara Lipszyc
210 Arnold Avenue
Thornhill, ON L4J 1B9
Tel: 905-771-0276

APPLICATION

1. The Applicants make an application for:
   a. An order setting aside the Arbitral Award of the Rabbinical Court of Mechon L'Hoyroa (the "Arbitral Tribunal") made on August 15, 2013, concerning disputed matters between the Applicants and the Respondents;
   b. The costs of this application on a substantial indemnity basis together with the applicable Harmonized Sales Tax thereon in accordance with the *Excise Tax Act*, R.S.C. 1985, c. E-15, as amended; and
   c. Such further and other relief as to this Honourable Court may seem just.
2. The grounds for the application are:
   a. By an Agreement to Submit to Arbitration, in writing and dated November 10, 2010, and an Arbitration Agreement Addendum, in writing and dated January 11, 2011, the parties agreed to submit to binding arbitration all the claims and counterclaims between them to three arbitrators, Rabbi Mordcha Babad, Rabbi Abraham Brownstein, and Rabbi Moshe Fleischman, from the Rabbinical Court of Mechon L'Hoyroa of Monsey and Brooklyn, New York (the "Arbitral Tribunal"), and to give to the Arbitral Tribunal exclusive jurisdiction to hear and adjudicate the matters in dispute between the parties in substitution for the jurisdiction of the Crown Heights Beth Din under the auspices of Rabbi Jacob Schwei, and that the Arbitral Tribunal would sit in Toronto, Ontario, as a foreign tribunal subject to Ontario's *International Commercial Arbitration Act*;
   b. At the time that the Agreement to Submit to Arbitration and the Arbitration Agreement Addendum were entered into and concluded by the parties, the place of business and habitual residence of the Applicant, Joseph Popack, was in the city of New York, in the State of New York, United States of America and the Respondents' places of business and habitual residences were in Ontario, Canada;
   c. The parties were afforded and took up the opportunity to be represented by counsel including legal counsel and rabbinical

counsel throughout the arbitration process before the Arbitral Tribunal;

d. The arbitration hearing went ahead in Toronto, Ontario, before the Arbitral Tribunal, on various dates between January 9, 2011 and March 13, 2013, as a form of adversarial adjudication at which the Arbitral Tribunal heard opening and closing statements of the parties, heard testimony and cross-examination of the parties and witnesses, reviewed documents and admitted documentary exhibits into evidence, made rulings on objections, heard and read final submissions of the parties, and reserved their final decision;
e. By a final Rabbinical Court Ruling, dated August 15, 2013 (the "Arbitral Award"), which terminated the arbitral proceeding, the Arbitral Tribunal, after hearing the arguments of the parties and their evidence, an analysis of their statements, and deliberations among the members of the Arbitral Tribunal, ordered that the sum of $440,000.00 held in escrow by the Arbitral Tribunal shall be returned to the Applicants, and that the Respondents shall pay the Applicants the sum of $400,000.00, whereby the parties are released from each other;
f. The Applicants received a copy of the Arbitral Award on September 2, 2013 by email correspondence from the Arbitral Tribunal;
g. However, on July 8, 2013, unbeknownst to the Applicants, the Arbitral Tribunal met privately with, interviewed, and obtained evidence from Rabbi Jacob Schwei, a material witness, in the absence of the Applicants, and without their consent, following which the Arbitral Tribunal rendered its final decision, the Arbitral Award;
h. Rabbi Jacob Schwei was a material witness whose testimony would or could have borne upon facts or law in issue or the credibility of witnesses or the parties in the arbitration proceeding before the Arbitral Tribunal; and
i. In consequence, the Arbitral Tribunal:
    i. Failed to treat the Applicants with fairness and with equality;

ii. Failed to give the Applicants a full opportunity of presenting their case;
iii. Followed an arbitral procedure that was in conflict with and not in accordance with the Model Law on International Commercial Arbitration adopted by the United Nations Commission on International Trade Law on June 21, 1985, being the Schedule to the *International Commercial Arbitration Act*, R.S.O. 1990, c. I.9, as amended (the "Model Law"), and Ontario law;
iv. Rendered the Arbitration Award which is in conflict with the public policy of Ontario, and which offends not only the local principles of justice and fairness, and notions of morality, in a fundamental way, but also offends shared notions of morality and justice that are common to legal systems throughout the world, and where the misconduct of the Arbitral Tribunal cannot be seen to be tolerated or condoned by the courts in Ontario;
v. Rendered an Arbitration Award which undermines the integrity of the system of international arbitration that was put in place by the Model Law;
vi. Engaged in intentional impropriety of conduct by questioning a material witness and receiving statements in the absence of the Applicants and without their knowledge or consent in circumstances where the possibility that the Arbitral Tribunal's mind may possibly have been influenced against the Applicants by the private communication;
vii. Failed to give the Applicants an opportunity to comment or deal with the evidence obtained by the Arbitral Tribunal from Rabbi Jacob Schwei, by questioning Rabbi Schwei, calling further evidence, or addressing arguments on the facts or the law to the Arbitral Tribunal;
viii. Failed to observe substantive and procedural fairness by not giving the Applicants any notice or opportunity to obtain disclosure of Rabbi Schwei's evidence at issue or to comment on it, or to obtain an adjournment if the Applicants thought that there was a case to meet; and neither were

the Applicants given any options to pursue by the Arbitral Tribunal which simply and impermissibly rendered its Arbitral Award without regard for the Applicants' rights;

ix. Engaged in a private activity by an arbitral tribunal in determining a matter which was antithetical to meaningful participation by the Applicants;

x. Violated the fundamental principle that an arbitral tribunal must act in a quasi-judicial manner by evaluating and deciding the case before it on the evidence as presented by the parties;

xi. Wrongfully engaged in an independent factual investigation and acted as "ad hoc investigators and researchers," thereby obtaining evidence following which they rendered their Arbitral Award, which was inconsistent with the Model Law, and contrary to the public policy of Ontario;

xii. Based the Arbitral Award on evidence that the Arbitral Tribunal had obtained through its own investigations without notice to or the consent of the Applicants;

xii. Exceeded the jurisdiction conferred on it by the parties and under the Model Law, by improperly conducting the hearing, improperly meeting with and obtaining evidence from a material witness, without notice to or the consent of the Applicants, after the close of evidence and final arguments, and thereby denied the Applicants the right to respond to that evidence and to fully present their own case to the Arbitral Tribunal;

xiv. Failed to meet the requirements of fundamental fairness which means that the minimal requirements of fairness — adequate notice, a hearing on the evidence, and an impartial decision — have not been met;

xv. Failed to observe the principles of natural justice — fair play in action — in the conduct of the arbitration proceeding;

xvi. Failed to allow the Applicants to make submissions on issues upon which the Arbitral Tribunal proposed to base or based its Arbitral Award and thereby engaged in a denial of natural justice;

xvii. Exceeded its jurisdiction by making a decision, the Arbitral Award, that amounts to a denial of natural justice;

xviii. Denied the Applicants' right to be heard in circumstances which affected or may have affected the outcome of the arbitration;

xix. Denied the Applicants the right to know the case they had to meet;

xx. Failed to deal with the evidence and submissions in an open and fair manner and thus prevented the Applicants from fully presenting their case to the Arbitral Tribunal;

xxi. Engaged in conduct giving rise to a reasonable apprehension of unfairness or bias;

xxii. Has thus lost jurisdiction and has denied fundamental and natural justice to the Applicants; and/or

xxiii. Seriously prejudiced the Applicants and deprived them of their right to a fair and just arbitration hearing.

3. Accordingly, the Arbitral Award should be set aside as being contrary to the *International Commercial Arbitration Act*, R.S.O. 1990, c. I.9 (the "Act"), Articles 18, 24 and 34(2)(a)(ii) and (iv) and (b)(ii) and 34(3) of the Model Law, being the Schedule to the Act, and Ontario law.
4. The following documentary evidence will be used at the hearing of the application:
   a. The Affidavit of Joseph Popack affirmed on November 7, 2013, and the exhibits attached thereto; and
   b. Such further and other documents as counsel may advise and that this Honourable Court may permit.

Date: November 7, 2013

SACK, GOLDBLATT, MITCHELL LLP
Barristers & Solicitors
20 Dundas Street West, Suite 1100
Toronto, ON M5G 2G8
Marlys A. Edwardh (LSUC #15939K)
Tel: 416-977-6070 ext. 4380
Fax: 416-591-7333
Lawyers for the Applicants

Court File No.

JOSEPH POPACK ET AL. - and - **MOSHE LIPSZYC ET AL.**

Applicants Respondents

ONTARIO

SUPERIOR COURT OF JUSTICE

(Proceedings Commenced at Toronto)

NOTICE OF APPLICATION

SACK, GOLDBLATT, MITCHELL LLP
Barristers & Solicitors
20 Dundas Street West, Suite 1100
Toronto, ON M5G 2G8
Marlys A. Edwardh (LSUC #15939K)
Tel: 416-977-6070 ext. 4380
Fax: 416-591-7333 Lawyers for the Applicants

APPENDIX 2

Precedent Notice of Application for Enforcement of an Arbitration Award

Court File No. ____________________

ONTARIO
SUPERIOR COURT OF JUSTICE

B E T W E E N :

JOSEPH POPACK, UNITED NORTHEASTERN RETAIL PORTFOLIO INC., UNITED BURLINGTON RETAIL PORTFOLIO INC., CAPTURE REAL ESTATE LLC, MIRIAM POPACK, EPHRIAM PIEKARSKI, MENDEL HENDEL, SCHNEUR ZALMEN HENDEL, SHOLOM BER HENDEL, RIVKA FELDMAN, and DEBORAH ZISSY RASKIN

Applicants

- and -

MOSHE LIPSZYC and SARA LIPSZYC

Respondents

APPLICATION UNDER Article 35 of the *UNCITRAL Model Law on International Commercial Arbitration*, being the Schedule to the *International Commercial Arbitration Act*, R.S.O. 1990, c. I.9, and Rule 14.05(2) of the *Rules of Civil Procedure*, R.R.O. 1990, Reg. 194

NOTICE OF APPLICATION

TO THE RESPONDENTS:

A LEGAL PROCEEDING HAS BEEN COMMENCED by the Applicants. The claim made by the Applicants appears on the following page.

THIS APPLICATION will come on for a hearing on ________________, 2016, at 10:00 a.m. at 393 University Avenue, 10th Floor, Toronto, Ontario.

IF YOU WISH TO OPPOSE THIS APPLICATION, to receive notice of any step in the application, or to be served with any documents in the application, you or an Ontario lawyer acting for you must forthwith prepare a notice of appearance in Form 38A prescribed by the *Rules of Civil Procedure*, serve it on the Applicants' lawyer or, where the Applicants do not have a lawyer, serve it on the Applicants, and file it, with proof of service, in this court office, and you or your lawyer must appear at the hearing.

IF YOU WISH TO PRESENT AFFIDAVIT OR OTHER DOCUMENTARY EVIDENCE TO THE COURT OR TO EXAMINE OR CROSS-EXAMINE WITNESSES ON THE APPLICATION, you or your lawyer must, in addition to serving your notice of appearance, serve a copy of the evidence on the Applicants' lawyer or, where the Applicants do not have a lawyer, serve it on the Applicants, and file it, with proof of service, in the court office where the application is to be heard as soon as possible, but at least four days before the hearing.

IF YOU FAIL TO APPEAR AT THE HEARING, JUDGMENT MAY BE GIVEN IN YOUR ABSENCE AND WITHOUT FURTHER NOTICE TO YOU. IF YOU WISH TO OPPOSE THIS APPLICATION BUT ARE UNABLE TO PAY LEGAL FEES, LEGAL AID MAY BE AVAILABLE TO YOU BY CONTACTING A LOCAL LEGAL AID OFFICE.

Date: ____________________ Issued by: ____________________

Registrar

Address of Court Office:
393 University Avenue
10th Floor
Toronto, ON M5G 1E6

TO: Moshe Lipszyc
210 Arnold Avenue
Thornhill, ON L4J 1B9
Tel: 905-771-0276

AND TO: Sara Lipszyc
210 Arnold Avenue
Thornhill, ON L4J 1B9
Tel: 905-771-0276

APPLICATION

1. The Applicants make an application for:
   a. An order recognizing and enforcing the Arbitral Award of the Beth Din of Mechon L'Hoyroa, dated August 15, 2013, made pursuant to the Agreement to Submit to Arbitration, dated November 10, 2010, and the Arbitration Agreement Addendum, dated January 11, 2011, awarding US$400,000.00 to the Applicants;
   b. An order requiring payment of the amount of US$400,000.00 to the Applicants by the Respondents by means of the amount of Canadian currency sufficient to purchase US$400,000.00 at a chartered bank in Ontario in accordance with the rate established by section 121 of the *Courts of Justice Act*, R.S.O. 1990, c. C.43;
   c. The costs of this application on a substantial indemnity basis; and
   d. Such further relief as this Honourable Court may deem just.
2. The grounds for the application are:
   a. The Applicant Joseph Popack (Popack) and the Respondent Moshe Lipszyc (Lipszyc) were originally business partners involved in commercial real estate transactions in Ontario;
   b. At all material times, Popack was habitually resident in the State of New York, United States of America and Lipszyc was habitually resident in the Province of Ontario, Canada;
   c. The business relationship between Popack and Lipszyc began to break down sometime between 2001 and 2005;
   d. After various attempts to resolve their disputes before a number of forums, Popack and Lipszyc entered into an Agreement to Submit to Arbitration, dated November 10, 2010, and an Arbitration Agreement Addendum, dated January 11, 2011. These agreements provided that all of the parties' outstanding disputes would be adjudicated by the Beth Din of Mechon L'Hoyroa, a Jewish Rabbinical Court that for the purposes of the dispute, constituted an international commercial arbitral panel seated in Toronto, Canada;

e. On August 15, 2013, the Beth Din released its award, ordering that the sum of US$440,000.00 be paid out of escrow with the Tribunal to the Applicants, and that the Respondents pay the Applicants a further $US400,000.00;

f. On November 7, 2013, Popack brought an Application to have the Beth Din's August 15th award set aside pursuant to Article 34 of the *UNCITRAL Model Law on International Commercial Arbitration;*

g. On June 1, 2015, Matheson J. of the Superior Court of Justice released her decision on the setting-side application, finding that while Popack had established grounds upon which the Beth Din's award could be set aside, she would exercise her discretion to nevertheless uphold it;

h. On February 18, 2016, the Court of Appeal for Ontario dismissed an appeal against Matheson J.'s decision;

i. On April 11, 2016, costs of the appeal were finally resolved. On the same day, counsel for the Applicants requested that the Respondents honour the Beth Din's award;

j. On April 22, 2016, counsel for the Respondents indicated that Lipszyc intended to return to the Beth Din to seek a reduction in the award due to the setting-aside application before the Ontario Courts. The Applicant has not been notified of any such proceeding;

k. The Award of the Beth Din, dated August 15, 2013 is final and not subject to revision or modification;

l. The *International Commercial Arbitration Act*, R.S.O. 1990, c. I.9, ss. 10–11;

m. The *UNCITRAL Model Law on International Commercial Arbitration*, being the Schedule to the *International Commercial Arbitration Act*, Arts. 34–36;

n. The *Rules of Civil Procedure*, R.R.O. 1990, Reg. 194, r. 14.05(2);

o. The *Courts of Justice Act*, R.S.O. 1990, c. C.43, s. 121; and

p. Such further and other grounds as counsel may advise and that this Honourable Court may permit.

3. The following documentary evidence will be used at the hearing of the application:

a. The Affidavit of Joseph Popack, to be affirmed, and the exhibit attached thereto;
b. The Award of the Beth Din of Mechon L'Hoyroa, dated August 15, 2013;
c. The Agreement to Submit to Arbitration, dated November 10, 2010;
d. The Arbitration Agreement Addendum, dated January 11, 2011; and
e. Such further and other material as counsel may advise and that this Honourable Court may permit.

Date:

GOLDBLATT PARTNERS LLP
20 Dundas Street West, Suite 1100
Toronto, ON M5G 2G8
Marlys A. Edwardh (LSUC# 15939K)
Tel: 416-979-4380
Fax: 416-979-4430
medwardh@goldblattpartners.com
Daniel Sheppard (LSUC# 59074H)
Tel: 416-979-6442
Fax: 416-979-4430
dsheppard@goldblattpartners.com
Lawyers for the Applicants

Court File No.

JOSEPH POPACK ET AL. - and - **MOSHE LIPSZYC ET AL.**

Applicants Respondents

ONTARIO

SUPERIOR COURT OF JUSTICE

(Proceedings Commenced at Toronto)

NOTICE OF APPLICATION

GOLDBLATT PARTNERS LLP
20 Dundas Street West, Suite 1100
Toronto, ON M5G 2G8
Marlys A. Edwardh (LSUC# 15939K)
Tel: 416-979-4380
Fax: 416-979-4430
medwardh@goldblattpartners.com
Daniel Sheppard (LSUC# 59074H)
Tel: 416-979-6442
Fax: 416-979-4430
dsheppard@goldblattpartners.com
Lawyers for the Applicants

chapter sixteen

The Art of Appellate Advocacy in the Arbitral Context and Outside It

PAUL J PAPE[1]

A. OVERVIEW

This chapter is about how I practice law. It applies to all litigious matters I deal with: motions, applications, trials, and appeals. However, it is particularly applicable to appeals. Many other skilled advocates will approach matters differently. Advocacy is an art, not a science. I have, however, concluded that what I elucidate here makes a difference between winning and losing — not always, but often enough that the result makes the effort worthwhile.

How, then, do you craft and deliver an argument that may influence the outcome of an appeal? In my view, the best arguments are those that tell a convincing story.[2] In the first half of this chapter, I discuss effective storytelling in three parts:

1) the content and form of the story
2) the credibility of the story
3) the conviction in telling the story

1 I would like to thank Andrea M Bolieiro and Justin H Nasseri, lawyers at Pape Barristers, for their assistance in preparing this chapter.

2 I have written about this before and spoken about it several times: see, for example, Paul J Pape, "Advocacy in the Court of Appeal: One Lawyer's Perspective" (2009) 28:3 *Advocates' Journal* 3.

Does the same approach apply in appeals from arbitral awards? Yes and no. In the second half of this chapter, I discuss the different considerations that must be kept in mind when appealing from arbitral awards. Such appeals are rare. There are no rights of appeal from international arbitral awards, and with respect to domestic arbitral awards, recourse must be had to the arbitration agreement and governing legislation to see what rights of appeal (if any) are provided for. Most importantly, arbitral appeals are centred on pure questions of law. Thus while these appeals are still about storytelling, the nature of the story is different: It is a legal story rather than a factual one.

B. THE ART: TELLING A CONVINCING STORY

1) The Content and Form of the Story

I have always guided myself by my friend Professor Charles Nesson's approach to advocacy. Charlie is the William F Weld Professor of Law at Harvard University.[3] He says that the way to win an argument in court is by telling a short story that will convince your mother of the righteousness of your position. This approach addresses the three necessary features of your argument: the auditor (your mother), medium (a story), and objective (to convey the righteousness of your position).

First, imagine that the adjudicator is *your mother*.[4] Selecting your mother as the auditor implicitly recognizes what Charlie and I believe: Judges are swayed, influenced, and governed by the same considerations as ordinary people. Judges come to their task with a sense of humanity and a sense of justice. This does not change when they take the judicial oath. Judges recognize that their job is to do justice between the parties. Your mother in making a decision would try to do the same. If you cannot persuade

3 Charlie is also the founder of the Berkman Klein Center for Internet and Society. He teaches the law of evidence and tort litigation.

4 I have maintained Charlie's choice of parent notwithstanding that some may see it as biased. I use your mother because, in my mind, she is reasonable, commonsensical, and humane. Your father is not.

your mother, then you certainly will not be able to persuade the court. Your mother (generally speaking) is also practical and sensible. She tries to solve family problems with a dollop of common sense. The same is true of most judges. Your argument should therefore appeal to the judges' common sense.

Next, Charlie requires that what you present to your mother is *a story*, not a submission, presentation, or argument. You need to capture your mother's attention and keep her interest. A story will do just that. Most everything we learn comes through the medium of the story. Think of the diet of information we receive from the media: It is invariably delivered in the form of stories. As Drew Westen of the *New York Times* wrote in 2011,

> The stories our leaders tell us matter, probably almost as much as the stories our parents tell us as children, because they orient us to what is, what could be, and what should be; to the worldviews they hold and to the values they hold sacred. Our brains evolved to "expect" stories with a particular structure, with protagonists and villains, a hill to be climbed or a battle to be fought. Our species existed for more than 100,000 years before the earliest signs of literacy, and another 5,000 years would pass before the majority of humans would know how to read and write.
>
> Stories were the primary way our ancestors transmitted knowledge and values. Today we seek movies, novels and "news stories" that put the events of the day in a form that our brains evolved to find compelling and memorable. Children crave bedtime stories; the holy books of the three great monotheistic religions are written in parables; and as research in cognitive science has shown, lawyers whose closing arguments tell a story win jury trials against their legal adversaries who just lay out "the facts of the case."[5]

All people, including judges, are accustomed to receiving information in this way. An appeal argument should be no different.

5 Drew Westen, "What Happened to Obama?" *New York Times* (7 August 2011) SR1, online: https://nyti.ms/2kVPBJb.

How does one tell a good story? The story must be brief, detailed, and organized. We live in the age of the sound bite. Now that Twitter has entered the mainstream, shorter is better. Less is always more. Everyone has grown up watching the opening monologue and the sixty-second news item. In reporting Margaret Thatcher's death, the media reduced her life to two minutes of airtime. Most people have not only never read James Joyce, they have never even heard of him. By keeping the story brief, I am merely giving my auditors what they are accustomed to hearing.

There are practical reasons why less is always more on appeal. The panel sits for a fortnight, which is followed by a fortnight off to prepare for the next sitting. While sitting, the panel hears, on average, two appeals per day or twenty appeals in ten hearing days. This means that each judge must read at least forty factums and twenty sets of reasons. Many of these will not be models of clarity, and that includes the reasons. If your mother had a choice between long and short when burdened with twenty appeals, and maybe more, which would she or anyone else choose? To ask the question is to answer it. As a long-serving judge of the Ontario Court of Appeal once remarked to me, "If you haven't got me in 30 pages, you're never going to get me."

I write using short paragraphs, trying to limit each to one or two facts. I try to use short sentences. I shun, in no particular order, conjunctions, the intricate, the convoluted, the complex, the dense, the verbose, and the legalistic. The oral argument is even more limited and narrow than the factum.

While the story must be brief, it must also be detailed and specific. Generalities are anathema. Details are the colours on your palette. They should be used for both interest and persuasion. A plaintiff or appellant who is a single mother of three preschool children and works night and day immediately becomes more sympathetic than a mere shareholder or policy owner. While these details may be irrelevant to a determination of the case before the court, they are highly relevant to your story.

The story must also be organized. It should have a beginning, middle, and end. It should also anticipate your argument. By the time the judges reach the issues and argument sections of your factum, they should understand your case. The best way to ensure this is using point-first advocacy or signposting. Signposting your argument, whether written or oral, is critical. It is what I facetiously call idiot-proofing the argument. Tell the court where you are going clearly and simply so that anyone can follow you. As John Laskin JA has famously written, "forget the windup and make the pitch."[6]

The last feature of the argument that Charlie describes is its objective: *to convey the righteousness of your client's position.* As Justice Laskin puts it in his paper on appeals, an appeal involves a struggle for the "moral high ground."[7] Whatever way you wish to describe it, the point is that the aim of your story is to convince the court that justice is on your side. The way to achieve this aim is through the facts of the case. Appeals, in the end, are all about people. The goal is to convince the judges to *want* to help your client, and to invoke their inherent sense of justice and right from wrong. In this respect, you have the advantage: You know the record better than the court. You are able to control how the story is told, particularly as the appellant.

I have always recommended, where possible, focusing on the facts in the argument and minimizing the role of the law. Most appeals do not involve real disputes over questions of law. They are really about the facts and the reasoning process of the judge below. In this type of appeal, the law can be distracting. It is complex and tedious, and it gets in the way of telling a good story. Moreover, the judges know the law far better than any of us lawyers. That said, it is important to give the court the essential tools to find in your client's favour. I therefore briefly cite the applicable principle or principles, relying on one or two leading cases instead of a long list of decisions from lower courts that are simply unnecessary.

---

6 John I Laskin JA, "Forget the Wind-Up and Make the Pitch: Some Suggestions for Writing More Persuasive Factums" (1999), online: www.ontariocourts.ca/coa/en/ps/speeches/forget.htm.

7 Quoted in Laskin, *ibid.*

It is, of course, vital to keep in mind the standard of review when crafting your story. When it comes to the trier's factual findings, appeal courts are highly deferential. The starting point on standard of review is the Supreme Court of Canada's decision in *Housen v Nikolaisen*.[8] You will cite this decision in virtually every civil appeal you do. In *Housen*, the Court explained that the applicable standard of review depends on whether the question on appeal is one of law, fact, or mixed fact and law. Questions of law are reviewable on a correctness standard: The judge below has to get the law right, or the appellate court is entitled to interfere. By contrast, with respect to questions of fact, the trier's factual findings are entitled to deference on appeal absent a "palpable and overriding error."[9] This deference is not limited to discrete determinations of fact. It is also granted to the trier's interpretation of the evidence as a whole, to decisions to draw (or decline to draw) inferences, and even to findings of mixed fact and law — that is, where a legal standard has been applied to a set of facts.[10]

It is a tall order to convince an appellate court to overturn factual findings. This is because many appellate judges do not view deference to factual findings — even findings that lead to an unjust result — as antithetical to doing justice between the parties. Under this view, there was a trial, findings were made, and justice was therefore done. What would be unjust is to intervene and impose the appeal court's own sense of justice. Notwithstanding this, as one judge has said to me, "There is much play in the joints." In other words, there is no sure way of determining where the line of deference will be drawn in any particular case. Accordingly, if I must challenge the trier's factual findings to tell the story on appeal, I make sure to identify precisely which factual findings were palpably wrong and altered the outcome of the case.

In my experience, Charlie's approach to advocacy often makes the difference between a successful and an unsuccessful argument

8 2002 SCC 33 [*Housen*].

9 *Ibid* at paras 1 and 36.

10 See *ibid* at paras 27–28 and 36. See also *Benhaim v St-Germain*, 2016 SCC 48 at paras 37–39, 42, and 78.

on appeal. As I discuss further in the second half of this chapter, Charlie's approach applies, with modifications, to arbitral appeals. Those appeals are generally limited to pure questions of law. Thus, the story requires greater emphasis on legal concepts and less emphasis on the particular facts of the case.

2) The Credibility of the Story

The story you present must be truthful, frank, and free of exaggeration. Everything you do in court must be infused with authenticity and credibility. I cannot overemphasize the critical importance of accurately reciting the facts and evidence. Nothing could be more damaging to your case than misstating the evidence. It undermines the justice of your position and your credibility as an advocate. Your mother would not be happy if she thought you were trying to fool her. If you are trying to mislead the court, how just can your case really be? I read every line of evidence that impacts the fact I am stating or the point I am making to ensure the accuracy of my writing and what I say in court. The judges have read and absorbed the record in advance and will read it again after you sit down. I cannot count the number of times that I have watched a judge call out counsel who has misstated the record.

Use language carefully, particularly adjectives. I try not to use superlatives or evocative terms. They add nothing and generally detract from the story. For example, if there is no evidence to support a finding of fact, simply say so. To add that there is not a "scintilla" or "shred" of evidence is, in my view, counterproductive. It will put off the judge. Furthermore, descriptions such as "egregious" and "scandalous" are also off-putting. They effectively usurp the judge's role. Let the court reach those conclusions on its own. If the underlying facts do not drive the court there, your heated or colourful language will not either. The heat and colour, while important to the story, are to be found in the facts themselves. Leave the characterization of those facts to the panel. Hyperbole undermines your credibility as an advocate.

Do not oversell your case. Put yourself in the judge's seat. Wouldn't you want it with the bark off? Be blunt. Be frank. Be forthright. If you are, you will immediately become more credible in the court's eyes, and the court will be more amenable to your argument. This, of course, means you must know and recognize the strengths and, more importantly, the weaknesses of your case. A weak submission undermines a good one. So I lead with my strengths and scrap weak and secondary points. I make concessions whenever possible. I always ask myself, what will the panel say in response to this submission? How will it respond? If I am unsure, I will parade the submission before one or more of the lawyers in the office first to see whether it will fly.

Preparation is essential when sorting strong arguments from weak ones. I cannot do it on my own. I need the help of someone in the office. She or he will be a sounding board, critic, and additional intelligence. I use what I call the Talmudic method: There are no answers, there are only questions, and it never ends. By this, I mean that I question everything. I run down every idea, every thought, to see where it may or may not lead. These questions produce answers, and these answers produce more questions, which produce more answers, and so on and so on. My colleagues are part of this game of appellate "catch." They are indispensable.

Do not be wedded to your argument. It is fluid and organic; it changes, and it grows. I sometimes find myself rewriting my argument as the judges enter the courtroom. It often changes while I am on my feet. I am able to do this because I have prepared the case from every angle. So when the inevitable surprise occurs — the unanticipated question, unanticipated answer, missed document leaving me to wonder how I could have been stupid enough to miss it — I have a framework to help me recover and respond. The preparation is lengthy and requires much more than reading the documents. It requires thinking about their meaning and, more importantly, what they will mean to my mother.

Your compendium on appeal is essential. Beyond the contents specified by the *Rules of Civil Procedure*, I ask myself what the court will want to read. For example, in a jury trial I always include the entire charge. In a contract case, I include the entire contract, not simply excerpts. I try to include sufficient excerpts of the evidence so that the particular item referred to in the factum is placed in context. I tend to include more rather than less. Do not underestimate the importance of the compendium. In telling the story, you will refer to the compendium much more than you will to your brief of authorities.

When you arrive in court to make your oral argument, your primary goal should be to help the panel. Your time to argue will be limited. You will neither be able to tell the story that is in your factum nor want to. Instead, be prepared to engage in a discussion with the panel about the case and, above all, to answer the judges' questions. The court will probe for the strengths and weaknesses in your story. Do not fear these questions; welcome them. They are windows into the judges' minds. I try to use the judges' questions to make my argument. They are my sprinters' starting blocks. Doing this requires you to anticipate the judges' questions. What will they want to know? Why will they want to know it? I craft my oral argument to answer anticipated questions.

I also prepare a second compendium to support my oral argument. I prepare it the day before I argue, and I hand it up to the panel. It is substantially smaller than the compendium mandated by the *Rules of Civil Procedure* and organized to follow my oral submissions. By this, I mean that I hope to start at the beginning and move numerically through the tabs. I want my argument to be seamless. More importantly, I want to make things easy for the panel. I do not want the judges fishing for their place in the volume or searching on their desk for other volumes. That is a waste of time, and it is distracting.

3) The Conviction in Telling the Story

What convinces is conviction. Lyndon Baines Johnson biographer Robert Caro writes the following about Johnson when he engineered the United States of America's first civil rights bill:

> He understood that all his life — as is shown by the fact that as a boy "he was always repeating" the salesman's remark that "You've got to believe in what you're selling," and that decades later, in his retirement, he would say: "What convinces is conviction. You simply *have* to believe in the argument you are advancing: if you don't, you're as good as dead. The other person will sense that something isn't there . . ." And Lyndon Johnson could *make* himself believe in an argument even if he had never believed in it before, even if he had believed in an opposite argument — and even if the argument did not accord with the facts.[11]

You must believe in the story you are telling. If you do not, no one else will.

At the same time, you must always be gauging the panel. You may come to a point in your oral argument where it is apparent that your thesis has been rejected. You may choose to persevere. Perhaps one or more silent judges are, in fact, with you on the point. However, you should recognize the point where no one is buying what you are selling and move on. This is essential to maintaining your credibility.

You may find yourself badgered by a judge. Do not despair. If that happens, politely say you can be of no further help on the point and move on to the next one.

C. THE ARBITRAL APPEAL: A RARE EVENT AND A DIFFERENT STORY

Much of what I discuss in the first half of this chapter also applies to appeals from arbitral awards. Brevity, clarity, credibility, and conviction are hallmarks of good advocacy in any context.

But appeals from arbitral awards are different. For one thing, they are rare.[12] One of the reasons that parties submit their dispute to an arbitrator in the first place is to avoid judicial proceed-

11 Robert A Caro, *Master of the Senate*, vol 3 (New York: Alfred A Knopf, 2002) at 886.

12 See *Sattva Capital Corp v Creston Moly Corp*, 2014 SCC 53 at para 67 [*Sattva*].

ings, and they certainly want to avoid multiple proceedings. They agree to be bound by the arbitrator's decisions on all issues, both factual and legal.[13] The arbitrator's decisions are intended to be final, and the statutory regime governing arbitrations reflects this. In some cases, there is no right of appeal at all. In most cases, the right of appeal is very limited in scope. Appeals are typically limited to questions of law and available only with leave. Moreover, the courts apply a more deferential standard of review to arbitral decisions than they apply to judicial decisions.

As a result, the focus in arbitral appeals must be placed on issues of law that transcend the immediate interests of the parties. The relevant legal questions should be extracted from the underlying facts and argued broadly rather than narrowly. The story must focus on law, policy, and consequences rather than simply the facts of the parties' case.

1) How to Determine Whether You Have a Right of Appeal from an Arbitral Award

The first step is, of course, to determine whether and what rights of appeal exist from an arbitral award.

a) International Arbitration

Generally speaking, there are no rights of appeal from international arbitral awards. Canada has adopted the *UNCITRAL Model Law on International Commercial Arbitration*.[14] All Canadian provinces and territories have enacted legislation expressly adopting the model law as well as the United Nations *Convention on the Recognition and Enforcement of Foreign Arbitral Awards* (the *New York Convention*).[15]

---

13 See Duncan W Glaholt & Markus Rotterdam, *Halsbury's Laws of Canada: Alternative Dispute Resolution* (Markham, ON: LexisNexis, 2014) at HDR-62.

14 21 June 1985, UN Doc A/40/17, annex 1, with amendments adopted 7 July 2006, UN Doc A/61/17, annex 1, online: www.uncitral.org/pdf/english/texts/arbitration/ml-arb/07-86998_Ebook.pdf [*UNCITRAL Model Law*].

15 10 June 1958, 330 UNTS 3, online: www.uncitral.org/pdf/english/texts/arbitration/NY-conv/New-York-Convention-E.pdf.

Under this regime, there is *no right of appeal* from an international arbitration award. As Duncan Glaholt and Markus Rotterdam explain,

> Canadian courts have recognized that the purpose of the legislation adopting the United Nations conventions is to ensure that the method of resolving disputes, in the forum and according to the rules chosen by the parties, is respected. Predictability in the enforcement of dispute resolution provisions is an indispensable precondition to any international business transaction and facilitates and encourages the pursuit of freer trade on an international scale.[16]

If an agreement to arbitrate has been made pursuant to the *UNCITRAL Model Law*, you cannot appeal the award. Article 5 of the model law states that "no court shall intervene except where so provided in this Law."[17] The only recourse to interfere with an international arbitral award is found in article 34 of the *UNCITRAL Model Law*, which provides for an application to set aside the award.[18] Courts have construed their authority to do so narrowly.[19]

See *Foreign Arbitral Awards Act*, RSY 2002, c 93; *International Commercial Arbitration Act*, RSY 2002, c 123; *International Commercial Arbitration Act*, RSNWT 1988, c I-6; *International Commercial Arbitration Act*, RSNWT (Nu) 1988, c I-6; *Foreign Arbitral Awards Act*, RSBC 1996, c 154; *International Commercial Arbitration Act*, RSBC 1996, c 233; *International Commercial Arbitration Act*, RSA 2000, c I-5; *The Enforcement of Foreign Arbitral Awards Act, 1996*, SS 1996, c E-9.12; *The International Commercial Arbitration Act*, SS 1988–89, c I-10.2; *The International Commercial Arbitration Act*, CCSM c C151; *International Commercial Arbitration Act, 2017*, SO 2017, c 2, Schedule 5; *International Commercial Arbitration Act*, RSNB 2011, c 176; *International Commercial Arbitration Act*, RSNS 1989, c 234; *International Commercial Arbitration Act*, RSPEI 1988, c I-5; *International Commercial Arbitration Act*, RSNL 1990, c I-15.

16 Glaholt & Rotterdam, above note 13 at HDR-73.

17 Above note 14, art 5.

18 *Ibid*, art 34.

19 For example, see *Kaverit Steel & Crane Ltd v Kane Corp*, [1992] AJ No 40 (CA); *Quintette Cole Ltd v Nippon Steel Corp*, [1990] BCJ No 2241 (CA); *Corporacion Transnacional de Inversiones, SA de CV v STET International, SpA*, [1999] OJ No 3573 (SCJ), aff'd [2000] OJ No 3408 (CA), leave to appeal to SCC refused, [2000] SCCA No 581; *Bayview Irrigation District #11 v Mexico*, [2008] OJ No 1858 (SCJ); *United Mexican States v Karpa*, [2005] OJ No 16 (CA); *Automatic*

The grounds for setting aside an international arbitral award are limited and go beyond the scope of this chapter.[20]

b) Domestic Arbitration

There is more flexibility when it comes to appeals from domestic arbitral awards. These awards are made locally pursuant to the laws of the province or territory, rather than pursuant to the *UNCITRAL Model Law*. To determine what rights of appeal exist from such an award, recourse must be had to the arbitration agreement itself, which may contain terms about the scope of any appeal, and the governing provincial or territorial statute, which provides the appeal route.[21] In Ontario, for example, an appeal from the arbitrator's decision is made to a single judge of the Superior Court with leave.[22] A further appeal from that court's decision may be made to the Court of Appeal, again, only with leave.[23]

I should note that Quebec is an exception. Under the Quebec *Code of Civil Procedure*, as under the *UNCITRAL Model Law*, a party may interfere with an arbitral award only by applying to the court for an annulment.[24] Such an application must be made within three months of the arbitral award being rendered.[25] In addition, the court has a discretion to stay such an application to allow the arbitrator to take steps to address the stated grounds for annulment.[26]

Systems Inc v Bracknell Corp, [1994] OJ No 828 (CA); *Canada (AG) v SD Myers, Inc*, [2004] FCJ No 29 (FC).

20 See Chapter 15, Section E.

21 See *Arbitration Act*, RSY 2002, c 8, s 25 [YT *AA*]; *Arbitration Act*, RSNWT 1988, c A-5, s 26; *Arbitration Act*, RSNWT (Nu) 1988, c A-5, s 26; *Arbitration Act*, RSBC 1996, c 55, s 14 [BC *AA*]; *Arbitration Act*, RSA 2000, c A-43, s 37 [AB *AA*]; *The Arbitration Act, 1992*, SS 1992, c A-24.1, s 38 [SK *AA*]; *The Arbitration Act*, CCSM c A120, s 37 [MB *AA*]; *Arbitration Act, 1991*, SO 1991, c 17, s 37 [ON *AA*]; *Arbitration Act*, SNB 2014, c 100, s 45(1) [NB *AA*]; *Arbitration Act*, RSNS 1989, c 19, s 5; *Arbitration Act*, RSPEI 1988, c A-16, Schedule, s 11; *Arbitration Act*, RSNL 1990, c A-14, s 36.

22 ON *AA*, above note 21, ss 45 and 49.

23 *Ibid*, s 49.

24 CQLR c C-25.01, art 648.

25 *Ibid*, art 648.

26 *Ibid*.

2) Recognize the Limited Scope of the Appeal

Unlike appeals from judicial awards, appeals from arbitral awards are generally restricted to questions of law and even then only with leave.[27] Appeals on questions of fact or mixed fact and law are allowed only if the arbitration agreement so provides.[28] Where the agreement does not so provide, appeals on these questions will be dismissed.[29] Where the agreement states only that rights of appeal are to be determined under the arbitration statute, the parties will be taken to have intended to restrict appeals to questions of law with leave.[30]

Beyond requiring a legal question, most provincial statutes permit leave to be granted only where the court is satisfied that the matters at stake are of sufficient importance to the parties and that the determination of the legal question will significantly affect the parties' rights.[31] In British Columbia, the statute further requires the court to be satisfied that determining the legal question may "prevent a miscarriage of justice" or that the legal question "is of general or public importance."[32] Generally speaking, the legal issue should be "material"; that is, it should go to the "heart" of the arbitrator's decision such that if decided differently, it would affect the result.[33] This requires the court to engage in some assessment of the merits at the leave stage to determine whether the appeal has "some possibility of succeeding."[34]

---

27 See, for example, AB *AA*, above note 21, s 44; ON *AA*, above note 21, s 45.

28 See AB *AA*, above note 21, s 44(1); SK *AA*, above note 21, s 45(1); MB *AA*, above note 21, s 44(1); ON *AA*, above note 21, s 45(3); NB *AA*, above note 21, s 45(3).

29 See *Costa v Costa*, [2008] OJ No 930 at para 34 (SCJ), where the court dismissed an appeal that concerned questions of mixed fact and law because the agreement provided for appeals only on questions of law. See also *Sherman v Classic Landmarks Master Builder Inc*, [2009] AJ No 446 at paras 13–16 (QB).

30 See *Costa v Costa*, above note 29 at paras 34–37.

31 See YT *AA*, above note 21, s 24; BC *AA*, above note 21, s 31; AB *AA*, above note 21, s 44; SK *AA*, above note 21, s 45(1); MB *AA*, above note 21, s 44(2); ON *AA*, above note 21, s 45(1); NB *AA*, above note 21, s 45(1).

32 BC *AA*, above note 21, s 31(2).

33 *Sattva*, above note 12 at paras 69–70.

34 *Ibid* at paras 71–74.

3) Appreciate the Different Standard of Review

The Supreme Court of Canada has held that instead of the correctness standard that typically applies when reviewing legal questions on appeal from judicial proceedings, the standard of review that "almost always" applies on arbitral appeals is one of *reasonableness*.[35] It is only in "rare circumstances" that the legal issue in an arbitral appeal will attract the stricter correctness standard of review. To attract that standard, the legal issue must involve a constitutional question or "a question of law of central importance to the legal system as a whole and outside the adjudicator's expertise."[36]

The reasonableness standard is extremely deferential to the arbitrator: The appeal court does not decide whether the decision on the legal issue is correct but rather whether it is reasonable. "Reasonable" means that "'the reasons do in fact or in principle support the conclusion reached.'"[37] When conducting a reasonableness review, the appeal court may "supplement" the reasons of the original decision maker as part of the analysis: "the decision-maker is not required to refer to all the arguments, provisions or jurisprudence or to make specific findings on each constituent element, for the decision to be reasonable . . . ."[38] Or as David Dyzenhaus describes it,

> even if the reasons in fact given do not seem wholly adequate to support the decision, the court must first seek to supplement them before it seeks to subvert them. For if it is right that among the reasons for deference are the appointment of the tribunal and not the court as the front line adjudicator, the tribunal's proximity to the dispute, its expertise, etc., then it is also

35 *Ibid* at paras 75 and 106.

36 *Ibid* at para 75.

37 David Dyzenhaus, "The Politics of Deference: Judicial Review and Democracy" in Michael Taggart, ed, *The Province of Administrative Law* (Oxford: Hart, 1997) 279 at 304, cited in *Sattva*, above note 12 at para 110.

38 *Sattva*, above note 12 at para 75.

> the case that its decision should be presumed to be correct even if its reasons are in some respects defective.[39]

The rationale for this highly deferential standard of review in the arbitral context is that arbitrations differ in character from judicial proceedings. Arbitrations are decided by nonjudicial decision makers who have been selected by the parties and who have special expertise.[40] Thus, arbitral appeals take place under a "tightly defined regime" that has been tailored to the specific objectives underlying commercial arbitrations.[41]

4) Properly Identify the Question of Law

Since appeals from arbitral awards are generally limited to pure questions of law, it is important to understand what "pure" means. Pure legal issues typically involve (1) the application of an incorrect principle, (2) the failure to consider a required element of a legal test, or (3) the failure to consider a relevant factor.[42] For example, if a particular legal test requires the arbitrator to consider four elements and if she has considered only three of them, her failure to consider the fourth required element is a pure, extricable error of law.[43]

Faced with the need to identify a pure legal issue, counsel will often go to extreme lengths to characterize the arbitrator's error as a legal one rather than a factual one. Tempting though this may be, the courts generally catch on to counsel's attempts in arbitral appeals to "frame any alleged errors as questions of law."[44] Indeed, the Supreme Court of Canada has recently instructed lower courts to "exercise caution" and "be careful to ensure that the proposed ground of appeal has been properly characterized."[45] The Court

39 Dyzenhaus, above note 37 at 304, cited in *Sattva*, above note 12 at para 110.
40 See *Sattva*, above note 12 at para 105.
41 *Ibid* at para 104.
42 See *ibid* at para 53.
43 See *Housen*, above note 8 at paras 8 and 27–28.
44 See *Sattva*, above note 12 at para 54.
45 *Ibid.*

specifically noted that in cases about contractual interpretation — the most frequent subject of arbitral disputes — the circumstances where a question of law can be extricated from the contractual interpretation process are "rare."[46] In most cases, contractual interpretation is largely intertwined with the facts underlying the agreement. The interpretation therefore is an issue of mixed fact and law, not pure law.[47]

5) The Law Is a Story Too

In an arbitral appeal, as in any appeal on a question of law, the story is a legal one, but it is still a story. The story is about how the decision maker got the law wrong and what this did to his ultimate conclusion. Depending on the case, the story may also be about why the law is the way it is. In some instances, the legal principles themselves may be in dispute, and in these cases the story may be about what the law should be and why.

In many ways, telling a legal story is more challenging than telling a factual story. It is less intuitive, and it requires in-depth knowledge of the area of law. To do it successfully, you must not only be well versed in the relevant legal principles and caselaw interpreting them; you must also prepare using the Talmudic method described above.[48] Asking every question and going down every alley you can think of will lead you to a sensible, defensible position on the law and give you the confidence to withstand the appellate court's questioning. Ultimately, the object in preparing

46 *Ibid* at para 55.

47 See *ibid* at para 50. In the two years following the Court's release of *Sattva*, appellate courts throughout Canada have struggled with its conclusion that contractual interpretation is an issue of mixed fact and law. Many courts have been hostile to the decision, particularly as it applies to standard form contracts. The Supreme Court has recently heeded these criticisms in *Ledcor Construction Ltd v Northbridge Indemnity Insurance Co*, 2016 SCC 37 at paras 4 and 20–24, where it held that in the case of standard form contracts, there are instances where contractual interpretation may give rise to pure questions of law.

48 See Section B(2), above in this chapter.

for a law-based appeal is the same as for a fact-based appeal: You are constructing a narrative to persuade the court of the correctness and the righteousness of your position.

It is important to elevate the broad legal question above the facts of the case, but it is equally important to then tie them back together — applying the law as you have argued it to the facts of the case. In a legal appeal, the facts are there to help illustrate your argument and demonstrate its correctness. Use them judiciously, but use them. You will need them to explain the law to your mother.

D. CONCLUSION

The art of advocacy is the art of telling stories. In a typical civil appeal, the story is in the facts. In a legal or arbitral appeal, the story extends beyond the facts and revolves around the broader issues of law. These are different exercises, but they are also the same. In all cases, the job of the advocate is to persuade the court through a story told with clarity, concision, credibility, and conviction.

chapter seventeen

Commercial Arbitration without Hearings: The Court of Innovative Arbitration

RICHARD McLAREN & KALEIGH HAWKINS-SCHULZ

A. INTRODUCTION TO THE COURT OF INNOVATIVE ARBITRATION

The Court of Innovative Arbitration (COIA) was established in late 2015 to provide an expedited commercial arbitration process in response to the reality that commercial arbitrations were becoming more lengthy and costly.[1] The COIA is modelled after the Basketball Arbitral Tribunal (BAT), which was established in 2007. This chapter describes the principles and procedures underlying the COIA, and it describes how the BAT, as the parent from which the COIA emerged, operates to explain how the COIA is likely to develop. The chapter also discusses how the conceptual principles underlying the COIA are gaining international momentum and posits that the COIA is emerging as a strong contender to be a successful and widely used mode of commercial dispute resolution in the future.

1 See Dirk-Reiner Martens & Heiner Kahlert, "Back to the Roots of Arbitration" *Kluwer Arbitration Blog* (26 October 2015), online: http://kluwerarbitrationblog.com/2015/10/26/back-to-the-roots-of-arbitration.

B. FOUNDATIONAL PILLARS OF THE COIA

1) *Ex aequo et bono*

The foremost foundational pillar of the COIA is that decisions can be based on principles of *ex aequo et bono*, that is, justice and fairness as recognized internationally. The *COIA Arbitration Rules* state, "If the Arbitrator is authorized by the parties to decide the dispute *ex aequo et bono* . . . , he shall apply general considerations of justice and fairness instead of any particular national or international law."[2] This is the case irrespective of the parties' domicile or the seat of arbitration.

The application of a foreign national or international law very often causes significant delay as the arbitrator is most likely not familiar with such law. Under traditional principles of commercial arbitration, the proof of foreign legal systems must be obtained through expert testimony. Having been educated on the content of the foreign legal principles, the arbitrator must then interpret the contract and other aspects of the dispute in accordance with the applicable domestic laws. To apply foreign law is both time-consuming and expensive. An expert in the foreign law to be utilized must first be accepted by the parties and the arbitrator as being such. If accepted, the expert must then opine upon the parameters of the foreign law applicable to the dispute at arbitration. This is an especially relevant consideration for cases that may be submitted to the COIA since many commercial matters have an international dimension.

The clash of conflicting local domestic laws in an international commercial arbitration is at the centre of the difficulties in international commercial law disputes, and relying on *ex aequo et bono* avoids this pitfall. The use of the principle of *ex aequo et bono* also eliminates the possibility of conflict or unfairness surrounding the use of expert witnesses.[3] For example, one party may not be in

---

2 *COIA (Court of Innovative Arbitration) Arbitration Rules* (in force as of 1 October 2015) art 16.3, online: http://coia.org/wp-content/uploads/2015/10/151001-COIA-Arbitration-Rules.pdf [*COIA Rules*].

3 See Martens & Kahlert, above note 1.

a financial position to submit an expert opinion, or both parties may submit conflicting expert opinions.[4]

The parties can alternatively request that the dispute be decided according to specific rules of law, such as a national or international law.[5] In respect of international law, the parties may frequently select an international regime designed for a specific purpose, such as the *United Nations Convention on Contracts for the International Sale of Goods*[6] or *UNIDROIT Model Law on Leasing*.[7] If the parties cannot agree on the applicable law, then by default they authorize the arbitrator to decide the dispute *ex aequo et bono*.[8]

2) Swiss Law as the Seat of Arbitration

The second foundational pillar of the COIA is that the arbitral proceedings are governed by Chapter 12 of the Swiss *Federal Act on Private International Law*.[9] This is so regardless of whether or not the dispute originated outside of Switzerland.[10] If all the parties to the arbitration procedure are domiciled in Switzerland, they may agree to waive the applicability of Part 3 of the Swiss *Civil Procedure Code*, which outlines a different set of arbitral procedural principles and requirements.[11]

Adopting Swiss law as the governing procedural law, being that the seat of arbitration is Zurich, Switzerland, allows the COIA to deal with cases that encompass employment contracts. While Swiss law permits the arbitration of employment disputes, other

4 See *ibid*.

5 *COIA Rules*, above note 2, art 16.1.

6 11 April 1980, 1489 UNTS 58, online: www.uncitral.org/pdf/english/texts/sales/cisg/V1056997-CISG-e-book.pdf.

7 13 November 2008, online: www.unidroit.org/english/documents/2008/study59a/s-59a-17-e.pdf.

8 *COIA Rules*, above note 2, art 16.2.

9 18 December 1987 [*PILA*] (English translation, online: www.andreasbucher-law.ch/images/stories/pil_act_1987_as_from_1_1_2017.pdf; *COIA Rules*, above note 2, art 2.3.

10 *COIA Rules*, *ibid*, art 2.3.

11 19 December 2008, online: www.admin.ch/opc/en/classified-compilation/20061121/index.html.

countries do not allow employment disputes to be submitted to arbitration.[12] In many of these other countries, employment disputes are required to go before specialized labour courts or administrative law judges and cannot be resolved via private arbitration. Making Zurich, Switzerland, the seat of arbitration allows employment disputes from foreign countries to be arbitrated under the COIA as a matter of Swiss procedural law even if there is a hearing conducted elsewhere.[13] Although the COIA may hear employment disputes, enforcement of any arbitral award within the parties' countries may be refused if the subject matter of the dispute is not capable of settlement by arbitration under the laws of the relevant country.[14]

3) Enforcement of Awards If Parties Do Not Voluntarily Comply with Orders

Like traditional commercial arbitration, the enforcement of arbitral orders under the COIA relies upon the parties' voluntary compliance. This is unlike the BAT system of arbitration, which has a unique enforcement method through the Fédération Internationale de Basketball (FIBA).

Part of the immediate and widespread acceptance of the BAT mechanism for arbitration of monetary issues between basketball clubs, players, and agents has been due to the role that FIBA plays in the enforcement of BAT awards. Being the worldwide governing body for basketball, FIBA can upon request of a party seeking enforcement of a BAT award impose varying sanctions on the noncompliant party until there is compliance with the or-

12 See Dirk-Reiner Martens, "Basketball Arbitral Tribunal — An Innovative System for Resolving Disputes in Sport (Only in Sport?)" (2011) 1:2 *International Sports Law Journal* 54 at 56.

13 *COIA Rules*, above note 2, art 2.1.

14 See *Convention on the Recognition and Enforcement of Foreign Arbitral Awards*, 10 June 1958, 330 UNTS 3, art 5, online: www.uncitral.org/pdf/english/texts/arbitration/NY-conv/New-York-Convention-E.pdf.

ders of the arbitrator.[15] The type of sanction imposed will depend on the identity of the noncompliant party, whether it be a professional basketball player, FIBA-registered agent, or club playing in FIBA-sanctioned events and leagues. The available sanctions are diverse and can include a monetary fine (which can be applied more than once), the withdrawal of a FIBA licence if the noncompliant party is a player's agent, a ban on international transfers if the noncompliant party is a FIBA-registered player, and a ban on the registration of new players or on international club competitions if the noncompliant party is a club.[16] In essence, FIBA can temporarily paralyze a team or agent or frustrate a player's ability to fully participate within the international basketball community until such time as the team, agent, or player complies with the orders of the BAT award. The sanctions can be applied cumulatively and numerously. They may also be extended, in FIBA's sole discretion, to natural or legal persons directly or indirectly linked to the noncompliant party, either from a legal or a sporting perspective (e.g., a different entity with a similar name).[17] The availability of such enforcement mechanisms has contributed significantly to the success of the overall mechanism and now encourages voluntary compliance with the orders of a BAT arbitrator so that sanctions do not have to be, and are not, imposed by FIBA.

The COIA arbitration mechanism does not have the special enforcement features available as part of the BAT arbitration. The COIA depends primarily upon voluntary compliance with the arbitrator's orders. In this respect, the COIA is no different from other forms of international commercial arbitration. It relies upon the enforcement mechanism of the United Nations *Convention on the Recognition and Enforcement of Foreign Arbitral Awards* (the *New York Convention*).[18] Unfortunately, there is no international organization

15 Fédération Internationale de Basketball, *Internal Regulations: Book 3 — Players and Officials* (January 2017) at paras 331–33, online: www.fiba.com/documents/2015/FIBABook3AG.pdf.

16 *Ibid.*

17 *Ibid.*

18 Above note 14.

like FIBA to provide a fail-safe mechanism for the enforcement of COIA arbitration awards. The *New York Convention* has been thoroughly explained in many law journal articles and does not require further discussion here.[19]

C. PROCEDURE TO INVOKE THE COIA AS THE DISPUTE RESOLUTION MECHANISM AND THE ARBITRATION PROCESS

1) Contract Requirements

To have a dispute resolved by the COIA, both parties must submit the dispute to the COIA (1) voluntarily and (2) in writing.[20] In the majority of cases, the first step is inserting an arbitration clause in the parties' contract. The arbitration clause should indicate a desire to use the COIA in the event of a dispute and an understanding of the core features of the procedure including the following:[21]

1) the use of Swiss Law;
2) that the arbitration shall be in English; and
3) that the arbitrator may decide the dispute *ex aequo et bono*.

19 See, generally, Ihab Amro, *Recognition and Enforcement of Foreign Arbitral Awards in Theory and in Practice: A Comparative Study in Common Law and Civil Law Countries* (Newcastle upon Tyne, UK: Cambridge Scholars, 2013); Alex Baykitch & Lorraine Hui, "Celebrating 50 Years of the New York Convention" (2008) 31:1 *University of New South Wales Law Journal* 364, online: www.unswlawjournal.unsw.edu.au/sites/default/files/20_baykitch_2008.pdf; Gary B Born, *International Commercial Arbitration: International Arbitral Awards*, vol 3 (Alphen aan den Rijn, NL: Kluwer Law International, 2014) ch 26 at 3394; Peter Gillies, "Enforcement of International Arbitration Awards — The New York Convention" (2005) 9:1 *International Trade and Business Law Review* 19, online: www.austlii.edu.au/au/journals/IntTBLawRw/2004/2.html. See also Chapter 1, Section D(3)(a).

20 *COIA Rules*, above note 2, art 1.1.

21 See Dirk-Reiner Martens & Heiner Kahlert, "*Ex aequo et bono*: The Court of Innovative Arbitration (COIA): An Alternative in the International Commercial Arbitration" *Dispute Resolution* (22 June 2016) at 12, online: www.disputeresolution-magazin.de/ex-aequo-et-bono/#more-1432.

The *COIA Rules* encourage parties wishing to submit a future dispute to the COIA to use the following model clause when entering into a contract:

> Any dispute arising out of or in connection with the present contract, including the (in)validity, breach, or termination thereof, shall be finally resolved by a sole arbitrator in accordance with the Arbitration Rules of the Court of Innovative Arbitration (COIA). The seat of the arbitration shall be Zurich (Switzerland). The arbitrator shall decide ex aequo et bono.[22]

Agreement to use the COIA can also occur *after* a dispute has arisen, and the same requirements of a voluntary and written submission apply.[23]

The model arbitration clause for the BAT is very similar to that for the COIA. Although use of the BAT is voluntary, due to its success many basketball agents uncompromisingly insist on the standard arbitration clause found in the preamble of the BAT *Arbitration Rules*.[24] In the future, commercial parties may similarly insist on the COIA as the dispute resolution mechanism when entering into agreements.

2) Use of the COIA by a Third Party

It is possible that the COIA will allow an arbitration agreement to extend to a third party. An illustration of this can be taken from BAT jurisprudence, which can be found on the BAT website.[25] Prior

---

22 Court of Innovative Arbitration, "Implementing COIA into Contracts: English Model Arbitration Clause," online: http://coia.org/implementing-coia-into-contracts; *COIA Rules*, above note 2, art 0.2.

23 See *COIA (Court of Innovative Arbitration) User Guide* (1 July 2015) at para 2, online: http://coia.org/wp-content/uploads/2015/10/150701-COIA-User-Guide.pdf.

24 *Basketball Arbitral Tribunal (BAT) Arbitration Rules* (1 January 2017) art 0.3, online: www.fiba.com/bat/process/arbitration-rules-january-1-2017 [*BAT Rules*]. See Martens, above note 12 at 55.

25 Fédération Internationale de Basketball, "Basketball Arbitral Tribunal (BAT): Awards," online: www.fiba.com/bat/awards.

cases suggest that although a player, agent, or club may not be a party to the contract, this does not automatically preclude a dispute involving that party from being heard.

For example, the award in *Dunston v Aris BSA 2003* demonstrates that the legal relationship between a party to the contract and a third party can be of sufficient intensity to justify the extension.[26] In that case, the club (contrary to its agreement) failed to pay both the player and the agents. The player and the agents submitted the dispute to the BAT. However, the agents had not signed the agreement between the player and the club and were therefore not initial parties to the contract. In fact, two unknown individuals had signed in place of the agents. In deciding whether the agents could be a party to the arbitration, the arbitrator referred to a decision of the Swiss Federal Tribunal from October 2003.[27] While the arbitration agreement between the initial parties had to follow the proper format required by article 178(1) of the *PILA*,[28] the extension to third parties did not need to follow the formal requirement.[29] Therefore, it was irrelevant whether the agents had signed the agreement or not, and it could be extended to third parties if there was a legal relationship of a certain intensity. As the agents were specifically mentioned in the preamble of the agreement, the arbitrator found that there was a sufficient legal relationship and allowed the extension.

Similarly, in *Funiciello v El Jaish Sports Club*, the third party was explicitly named in the contract as the player's agent, and the contract obligated the club to make payments to the agent.[30] These two factors led the arbitrator to find that there was jurisdiction to adjudicate the agent's claim against the club.

---

26 BAT 0328/12, online: http://goldengate-law.com/pdf/bat/bat_award_0328.pdf.

27 *X v Z*, 4A_115/2003 (English translation, online: www.swissarbitrationdecisions.com/sites/default/files/16%20octobre%202003%204P%20115%202003.pdf).

28 *PILA*, above note 9, art 178(1).

29 *X v Z*, above note 27.

30 BAT 0664/15, online: www.fiba.com/en/Module/85132837-66aa-4ff3-a063-8cdfe44ea14d/87125d51-c898-4cea-bef7-c9dacb3b1c6d.

3) Predictability

Although there has been some criticism regarding the predictability of having a dispute resolved by a single arbitrator using the principle of *ex aequo et bono*, three factors give the process consistency.

First, a summary of each award is published online in anonymized form to enhance the ability of a party (or party's counsel) to review precedent and determine the likely outcome of its case.[31] Before the COIA secretariat publishes the anonymized award, the parties are given a copy and may suggest further redactions to guard their interests.[32] This is a significant departure from the traditional commercial arbitration process where awards are considered to be confidential and of no precedential value due to issues and agreements of confidentiality. The protection of disputants' confidential proprietary information is an important reason why traditional commercial arbitration is chosen over litigation in the courts.

Second, and except in situations of gross and inequitable unfairness, the arbitrator primarily applies the parties' contract. This means that the dispute will be decided based on the objective provisions of the parties' contract, and will not turn on the principles of *ex aequo et bono*, which may produce a result not contemplated by the parties at the time at which they entered into the contract. Instead, this method of deciding the dispute by applying the contract provides parties with greater certainty that the decision will reflect what the parties agreed to.[33]

Third, the president of the COIA, with a view to developing consistent COIA jurisprudence, may allow an arbitrator to consult with other COIA arbitrators provided that the parties remain anonymous.[34] In exercising this right to consultation, the arbitrator can discuss issues of principle or novel matters. Such consultation broadens the judgment beyond that of the particular arbitration

31 *COIA Rules*, above note 2, art 17.5.

32 *Ibid.*

33 See Martens & Kahlert, above note 22.

34 *COIA Rules*, above note 2, art 17.2.

and thereby enables a better quality of decision making. The diverse multidisciplinary backgrounds of the current COIA arbitrators (in engineering, financial services, sports law, etc.) provide a rich environment for problem solving that allows those who hold expertise in the subject area being adjudicated to be of assistance. Given that many commercial issues cross lines of expertise and academic discipline, consultation with multiple arbitrators may provide the insight needed to resolve complicated or novel disputes in a meaningful and effective way.

Therefore, the COIA offers parties a unique opportunity to resolve disputes in a more predictable environment. Parties may also opt to keep their case confidential. To do so, one party must object to publication within thirty days of notification of the award.[35]

4) Submitting a Dispute to the COIA

The COIA mechanism to resolve disputes is designed to be simple, quick, inexpensive, and effective. The agreement to arbitrate must include the required arbitration clause or an agreement to use the *COIA Rules*. To found jurisdiction, the agreement must provide for the arbitration to be procedurally conducted in accordance with the *PILA*.[36] In selecting the COIA mechanism, the parties implicitly empower the arbitrator to find that a hearing is unnecessary.

The claimant begins the process by filing a request for arbitration, preferably by email,[37] which must include (1) a statement of facts and legal arguments and (2) the claimant's request for relief.[38] Unless the arbitrator orders otherwise, there should be only one written submission per party.[39] The request must also include a copy of the contract containing the arbitration clause or written evidence of the agreement to have the dispute resolved by the

35 *Ibid.*

36 Above note 9.

37 *COIA Rules*, above note 2, art 5.2.

38 *Ibid*, art 8.

39 *Ibid*, art 8.2.

COIA.[40] Arbitration under the COIA requires cooperation by the parties and their counsel because of the limited number of written submissions and the short time limits that are applied. The parties need to select counsel capable of acting and implementing the restriction of a no-hearing procedure with short timelines and limited submissions. Thus, the parties have a significant impact on the potential success of the procedural aspects of the arbitration mechanism.

Upon receiving the completed request, the COIA secretariat, which consists of the COIA president and case managers, determines whether there is *prima facie* jurisdiction for the arbitration to be initiated.[41] The final aspect of the application process is the payment of a nonrefundable handling fee that is proportionate to the sum in dispute, somewhere between EUR 2,500 and up to, in rare cases, EUR 25,000.[42]

Once jurisdiction is confirmed and once full payment of the filing fee has been received, the COIA secretariat notifies the respondent of the pending case and also informs the parties of the amount of the advance on costs to pay for the arbitration mechanism and the time limit for its payment.[43] When fixing the amount of the advance on costs, the COIA secretariat takes into account, among other things, the monetary value of the dispute and the complexity of the case.[44] If a party fails to pay its share, the other party may pay it, as the arbitration will not and cannot proceed until the COIA secretariat receives the full amount of the advance on costs.[45] These funds are used to cover the costs of the procedure and pay the arbitrator's fees.

---

40 *Ibid*, art 8.1.

41 *Ibid*, art 11.3.

42 See *COIA (Court of Innovative Arbitration) Cost Schedule* (1 October 2015), online: http://coia.org/wp-content/uploads/2015/10/151001-COIA-Cost-Schedule.pdf [*COIA Cost Schedule*].

43 *COIA Rules*, above note 2, art 11.3.

44 *Ibid*, art 9.1.

45 *Ibid*, art 9.3 & 9.4.

The respondent must submit its answer within the time limit established by the arbitrator.[46] There is no uniform time limit, and the arbitrator has discretion to set, and extend, time limits according to the specific facts of the case.[47] The answer should include any defences, any counterclaims, and all written evidence upon which the respondent intends to rely.[48] The COIA secretariat will forward all documents submitted to the other party and the arbitrator.

5) Role of the Arbitrator

Disputes before the COIA are decided by a sole arbitrator chosen from a list of (currently eight) arbitrators, the names of whom can be found on the COIA website.[49] The parties may select an arbitrator from the list by agreement. If there is no such agreement, the arbitrator is selected by the COIA secretariat.[50]

Following proper appointment, the arbitrator plays the role of an inquisitor. She will ask questions concerning the nature of the dispute, receive the parties' documents and statements, assess the information, and issue an award. Typically, there is no hearing unless requested by both parties or unless the arbitrator decides to hold a hearing.[51] Therefore, there are generally no witnesses, which is a significant factor in expediting the procedure and containing the costs of the arbitration. Since there has not yet been a case submitted to the COIA, it is unknown whether the COIA will experience a greater frequency of hearings than that experienced by the BAT. Nonetheless, this ability of the COIA to keep costs low and reduce the time needed to render a decision is a salutary advantage of the COIA dispute resolution mechanism.

---

46 *Ibid*, art 11.3.

47 *Ibid*, art 6.

48 *Ibid*, art 12.1.

49 Court of Innovative Arbitration, "Who We Are," online: http://coia.org/who-we-are. See Martens & Kahlert, above note 22.

50 *COIA Rules*, above note 2, art 7.1.

51 *Ibid*, art 14.1.

Both parties can request an in-person hearing, where the traditional procedure of commercial arbitration would be used, including the calling and hearing of witnesses. However, the BAT jurisprudence suggests wide acceptance of the underlying idea that there will be no hearings or witnesses: From 2007 to 2011, an oral hearing was requested twice out of a total of 243 requests for arbitration.[52]

In furtherance of the arbitrator's active inquisitorial role, there are certain circumstances in which the arbitrator is authorized to attempt to bring about a settlement of the dispute.[53] In the context of the BAT, jurisprudence suggests that though this is not the norm, it is not insignificant either, as from 2007 to 2015 roughly 10 to 20 percent of the cases were settled.[54] It is more common, though, for the arbitrator to examine the legal documents, request parties to submit their summary of legal fees and expenses, and draft the award with reasons.[55] Unless the matter is exceptionally complex, the COIA arbitrator shall render the award no later than six months after the advance on costs is received.[56] At the parties' request, the award can also be given without reasons.

It is common practice for certain BAT awards to be given without reasons. This is the default outcome for disputes that do not exceed EUR 100,000 in value unless one party requests a reasoned award and pays an additional cost.[57] Such a procedure assists greatly in keeping arbitration costs low and encourages players from all salary ranges to seek justice by submitting a dispute. The BAT began allowing and issuing awards without reasons in May 2010. Before this, certain parties (especially female basketball players

52 See Martens, above note 12 at 55.

53 *COIA Rules*, above note 2, art 13.4.

54 Fédération Internationale de Basketball, "Basketball Arbitral Tribunal: Statistics" (31 December 2015), online: www.fiba.com/en/Module/c9dad82f-01af-45e0-bb85-ee4cf50235b4/984a5df1-a490-49a5-8aa4-86d985e703d9 ["BAT 2015 Statistics"].

55 See *COIA Rules*, above note 2, art 17.1.

56 *Ibid*, art 17.4.

57 *BAT Rules*, above note 25, art 16.2.

with lower salaries) had restricted access to the BAT due to costs.[58] On top of having lower salaries, players frequently had to advance the respondent's share of the costs (the respondent often being an uncooperative club) for the proceedings to move forward.[59] Since the change to the *BAT Rules* allowing for awards without reasons, the number of cases submitted to the BAT with a low value has jumped from only four in 2009 to sixty-one in 2013—a growth rate five times faster than that of all cases submitted to the BAT during that period.[60] Lower costs, therefore, seem to be a driving factor for some categories of users, and awards without reasons contribute greatly to access to justice at a lower cost.

6) Closing the Case

COIA awards are deemed to be final and binding upon communication to the parties by email.[61] The COIA secretariat determines the final amount of the arbitration costs, and the arbitrator determines whether one party shall partially or fully reimburse the other for its expenses and legal fees.[62] The maximum reimbursement of a party's expenses and legal fees is EUR 75,000 and is proportionate to the amount in dispute.[63]

D. APPEALING AN AWARD

1) Grounds for Appeal

A COIA award can be appealed only to the Swiss Federal Tribunal because the seat of the arbitration has been designated to be Zurich, Switzerland. The grounds for appeal are extremely narrow and are described in article 190(2) of the *PILA*. An appeal may be initiated only

58 See Martens, above note 12 at 56.

59 See *ibid*.

60 See "BAT 2015 Statistics," above note 55.

61 *COIA Rules*, above note 2, art 17.6.

62 *Ibid*, art 18.4.

63 See *COIA Cost Schedule*, above note 42.

a. where the sole arbitrator has been improperly appointed or where the arbitral tribunal has been improperly constituted;
b. where the arbitral tribunal has wrongly accepted or denied jurisdiction;
c. where the arbitral tribunal has ruled beyond the claims submitted to it, or failed to decide one of the claims;
d. where the principle of equal treatment of the parties or their right to be heard in an adversary procedure has not been observed; [or]
e. where the award is incompatible with public policy.[64]

The limited appeal process under the *PILA* has resulted in very limited judicial interference in any of the BAT procedures. There is no reason to think that it will be any different for the COIA dispute resolution mechanism. The recent experience of the BAT has been that the absence of full appeal review has no discernible effect on the BAT arbitration procedure. Before 2010, the BAT allowed appeals to be heard by the Court of Arbitration for Sport (CAS).[65] At that time, the appeal was required to be made within twenty-one days from the communication of the award, and the CAS was to decide the appeal *ex aequo et bono*.[66] After the possibility of an appeal to the CAS was eliminated, the only avenue for an appeal of a BAT award was through the narrow grounds under the *PILA*. Such narrow grounds for appeal promote meaningful participation in the arbitration and reduce the number of intentional breaches of a contract.[67] They also make it much more difficult for a party to appeal solely to postpone enforcement of a BAT award, which is often either a sanction or an order to pay.[68] Similarly, the narrow appeal process of the COIA may also maximize meaningful participation in the arbitration, reduce the number of intentional breaches, and

64 *PILA*, above note 9, art 190(2).
65 See Martens, above note 12 at 56.
66 See IBPA: International Basketball Players Association, LCC, "Appealing a BAT Award" (9 September 2013), online: http://playersassociation.org/appealing-a-bat-award.
67 See *ibid*.
68 See *ibid*.

limit the opportunity to intentionally postpone cooperation with an award.

2) Frequency of Appeals

Given the narrow grounds for appeal under the *PILA*, it is unlikely that the COIA will experience a high frequency of appeals. The same prediction can be supported by referring to the BAT's statistical outcomes. From the BAT's origin in 2007 to 31 December 2013, there were two appeals to the Swiss Federal Tribunal and twenty-two appeals to the CAS, which was the appeal-deciding body before the *BAT Rules* changed.[69] From 2013 to 2015, the number of appeals decreased significantly: None was reported.[70] Given that the COIA follows the same appeal guidelines, it is likely that it will see a similar frequency, and near inexistence, of appeals.

E. TODAY AND BEYOND

As of the time of publication, there have been no commercial cases submitted to the COIA.[71] This is because the parties must first insert the required arbitration clause into their agreement and then wait for a dispute requiring adjudication. Of course, the parties could have already become embroiled in a dispute, in which case jurisdiction over the dispute can be conferred by an agreement to arbitrate that fits the parameters of the *COIA Rules*. To date, neither method of commencing the use of the COIA has occurred. Given that the COIA was launched only in September 2015, more time is needed before a case will emerge using this new international commercial arbitration mechanism.

---

69 Fédération Internationale de Basketball, "Basketball Arbitral Tribunal: Statistics" (20 December 2013), online: www.fiba.com/downloads/v3_expe/bat/BAT%20Statistics%2031%20December%202013.pdf.

70 Email exchange between Dr Heiner Kahlert and Kaleigh Hawkins-Schulz (2 August 2016).

71 See Dr Heiner Kahlert (lawyer at Martens Rechtsanwälte and co-creator of the COIA), interview by Kaleigh Hawkins-Schulz (23 August 2016).

There were, however, three instances where parties notified the COIA that they had inserted the COIA arbitration clause into their contract and two more instances where parties negotiated to insert the clause into their contract but where, in the end, the contract itself was not proceeded with.[72] In all likelihood, there may be more cases where parties have agreed to insert the COIA arbitration clause but have not notified the COIA of having done so.

Although there have been no COIA cases to date, the COIA model of simple, quick, and inexpensive commercial arbitration is the precursor of coming changes in international commercial arbitration. In April 2016, the Indian National Bar Association (INBA) entered into a joint venture with the COIA.[73] The INBA is scheduled to launch its own parallel model of the COIA called the Centre for Innovative Conflict Resolution (CICR) in early October 2016.[74]

The CICR will have several modifications, but it will not disturb the overall essence and foundational pillars of the COIA, such as *ex aequo et bono*.[75] The CICR will focus on domestic commercial disputes and refer disputes with an international dimension to the COIA. The CICR is anticipated to have its own list of arbitrators, which will not necessarily be limited to Indian nationals but may include international arbitrators as well.[76] Whether the CICR will be seated in Swiss law and what its rules of arbitration will be are not yet finalized. Other modifications will likely be minor and undertaken to account for factors specific to the Indian market.[77] An example of such an anticipated modification relates

72 See *ibid.*

73 See Court of Innovative Arbitration, "Press Release" (6 April 2016), online: http://martens-lawyers.com/wp-content/uploads/2016/04/160406-EN-INBA-COIA-press-release.pdf.

74 See Indian National Bar Association, "Court of Innovative Arbitration (COIA) Germany Entered in Joint Venture with Indian National Bar Association" (6 April 2016), online: www.indianbarassociation.org/court-of-innovative-arbitration-coia-germany-entered-in-joint-venture-with-indian-national-bar-association.

75 See *ibid.*

76 See Kahlert, above note 71.

77 See *ibid.*

to the cost of using the CICR.[78] It would better encourage and facilitate use of the CICR if the cost schedule was revised to reflect what commercial parties to a domestic dispute in India can afford. The cost schedule will, therefore, likely be lower than that of the COIA, making it more attractive to the Indian market. The CICR is neither a subsidiary nor an affiliate of the COIA. The COIA will, however, be involved in training CICR arbitrators in *ex aequo et bono* arbitration before and after its launch.[79] The COIA will also advise the CICR on finalizing the CICR arbitration rules and other aspects involved in designing and managing the CICR.[80]

F. CONCLUSION

Both the COIA and the BAT offer a simple and effective method of dispute resolution through a modified form of traditional commercial arbitration. Since the BAT's inception in 2007, there have been almost 900 cases submitted to it, and the number of submissions increases each year. The BAT has provided a meaningful alternative to the lengthy and costly court battles that parties previously faced and has facilitated justice and fairness in dispute resolution in the world of international basketball. In time, it is expected that the COIA, and its parallel models, will bring the same success and efficiency to the world of traditional commercial arbitration.

78 See *ibid.*

79 See *ibid.*

80 See *ibid.*

Arbitration Resources

COMPILED BY JOAN RATAIC-LANG & LINDA ZARDO

Texts

AMRO, IHAB. *Recognition and Enforcement of Foreign Arbitral Awards in Theory and in Practice: A Comparative Study in Common Law and Civil Law Countries* (Newcastle upon Tyne, UK: Cambridge Scholars Publishing, 2013).

BALTHASAR, STEPHAN, ED. *International Commercial Arbitration: International Conventions, Country Reports and Comparative Analysis* (Oxford: Hart, 2016).

BARIN, BABAK, ANDREW D LITTLE, & RANDY A PEPPER. *The Osler Guide to Commercial Arbitration in Canada: A Practical Introduction to Domestic and International Commercial Arbitration* (The Hague: Kluwer Law International, 2006).

BERNSTEIN, RONALD, JOHN TACKABERRY, & ARTHUR MARRIOTT. *Bernstein's Handbook of Arbitration & Dispute Resolution*, 4th ed (London: Sweet & Maxwell, 2003).

BINDER, PETER. *International Commercial Arbitration and Conciliation in UNCITRAL Model Law Jurisdictions*, 3d ed (London: Sweet & Maxwell, 2011).

BORN, GARY. *International Arbitration: Law and Practice* (Alphen aan den Rijn, NL: Kluwer Law International, 2016).

———. *International Commercial Arbitration* (Alphen aan den Rign, NL: Wolters Kluwer Law & Business, 2014).

BROWN, HENRY J, & ARTHUR L MARRIOTT. *ADR Principles and Practice*, 3d ed (London: Sweet & Maxwell, 2011).

CASEY, J BRIAN. *Arbitration Law of Canada: Practice and Procedure*, 2d ed (Huntington, NY: Juris, 2011).

———. *International and Domestic Commercial Arbitra*tion (Toronto: Carswell, 1993–) (Loose-leaf).

COOLEY, JOHN W, & STEVEN LUBET. *Arbitration Advocacy*, 2d ed (Notre Dame, IN: National Institute for Trial Advocacy, 2003).

DOMKE, MARTIN, GABRIEL M WILNER, & LARRY E EDMONSON. *Domke on Commercial Arbitration (The Law and Practice of Commercial Arbitration)* (St Paul, MN: Thomson/West, 2003–) (Loose-leaf).

EARLE, WENDY J. *Drafting Arbitration and ADR Clauses for Commercial Contracts: A Solicitor's Manual* (Toronto: Carswell, 2002–) (Loose-leaf).

FRIEDLAND, PAUL D. *Arbitration Clauses for International Contracts*, 2d ed (New York: JurisNet, 2007).

FRY, JASON, SIMON GREENBERG, & FRANCESCA MAZZA. *The Secretariat's Guide to ICC Arbitration* (Paris: International Chamber of Commerce, 2012).

GAILLARD, EMMANUEL, & JOHN SAVAGE, EDS. *Fouchard, Gaillard, Goldman on International Commercial Arbitration* (The Hague: Kluwer Law International, 1999).

GAITIS, JAMES M, ED. *College of Commercial Arbitrators Guide to Best Practices in Commercial Arbitration*, 3d ed (Huntington, NY: JurisNet, LLC, 2014).

GARNETT, RICHARD ET AL. *A Practical Guide to International Commercial Arbitration* (Dobbs Ferry, NY: Oceana Publications, 2000).

GRENIG, JAY E. *International Commercial Arbitration* (St Paul, MN: Thomson Reuters, 2016).

HARRIS, BRUCE, ROWAN PLANTEROSE, & JONATHAN TECKS. *The Arbitration Act, 1996: A Commentary*, 4th ed (Oxford: Wiley-Blackwell, 2007).

INTERNATIONAL CHAMBER OF COMMERCE. *Arbitration and ADR Rules* (Paris: International Chamber of Commerce, 2011).

JACYK, DAVID WILLIAM. *Arbitration in WTO Disputes: The Forgotten Alternative* (Vancouver: University of British Columbia, 2007).

JARVIN, SIGVARD, & ANNETTE MAGNUSSON. *International Arbitration Court Decisions* (Huntington, NY: JurisNet, 2006).

JOHNSON, INDIA. *Handbook on Commercial Arbitration* (Huntington, NY: Juris, 2016).

JOSEPH, DAVID. *Jurisdiction and Arbitration Agreements and Their Enforcement* (London: Sweet & Maxwell, 2005).

KURKELA, MATTI, & HANNES SNELLMAN. *Due Process in International Commercial Arbitration* (Dobbs Ferry, NY: Oceana, 2005).

LOWENFELD, ANDREAS F. *Lowenfeld on International Arbitration: Collected Essays over Three Decades* (Huntington, NY: Juris, 2005).

MACLACHLAN, CAMPBELL, LAURENCE SHORE, & MATTHEW WEINIGER. *International Investment Arbitration: Substantive Principles* (Oxford: Oxford University Press, 2017).

MCEWAN, QC, KENNETH, & LUDMILLA BARBARA HERBST. *Commercial Arbitration in Canada: A Guide to Domestic and International Arbitrations* (Aurora, ON: Canada Law Book, 2013–) (Loose-leaf).

MUSTILL, SIR MICHAEL, & STEWART C BOYD. *Commercial Arbitration*, 3d ed (London: LexisNexis Butterworths, 2018).

PARK, WILLIAM W. *The Arbitrator's Jurisdiction to Determine Jurisdiction* (Alphen aan den Rijn, NL: Kluwer Law International, 2007).

REDFERN, ALAN, & MARTIN HUNTER. *Law and Practice of International Commercial Arbitration*, 4th ed (London: Sweet & Maxwell, 2004).

ROWLEY, JOHN WILLIAM. *Arbitration World: Jurisdictional Comparisons*, 2d ed (London: European Lawyer, 2006).

SUTTON, DAVID ST JOHN ET AL. *Russell on Arbitration*, 24th ed (London: Sweet & Maxwell, 2015).

VAN DEN BERG, ALBERT JAN ET AL. *International Arbitration 2006: Back to Basics* (Alphen aan den Rijn, NL: Kluwer Law International, 2007).

VERBIST, HERMAN, ERIK SCHÄFER, & CHRISTOPHE IMHOOS. *ICC Arbitration in Practice*, 2d rev ed (Alphen aan den Rijn, NL: Kluwer Law International, 2016).

VON THÜLEN RHOADES, RUFUS, DANIEL M KOLKEY, & RICHARD CHERNICK. *The Practitioner's Handbook on International Arbitration and Mediation* (Huntington, NY: Juris, 2002–) (Looseleaf).

WADE, SHAI ET AL. *A Commentary on the LCIA Arbitration Rules* (London: Sweet & Maxwell/ Thomson Reuter, 2015).

WEBSTER, THOMAS H, & MICHAEL BÜHLER. *Handbook of ICC Arbitration: Commentary, Precedents, Materials*, 2d ed (London: Sweet & Maxwell, 2008).

WEIGAND, FRANK-BERND, ED. *Practitioner's Handbook on International Commercial Arbitration*, 2d ed (Oxford: Oxford University Press, 2009).

Continuing Legal Education Seminars

"Conducting the Commercial Arbitration" (Law Society of Upper Canada Continuing Legal Education program, delivered at the Law Society of Upper Canada, Toronto, 2001).

"Advanced Commercial Arbitration" (Law Society of Upper Canada Continuing Legal Education program, delivered at the Law Society of Upper Canada, Toronto, 2007).

"Successfully Navigating an International Commercial Arbitration" (Ontario Bar Association Continuing Professional Development program, delivered at the Ontario Bar Association, Toronto, 2013).

"Internationalizing Commercial Contracts" (Institute of Continuing Professional Development program, delivered at the Ontario Bar Association, Toronto, 2014).

Journals and Periodicals

Arbitration Brief (Washington, DC: American University Washington College of Law, 2011–).

Arbitration International (Oxford: Oxford University Press, 1985–).

Canadian Arbitration and Mediation Journal/Journal d'arbitrage et de médiation canadien (Toronto: ADR Institute of Canada, 1992–).

Commercial Arbitration (New York: Practising Law Institute, 2010–).

Commercial Litigation and Arbitration Review (previously *Commercial Litigation Review*, 2003–2011) (Markham, ON: LexisNexis, 2012–).

Journal of International Arbitration (The Hague: Kluwer Law International, 1984–).

Revue d'arbitrage et de médiation/Journal of Arbitration and Mediation (Cowansville, QC: Yvon Blais, 2010–).

Arbitration Centres and Associations

Canada

ADR Chambers Canada, online: http://adrchambers.com/ca
ADR Institute of Canada, online: www.adric.ca
ADRIC Arbitration Rules, online: http://adric.ca/arbrules
ADR Institute of Ontario, online: http://adr-ontario.ca
Amicus Chambers, online: www.amicuschambers.com
Arbitration Place, online: www.arbitrationplace.com
Arbitrators Association of British Columbia (AABC), online: www.labour-arbitrators.bc.ca

Bay Street Chambers, online: http://baystreetchambers.com
British Columbia Arbitration and Mediation Institute, online: http://bcami.com
British Columbia International Commercial Arbitration Centre, online: http://bcicac.com

Canadian Commercial Arbitration Centre (CCAC), online: www.ccac-adr.org/en
Coe ADR Management, online: http://coeadrmanagement.com

Ontario Bar Association, Alternative Dispute Resolution Section, online: www.oba.org/adr
Ontario Labour-Management Arbitrators' Association, online: www.labourarbitrators.org

Toronto Commercial Arbitration Society (TCAS), online: http://torontocommercialarbitrationsociety.com

Western Canada Commercial Arbitration Society (WCCAS), online: https://wccas.ca
Winkler Institute for Dispute Resolution, online: https://winklerinstitute.ca

International

For exhaustive list, please see Happ's Arbitration Links, online: www.arbitration-links.de

American Arbitration Association (AAA) [United States], https://adr.org
Commercial Arbitration Rules and Mediation Procedures, online: www.adr.org/sites/default/files/Commercial%20Rules.pdf

Arbitration Institute of the Stockholm Chamber of Commerce (SCC) [Sweden], online: www.sccinstitute.com
  Rules, online: www.sccinstitute.com/dispute-resolution/rules/

Australian Centre for International Commercial Arbitration (ACICA), online: https://acica.org.au
  ACICA Rules 2016, online: https://acica.org.au/acica-rules-2016

Bahrain Chamber for Dispute Resolution (BCDR-AAA), online: www.bcdr-aaa.org/en

Cairo Regional Centre for International Commercial Arbitration (CRCICA) [Egypt], online: crcica.org

Chartered Institute of Arbitrators (CIArb), online: www.arbitrators.org

China International Economic and Trade Arbitration Commission (CIETAC), online: cietac.org/?l=en

Dubai International Arbitration Centre (DIAC), online: www.dubaichamber.com

German Institute of Arbitration (DIS), online: www.disarb.org/en
  DIS-Arbitration Rules 98, online: www.disarb.org/en/16/rules/dis-arbitration-rules-98-id10

Hong Kong International Arbitration Centre (HKIAC), online: www.hkiac.org

International Centre for Dispute Resolution (ICDR), online: www.icdr.org

International Centre for Settlement of Investment Disputes (ICSID), online: https://icsid.worldbank.org/en

International Chamber of Commerce International Court of Arbitration, online: https://iccwbo.org
  Arbitration Rules, online: https://iccwbo.org/dispute-resolution-services/arbitration/rules-of-arbitration/

International Council for Commercial Arbitration (ICAA), online: www.arbitration-icca.org/ (CPR), online: www.cpradr.org
  Rules, online: www.cpradr.org/resource-center/rules/arbitration

International Islamic Mediation & Arbitration Centre (IMAC), online: www.arabcci.org/IMAC_aboutus.htm

JAMS International, online: www.jamsinternational.com/

Japanese Commercial Arbitration Association (JCAA), online: www.jcaa.or.jp/e
Commercial Arbitration Rules, online: www.jcaa.or.jp/e/arbitration/docs/Arbitration_Rules_2015e.pdf

London Court of International Arbitration (LCIA), online: www.lcia.org
Arbitration Rules, online: www.lcia.org/Dispute_Resolution_Services/lcia-arbitration-rules-2014.aspx

Mediation.org, online: https://mediation.org

Netherlands Arbitration Institute (NAI), online: www.nai-nl.org/en/
Arbitration Rules, online: www.nai-nl.org/downloads/NAI%20Arbitration%20Rules%20and%20Explanation.pdf

New York International Arbitration Center (NYIAC), online: https://nyiac.org
NYIAC Rules, online: https://nyiac.org/about/rules

Shanghai International Economic and Trade Arbitration Commission, online: www.shiac.org/SHIAC/arbitrate_items_E.aspx

Singapore International Arbitration Centre (SIAC), online: www.siac.org.sg
SIAC Rules 2016, online: www.siac.org.sg/our-rules/rules/siac-rules-2016

Swiss Arbitration Association (ASA), online: www.arbitration-ch.org/en/home/index.html

Vienna International Arbitral Centre, online: www.viac.eu/en

Young International Arbitration Group (YIAG), online: www.lcia.org/Membership/YIAG/Young_International_Arbitration_Group.aspx

Canadian Legislation

Available online: www.canlii.org

Canada

Commercial Arbitration Act, RSC 1985, c 17 (2nd Supp)

Alberta

Arbitration Act, RSA 2000, c A-43
International Commercial Arbitration Act, RSA 2000, c I-5

British Columbia

Arbitration Act, RSBC 1996, c 55
International Commercial Arbitration Act, RSBC 1996, c 233

Manitoba

Arbitration Act, CCSM c A120
International Commercial Arbitration Act, CCSM c C151

New Brunswick

Arbitration Act, SNB 2014, c 100
International Commercial Arbitration Act, RSNB 2011, c 176

Newfoundland & Labrador

Arbitration Act, RSNL 1990, c A-14
International Commercial Arbitration Act, RSNL 1990, c I-15

Northwest Territories

Arbitration Act, RSNWT 1988, c A-5
International Commercial Arbitration Act, RSNWT 1988, c I-6

Nova Scotia

Arbitration Act, RSNS 1989, c 19
Commercial Arbitration Act, SNS 1999, c 5
International Commercial Arbitration Act, RSNS 1989, c 234

Nunavut

Arbitration Act, RSNWT (Nu) 1988, c A-5
International Commercial Arbitration Act, RSNWT (Nu) 1988, c I-6

Ontario

Arbitration Act, 1991, SO 1991, c 17
International Commercial Arbitration Act, 2017, SO 2017, c 2, Schedule 5
Municipal Arbitrations Act, RSO 1990, c M.48

Prince Edward Island

Arbitration Act, RSPEI 1988, c A-16
International Commercial Arbitration Act, RSPEI 1988, c I-5

Quebec

Civil Code of Québec, CQLR c CCQ-1991
Code of Civil Procedure, CQLR c C-25.01

Saskatchewan

Arbitration Act, 1992, SS 1992, c A-241
International Commercial Arbitration Act, SS 1988–89, c I-10.2

Yukon

Arbitration Act, RSY 2002, c 8
International Commercial Arbitration Act, RSY 2002, c 123

Uniform Law Conference of Canada

Uniform Arbitration Act (1990, amended 2002), online: www.ulcc.ca/en/home/117-josetta-1-en-gb/uniform-actsa/arbitration-act

International Legislation, Treaties, and Instruments

Arbitration Act, 1996 (UK), 1996, c23, online: www.legislation.gov.uk/
ch 1 (General Provisions)
ch 2 (*Convention on Recognition & Enforcement of Foreign Arbitral Awards*)
ch 3 (*Inter-American Convention on International Commercial Arbitration*)

Federal Arbitration Act, 9 USC, online: www.gpo.gov

Organization of American States (OAS) *Inter-American Convention on International Commercial Arbitration*, 30 January 1975, OASTS 42 [the "Panama Convention"], online: www.oas.org/en/sla/dil/inter_american_treaties_B-35_international_commercial_arbitration.asp.

Uniform Law Commission *Uniform Arbitration Act* (1956, revised 2000), online: www.uniformlaws.org/shared/docs/arbitration/uaa55.pdf

United Nations Commission on International Trade Law (UNCITRAL) "Notes on Organizing Arbitral Proceedings," online: www.uncitral.org/pdf/english/texts/arbitration/arb-notes/arb-notes-e.pdf

United Nations Commission on International Trade Law (UNCITRAL) *Arbitration Rules*, GA Res 31/98, UNGAOR, 1976, with amendments as adopted in 2013, online: www.uncitral.org/uncitral/en/uncitral_texts/arbitration/2010Arbitration_rules.html

United Nations Commission on International Trade Law (UNCITRAL) *Convention on the Recognition and Enforcement of Foreign Arbitral Awards*, 10 June 1958, 330 UNTS 3 [the "New York Convention"], online: www.uncitral.org/uncitral/en/uncitral_texts/arbitration/NYConvention.html.

United Nations Commission on International Trade Law (UNCITRAL) *UNCITRAL Model Law on International Commercial Arbitration*, GA Res 40/72, UNGAOR, 1985, with amendments as adopted in 2006, online: www.uncitral.org/uncitral/en/uncitral_texts/arbitration/1985Model_arbitration.html

Contributors

THE EDITOR

Marvin J Huberman, LLB, LLM (ADR), CS (Civil Litigation), C Arb, is a senior barrister, mediator, and chartered arbitrator with over thirty years' experience. He represents individual and business clients, financial institutions, insurers, and governments in Toronto and has acted in cases in the United States, Europe, and internationally.

Marvin has mediated hundreds of insurance cases and a wide variety of corporate and commercial matters. He is the recipient of the 2017 *Corporate INTL Magazine* Global Award for Partnership Disputes Mediator of the Year in Canada. He has acted as a commercial arbitrator in complex cross-border matters and disputes in corporate law, employment law, real estate and leasing, insurance disputes, intellectual property and high-technology, administrative and constitutional law, motor vehicle accident, and statutory accident benefit cases for the Financial Services Commission of Ontario. He has been awarded the Lawyer International Global Award in 2017 for Law Firm of the Year — Commercial Arbitration — Canada.

Marvin is a founding member of the Chief Justice of Ontario's Advisory Committee on Professionalism and was appointed by the Chief Justice as a member of the Ontario Civil Rules Committee. He is passionate about commercial arbitration and serves as an executive committee member of the Toronto Commercial Arbitration Society.

AUTHORS AND CONTRIBUTORS

Robert Armstrong

The Honourable Robert P Armstrong, QC, was appointed directly from the bar to the Court of Appeal for Ontario on 25 January 2002 and served on that court until 6 March 2013. During his eleven years on the court, he sat on nearly 2,000 cases covering a wide range of commercial, civil, public, administrative, and criminal law matters. Before his appointment to the Court of Appeal, he was engaged in a busy litigation practice at Torys. His practice also covered a variety of matters including cases at all levels of court and before arbitration panels and administrative tribunals. He appeared at both the trial and the appellate levels including the Court of Appeal for Ontario, the Federal Court of Appeal, and the Supreme Court of Canada. He also acted as commission counsel to a number of commissions of inquiry.

Mr Armstrong was commission counsel to the Dubin Inquiry into the use of drugs and banned substances in sport. While at the bar, he was an active member of several legal organizations. He was Treasurer (Head) of the Law Society of Upper Canada from 1999 to 2001. He is a fellow of the American College of Trial Lawyers and was a member of its Board of Regents for a brief period before his appointment to the court. He was the chair and president of the Canadian Institute for Advanced Legal Studies from 2003 to 2014.

Mr Armstrong is presently a resident arbitrator at Arbitration Place in Toronto, where he presides over a wide variety of cases. He received a BA (Hons) from Carleton University, an MA and LLB from the University of Toronto, and an honorary LLD from the Law Society of Upper Canada.

Ian Binnie

The Honourable Ian Binnie, CC, QC, is counsel at Lenczner Slaght, Toronto. One of Canada's most respected lawyers, he served for nearly fourteen years as a justice of the Supreme Court of Canada. When he retired in 2011, he was described by the *Globe and Mail* as "arguably the country's premier judge" and by *La Presse* as "peut-être le juge le plus influent au Canada dans la dernière décennie."

During his time on the country's top court (as only the third modern justice appointed directly from the bar), Ian authored more than 170 opinions including on landmark cases involving patent interpretation and validity, protection of trade-marks, media law, Indigenous law, commercial disputes, punitive damages, expert evidence, and many aspects of constitutional, criminal, and administrative law. Over the course of three decades as a litigator, he argued cases in most of the common law provinces and appeared regularly before the Supreme Court on a range of constitutional, civil, and criminal matters.

Ian has often taken on public service roles as well. In the early 1980s, he served for four years as Canada's associate deputy minister of justice. He was later appointed special parliamentary counsel to the Joint Committee of the Senate and the House of Commons on the Amendment of the Constitution. He is an elected member of the International Commission of Jurists and has appeared as counsel on behalf of Canada before the International Court of Justice and various international tribunals.

Sheila R Block

Sheila R Block is the chair of Torys' Litigation and Dispute Resolution Practice. She is a trial and appellate counsel with a broad civil litigation practice—acting as counsel on leading cases in a diverse range of matters across many disciplines. She has appeared before all levels of court including the Supreme Court of Canada and in domestic and international arbitrations. She is the chair of the Touching Tiny Lives foundation, the president of The Harold G Fox Education Fund, a trustee of the Foundation for International Arbitration Advocacy in Geneva, and a member of the President's Council of the University of Ottawa. She has been ranked by *Lexpert* as one of Canada's top twenty-five corporate litigators and top twenty-five women lawyers and by *Canadian Lawyer* as one of Canada's top twenty-five most influential lawyers in 2015. She has taught trial and arbitration advocacy in North and South America, Great Britain, Europe, India, Singapore, Hong Kong, and New Zealand, and at the war crimes tribunals in Rwanda and Sierra Leone. She has worked on the Canadian edition of *Modern Trial Advocacy* by Steven Lubet.

Ms Block received her LLB (Gold Medalist) in 1972 from the University of Ottawa, was called to the Ontario bar in 1974, and became a member of the American College of Trial Lawyers and of the International Society of Barristers in 1992. She was awarded The Douglas K Laidlaw Medal for Excellence in Advocacy in 1999, inducted into the University of Ottawa's Common Law Honour Society in 2003, and presented with the Toronto Lawyers Association Award of Distinction in 2004, the Law Society of Upper Canada's Law Society Medal and the Ontario Bar Association's Award for Excellence in Civil Litigation in 2006, The Advocates' Society Medal in 2008, the University of Ottawa's Meritas Tabaret Award for Alumni Achievement in 2012, an honorary LLD from the University of Ottawa in 2014, and an honorary LLD from the Law Society of Upper Canada in 2015. In 2016, she was named the *Benchmark* Trial Lawyer of the Year.

Will Bortolin

William Bortolin has a general commercial litigation practice with an emphasis on high-stakes litigation involving complex subject matter. He has specific experience with shareholder and partnership disputes, intellectual property litigation (including *Patented Medicines (Notice of Compliance) Regulations,* Trademark Opposition Board, and section 45 expungement proceedings), injunctions, appeals, *Companies' Creditors Arrangement Act* proceedings, class action proceedings, and fraud claims.

William brings a science background to his work, having obtained an undergraduate degree in medical sciences. He is also known for his technological savvy, which is increasingly valuable as courts modernize and opportunities arise to leverage technology to run litigation more efficiently and cost-effectively.

J Brian Casey

J Brian Casey received a bachelor of engineering degree from Carleton University and graduated *magna cum laude* with a JD from the University of Ottawa. He was called to the bar in 1976. He has practised at all levels of the courts in Canada including the Supreme Court of Canada.

Brian also holds a master of laws in International Business Law from York University, having focused his studies on international commercial arbitration. He is a former principal of Baker & McKenzie International and a former chair of that firm's North American Litigation Practice Group. In 1995, he was designated a fellow of the Chartered Institute of Arbitrators. In 2012, he formed Bay Street Chambers to continue his practice as an independent commercial arbitrator providing arbitration and consulting services to both the Canadian and the international business community. He is an adjunct professor at the University of Toronto's Faculty of Law and on the Council of the American Arbitration Association. He is also chair of the Canadian Advisory Committee to the International Centre for Dispute Resolution.

Brian is the author of *Arbitration Law of Canada: Practice and Procedure* and a contributor to *International Arbitration Checklists*, both by Juris Publishing. He has also contributed to *Alternative Dispute Resolution*, by Aspatore Books, the CCH *Ultimate Corporate Counsel Guide*, and the fourth edition of *Arbitration World*, by Sweet & Maxwell.

Shantona Chaudhury

Shantona Chaudhury is a partner at Pape Barristers. Her civil litigation practice includes tort, class actions, commercial litigation, civil procedure, professional discipline, administrative, and constitutional law. She has extensive experience in appellate litigation, having been counsel in over twenty cases at the Court of Appeal for

Ontario and in several Divisional Court appeals, and also having argued at the Supreme Court of Canada.

Shantona is ranked in *Chambers Canada: Canada's Leading Lawyers for Business, 2016*, which describes her as follows: "Shantona Chaudhury is building an impressive reputation for herself in the appellate litigation space. One peer noted: 'She is fantastic. She is one of the smartest lawyers out there right now. Her written work is outstanding.' Clients describe her as a 'brilliant advocate.'" She was also listed in the *Best Lawyers in Canada* in 2017 and named a litigation future star by *Benchmark Canada* in 2014, 2015, and 2016. In 2013, she was recognized with a Precedent Setter award from *Precedent* magazine.

Before starting practice, Shantona clerked for Justice Ian Binnie at the Supreme Court, trained as a Fox Scholar and pupil barrister in England, and obtained a master's degree in law from the University of Oxford. Her early experience also includes internships at the International Criminal Tribunal for Rwanda and at the Parliament of Canada.

Shantona is fluently bilingual, and she was called to the bars of both Ontario and Quebec in 2007. She holds a BCL from the University of Oxford, a BCL/LLB from McGill University, and a BA (Hons) in French Studies and an MA in eighteenth-century French literature from Queen's University.

Anthony Daimsis

Professor Anthony Daimsis has been teaching at the University of Ottawa since 2003 and is the director of the bijural (common law and civil law) National Program. He teaches contract and tort law, international sales law, international commercial arbitration, and legal writing. In addition to his teaching at the law faculty, he works with the National Judicial Institute, a not-for-profit institution committed to building better justice through leadership in the education of judges in Canada and internationally. He is the lead instructor for the Professional Certificate in International Arbitration and is a member of the Ontario bar.

Before teaching at the university, Professor Daimsis worked as an associate at an international law firm in Austria. His work focused on foreign investment disputes, telecommunications, and underground resources in addition to a number of international commercial contract and construction disputes resolved under the auspices of the World Bank Group (International Centre for Settlement of Investment Disputes) and various other international commercial arbitration institutions. He is frequently approached to serve as an arbitrator in domestic and international commercial disputes. He is also a sought-after speaker on international arbitration, international sales law, and foreign direct investment and has given talks in the United States, England, Sweden, Austria, Iran, and Myanmar, to name a few, in addition to advising Southeast Asian governments on their foreign direct investment policies.

Leslie Dizgun

Leslie Dizgun, MA, LLM, C Med, is a mediator and arbitrator with ADR Chambers. He has twenty-seven years' experience in dispute resolution. His areas of expertise include contracts, libel, commercial disputes, wrongful dismissal, workplace, franchise, real estate, and construction matters.

Leslie received his master of laws in Alternative Dispute Resolution from York University's Osgoode Hall Law School and his master of arts from Concordia University. He is a chartered mediator and a member of The Advocates' Society and has recently been awarded The Advocates' Society Award for Excellence in Teaching.

Leslie is a frequent speaker and instructor on ADR and dispute resolution topics. He is an adjunct professor at Osgoode Hall Law School, teaching dispute settlement in the civil justice system. He has also taught civil procedure and the capstone colloquium in litigation, dispute resolution, and administration of justice. Leslie has provided training in mediation techniques and mediation advocacy to government lawyers for the Office of the Attorney General and acted as a coach in settlement conference training for judges and masters for the National Judicial Institute. He was the sole mediator for the pilot program for professional misconduct complaints at the Royal College of Dental Surgeons. He is also the author of many publications on ADR. He can be reached through the Toronto office of ADR Chambers.

Wendy Earle

Wendy Earle, LLB, FCIArb, is a mediator, an arbitrator, and counsel specializing in commercial litigation in Toronto. She has served as appellate counsel in disputes involving real estate and focused on all manner of commercial disputes with specific emphasis on commercial real estate, solicitor's negligence, and franchise disputes. In the course of her career, she has appeared before all levels of the Ontario Superior Court and before the Supreme Court of Canada. She was the national leader of Borden Ladner Gervais LLP's Real Estate Litigation Focus Group. In the last ten years, her practice has shifted toward an emphasis on ADR and arbitrations, specifically, designing dispute resolution regimes for complex commercial relationships and advising on the drafting of ADR and arbitration clauses for commercial contracts and self-regulating industry associations.

Wendy is a fellow of the Chartered Institute of Arbitrators and the author of the loose-leaf text *Drafting ADR and Arbitration Clauses for Commercial Contracts*, published by Carswell. Since 2016, she has been the chair of The Law Foundation of Ontario's Class Proceedings Committee, on which she has served since 2006, having been appointed jointly by the Attorney General of Ontario and The Law Foundation.

Kenneth J Glasner

Kenneth J Glasner, QC, is an experienced mediator and arbitrator based in Vancouver. He has practised as a neutral since 1967, and he was appointed as a federal Queen's Counsel in 1990.

Ken has been involved in hundreds of disputes over a range of civil matters as a neutral and has been a frequent lecturer and panel member speaking on subjects dealing with ADR and designing mediation systems in Canada. He also sits on discipline panels. A number of his papers have been published. He retired some years ago as an adjunct professor of law at the University of British Columbia's Faculty of Law.

Ken participates with other colleagues as a special adjudicator and judicial justice of the peace in a highly successful small claims project for the Provincial Court of British Columbia that has resulted in cleaning up the backlog of cases. He is also on the International Institute for Conflict Prevention & Resolution's panel of distinguished neutrals based in New York. He is a former trustee of the British Columbia International Commercial Arbitration Centre and member of the working group dealing with domestic arbitration for the Uniform Law Conference of Canada. Recently, the minister of justice for British Columbia appointed him to an arbitration advisory group.

Stephen Goudge

The Honourable Stephen Goudge, QC, articled to The Honourable Ian G Scott, QC, and was called to the bar of Ontario in 1970, appointed as Queen's Counsel in 1982, and appointed to the Order of Ontario in 2016. He is currently engaged in mediation, arbitration, and advising government and has been a lecturer in professional responsibility at Osgoode Hall Law School since 2014.

Mr Goudge practised with the small litigation firm Cameron, Brewin & Scott until it merged with Gowling and Henderson in 1983. He was managing partner of Gowling, Strathy & Henderson in Toronto, where he had a general litigation practice. He has appeared before many administrative tribunals, courts at all levels in Ontario, and the Supreme Court of Canada. He was a lecturer in labour law and Native rights from 1974 to 1985 and in professional responsibility from 2001 to 2012 at the University of Toronto's Faculty of Law. He has been active in the Ontario Bar Association and Canadian Civil Liberties Association, and he was elected bencher of the Law Society of Upper Canada from 1991 to 1996. He is a fellow of the American College of Trial Lawyers.

Mr Goudge was appointed to the Court of Appeal for Ontario in 1996. He was a board member of Pro Bono Law Ontario from 2002 to 2006 and member of the Civil Rules Committee from 2009 to

2014, and he has been a member of the Chief Justice of Ontario's Advisory Committee on Professionalism since 2001, a member of the Law Commission of Ontario's Board of Governors since 2009, and board chair of the Pediatric Oncology Group of Ontario since 2014. In April 2007, he was appointed by Ontario to conduct the Inquiry into Pediatric Forensic Pathology, which reported in October 2008. In April 2014, he resigned from the judiciary, and as of May 2014 he has been counsel to Paliare Roland Rosenberg Rothstein LLP.

Mr Goudge received a BA (Hons) in Political Science and Economics from the University of Toronto in 1964, an MSc in Economics from the London School of Economics in 1965, and an LLB and the Dean's Key from the University of Toronto in 1968. He is the recipient of honorary doctorates from the Law Society of Upper Canada and Assumption University.

Kaleigh Hawkins-Schulz

Kaleigh Hawkins-Schulz, BA, JD (expected 2018), is a law student at Western University and obtained her BA from McGill University. She is the Chief Research Assistant to Professor Richard McLaren and has assisted in numerous arbitrations and sports integrity cases. Most recently, she was a member of the team led by Professor McLaren investigating allegations of sample-tampering at the 2014 Sochi Winter Games. She also serves as a Managing Editor of the Western Law Review and is an active mentor to first year law students. In the fall of 2017, she travelled to Hong Kong to complete a semester abroad at the University of Hong Kong, Faculty of Law.

William G Horton

William G Horton, C Arb, FCIArb, practises as an arbitrator of Canadian and international business disputes. Before establishing his current practice, he served as the head of litigation at two major Canadian law firms. He has been appointed tribunal chair, party nominee, or sole arbitrator in over 100 substantial disputes. His arbitration appointments have included cases involving nuclear facilities, telecommunication, satellite and wireless industry disputes, oil and gas and alternative energy disputes, government privatization contracts, national advertising campaigns, and cross-border distribution, shareholder, software licensing, and other intellectual property agreements.

Mr Horton is a fellow of the Chartered Institute of Arbitrators, former chair of the International Bar Association's International Litigation Committee, former Co-Chair of ADR Chambers' international and commercial panels, and former executive member of International Chamber of Commerce Canada. He is on the arbitration roster of many international arbitration institutions including the International Centre for Dispute Resolution, International Institute for Conflict Prevention & Resolution, China International Economic and Trade Arbitration Commission, and ADR Institute of Canada. Until recently, he served as a member of the NAFTA 2022 Committee. He is the editor-in-chief of the *Canadian Arbitration and Mediation Journal* and Course Director and principal instructor of the Toronto Commercial Arbitration Society's Gold Standard Course in Commercial Arbitration.

Mr Horton is widely recognized in Canadian and international surveys as a leading arbitrator of commercial disputes. His recognitions include the Lionel J McGowan Award of Excellence in Dispute Resolution, *Who's Who Legal* (arbitration), *Chambers Canada: Canada's Leading Lawyers for Business* (leading individuals in arbitration — band 1), *Canadian Legal Lexpert Directory* (international commercial arbitration — most frequently recommended category), *Lexpert Guide to the Leading US/Canada Cross-border Litigation Lawyers in Canada*, 2014 *Euromoney* (shortlist for Canadian arbitrator of the year), 2012 *Best Lawyers in Canada* (best Toronto international arbitration lawyer), and 2007 *Who's Who Legal: International Who's Who of Business Lawyers* (ten most highly regarded individuals — global — in the field of commercial litigation).

Dominique T Hussey

Dominique T Hussey is the head of the Intellectual Property Litigation Practice Group at Bennett Jones LLP. Her practice involves patent, trade-mark, copyright, and commercial litigation and counselling, brand portfolio management, and advice on advertising, marketing, packaging, labelling, and regulatory matters. She is depended on to negotiate complex strategic settlements and business arrangements with a view to positive business and litigation outcomes.

Dominique was named one of *Lexpert*'s "Rising Stars: Leading Lawyers under 40" in 2012, and she has been recognized for intellectual property litigation in *Lexpert*, *Chambers Global: The World's Leading Business Lawyers*, *IAM Patent 1000 — The World's Leading Patent Professionals*, *World Trademark Review 1000 — The World's Leading Trademark Professionals*, *Managing Intellectual Property*'s IP Stars (patent, trade-mark, and copyright), *Benchmark* (intellectual property), and *Who's Who Legal: Canada* (life sciences).

Dominique is deeply involved in the intellectual property and advocacy communities through committee work and teaching in association with the Intellectual Property Institute of Canada, the International Trademarks Association, the Professional Development Committee of The Canadian Bar Association's Intellectual Property Section, and Osgoode Hall Law School's LLM program, as an adjunct professor supporting the moot program at the University of Toronto's Faculty of Law, and as a board member of and trainer at The Advocates' Society. Before joining Bennett Jones LLP, she litigated for three years at a New York law firm in the areas of patents, trade secrets, and false advertising, with a particular focus on pharmaceutical patent litigation.

John AM Judge

John AM Judge is an arbitrator and barrister with 39 Essex Chambers in London, England, where he carries on his international arbitration practice, and a resident arbitrator at Arbitration Place in Toronto, where he sits as arbitrator in domestic Canadian arbitrations. He also acts as counsel in Ontario court proceedings arising from international arbitration.

John was a partner at Stikeman Elliott, where he carried on a counsel practice for thirty-five years, appearing before administrative and arbitral tribunals and trial and appellate courts including the Supreme Court of Canada. He has over sixteen years' experience in international arbitration as an arbitrator and has been recognized in all major rankings for international arbitration, most recently in *Chambers Global: The World's Leading Business Lawyers* (band 1 in Canada) in 2017 as well as *International Who's Who of Commercial Arbitration* and *Best Lawyers in Canada*. He has experience in ad hoc arbitration and arbitration with the leading arbitral institutions including the International Chamber of Commerce, International Centre for Dispute Resolution, London Court of International Arbitration, Singapore International Arbitration Centre, and Kuala Lumpur International Arbitration Centre.

John has broad dispute experience in the following industries: mining, oil and gas, and energy; construction, engineering, infrastructure, and real estate; technology, Internet, and telecommunications; insurance and reinsurance; banking and investment; and transportation. He may be reached at john.judge@39essex.com or jjudge@judgearbitration.com.

Lucas Kittmer

Lucas Kittmer graduated from the University of Toronto's Faculty of Law in 2015 and completed his articles at a broad commercial litigation firm before being called to the Ontario bar in 2016. He then joined Paterson MacDougall LLP as an associate and focused his practice on aviation law, municipal liability, and estates. He is a member of the Toronto Lawyers Association, Canadian Defence Lawyers, and The Advocates' Society.

Ken McEwan

Ken McEwan, QC, practises as general counsel with a particular focus on complex corporate commercial litigation and arbitration, and administrative law. Among many favourable peer reviews, he is ranked by *Chambers Canada: Canada's Leading Lawyers for Business* in the highest band for dispute resolution, and Martindale-Hubbell has given him a ranking of "AV Preeminent." He regularly acts as both mediator and arbitrator of commercial disputes.

Mr McEwan is a co-author of *Commercial Arbitration in Canada: A Guide to Domestic and International Arbitrations*, published by Canada Law Book, which has been cited as authority in judgments across Canada. He is a member of the Chartered Institute of Arbitrators and Western Canada Commercial Arbitration Society, the secretary and treasurer of the International Society of Barristers, a fellow of the American College of Trial Lawyers, and a director of The Advocates' Society. The Law Society of British Columbia has appointed him to the Committee on Relations with the Judiciary, and the Attorney General appointed him to the Supreme Court Rules Revision Committee, where he served several terms until it disbanded in April 2016.

Mr McEwan is the author of the third edition of *Sopinka on the Trial of an Action*, published by LexisNexis. He is an adjunct professor of law teaching trial advocacy at the University of British Columbia. He is a past president of the Sopinka Cup Society and a regular contributor to both the Continuing Legal Education Society of British Columbia and The Advocates' Society on topics related to litigation and arbitration. He chairs a panel of the British Columbia Inns of Court project.

Richard McLaren

Professor Richard McLaren, OC, HBA, LLB, LLM, DD, C Arb, is a recipient of the Order of Canada, one of the country's highest civilian distinctions, which recognizes exceptional achievement, service, and contribution to the country and the international community.

An internationally recognized expert in sports law and arbitration, Professor McLaren has spent his career working at the highest levels to protect the integrity of sports. He is an adjudicator of sports-related disputes at both the amateur and the professional levels. He is the president of the Basketball Arbitral Tribunal, which deals with monetary disputes involving professional basketball players, agents, and clubs primarily in Europe but increasingly in South America, Africa, the Middle East, and Asia, in particular, China. As a long-standing member of and arbitrator for the Court of Arbitration for Sport, based in Lausanne, Switzerland, he has arbitrated cases worldwide, and as an ad hoc panel member of that court, he has participated in five Olympic Games. He has served as an arbitrator for the National Hockey League, dealing with salary arbitrations and player-agent disputes for the NHL Players' Association. As a member of the World Anti-doping Agency's 2015 Independent Commission, he examined systemic doping and corruption in Russian athletics. In 2016, he led the investigation into allegations of sample tampering at the 2014 Sochi Winter Games.

Professor McLaren is an arbitrator for the British Columbia International Commercial Arbitration Centre and has acted as arbitrator in disputes for the International Chamber of Commerce and the International Centre for Settlement of Investment Disputes, as well as being a member of a number of international commercial arbitration centres such as the Beijing Arbitration Commission, London Court of International Arbitration, and Dubai International Arbitration Centre.

Professor McLaren has published in a wide range of areas including dispute resolution and bankruptcy. He is a professor of law at Western University in London, Ontario, chairman of the National Sports Law Institute's Emeritus Advisory Board at Marquette University, and a special adviser to the Straus Institute for Dispute Resolution at Pepperdine University. He is also counsel to McKenzie Lake Lawyers LLP and has extensive experience as a labour and commercial mediator and arbitrator.

Graeme Mew

The Honourable Justice Graeme Mew was appointed to the Ontario Superior Court of Justice in December 2013. Previously, he practised as an advocate, mediator, and arbitrator with Clyde & Co in Toronto and as a member of chambers at 4 New Square in London, England. He holds law degrees from Kingston University in England and the University of Windsor in Canada. He was a member of the bars of England and Wales (Middle Temple, 1982), Ontario (1987), and British Columbia (2010). His practice concentrated on civil litigation, insurance law, commercial mediation and arbitration, and sports disputes.

Mr Mew is the author of *The Law of Limitations*, published by LexisNexis. He has been a judicial and appeals officer for World Rugby since 2001 and member of World Rugby's Anti-doping Advisory Committee since its establishment in 2000. He was a member of the ad hoc panels of the Court of Arbitration for Sport at the 2010 New Delhi Commonwealth Games and the 2012 London Summer Games. He currently serves as a director of the Sport Dispute Resolution Centre of Canada and the Ontario Superior Court Judges' Association. He is a bencher of the Honourable Society of the Middle Temple.

Neal Mizrahi

Neal Mizrahi, CPA, CA, CBV, is a managing director in the Economic and Financial Consulting, International Arbitration Practice at FTI Consulting. He is a chartered professional accountant and chartered business valuator. He has been ranked in the 2014, 2015, 2016, and 2017 editions of Global Arbitration Review's *International Who's Who of Commercial Arbitration*, which lists the most highly regarded experts globally. In the independent survey, he is described as "the engine room and brains behind FTI's most high-profile mandates" and as being held in "universally high esteem."

Mr Mizrahi has more than twelve years' experience in business valuation and quantification of economic loss and has authored over 100 reports relied on by courts and arbitral institutions globally. He obtained his CA designation while working at PricewaterhouseCoopers in Toronto, practising in the Audit and Assurance Group and servicing clients, including financial institutions, in a variety of industries. He has been qualified as an expert witness by the Ontario Superior Court of Justice and the Federal Court of Canada, where he has provided oral testimony in a number of complex disputes. He has also testified in investor-state and commercial arbitration. In addition to his experience in Canada, he deals with international trade and investment arbitration for the International Centre for Settlement of Investment Disputes and with international commercial arbitration for the International Chamber of Commerce, London Court of International Arbitration, and Dubai International Arbitration Centre. He also provides expert and advisory services to companies and governments in North and South America, Europe, Africa, and Asia.

Mr Mizrahi is an adjunct professor at York University's Schulich School of Business and the University of Toronto's Rotman School of Management. For the past decade, he has been teaching courses in accounting and business valuation in graduate and undergraduate programs. And for the past five years, he has been extensively involved in a leading three-day training program, Questioning Expert Witnesses in International Arbitration, offered by the Foundation for International Arbitration Advocacy.

Stephen Richard Morrison

Stephen Richard Morrison, LLB (Hons), C Med, C Arb, FCIArb, graduated with honours from Osgoode Hall Law School in 1976 and was called to the Ontario bar in 1978. Following a career in criminal law, in 1982 he cofounded The Rose Corporation, a land development and investment company, where he served as president and in-house legal counsel until 1999. Until the end of 2014, he was a partner in a leading Canadian law firm and was regularly engaged in the resolution of commercial disputes including matters arising from development and construction projects, financing failures, delay and impact claims, contract tendering issues, environmental problems, insurance coverage disputes, and breach of trust claims.

Through Stephen Richard Morrison ADR Inc, he now brings his over forty years of legal and business experience to the resolution of complex commercial disputes as a neutral mediator and arbitrator. As a mediator, he understands that the parties prefer workable solutions to protracted litigation and brings creativity and persistence to the resolution of difficult conflicts. As an arbitrator, he understands that the parties are entrusting to him the fair, equitable, and legally correct resolution of a dispute that they have been unable to settle themselves. He is also committed to ensuring that regardless of the outcome all parties feel confident that they have been heard and understood. He has been recognized by the ADR Institute of Canada with the designations chartered mediator and chartered arbitrator, and he is a fellow of the Chartered Institute of Arbitrators.

Paul J Pape

Paul J Pape's litigation practice in Toronto focuses on complex commercial, securities, class action, professional negligence, and administrative matters with special emphasis on appeals in these and other areas.

Paul has over forty-five years' experience as both trial and appellate counsel and has acted in many cases of significance. He is a fellow of the American College of Trial Lawyers and International Academy of Trial Lawyers, is regularly listed in the *Lexpert/American Lawyer Guide to the Leading 500 Lawyers in Canada*, and is recommended in *Chambers Global: The World's Leading Business Lawyers*. He is also listed in the *Lexpert Guide to the 100 Most Creative Lawyers in Canada* and the recipient of a Lexpert Zenith Award. He is an honorary member of The Commercial Bar Association in England, past chair of the Ontario Bar Association's Civil Litigation section, and member of the Holland Access to Justice in Medical Malpractice Group. He was an instructor in civil litigation at the Law Society of Upper Canada's Bar Admission Course for many years and holds a master of laws from the University of London in England. He was called to the Ontario bar in 1971.

Marina Pavlović

Marina Pavlović is an assistant professor at the University of Ottawa's Faculty of Law—Common Law Section, where she is a member of the Centre for Law, Technology and Society and the coordinator of the option in Dispute Resolution and Professionalism. Her teaching and research are in the areas of dispute resolution, access to justice, private international law, consumer protection, and technology policy. She holds a law degree from the University of Belgrade in Serbia and a master of laws in Law and Technology from the University of Ottawa, and she has been called to the Ontario bar.

Harvin Pitch

Harvin Pitch is a partner with the firm Teplitsky, Colson LLP. He was called to the bar in 1970, and he has practised civil litigation ever since. He holds a master of laws from Harvard Law School and is the author of the loose-leaf text *Damages for Breach of Contract*, published by Carswell and updated quarterly.

Mr Pitch has lectured at The Canadian Institute, the Canadian Bar Association (Ontario), Osgoode Hall Law School, the Law Society of Upper Canada, and The Advocates' Society. He was an instructor in civil litigation at the Law Society of Upper Canada's Bar Admission Course for ten years.

Mr Pitch's practice is primarily in the areas of commercial litigation, class actions, and torts. With respect to class actions, he has been involved in the hepatitis C class action and, more recently, the Sunrise Propane explosion as one of the lead counsel for the plaintiffs. With respect to torts, he acted for plaintiffs who had been sexually abused at Maple Leaf Gardens, in 1999 and again in 2009 when new cases came to light. He has practised before all of the courts in Ontario. In addition, he is an expert in commercial litigation with emphasis on real estate litigation.

Joan Rataic-Lang

Joan Rataic-Lang, MLIS, is the executive director of the Toronto Lawyers Association and the library director of the Toronto Lawyers Association Court House Library. Before coming to the TLA, she spent twenty years managing large law firm libraries. In those years, she answered thousands of legal and business research questions, trained hundreds of articling students on how to do legal research, and oversaw the functioning of a number of law firm libraries.

Linda Zardo

Linda Zardo, MLS, has been a law librarian since the mid-1980s, when a land-line telephone functioned as the Internet and when

Quicklaw was the only game in town. She has worked in a variety of law firms over the years and is currently the research librarian at the Toronto Lawyers Association Court House Library. In that capacity, she uses the library's exhaustive collection of both digital and analog resources to assist lawyers, articling students, and self-represented litigants (the few who manage to find their way to the beautiful, architecturally renowned library) with research at all levels and in many disciplines.

Table of Cases

Printed and bound by CPI Group (UK) Ltd, Croydon, CR0 4YY

15/09/2026

14962400-0007